What Others Say About This Book

"*Worship God! Exploring the Dynamics of Psalmic Worship* is an excellent, biblically based book that has been decades in the making. It has been my joy to know Ernest Gentile for more than 30 years. His teaching and concepts on worship have made a great impact upon Bible Temple and I credit the revelation of worship as the key to our growth and expansion. This book provides a wealth of information and is full of inspiration as well."
Dick Iverson . . . . . . Founder and Chairman of Ministers Fellowship International, Founding Pastor of Bible Temple, Portland, OR, and author of The Holy Spirit Today

"I believe your book will do a service to provide scriptural and theological support and, yes, justification for using the key of David to open the windows of heaven to the modern church."
David Fischer . . . . .Pastor of Living Waters Christian Fellowship, Pasadena, CA, a director of the International Worship Symposium

"Ernest Gentile's new book, *Worship God! Exploring the Dynamics of Psalmic Worship*, is a refreshingly non-sectarian, sound theological masterpiece. It is a passionate plea to recapture the priority of Worship. This book is a mandatory syllabus for those seeking a spiritual rebirth."
David Kiteley . . . . . Pastor of Shiloh Christian Fellowship, Oakland, CA, expert on innercity ministry, and missionary statesman

"This outstandingly researched book will strengthen the roots of the modern worshiper in the rich resources of the Psalms. You will emerge from the pages of this book with fresh understanding of the great continuity of worship from David's day to our own time."
J. Michael Herron . . Pastor of Willamette Christian Fellowship, Salem, OR,worship conference speaker, and prolific composer of praise music

"*Worship God!* is a much needed book focusing on the real issues of worship. The truth in this dynamic book will empower your worship. Believers' from all Christian backgrounds will be inspired when reading *Worship God!* I highly recommend it to all church leaders. It richly fed my spirit."
LaMar Boschman . . . Dean of the Worship Institute, Bedford TX

WORSHIP
GOD!

WORSHIP GOD!

Exploring the Dynamics of Psalmic Worship

ERNEST B. GENTILE

Published by BT Johnson Publishing
www.btjohnsonpublishing.com

Printed in the U.S.A.

Dedication

To my beloved family and church
who have joined with me
in the adventure of
exploring the wonders of worship.

Acknowledgments

This book would not exist without the interest and cooperation of the members and staff of Christian Community Church in San Jose, California, who for 32 years joyfully cooperated with me in the grand adventure of worshiping God and making His praise glorious. That fine group included my four children, Sharon, Debbie, Janice, and Ernie, their spouses and children.

And what can I say about my wife, Joy, and her loving support for more than 50 years? Worship has been a major part of our lives and she has been a constant source of encouragement. Thanks, Joy, for our many helpful discussions on the meaning and heart of worship.

A large number of people, including ministers and professors, have shared their insights with me. To all of them, especially those who have critiqued sections of this book, I say a heartfelt thank you.

I also wish to express my deep appreciation to Pastor Dick Iverson, founding pastor of Bible Temple Church (now City Bible Church) in Portland, Oregon, for his personal encouragement.

Foreword

For too long, churches' worship forms hampered unity in the body of Christ. The lack of unity hurt Christian evangelism all over the world.

Today, interest in biblically directed worship is rising. Recordings of new worship songs sell by the thousands, and large conferences draw people from all christian groups to learn worship principles and methods from the Psalms.

In this book, Ernest Gentile gives the church of Jesus Christ an invaluable, universal worship guide. It is not just a theological treatise. It is the result of his lifelong passion for worship. He is, first, a fervent worshiper. In addition, his academic background equipped him to research and prepare this material. Biblical truth revealed in these pages will inspire readers' devotional lives and encourage leaders who oversee corporate worship services. The information is well documented and supported with quotes from leaders in every stream of historic, orthodox Christianity.

As the third millennium approaches, Christians who travel to foreign lands find more believers involved in this Psalmic-style worship. The resulting unity has made possible the final thrust of world evangelization. This book inspires all Christians to help restore the jewel of the church of the twenty-first century: powerful worship!

Frank Damazio
Portland, Oregon

xiii

Preface

The kind of worship described in the book of Psalms can and should be used in churches throughout the world. Christians everywhere have been trained through Sunday Scripture readings to extol the virtues of this type of worship. Therefore, it is no surprise to see an increasing number of people wanting to participate in these inspiring worship modes, especially believers who want to reaffirm genuine, God-centered worship as the first priority of a local church's *worship* service.

Great benefits come to individuals and local churches that follow this biblical pattern. It is meaningful, celebrative, expressive, and participatory.

I use the term *Psalmic* worship to describe this marvelous approach to God, capitalizing Psalmic to emphasize the focus of the book of Psalms. Psalms stands as the great Rock of Gibraltar of all worship discussion. It epitomizes the biblical ideals of human effort to reach out to God in adoration, praise, celebration, and thanksgiving.

In recent years, God has been discussed and explained, yet many people have not experienced Him as they would like. You might say they have come to a spiritual barbecue only to find the steaks still frozen. People now seek to understand the exuberant worship presented in the book of Psalms and practiced by the early church. They want to thaw out the frozen teachings. They want to participate in the Psalmic worship they have read about in the Bible, and they want to enjoy it!

Spiritual renewal today sweeps through Christendom. It sparks liturgical change and encourages all of us to examine our worship heritage. The refreshing breeze of the Spirit brings inspiration, excitement, and restoration. Scriptural forms of worship now command particular interest among Bible-believers.

Worship renewal holds the key for overall renewal of the church for two reasons. First, it encourages a heightened activity of the Holy Spirit as believers give greater glory to God the Father and the Lord Jesus Christ. Second, sincere worship creates an awareness of the presence of God that is desperately needed by today's confused generation.

This book is both objective and subjective. It is objective in its honest attempt to present a balanced, biblical perspective. It is subjective because I joyfully participate in Psalmic worship and have tasted its fruits. I also offer practical advice from my personal quest to renew worship in the local church.

I hope every reader will explore the dynamics of Psalmic worship and will discover how this biblical approach can enhance personal and corporate worship experiences. I pray that God will revitalize every church with meaningful worship that glorifies Him and inspires people.

Contents

CONTENTS

Part V: David's Revelation

Part VI: Nine Psalmic Worship Forms for Today's Church

Part VII: Psalmic Worship In The New Testament

Part VIII: Christ Is Actually Present In Our Corporate Worship Times

List of Abbreviations

AMP   *The Amplified Bible*
ANCHOR   *The Anchor Bible*
BECK   *The New Testament in the Language of Today* (William F. Beck), 1963.
DEWITT   *Praise Songs of Israel: A rendering of the Book of Psalms* (John DeWitt).
GDSP   *The Complete Bible: An American Translation* (J.M. Powis Smith and E.J. Goodspeed).
JB   *The Jerusalem Bible*
KD   *Commentary on the Old Testament* (C.F. Keil and F. Delitzsch).
KJV   *The King James Version*
LB   *The Living Bible: Paraphrased* (Kenneth Taylor)
M   *The Interlinear Greek-English NT with Literal English Translation* (Alfred Marshall).
MOF   *A New Translation* (James Moffatt).
ML   *The Modern Language Bible: The New Berkeley Version in Modern English*
NAS   *The New American Standard*
NEB   *The New English Bible*
NIV   *The New International Version*
NKJV   *New King James Bible*, 1979
NT   *New Testament*
OT   *Old Testament*
PHILLIPS   *The New Testament in Modern English* (J.B. Phillips).
RHM   *The Emphasized Bible: A New Translation* (J.B. Rotherham).
SEPT   *The Septuagint*
RSV   *The Revised Standard Version*
TEV   *The Bible in Today's English Version* (Good News Bible)
W   *The New Testament in the Language of the People* (Charles B. Williams).

xix

Then a voice came from the throne saying:
"Praise our God all you his servants. . ."
Worship God! . . . Worship God!
—Rev. 19:5, 10; 22:9 (NIV)

Part I

Blow Upon Us Holy Spirit

This is a time of heightened Holy Spirit activity. He is restoring true corporate worship to the church. This worship must be in Spirit and Truth and use the ideal Psalmic modes.

- Chapter 1 **What is Psalmic Worship?**
  The emotional and physical responses, which are a natural part of our human makeup, find their finest expression and highest fulfillment when quickened by the Holy Spirit to worship Almighty God.

- Chapter 2 **The Wind is Alive!**
  The Holy Spirit is now moving to transform our mere ideas about God into actual experiences of greater intimacy with Him.

- Chapter 3 **Worship in Spirit**
  Major consideration must be given to Jesus' classic statement about Spirit and Truth in John, chapter 4.

- Chapter 4 **Worship in Truth**
  There can be no true worship apart from Christ, who embodies truth, and the Bible, which is God's written record of truth.

1

What is Psalmic Worship?

This will be written for the generation to come;
That a people yet to be created may praise the Lord.
—Psalm 102:18

The term Psalmic worship refers to the heartfelt, enthusiastic, expressive worship found throughout the Bible and described in detail in the book of Psalms. King David initiated Psalmic worship on Mount Zion in Jerusalem. After practicing these forms or modes of expression in his personal communion with God, David shared his discoveries with the world by writing a formula for public, congregational worship. His expressive musical instructions were gathered in the Psalter, the book of Psalms.

Other Bible characters were expressive worshipers but David, through his life, writings, and leadership, became God's principal spokesman on this vital subject. Singing, musical priests and leaders perpetuated the Davidic approach in Solomon's temple and in every succeeding revival.

The book of Psalms usually is credited to David, but other authors did contribute to it. David and the other psalmists uncovered a wonderful, foundational truth: emotional and physical responses that are a natural part of our human makeup find their highest fulfillment in the worship of almighty God. They described warm, satisfying, loving, emotional worship involving the total person. Psalmic worship uses the voice (speaking, singing, shouting), the hands (lifting, playing instruments, clapping), and body posture (bowing, standing, dancing). These nine forms receive detailed explanation in Part VI.

Psalmic worship involves more than religious emotion and body movement. It originates in man's hunger for intimacy with God. David discovered that God delights in man's passionate pursuit of Him!

Psalmic worship in New Testament times

The singing prophets and priests who wrote the Psalms introduced concepts that eventually broke into full bloom under the warming influence of the Holy Spirit and the tender care of the apostles of Jesus. The worship forms found in the book of Psalms provided an ideal way for the lively, Spirit-filled Christians of Bible days to

3

express themselves in personal and corporate worship. The New Testament compels the serious reader to conclude that the sincere fervency of the early church grew from its dynamic, ongoing worship experience.

Psalmic worship in the early church also created the atmosphere most suitable for manifestations of the gifts of the Holy Spirit mentioned in the New Testament. Powerful prophetic messages were received in their congregational gatherings. This happened to a degree in Old Testament times, but the early church, which had been filled with the Holy Spirit and had observed the behavior of Jesus, exalted Psalmic worship and prophetic activity to a level never consistently experienced by David and his followers.

In an environment of praise, God often is pleased to manifest His Spirit through the prophetic word. In fact, Scriptures such as 1 Corinthians, chapter 14, and the book of Revelation, together with personal observations, make me think that God seems to prefer the worship setting to release prophetic messages.

'Dynamic' does not imply 'fanatic'

The Psalms use strong, passionate language in celebrating God. Active, dynamic terms used in original biblical texts seem by modern standards to border on fanaticism. Many in our day categorize religious excitement and involvement as excessive or unnecessary. In contrast, the Bible shows we can truly enjoy God! To be emotionally and spiritually involved with the God of the Bible is not fanaticism at all. It is the heart of true worship!

Psalmic worship involves the enthusiasm of both God and man. It is free-flowing, spontaneous, joyful, and Spirit-inspired. It is devotional and personal but also congregational. It allows and encourages every church member to participate within a format that edifies everyone.

The full adoration of the heart is involved. Psalmic worship embraces the full range of human emotional expression from silence to jubilation. It can be expressed by a happy congregation or by a single, penitent soul. It is holistic worship in the true sense of the word. Accordingly, even heaven's worship is Psalmic, differing from ours only in intensity and depth.

The vision of a praying, worshiping church is too grand to be canceled by the attitudes of either excited zealots or uncommitted, lukewarm believers. The Bible prescribes a dynamic relationship, and it teaches that God gives wisdom for balance if we ask for it. Joyful anticipation replaces fear in those who seek to be true worshipers!

My introduction to Psalmic worship

I stared and listened in amazement the first time I observed a large congregation worship God in a genuine Psalmic fashion. People were caught up in the joy of praising God. Sincere, fervent worship continued for nearly an hour as I watched with awed interest. It disturbed me that I was so unprepared emotionally and spiritually to participate freely in such a glorious, lengthy, total, and intense adoration of God.

As I watched the service progress, I was astounded at the order, the intensity, and the spiritual flow. The people employed Psalmic worship forms in a natural, free-flowing style. With hands raised, they audibly praised the Lord. They stood and worshiped for a long time, yet their awareness of God seemed to dispel their tiredness. Prophetic messages were spoken, and the service was well controlled by the leaders. I

4

was seeing the worship I had read about in the book of Psalms, and it was coupled with the special emphases and manifestations of the early church's worship.

Something else particularly impressed me. An hour before the service began, people had gathered at the altar to pray. Many knelt while others stood or sat, but all of them prayed with fervency. Many spoke or sang praises to the Lord. I returned from the services that week with a great hunger to worship the way those people did.

I had attended demonstrative services before, and I had seen radical religious behavior, but the spiritual letdown always had been frustrating after the momentary excitement was over. I hungered for worship that was biblical and enthusiastic with lasting, meaningful results.

I first experienced Psalmic worship in 1950 when I was a searching, twenty-year-old minister. Now I participate in the inspiring worship that was so awesome to me. I have been delighted to discover a great deal in the Bible about worship and to find that biblical worship has gained the interest of Christians worldwide. Such worship truly does have a dynamic, positive effect on individuals and entire congregations.

My great adventure

My search to understand these things became an intense, far-ranging adventure and study. I discovered that Christendom's worship is like a great treasure vault loaded with rich truths. It has been a delight to find many Christians with serious, devoted attitudes on this subject.

New appreciation was born in my heart for the whole church, which is Christ's body. I was grateful to learn how Christians down through the church age have sought to revive the worship of the early church. They deserve special thanks.

This generation must now accept the responsibility to hear what the Holy Spirit is saying to it. What is relevant, meaningful, and scriptural for the church today? How can we be responsive to our generation and yet maintain the important ancient landmarks laid down by the church fathers?

The church of Bible days provides the principal benchmark as we seek to be faithful to meet the needs of today's generation. A true renewal will be biblical in the best sense of the word, and it certainly should contain the best contributions from the sacramental, the evangelical, and the charismatic. The result certainly will be an awakened, enthusiastic church producing authentic Christians.

The responsibility of every leader is to provide a congregational setting where the Holy Spirit is welcome, comfortable, and pleased. This requires wise leadership, willing followers, and sincere prayer. It also requires a format that fosters spirituality and freedom without encouraging fanaticism or license.

How exciting to be part of a local church whose worship is marked by freshness, stability, vigor, and power! It releases a remarkably creative energy that will work in believers' minds, emotions, and bodies. May every reader have the privilege of close association with such a church body.

Reflections

At this moment, we see in the sky of the Church manifestations of the Holy Spirit's action which seem to be like those known to the early Church. It is as though the Acts of the Apostles and the letters of St. Paul were coming to life again, as if God were once more breaking into our history.

—*Leon Joseph Cardinal Suenens[1]*

We can speak of modern worship as being like New Testament worship in type only if its several elements—music, prayers, sermons, and so on—contain this quality of spontaneity. If worship is to be made fully christian, fully alive, in the New Testament sense, it must provide an open channel for the incoming of the Holy Spirit, 'who works when and where and how he pleases.'

—*Illion T. Jones[2]*

If the mind of our time is growing dull to the meaning of Christianity the reason may be largely this, that in our worship there is so little of the fire, that active manifestation of the Spirit, which was present in the early church and which belongs to the intrinsic nature of our religion.

—*Ernest F. Scott[3]*

There is a technique and proper procedure for doing almost everything—using the dishwasher or the vacuum cleaner, driving an automobile, and using a typewriter. What is more natural than breathing? One does not "learn" to breathe, he just breathes. Yet, doctors tell us that many of our ills come from improper breathing. Walking is a simple activity, we assume. Did you ever help a child to walk? We are assured by those who should know that most people never learn to walk or sit correctly. One of the first things that any good 'house of charm' does is to teach a student how to walk and to sit! Talk? Who needs to be taught that art? Yet, one day you meet someone who is trained, disciplined, and experienced in the art of conversation, then you know how ineffective you are in communication . . . . WHY, THEN, SHOULD WE BE SURPRISED THAT IT IS POSSIBLE TO 'LEARN' TO BE MORE EFFECTIVE IN WORSHIP?

—*J. Winston Pearce[4]*

2

The Wind is Alive!

You give breath, fresh life begins,
you keep renewing the world.
—Psalm 104:30 JB

A church breathes through its worship system! The vitality of a local church is linked to its devotion. God's people thrive on meaningful worship and it, in turn, produces spiritual people. In a sense a church's theology and structure are validated by the worthwhile experience of her people in worship. That is why Paul said:

For we are the true circumcision who worship in [lit. by] the Spirit of God and glory in Christ Jesus (Phil. 3:3).

Be filled [continuously] with the Spirit, speaking to one another in psalms and hymns and spiritual songs, singing and making melody with your heart to the Lord; always giving thanks for all things (Eph. 5:18,19).

Let the word of Christ richly dwell within you, with all wisdom teaching and admonishing one another with psalms and hymns and spiritual songs, singing with thankfulness in your hearts to God (Col. 3:16).

Meaningful and dynamic worship is an integral part of the life-force in healthy church bodies. Rhythms of a church's life and cycles of its faith are inextricably bound up in the vitality of its communion with God. Jaraslav Pelikan gives this rich insight: "Worship is the metabolism of the Christian life."[1] "It is by its worship that the church lives," says Reformed theologian J.J. von Allmen. "It is there that its heart beats."[2] When this principle is neglected, spiritual life stagnates. "At its 1968 Uppsala [Sweden] meeting," reported Marianne H. Micks, "the World Council of Churches acknowledged 'a crisis of worship and behind it a widespread crisis of faith.'"[3] A healthy faith encourages a healthy worship and vice versa. "When our worship is true, our thought about the church is likely to be true," reasons Paul W. Hoon of Union Seminary.[4]

Beautiful church structures and efficient organizations provide no guarantee that worship services will inspire and feed people. Worshipers' interest and energy will decrease if they do not feel they are meeting with God.

The problem in church renewal

The way worship is presented and modeled in local churches can hinder or encourage church renewal. People cry out for reality in worship and desire to experience God but may only hear Him analyzed. Traditionally, the God of the Bible was set on a heavenly pedestal as an object of sterile veneration rather than sought as a loving Father with whom we may have fellowship or as a heavenly King we may extol.

Church people want more knowledge of God but not through theology. Factual knowledge of God alone is cold and unpalatable. The average person craves to encounter—not just intellectualize—the presence of God. Worshipers who gather for congregational celebration want to see their spiritual leaders enjoy intimacy with God and an exciting freedom of the Spirit. Worshipers also want to see their leaders translate their experience into the church service itself so all the people may meet God in the same dynamic way.

People should enjoy their religious celebrations as if each meeting were a spiritual barbecue! David DuPlessis once likened the truth of the Bible to a frozen steak.[5] It cannot be eaten unthawed, but everyone knows when the steak is on the fire. Mouths water as the wonderful aroma rises from the broiling meat. The atmosphere becomes jovial as guests anticipate a delicious meal.

While hungry guests nervously wait to eat, a cook does not talk incessantly about the history of the steak's origin, its protein content, etc., yet this is exactly what churchmen do when they attempt to explain the Bible without experiencing or demonstrating it. Theology should not be discarded any more than the steak,[6] but we must take theology and allow the warming, transforming work of the Holy Spirit to make worship come alive.

Everyone has the inherent capability to enjoy God spontaneously, but people's spirits can be frozen in the ice of religious formalism, hindering joyful expression. God's chosen people then become God's *frozen* people. Clark Pinnock makes this astute observation in *Christianity Today:*

> It is not a new doctrine we lack. What we need is a new dynamism that will make all of the old evangelical convictions operational. We need not so much to be educated as to be vitalized. It is not a doctrine of the Spirit that we need, but a movement of the Spirit, pervading and filling us, setting our convictions on fire.[7]

It is time to lift people and their worship out of the religious deep-freeze. Like the apostles, people today find it easier to enjoy and experience God first and to theologize afterward.[8]

8

The Wind is Alive!

The Holy Spirit is moving
The Holy Spirit thaws out people's ideas about God and makes Bible truth alive in their hearts. He changes the religious climate just as springtime relieves winter's cold grip. When warm, spring winds begin to blow, frozen land and rivers thaw. Snow and ice melt. Soon streams and rivers begin to flow because warm, moving air breaks the shackles of winter.

This is the meaning of Ps. 147:18 which says God "causeth His wind to blow, and the waters flow" (KJV). Today, the church has entered a spiritual springtime. His Spirit causes people's spiritual lives to melt and flow again. Jesus compared the Spirit of God to moving, fresh, breathable air:

> That which is born of the flesh is flesh; and that which is born of the Spirit is spirit. . . . The wind blows where it wishes and you hear the sound of it, but do not know where it comes from and where it is going; so is every one who is born of the Spirit (John 3:6, 8).

Hebrew and Greek words translated *spirit* can also be translated as *wind* or *breath*. One leading lexicon aptly and correctly states: "The basic idea of *ruah* (Hebrew) or *pneuma* (Greek) is air-in-motion."[9] A natural illustration perfectly parallels a spiritual reality; air and spirit seem beautifully matched.

Like sealed tombs, religious gatherings can become heavy with the dead air of institutionalized religion. It is time to let the Spirit blow through churches, allowing people's spiritual respiratory systems to breathe and worship fully. Let the Spirit move now, just as God's breath moved on Ezekiel's bone yard, and Christ's church will joyfully worship with New Testament fervency!

> Thus says the Lord God to these bones. "Behold, I will cause breath to enter you that you may come to life . . . . And I will put My Spirit within you, and you will come to life." (Ezek. 37:5, 14).

The breath of God, the holy wind makes us live! It inspires people to worship. True, dynamic worship will be in, by, and of the Holy Spirit and not just an emotional expression. The early church esteemed the Holy Spirit as absolutely essential in individual and corporate worship:

- No one can say, "Jesus is Lord," except by the Holy Spirit (1 Cor. 12:3).

- I shall pray with the spirit and I shall pray with the mind also; I shall sing with the spirit and I shall sing with the mind also (1 Cor. 14:15).[10]

- Through Him we both have our access in one Spirit to the Father (Eph. 2:18).

- Building yourselves up on your most holy faith; praying in the Holy Spirit (Jude 20).

9

The Spirit brings balance

People flourish in a worship environment that supplies both flexibility and standards, free expressions and appropriate limitations, the evangelical spirit and historic substance. It is easy to flee binding restrictions of formalism only to arrive in a foolish fanaticism. On the other hand, it is easy to run from spiritual manifestations and free expressions only to be trapped in a stultifying liturgy.

Today's worship renewal does not force Christians to choose between the formal-liturgical and the free-form charismatic approaches. Churches should not abandon one in favor of the other. The apostle Paul valued both and promoted a harmonious combination in local churches. This spiritual balance produced greatness and uniqueness in the early churches' worship. Oscar Cullmann clearly stated this truth more than thirty years ago, and now we are in the position to implement his insight:

> Paul was able to bring freedom of the Spirit and the restrictions of liturgy together in the self-same service because he saw everything in the light of the one aim: the *oikodome* (building up of the Church) . . . . Paul does not fall into the error of reducing the worship life of the Church to a minimum from fear of the binding character of liturgy, nor yet does he, out of fear of sectarianism, fall into the error of eliminating on principle from the service of worship all free expressions of the Spirit.[11]

A broad spectrum of balanced activities spring out of the Spirit's freedom. A proper emphasis on the Holy Spirit does not encourage foolish fanaticism. Believers can trust Him to lead them into all truth (John 16:13; 1 John 2:20, 27).

Michael Green has done a great service to the worldwide church by writing his book *I Believe in the Holy Spirit.* I particularly appreciate the wisdom shown in the last chapter "What To Make of the Charismatic Movement?" He strongly advocates balance:

> It will prove to be a great tragedy if charismatics and non-charismatics cannot live together in peace and harmony in the same church; tragic if we have learned nothing in the centuries since Paul wrote to the Corinthians. Paul prized order in the church, for order was a mark of the faithfulness of the Lord the Spirit. Paul equally loved freedom in the church, for freedom was what the Spirit came to bring us. He knew that order could degenerate into the peace of the graveyard, and freedom turn into the chaos of the revel. The enthusiasts must remember not to do for the Spirit what he does not do for himself, and that is to seek the limelight. The traditionalists must remember that they do not control the Spirit, but that the Spirit creates, indwells and leads the community of the church.[12]

The inspiring worship of the early church rose out of meaningful encounters with her risen Lord. Believers seek the living Jesus in the midst of His church. They will find Him in a harmoniously blended format that allows His presence to be manifested in the Word, sacraments, spiritual gifts, and biblical expressions.

The present enthusiasm in the Pentecostal-charismatic movement certainly is not new or unique. Every generation of church history has seen manifestations of revival and free-form in worship. Today's emphasis on greater freedom is not a threat. Rather it is an encouraging sign of church renewal. Let us seriously consider the possibility that freedom and form can be reconciled biblically, and let us allow the Spirit to blow upon us!

O Breath of Life, come sweeping through us,
Revive Thy Church with life and power;
O Breath of Life, come cleanse, renew us,
And fit Thy Church to meet this hour.

O Wind of God, come bend us, break us,
Till Humbly we confess our need;
Then in Thy tenderness remake us,
Revive, restore, for this we plead.

O Breath of Love, come breathe within us,
Renewing thought and will and heart:
Come, Love of Christ, afresh to win us,
Revive Thy Church in every part.[13]

Reflections

When the spiritual life of a congregation is weak, it is most evident at the level of worship. In a positive sense, the vitality of the church is best indicated by the nature of its worship.
—*Joseph C. Aldrich[14]*

As pastors and as churches we evangelicals have not taken worship very seriously. But there are fresh winds blowing. Renewal in worship in beginning to sweep across the nation. The Holy Spirit is creating a hunger for God in the souls of weary saints. Believers everywhere are losing interst in merely going through the motions at church. People want to know God more deeply and to learn to worship Him more fully and to enjoy the priceless privilege of fellowship with Him.
—*Bruce H. Leafblad[15]*

The time has come for a revival of public worship as the finest of the fine arts . . . . While there is a call for strong preaching there is even greater need for uplifting worship.
—*Andrew W. Blackwood[16]*

There is a new wind blowing, born of a need that many Christians feel. The new wind blows across the city today, and finds its poets, and artists, and musicians, and call them to use their talents to praise God. The wind blows across the past, into the early Christian Church, and sweeps their excitement and spontaneity right into the Twentieth Century. The wind blows through all the nations of the earth, and the ethnic variety becomes a symbol of our oneness in Christ. With men of all cultures, all races, we praise God in a combination of very old and very new forms of worship.
—*Marilee Zdenek and Marge Champion[17]*

We are witnessing the end of a faith and worship characterized by passive noninvolvement, intellectualized propositions, and a seeming absence of God.
—*Robert Webber[18]*

12

3

Worship in Spirit

God is Spirit,
and those who worship Him
must worship in Spirit and truth.
—John 4:24 ANCHOR

Among remarks made to a Samaritan woman and recorded in John 4:5-24, Jesus capsulized the most fundamental information on worship His church needs to know. Robert G. Rayburn calls it "the most important single statement that was ever made concerning the vital subject of worship."[1]

> An hour is coming when neither in this mountain, nor in Jerusalem, shall you worship the Father . . . . But an hour is coming, and now is, when the true worshipers shall worship the Father in spirit and truth; for such people the Father seeks to be His worshipers. God is spirit; and those who worship Him must worship in spirit and truth (John 4:21-24).

Samaritans were considered by Jews to be a mongrel, semi-alien race. Several centuries earlier, when the Assyrians had taken Israel into captivity, the land had been repopulated by foreign peoples who mixed with the remaining Jews to form a hybrid race (2 Kings 17:24-41). Their religion became a type of spurious Judaism which accepted the five books of Moses and some of the Hebrew prophecies but rejected the historical books and the importance of Jerusalem.

Samaritans lived in an area bordered by Judea on the south and Galilee on the north. It was a location ideally suited to promote a smoldering, long-standing feud between the two peoples. Jews traveling north from Jerusalem could take the road which led directly through Samaria, or they could go around the area by traveling through the Jordan Valley. The disciples may have suggested the latter course, but Jesus felt that He "must needs go through Samaria" (v. 4, KJV). God had arranged a meeting of destiny for the whole world!

Eventually, Jesus and His friends approached the narrow valley formed by Mount Ebal on the north and Mount Gerizim on the south. They stopped at the ancient well of Jacob, located one-third of a mile from the tomb of the patriarch Joseph. While the disciples continued into the village to acquire food, Jesus remained behind, sitting on the edge of the well.[2] Although the travel-weary Jesus hardly appeared to be the majestic Son of God, his outward appearance belied the inner alertness of His Spirit. Like water springing up in the recesses of the well's 100-foot shaft, the Spirit moved deep within Jesus, the obedient Son.

A lowly woman approached with no inkling of the important discussion that was about to begin. In conversation, she addressed Him with terms appropriate to the insights that awakened her mind: Jew . . . Sir . . . Prophet . . . the Christ!

The divine gift of living water

Jesus' bold request, "Give Me a drink," actually began the subject of worship, for every aspect of this conversation was geared toward the grand climax of verses 20-24. Jesus quickly established the importance of the Holy Spirit who enables people to worship correctly. Although not fully explaining His meaning, He referred to the gift of God and to the *living water* (v. 10-14). Both refer to the Holy Spirit.[3]

An Easterner easily grasps Jesus' use of water to illustrate the Holy Spirit. Where drought is common, the value of water to sustain life is unquestioned. It is considered a true gift from God. In addition, the Old Testament's use of water to describe divine activity is well known.

> They have forsaken me the fountain of living waters (Jer 2:13).

> It shall come to pass in that day, that living waters shall go out from Jerusalem (Zech. 14:8).

> Everything shall live withersoever the river cometh (Ezek. 47:9).

Jesus compared the Holy Spirit to living water on another occasion.[4] He used the same terminology when he addressed a multitude gathered at the temple in Jerusalem during a Jewish festival.

> Now on the last day, the great day of the feast, Jesus stood and cried out, saying, "If any man is thirsty, let him come to Me and drink. He who believes in Me, as the Scripture said, 'From his innermost being shall flow rivers of living water.'" But this He spoke of the Spirit, whom those who believed in Him were to receive; for the Spirit was not yet given, because Jesus was not yet glorified (John 7:37-39).

The temple setting enhanced Jesus' discussion of the Holy Spirit. The festival scene, described by James Freeman, added dramatic color to Christ's message:

> Every morning the seven days of the feast proper, at daybreak, a priest went to the pool of Siloam and filled with water a golden pitcher, containing about two pints and a half. He was accompanied by a procession of the people and a band of music. On returning to the temple he was welcomed with three blasts from a trumpet, and going to the west side of

the great altar he poured the water from the golden pitcher into a silver basin, which had holes in the bottom through which the water was carried off. This ceremony was accompanied with songs and shouts from the people and with the sound of trumpets.[5]

Jesus shouted to the multitudes possibly at the very moment the officiating priest emptied the contents of his golden pitcher!

John's record seems conclusive: the Holy Spirit and His activity are likened to springing, artesian, fresh, flowing water that creates and maintains life. Jesus' application of this thought to worship is exciting: The indwelling Spirit quickens people to worship the Father. What transformation takes place when the inner person is caught up in the current of the Spirit! "It is the Spirit who gives life" (John 6:63). In no other instance is this truth more appropriate than in worship.

What is God's address?

Startled by Jesus' miraculous knowledge of her life, the Samaritan woman knew she was speaking with an extraordinary man. A question burst from her lips that only a prophet could answer: "Where must I go to worship God properly?"

For many years she had seen Jews travel through her city on their way to Mount Zion in Jerusalem. All the while, she had joined fellow Samaritans in the frustrating, empty worship at a decaying temple on a mountain not far from Jacob's well. Religious thoughts troubled her. Her search for the living God had found little fulfillment at either Mount Gerizim or at the Samaritan temple. Her lifestyle revealed an inner emptiness and she attempted to find peace and satisfaction in relationships with men. Although Jesus dramatically exposed the woman's extramarital affairs, He offered no condemnation. He merely confirmed her unending search for peace and introduced her to a loving, heavenly Father. God's choice of this woman for this important discourse may indicate that in her own way she had sought much after God. He who searches for true worshipers found in this woman a responsive heart to an important message. This event holds a warning for any who judge worship candidates by outward appearances.

Heathen worshipers commonly believe their gods reside in specific locations. The Reverend Paul Yonggi Cho, a Korean pastor, offers this insight into the woman's need:

Oriental people in particular require the address and location of the god they worship. Most Oriental people grow up under the influence of heathen worship, and they need the location or address of their god in order to go and worship it. When I needed my god in heathenism, I would go to a temple and kneel down before an idol, so I could address myself to him directly. In heathenism one has the address of his or her god or gods.[6]

Pastor Cho has described his agony in trying to find where God is, even after he had become a Christian. Finally he realized the wonderful truth taught in John, chapter 4.

Gradually I began to see that through the Holy Spirit, God the Father and God the Son dwelt right in me. I read in 2 Corinthians that God sealed us and sent His Holy Spirit

15

right into our own hearts. I found the address of God. I found that His address is MY address.

The person is indeed more important than a religious place, and the Holy Spirit makes the difference. If you are filled with God's Spirit, your body becomes a temple of worship, and your concern shifts from finding a proper location to finding the proper object and method of worship.[7] True worshipers come as children, not as fanatical cultists.

Do you not know that you are a temple [sanctuary] of God, and that the Spirit of God dwells in you? (1 Cor. 3:16).

Or do you not know that your body is a temple of the Holy Spirit who is in you, whom you have from God, and that you are not your own? (1 Cor. 6:19).

The hour of worship
The time of true worship, Jesus said, is coming—yet it exists at this moment![8]

But an hour is coming, and now is, when the true worshipers shall worship the Father in spirit and truth (John 4:23).

If we interpret Jesus' expression "in spirit and truth" to mean heartfelt worship, or sincere worship, or worship with a right motive, etc., the meaning becomes confused. Sincere, motivated people are in all religions. The Samaritan woman is a good example. However, capitalize *Spirit* and it becomes immediately apparent that Jesus referred to a Spirit-enabled worship that mankind had not yet experienced "for the Spirit was not yet given" (John 7:39). Spirit-enabled worship did exist at that time ("and now is"), because Jesus presented it to the Father. An unusual confirmation of this is found in the Gospel of Luke.

At that very time [lit. hour] He rejoiced greatly *in the Holy Spirit,* and said, 'I praise Thee, O Father, Lord of heaven and earth' (Luke 10:21, emphasis added).

This was certainly worship for He rejoiced, praised and prayed "in the Holy Spirit!"[9] A reference from Hebrews also suggests that Jesus' own worship was by the Holy Spirit:

How much more will the blood of Christ, who *through the eternal Spirit* offered Himself without blemish to God, cleanse your conscience from dead works to serve the living God? (Heb. 9:14, emphasis added).

The hour that "is coming" took place later on the day of Pentecost when the Holy Spirit came upon the church for the first time. Jesus meant that true worship—exemplified in His own life—would become possible within the church, and it actually happened!

16

Should *Spirit* be capitalized?

Jesus clarified what he meant by *spirit* when he said, "God is Spirit" (v. 24). Jesus referred to the Holy Spirit in this text. The primary, basic interpretation of Jesus' words must be found in the most literal application. It was not a reference to man's spirit or the need to have a right personal attitude, although both are important. Raymond E. Brown, one of the leading biblical scholars on the life of Christ, lends his weight to this interpretation:

> Today most exegetes agree that in proclaiming worship in Spirit and truth, Jesus is not contrasting external worship with internal worship. His statement has nothing to do with worshiping God in the inner recesses of one's own spirit; for the Spirit is the Spirit of God, not the spirit of man, as v. 24 makes clear.[10]

It is unfortunate that the word *spirit* was not capitalized in the King James Version. That would have enabled readers to quickly identify Jesus' meaning. Other commentators also agree that *spirit* means *Spirit*. George Ladd, for instance, comments, "'spirit' refers to the Holy Spirit and not to inner 'spiritual' worship as opposed to outward forms."[11] Robert Rayburn suggests a secondary meaning of "spiritual activities" that would utilize a person's "spiritual capacities," but he also feels that the primary meaning is that "worship must be in the Holy Spirit."[12] In his excellent book, *Jesus and the Spirit*, James D.G. Dunn gives this confirmation:

> 'In Spirit' must imply ' by inspiration of Spirit'—that is, charismatic worship—for in the immediate context worship in Spirit is set in pointed contrast to worship through temple and sacred place. The worship that God seeks is a worship not frozen to a sacred place. The worship that God seeks is a worship not frozen to a sacred building or by loyalty to a particular tradition, but a worship which is living, the ever new response to God who is Spirit as prompted and enabled by the Spirit of God.[13]

Christians must not neglect the activity of the Holy Spirit in making worship genuine and acceptable to God. In fact, the pneumatic dimension should receive priority consideration in today's renewal efforts where divine enablement is sorely lacking.

Abba, the cry of the Spirit

The Aramaic word *Abba* appears three times in English Bibles (Mark 14:36; Rom. 8:15; Gal 4:6). It sounds strange and unfamiliar to us, especially in the context of prayer in which it is used. In Jesus' time, Abba was commonly used as a family word. Children used it to address their fathers. It is similar to "dear father" or "daddy." It implied trust, courtesy, confidence, and above all a warm intimacy.

Apparently no one ventured to use the term to address God. However, Jesus broke the tradition. Joachim Jeremias comments:

17

Jesus' use of the word "Abba" (Mark 14:36) in addressing God is unparalleled in the whole of Jewish literature . . . . He spoke to his heavenly father in as childlike, trustful, and intimate a way as a little child to its father.[14]

Ralph Martin observes that Abba was avoided because "it was thought to be too daring and familiar an expression to be used of the King of the universe."[15] Nevertheless, Jesus walked in such close intimacy with God that He felt perfectly comfortable in using the word. Although Jesus' use of Abba was shocking to His contemporaries, it illustrates how distinctive and personal His relationship with the Father was. James D.G. Dunn says:

> Jesus experienced an intimate relation of sonship in prayer: he found God characteristically to be "Father"; and this sense of God was so real, so living, so compelling, that whenever he turned to God it was the cry "Abba" that came most naturally to his lips.[16]

The intensity of Jesus' Gethsemane experience illustrates the depth of His relationship with the Father and the power of His Spirit-sustained intercession. Being very distressed, He fell to the ground in an agony of prayer. From His lips burst the words that have come to characterize for Him and His church the intimacy of prayer, "Abba! Father!" (Mark 14:36).

When asked to teach the disciples to pray, Jesus showed them how to address "Our Father."[17] The prayer of Jesus became the prayer of the disciples as they learned how the Spirit makes possible relationship with the Father. Paul spoke of worshipful prayer in the Spirit which allows believers to experience intimacy with the Father:

> For you have not received a spirit of slavery leading to fear again, but you have received a (lit. the) spirit of adoption as sons by which we cry out, "Abba! Father!" The Spirit Himself bears witness with our Spirit that we are children of God (Rom. 8:15-16).

The RSV gives this wording:

> When we cry, "Abba! Father!" it is the Spirit himself bearing witness with our spirit that we are children of God.

To use this term, a person has to have the inner experience of the Spirit that generates it (Gal. 4:6). Only those born of the Spirit are capable of worshiping God the way He desires to be worshiped. The Spirit produces our sonship. This brings us into a dynamic, new relationship with God! He is now our heavenly Father!

When a person is so alive with the inner witness and reality of divine relationship, the most natural expression in prayer is one of loving endearment, such as Abba (note Ps. 89:26). I cannot help but agree with C.F.D. Moule when he says that with Abba "a new epoch is marked in the history of prayer to God."[18]

18

Reflections

Jesus replied, "The time is coming, Ma'am, when we will no longer be concerned about whether to worship the Father here or in Jerusalem. For it's not where we worship that counts, but how we worship—is our worship spiritual and real? Do we have the Holy Spirit's help? For God is Spirit, and we must have His help to worship as we should. The Father wants this kind of worship from us.

—John 4:21-24 LB

The Saviour's reply was as pregnant a statement on this theme as had escaped the lips of man. Indeed, once He had uttered it, it would be impossible thereafter for any man intelligently to ponder this theme without returning to consider those priceless words. As an utterance on worship they were timeless and absolutely definitive. . . .

—Zane Clark Hodges[19]

It is impossible to exhaust the wealth of this great declaration. GOD IS SPIRIT. That is the most fundamental proposition in theology.

—William Temple[20]

Heathen men are capable of recognizing the awesomeness of God and of worshiping him accordingly. But they will never know the intimacy of worshiping him in spirit and in truth. Spiritual worship is the exclusive privilege of those who have been quickened by the indwelling Holy Spirit!

—Bob Sorge[21]

The Spirit raises men above the earthly level, the level of the flesh, and enables them to worship properly.

—Raymond E. Brown[22]

To worship "in spirit" is to tap into the very source of worship himself, the inexhaustible, endlessly praising Spirit of God, and to allow him liberty to join with our own spirit in expressing through our mind and body the worth of our saviour Jesus, and the love of our heavenly Father.

—Graham Kendrick[23]

4

Worship in Truth

For we are the true circumcision,
who worship in the Spirit of God and glory in Christ Jesus
and put no confidence in the flesh.
—Philippians 3:3

I laid the two sacred books side by side on the small table between us. The eyes of my new Muslim friend moistened with appreciation as he reverently extended his trembling fingers to touch them.

Hussein seemed overwhelmed with gratitude for the gifts I had just presented to him: a copy of the Koran in modern English and a New Testament with Psalms. Almost identical in appearance, the two books had been printed beautifully in a compact size that made them excellent traveling companions. Truthfully, I hesitated when the benevolent thought first confronted me. I simply did not want to give the books away. They represented an effort of determined searching.

Long before making this first trip to Pune, India, to visit missionaries, I had carried in my heart a special burden for the Muslim world. Planning to do more overseas ministry, some of which would be in Muslim lands, I felt it could be advantageous to read the Koran, the sacred book of Islam. Finding this copy in a bookstore, I immediately liked its looks. Scanning the index, my eyes lit upon the word *Jesus*. Yes, Jesus is indeed in the Koran![1]

During our time in Pune, Joy and I stayed at the Holiday House. Fashioned like an Indian village inn, this old estate hosts visitors from near and far. The aging buildings, with their ancient tile roofs, are garnished with luxuriant shrubs and brilliant flowers. Six hotel-like rooms had been built in the rear of the compound, and this is where we stayed. Hussein, a tall, impressive Indian, was in charge of the servants. Usually wearing his Muslim hat, he padded around the compound in his slippers issuing orders and demanding immediate obedience from his subordinates. He was particularly gracious to us, somehow feeling that we were holy people.

On our last day, we packed in the morning, expecting to leave around noon. Hussein came to talk with me. While Joy continued to pack inside, I sat with my searching friend in the shade of the covered porch. It was a bright, sunny morning, and beautiful, bright-red hibiscus flowers were blooming on the vine-covered wall

21

facing our room. Indian kites (hawk-like birds) circled in the clear blue skies. A perfect setting for a two-hour discussion of truth.

Hussein is a member of Islam, one of the world's fastest-growing religions with over 700 million adherents. Nearly one out of every five people on earth is a Muslim. Over eighty percent of all Muslims have never heard the Gospel, but they regard the Bible as a holy book.[2] This man knew nothing of the contents of our Bible. Hussein had never heard of an Old or New Testament. He knew nothing of Matthew, Mark, Luke, and John. I braced myself for an argument, but instead I found a sponge-like mind thirsting to soak up what information I could share. It was a great challenge to me, having been a Christian for fifty-one years and preaching in over a dozen countries of the world, yet I had never personally witnessed to a Muslim!

For two hours I poured out everything I knew about Christ and the Bible that would help him. Frustrated that I was unable to lead my friend to Christ, I did feel gratified that I was able to raise his understanding one notch higher to God than it had been. Realizing that Hussein must know more before he could make an intelligent decision, I placed the two books before him. He promised to read them both.

I astounded myself! The New Testament, of course, would be an ideal gift. But, to give a Muslim a copy of the Koran—in a language that would be more understandable to him? Having read portions of the Koran, I now knew there would be no contest when the two books were compared. There is such an obvious clarity and logic, such a beauty in the life and ministry of Jesus the Christ, that I consider the New Testament fully able to defend itself! It is a record of truth about Him who embodies truth. I laid my hands on Hussein and prayed a fervent prayer for his guidance into the truth. He trembled and wept.

Hussein lives in the central portion of the vast "10-40 Window." This term of missions strategists refers to a narrow, elongated rectangle that has been superimposed on the map of the world. The southern boundary follows the 10° north latitude, and the northern follows the 40° north latitude. Stretching from the west African coast to the islands of Japan and the Philippines in the East, this invisible border encompasses thirty-seven of the least evangelized countries of the world. Ninety-seven percent of all the people in the least evangelized countries are here. Eighty-two percent of the poorest of the poor live here.

Rooted like large, stubborn weeds in the 10-40 Window are the seed-sowing centers for all the world's non-Christian religions. Over 700 million Muslims and over 700 million Hindus, as well as 1.2 billion Chinese, many of whom are Buddhists, are found in the 10-40 Window. The projected populations by AD 2000 are: 1.1 billion Muslims; 1.0 billion Hindus; and 600 million Buddhists.[3] This global picture presents an awesome challenge to the church of Jesus Christ. Is it possible to reach the world for Christ in our time?[4]

The heart of the issue

Missions and evangelism are geared to "save" and help people, and rightly so. The ultimate objective, however, is to make worshipers of these converts. Every religion finds its highest expression in worship. This is the heart of the religion package a person buys into when he believes. Conversion occurs when a person accepts a religion as truth. The way in which a person focuses on this truth will determine how he or she worships. Worship is really our most intense focus upon cherished religious beliefs and our expression and response to the divinity therein revealed. Until a Westerner visits the darkened lands of superstition and idolatry, he does not fully understand the significance of his worship system.

Walking the streets of India, I was startled to see cattle plodding along with the masses of humanity. From time to time, some person would reach out and rub a finger on the animal's body and then quickly rub that same finger over his own chest, thereby identifying with the spirits. Visit the towns and cities of Malaysia and you will be astounded at the number of temples with the innumerable idols, gods, and spirits. The air is heavy with the pungent odor of sacred incense as the masses worship in a society that has outlawed Christianity. And so it goes, through the world, superstitious mankind vainly seeks religious fulfillment. Meanwhile, the truth of Christ's teaching exists like a lush oasis in the midst of this barren spiritual wasteland, waiting for the weary traveler to seek shelter and help.

A call to the nations

Psalmic worship has an undeniable missionary theme. Although there is the expected "call to worship" for Israel in the Psalter, there is also a great cry to the nations to join in celebration of the God of all the earth! One cannot sing or use the Psalms in worship without noticing the missionary zeal of the psalmists to recruit the nations to seek and to exalt the one and only, true and living God.

When Jesus told the Samaritan woman, "You worship that which you do not know; we worship that which we know, for salvation is from the Jews" (John 4:22), He reflected the uncompromising Psalmic attitude. That is, all religions of the world, regardless of their size or influence, are false if they do not seek the God of the Bible and worship according to His truth.

C.K. Barrett, while commenting on Jesus' above statement, makes this wise, albeit prejudiced, statement: "Religion without, or apart from the main stream of revelation, may be instinctive but can be neither intelligent nor saving."[5] For a Christian church to pump the Psalms heavily into its worship scheme is to fuel the fires of world evangelization.

Notice one of the psalms of the sons of Korah in chapter 47. The chapter theme is "God the King of the Earth." All nations or people are urged to clap their hands and joyfully shout to the Lord most high, for this God is a great King over all the earth (vv. 2, 6-8). Also Psalm, chapter 67, exhorts the nations to praise God, "Let the peoples praise Thee, O God; Let all the peoples praise Thee. Let the nations be glad and sing for joy." The objective, given in verse 7, is "that all the ends of the earth may fear Him." This thought is repeated in the New Testament about the message of Christ being taken to "the remotest part of the earth" (Acts 1:8). Psalmic worship is meant for every ethnic group!

David prayed, "All nations whom Thou has made shall come and worship before Thee, O Lord" (Ps. 86:9), and this theme is picked up by the overcomers in Rev. 15:4. Psalmic worship carried a triumphal, uncompromising attitude about the worship of the one true God. Psalm 96 calls all the earth to sing to the LORD and to tell of His glory among the nations, saying "The Lord reigns!" Psalm, chapter 100, tells all nations to shout joyfully while serving the Lord with gladness.

23

This call to the nations is both missionary zeal and prophetic insight. When one worships the true God fervently, the Holy Spirit reveals the heart of Father God to bring all peoples before Him in worship.

Christ as the Truth

Pontius Pilate, the pagan Roman procurator of Judea, asked the bleeding, battered Jesus of Nazareth the classic question of all time: "What is truth?" (John 18:38). With gods and philosophers galore in his tradition, Pilate could not relate to Jesus' simplistic statement, "I have come into the world to bear witness to the truth. Everyone who is of the truth hears My voice" (John 18:37). Every adherent of every false religion who seeks true worship is like Pilate.

Christianity is not just another religion. It is not one of many roads leading to the same destination. Christ claims total allegiance, and the worship that He promotes is the only true worship. Jesus Himself claims to be the truth!

> Jesus said to him, "I am the way, and *the truth*, and the life; no one comes to the Father, but through me" (John 14:6, emphasis added).

> And the Word became flesh, and dwelt among us, and we beheld His glory, the glory as of the only begotten from the Father, full of grace and *truth* (John 1:14, emphasis added).

> Grace and *truth* were realized through Jesus Christ (John 1:17, emphasis added).

> And you shall know *the truth*, and the truth shall make you free (John 8:32, emphasis added).

Jesus goes beyond the dictionary meaning which links truth with whatever conforms to reality or fact. Charles Colson says:

> Jesus does not claim to be just one truth or one reality among many, but to be *the ultimate reality*--the root of what is and what was, the point of origin and framework for all that we can see and know and understand. It is the assertion that in the beginning was God, that He is responsible for the universe, for our very existence, and that He has created the order and structure in which life exists. Everything we know—all meaning—flows from Him.[6]

The ultimate reality and absolute truth has become repugnant to many people. George Barna in a 1991 poll claims that sixty-seven percent of the American people believe there is no such thing as absolute truth.[7] In contrast, we Christians believe that Jesus Christ embodies divine truth. We believe Christ is the only road that leads to God. Lawrence O. Richards succinctly expresses this evangelical perspective:

> In the Bible God presents truth, true information, from and about Himself. But God does more. He presents Himself in the information. God Himself confronts us in His truth.[8]

24

Most importantly, we Christians believe that authentic worship must involve—uncompromisingly—Jesus Christ at the heart of the worship. We are to worship in truth; i.e., in and through the Lord Jesus Christ. The invisible God of Old Testament Psalmic worship now has been made visible or "given a face" in the person of Jesus Christ, thus giving added enthusiasm and sharper focus to the Psalmic worship of the New Testament church.

True worship involves the Trinity

Christian worship is unique among world religions. It alone is directed to and involved with One Supreme and only God who is three-fold in nature and function. New converts are baptized immediately into Christ's church using an initiation formula that glorifies Father, Son, and Holy Spirit (Matt. 28:19; Acts 2:36, 38).

This confession of the tri-unity of God is apparent throughout the New Testament as well as the history of the church. Paul Hoon calls it "An inescapable form within which all thought about worship must move."9 Perhaps the clearest statement on how our worship involves Father, Son and Holy Spirit is: "for through *Him* we both have our access in one *Spirit* to the *Father*" (Eph. 2:18, emphasis added).10 Diagram 1 illustrates the concept.

TRINITARIAN WORSHIP *EPH 2:18*

GOD the Father

To The FATHER

JESUS the Son

Through HIM

MAN

In One SPIRIT

DIAGRAM 1.

25

The following Scriptures support the unity and three-ness of God:

Matt. 3:16, 17; 28:19; Acts 2:32, 33; Rom. 8:9-11; 11:36; 1 Cor. 12:4-6; 2 Cor. 13:14; Gal. 4:4-9; Eph. 1:17; 2:18; 3:14-17; 4:4-6; 2 Thess. 2:13, 14; Titus 3:4-6; 1 Pet. 1:2; 2:5; Rev. 1:4, 5.

In addition to Scripture and the creeds, the greatest expressions of this truth are in the prayerful, worshipful hymns and songs of the faith. A contemporary example would be this beautiful chorus by Jim Stipech that expresses so well the feelings of the responsive heart:

> Praise You Father, Bless You Jesus,
> Holy Spirit thank you,
> For being here, Being near, Lord![11]

An all-time great hymn of the church is *Come, Thou Almighty King*. Each of the first three verses glorifies Father, Son and Holy Spirit respectively, with the final verse magnifying the great God who is one, yet three.

> Come, Thou Almighty King.
> Help us Thy name to sing.
> Help us to praise.
> Father, all glorious,
> O'er all victorious,
> Come and reign over us,
> Ancient of Days.

> Come, Thou Incarnate Word,
> Gird on Thy mighty sword,
> Our prayer attend.
> Come, and Thy people bless,
> And give Thy Word success.
> Spirit of holiness,
> On us descend.

> Come, Holy Comforter,
> Thy sacred witness bear
> In this glad hour.
> Thou who almighty art,
> Now rule in every heart;
> And ne'er from us depart
> Spirit of pow'r.

> To the great One in Three
> Eternal praises be
> Hence evermore.

26

His sov'reign majesty
May we in glory see,
And to eternity
Love and adore.

In Spirit and Truth

Jesus' statement to the Samaritan woman in John, chapter 4, although somewhat veiled, shares this same concept of historic Christian worship. In fact, it may be considered the very foundation of all subsequent discussions on the subject! Notice His way of incorporating the tri-unity of God in true worship:

•**Father**	"worship the Father" (v. 21), "worship the Father" (v. 23), "the Father seeks . . . His worshipers" (v. 23), "worship Him" (v. 24)
•**Son**	"worship . . . in . . . truth" (v. 23), "worship in . . . truth" (v. 24)
•**Holy Spirit**	"worship . . . in spirit" (v. 23), "worship in spirit" (v. 24)

The expression "in spirit and in truth" is the well-established, but incorrect, wording of the King James Version. The Greek text says: *en pneumati kai aletheia dei proskunein*, which literally means "in spirit and truth it is necessary to worship." The word *in* appears only once in the Greek text, emphasizing the unity and equality of spirit and truth. Both *spirit* and *truth* are nouns without articles (anarthrous) and both share the common preposition *in*. This is a significant construction. Raymond E. Brown feels that "one could almost regard 'Spirit and truth' as a hendiadys equivalent to 'Spirit of truth.'"[12] A hendiadys is the expression of a complex idea using two nouns connected by *and* (as *to look with eyes and envy*) instead of a noun and adjective (as *with envious eyes*). Other leading commentators echo this thought.

Therefore, Jesus' use of *truth* in this setting must have special significance beyond mere truthfulness or sincerity. Truth appears in tandem with spirit. If Spirit can be capitalized to signify the Holy Spirit, then truth can be properly capitalized for it receives equal status in Jesus' statement. I agree with those who interpret *truth* to find its best meaning in the Lord Jesus Christ, not some secondary interpretation.[13]

The coupling of *Spirit* and *Truth* in verse 24 is a strong declaration of the Holy Spirit of God and the Son of God. This statement clarifies also that worship in Spirit is synonymous with worship in Truth. The revelation of God is so completely incarnated in Christ, He so satisfies "the faithful fulfillment of God's purposes,"[14] that it can be claimed that Jesus is exclusively the Truth of God.

The Holy Spirit, being the Spirit of Jesus (2 Cor. 3:17; Gal. 4:6; Acts 16:7) is without question the Spirit of truth. Jesus' favorite description of the Holy Spirit seems to be *to pneuma tes aletheias* (the Spirit of truth): John 14:17; 15:26; 16:13. John later writes, ". . . the Spirit is the truth" (1 John 5:7).

Worship of the Father is impossible without the help of the Son. After calling Himself the truth, Jesus declared that "no one comes to the Father, but through Me" (John 14:6). He is the mediator (1 Tim. 2:5; Heb. 8:6; 9:15; 12:24). He is our heavenly intercessor (Rom. 8:34; Heb. 7:25; 1 John 2:1). Therefore, the abundant

27

evidence indicates that to worship in Truth is to worship the Father, *through the Son*, by the Holy Spirit.[15] The worship Jesus spoke about in John, chapter 4, was the true worship that would be made possible by the revelation and exaltation of Christ and the release of the heavenly paraclete, the Holy Spirit. This would take place because of Jesus' death, resurrection and ascension.[16] Thomas F. Torance gives this beautiful description of such worship:

> Thus in our worship the Holy Spirit comes forth from God, uniting us to the response and obedience and faith and prayer of Jesus, and returns to God, raising us up in Jesus to participate in the worship of heaven and in the eternal communion of the Holy Trinity.[17]

The Father seeks such worshipers

Our God has all power, knows everything, exists in all places, and creates anything He wants. Yet He seeks and searches for worshipers who will be genuine, true, and proper in their adoration of Him (John 4:23).

Jesus' statement to the Samaritan woman indicates that God Himself must actively search to find people to worship the Father in Spirit and Truth because so few come on their own. Jesus' explanation is stated with tongue-in-cheek since God knows everything, but the point is strongly and clearly made!

This is remarkable! The emphasis now is on the *object* of our worship and *how* we worship more than *where* we worship. Jesus wanted even the most far-flung tribes of the earth to be able to worship the Father. Even the nomadic peoples of the earth must be able to worship. Jesus, wiser than some of his followers, anticipated the argument of one old Somali camel herder who said, "When you can put your church on the back of a camel, then I will believe that Christianity is for us."[18]

Our worship must be enabled by the Holy Spirit, directed to the Father through Jesus. We must have God's help to worship as we should, and this help is abundantly available! Such worship is true worship and most pleasing to the Father.

28

Reflections

The expression "Spirit and truth" then summarizes the new and authentic worship Jesus brings. It is a worship centered in Him and vivified by the Spirit.
—*George T. Montague*[19]

Worship in spirit and in truth means worship, under the direction and constraint of the Spirit, of the true God—God as He has revealed Himself through his saving acts recorded in the bible, and vivified in Him who is the way, the truth and the life.
—*Raymond Abba*[20]

When Jesus spoke of worshiping in truth, he meant that worship must involve the mind. Worship that involves only the spirit is insufficient; the mind must also be exerted. Some people wait for a floaty, ethereal feeling to come over them before they are sure they have really worshiped. They fail to realize that worship involves all of one's mental faculties and is experienced at the height of mental awareness. The more we exert our minds in worship, the more meaningful our worship is likely to be.
—*Bob Sorge*[21]

If a person is to worship in "spirit," he must be spiritually renewed and indwelt by the Spirit. He must be growing in the knowledge of the reality of Jesus Christ, which is growth in the truth. There must be a constant hungering for God, which is characteristic of all those who have truly sought after him with all their hearts (Ps. 42).
—*Calvin H. Chambers*[22]

True worship has always been both spiritual and in the Spirit, so when we worship God through Jesus Christ in the power of the Holy Spirit our worship will be both "in spirit and in truth."
—*Judson Cornwall*[23]

To worship in truth means to worship according to God's own revelation of himself and his purposes for mankind, and not according to religions, philosophies, ideas and inventions of man. So we worship according to the truth about Jesus, that he is our Saviour, Prophet, Priest and King—our supreme example of manhood, and an undistorted image of the Creator. Without the knowledge and application of these and other marvelous truths about Jesus, our worship would be shrouded by mists of ignorance and uncertainty.
—*Graham Kendrick*[24]

Part II

Our Quest for a Meaningful Worship

Significant corporate worship does not happen automatically. It flows from vital religious experience, meaningful tradition, intelligent communication and cooperative congregations.

* Chapter 5 **Today's Search For Roots and Reality**
  The church needs worship renewal. We turn to the church of Bible times to see its objective outlook and real experience.

* Chapter 6 **Four Important Safeguards**
  Worship will be genuine and not foolish if balanced by four factors: the Theological, the Biblical, the Historical, and the Pneumatic.

* Chapter 7 **Treasure New and Old**
  Worship needs both the old and the new, but the age-old tendency of religious man rejects the new and stays with old, familiar patterns. "The old is good enough," he says.

* Chapter 8 **Decades of Destiny**
  Worship renewal trends reflect dramatic events that occurred in society and in the church during the 1960s, 1970s, 1980s and 1990s.

Today's Search
for Roots and Reality

It is the glory of God to conceal a matter,
But the glory of kings is to search out a matter.
—Proverbs 25:2

During times of religious renewal, sincere students always turn back to the Bible to see if new insights can be gleaned from actions of the early church. The first expressions of theology and church practice are the apostolic roots or foundations of the Christian church. Today the worship practices of that original church undergo intensive investigation.

Surprisingly, New Testament books make little direct reference to the actual worship practices of that day. It may be disappointing not to find easy formulas to apply or forms to follow.[1] However, the total biblical context suggests the vitality of the early church can be traced to its worship practices. It was a living part of daily lifestyles and congregational gatherings. This why Paul said,

> Therefore, I urge you, brothers, in view of God's mercy, to offer yourselves as living sacrifices, holy and pleasing to God—which is your spiritual worship (Rom. 12:1 NIV).

Imagine how intense and impressive the worship atmosphere must have been in early church gatherings.

> And so he will fall on his face (the unbelieving or unlearned one) and worship God, declaring that God is certainly among you (1 Cor. 14:25).

> One day while they were offering worship to the Lord and keeping a fast, the Holy Spirit said, "I want Barnabas and Saul set apart for the work to which I have called them." So it was that after fasting and prayer they laid their hands on them and sent them off (Acts 13:2, 3 JB).

But earnest prayer was going up to God from the church for his [Peter's] safety all the time he was in prison (Acts 12:5 LB).

The initial outpouring of the Spirit, which brought the invisible presence of Jesus to the church, was perpetuated by an unaffected worship (see Acts, chapter 2). It was the source of the church's continuing exuberance and effectiveness. The Spirit was like "new wine" to the early disciples. They had found "joy inexpressible and full of glory" (1 Pet. 1:8).

Why the lack of explanation?

After God prescribed an order of worship and service so carefully for Old Testament Israel, did He ignore giving direction for His New Testament saints? Why is so little said of actual worship procedures in the New Testament? First, the early church adopted existing, workable worship forms. The first Christians inherited rich treasures from the Old Testament, particularly the Psalmic approach to song and praise which readily fit authentic Christian expression. The Davidic structure of the Psalms was not abrogated but enhanced by the gifts of the Holy Spirit. The new wine of the Gospel poured new vitality into the existing forms.

All Jewish Christians were accustomed to weekly services in the local synagogues. The first believers easily adopted familiar worship formats of prayer, singing psalms, reading Scripture and hearing exposition. New Testament writers made little mention of such activities since they assumed Psalmic forms would continue as part of the worship experience.

However, the difference between the synagogue service and the Christian service was not so much in the format or the location as much as in the worshipers themselves.[2] The church gatherings were radically different from the synagogue meetings because Christians came to minister to God and to each other with a whole new attitude, outlook, and experience. Their hearts overflowed with the joy of the Lord. The Spirit that filled and led them during the week broke forth like a living fountain when they gathered in Christ's name.

Second, their worship was such a vital part of their lifestyle—such a simple and natural function of their Christian existence—that they had no reason to take time to describe and explain something commonly done among them. Alexander B. Macdonald beautifully explains this point:

> As we read the New Testament afresh with minds alert for traces of the worship, we become increasingly aware that though it is not often mentioned, yet it is everywhere present behind the writers, giving form and colour and vitality to their modes of expression and thought; and ere long we reach the conclusion that their frequent silence regarding their worship must be due in great measure to the largeness of the place it filled in their lives. They speak so little about it for just the same reason that we speak and think so little about the air we breathe.[3]

A third reason is equally simple: God did not inspire His writers to record in detail the order of church meetings because He knew man's tendency to stylize, formalize and institutionalize worship. Jesus clearly stated in John 4:24 that the emphasis had shifted from sectarian concern of places and forms to the awareness of God's presence. He did not do away with meeting places and ways of worship, but He clearly established the priorities of Spirit and truth for His people when they gathered in His presence.

Worship in the universal church of Christ certainly has common elements, but the diversity of cultures, races, languages, and experiences demands variety of expression. Add to this the unpredictability of the Holy Spirit, and one can easily see that it would have been a major mistake to set an inflexible structure of liturgy in the canon of Scripture.

Today's church needs to reexamine the dynamic spontaneity of the New Testament church. We will find God has given stable components for worship services to be expressed through flexible forms.

The need for renewal

A confused society thirsts for reality. Modern man needs to see the enthusiastic devotion of the first century church. Vital worship could be the force in today's church that would draw these despondent souls. The people of God, living in the midst of a bewildered, secular society must exist like a fruitful oasis in the midst of the parched wilderness. Like springs of water, worship will draw thirsty souls.

The need in today's church for change or renewal in worship is declared by many church leaders. For instance:

- James F. White (Methodist): The times have changed . . . . We must realize that people changed . . . . And consequently the forms by which worship is expressed must change too.[4]

- Howard Hendricks (Baptist): Worship is the lost chord of evangelicalism.[5]

- Robert E. Webber (Episcopalian): There is a cancer at the heart of many churches—the failure to understand and practice public worship.[6]

- Robert G. Rayburn (Presbyterian): One of the most tragically neglected activities in the average evangelical church today.[7]

- Paul W. Hoon (Methodist): The fact is that ignorance of the meaning of worship is so widespread among the laity of free-church Protestantism as to be virtually disabling.[8]

Subjective vs. objective

One reason for power in the early church's worship was the objective attitude in individual Christians and in the corporate body of believers. Together the people believed that something wonderful was meant to happen in their times of celebration—that God by His Spirit would come among them, and they, in turn, would joyfully respond with sincere praise and adoration.

35

Therefore let us be grateful for receiving a kingdom that cannot be shaken, and thus let us offer to God acceptable worship, with reverence and awe (Heb. 12:28 RSV).

In contrast, today's typical Sunday morning worshiper is overly involved with himself and his problems. He fights for existence in a competitive, hostile world that stresses getting more than giving. It is hard for such a person to shake off this negative influence when entering a worship service. We know instinctively that this advice of Andrew W. Blackwood is right:

> The average man in the pew seems to direct his attention primarily to himself and his needs, whereas he should turn his mind and heart toward God, desiring to come into closer touch with him, to become right with him, and perhaps to make some desired effect upon him.[9]

Every worshiper must rid himself of the clutter of subjective thoughts that cling to his worship attitude. He must make a concerted effort to keep his personal feelings from eclipsing the important objectives of the church service—the adoration and magnification of God and the edification of His people.

An analysis of songs sung by congregations today reveals that the average hymnal abounds with testimonial songs and lyrics that glorify personal experience. I agree with Donald Gee who said:

> I would that more of our hymns were hymns of worship. Seventy-five per cent of our singing today is about ourselves, about our feelings and experiences. It is time we came to church to sing about the Lord. It would be a good thing to set aside one or two meetings where we came to minister to the Lord, came to bring HIM something.[10]

Subjective songs and hymns tend to reinforce the dilemma in the pews. Songs, particularly at the height of a service, should be objective, bringing man into living relationship with his God. For instance, contrast the difference in attitude between the man who sings from the heart, "How great thou art," and with equal sincerity sings "Count your blessings." Robert S. Simpson makes this appropriate comment:

> The tendency at times in Protestant worship is to suggest that the value of the worship lies in its effect upon the worshipper. That is not so. The central thing in worship is objective, not subjective. In worship we do not only receive, but primarily we give. Worship is offering.[11]

Churches are generally the result of some reformation, renewal, or revival movement of religion. In such a setting people become alert and sensitive to spiritual reality. It is as though the Spirit issues a call to worship, and the people respond:

> Come, let us go up to the mountain of the Lord,
> To the house of the God of Jacob;
> That He may teach us concerning His ways,

And that we may walk in His paths (Isa. 2:3).

In spiritual awakenings, people feel as if they are part of a living organism rather than involved in an organization. They feel the kingdom of God is working among them. There is a shift of center from self to God. As people praise the Lord, they relinquish occupation with self. "When praise becomes a way of life," Paul Billheimer wisely comments, "the infinitely lovely God becomes the center of worship rather than the bankrupt self."[12]

During renewal, the worshiper's mind becomes objective. His spiritual attention is directed outward and upward. His worship becomes the adoring expression of love to a personal God and Savior. His participation with other worshipers is an exciting, corporate adventure.

Today's mixed-up generation needs the experience common to the saints of early days. In those congregational gatherings, the celebration became absolutely electric! With minds centered on God, they found themselves a part of God's historical flow to redeem mankind. What a sense of destiny and participation stirs in the hearts of objective people! People who worship God in this frame of mind are active, healthy, productive Christians in every phase of life! "Every event in the service stands right in the movement of this salvation history and participates in it."[13]

Reflections

When men of faith look to their past, they do not see a different past from that of other human beings: they see the same past differently. Faith provides a framework of meaning by which the past is interpreted and a criteria by which facts and events are selected for a description of the past.

—*C. Ellis Nelson*[14]

Our roots lie in the New Testament Church and the early church fathers. In addition, there have been many "greenings" of spiritual renewal throughout history, each of which exhibits certain similar evangelical phenomena. Finally, although our recent traditions are mostly those of reaction against the formalism and sacerdotalism of the middle ages, it is helpful to identify what we have reacted against, in order to separate our true identity from any indulgence in blind iconoclasm.

—*Donald P. Hustad*[15]

Each evangelical congregation or denomination will have to make a commitment to recover worship, then pay the price in study, time, and change that it will take.

—*Robert E. Webber*[16]

There is a vital need for the Church today to reexamine the early Christian Community and to enter into the dynamic mode of expression that characterized the Christians of the first century, who were overpowered by the marvelous reality of the presence of God in their midst.

—*Calvin H. Chambers*[17]

6

Four Important Safeguards

*I felt the necessity to write to you appealing
that you should contend earnestly for the faith
which was once for all delivered to the saints.*
—Jude 3

Four important safeguards enable us to maintain a fervent, genuine experience in Christ yet keep ourselves from foolish fanaticism. A balanced worship program will be monitored by:

1. A sound *theological foundation.*
2. An accurate *biblical structure.*
3. A meaningful *historical substance.*
4. A living *pneumatic presence.*

These safeguards must do more than monitor. They must keep a dynamic tension within the church. One safeguard cannot be exchanged for another or chosen over another. The traditional this-is-the-way-it-has-always-been-done mindset must be exchanged for an open, prayerful attitude that seeks the best of God for today's generation.

Diagram 2 illustrates how balanced, corporate worship draws strength from twelve primary sources located in four quadrants. Within each quadrant, three circles identify complimentary thoughts that need serious consideration.

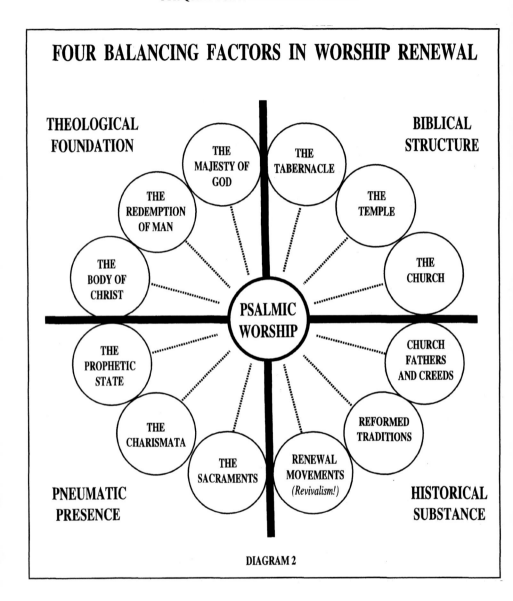

FOUR BALANCING FACTORS IN WORSHIP RENEWAL

THEOLOGICAL FOUNDATION

BIBLICAL STRUCTURE

THE MAJESTY OF GOD

THE TABERNACLE

THE REDEMPTION OF MAN

THE TEMPLE

THE BODY OF CHRIST

THE CHURCH

PSALMIC WORSHIP

THE PROPHETIC STATE

CHURCH FATHERS AND CREEDS

THE CHARISMATA

REFORMED TRADITIONS

THE SACRAMENTS

RENEWAL MOVEMENTS *(Revivalism!)*

PNEUMATIC PRESENCE

HISTORICAL SUBSTANCE

DIAGRAM 2

The theological foundation

Like a tree supported and nourished by roots, a church feeds on its theology. Everything done in a church flows from its understanding of God. The correctness and integrity of a group's theology is displayed in the people's authentic experience.

Theologians may debate deep implications of lofty concepts, but pastors occupy a more challenging place in church structure. Pastors must work with average people—who comprise the majority in the church—and give them an understanding of God and His ways.

God must be presented in an appealing and exciting manner. The people want to understand and experience the God of the Bible. This is where "the rubber meets the road." Here the theoretical has to become practical. Theology must be more than terminology to people. It must be more than just thoughts about God. It must be a personal, enjoyable relationship with God. Theology comes alive through vibrant worship. Paul Hoon states it this way:

> In short the living nerve of theology is touched in liturgy, and as the parish pastor conceives, plans, and conducts worship with his people, he has an unexcelled opportunity to match theology against experience, and from experience to apprehend theology.[1]

The majesty of God. The knowledge of God's attributes and majesty must be firmly established in people's minds.[2] Worship services will become powerful religious experiences for people if they believe God is loving, real, and approachable.

Among some Christians the false idea prevails that no one may know or understand God. They are told that God is incomprehensible, that He dwells in a high and holy state unapproachable by His creatures, and that it is impossible for finite man to understand the infinite God. Just the reverse is true! In Jesus Christ, God made Himself one of us, brought Himself down to our level, touched our humanity and partook of it, carried our infirmities, and bore all the reproach of our sin.

People must come for worship filled with reverential awe and fear but also eagerly anticipating an inspiring encounter with the God who loves them and calls them His children.

The redemption of man. Dynamic worship springs from liberated hearts. The worthiness of God, which is emphasized in worship, is best expressed through people who know they are worthy of such a noble activity. Redemption includes more than just salvation from hell and divine judgment. People must know that God forgives and makes covenant with them.

With a fresh understanding of Jesus' redeeming love, God's people can lift their heads, voices and hands without condemnation. It is so important that Christians appreciate their self-worth in Christ.[3] A person who knows his redemption in Christ will walk in dignity and self-esteem rather than in a morbid, self-destructive frame of mind. We are meant to be friends and confidants of the mighty God. We are made to look up!

> The Greeks had an interesting word for man; in this name there is an indication of why man is a worshiping creature. The word is *anthropos*: It means the "upward-looking creature."[4]

The church was redeemed by almighty God and invited to personal communion with Him. People who know their God and live confidently in His blessings will be worshipers indeed.

The body of Christ. Ecclesiology, the study of the church, needs a renewed, lively interpretation. The church of Christ is not only universal but also local. Each local church is not only an organization but also is an organism. Every congregation is comprised of many believers, and each individual has vital importance. Each individual makes significant contributions. This view of the church is not new but has revolutionary implications for worship.

The early church had a prophetic dimension that drew every member into the magnetic field of the Holy Spirit. People became participators instead of spectators. The Spirit used every member to make Jesus' presence real to the gathered saints. Body life, as Ray C. Stedman describes it, makes every member a contributing part.[5] This gracious open door enhances worship immeasurably.

The biblical structure

The three great habitations of God in Scripture have been the Tabernacle of Moses, the Zion of David, and the Church of Christ. The theme of worship runs through descriptions of each of these dwelling places.

The Tabernacle of Moses. The patriarchs revealed a few thoughts about worship, but Moses provided the first substantive teaching on it in Exodus and Deuteronomy. During his awesome experience on Mount Sinai, Moses observed and recorded a specialized worship system that startles modern minds.

Beginning with His thunderous, earth-shattering appearance on the mountain, God gave a whole liturgical system to the newly created nation of Israel to enable people to meet properly with Him. God outlined plans for the place of worship, and the people built it. Men of the tribe of Levi became priests and worship leaders. The book of Leviticus gave detailed instruction on how to approach God and bring sacrificial offerings. As priests employed the Levitical system, God's fiery power was present at the tabernacle.

The Mosaic system is a living parable from history symbolizing New Testament truths and informing believers today of the basic necessities of worship.[6] The emphasis on blood atonement and redemption pointed to Jesus' supreme sacrifice on the cross.

The Zion of David. By divine revelation, King David received a blueprint for the permanent temple structure and for worship conducted in it. Following David's death, his son, Solomon, constructed the building and formalized the singing priesthood. God's majestic presence dwelt in David's tabernacle and Solomon's temple because the priests applied David's revelation of worship. The reader will find more on this topic in succeeding pages; however, the book Christians read every Sunday, the book of Psalms, holds a key to the renewal of worship in our day.

Psalmic-style worship has been neglected too long! Although most Christian churches use the Psalms for responsive reading and singing, their actual worship services are geared more to the priestly, Levitical style than to the expressive Psalmic method.

Four Important Safeguards

The church of Christ. It is important to study what is said about worship in the early church and to understand the source of the early believers' devotion. A living awareness of Christ brought an electric quality to early church gatherings. "The *experience* of the early believers was at the *heart* of their gospel," explains James D.G. Dunn. "Their gospel was in large measure the expression of their experience."[7]

Like Old Testament Israel and the early church, the church today desires God's presence. God in Christ is revealed in the church through the activity of the Holy Spirit.

The historical substance

Religious people often suffer from "historical amnesia." They easily forget mistakes of the past—and repeat them! In vibrant, religious movements throughout the church age, certain tendencies and trends have reoccurred during transitions of leadership from the first to the second and third generations. These observations can help guide the modern-day church to renewal.

The church Fathers and creeds. The opening centuries of church history hold significance for the church today.[8] Church leaders who immediately followed the original apostles faced tremendous challenges including doctrinal dilemmas. During those trying times the Fathers produced creeds that articulated answers to the dilemmas. The creeds have kept the church's course steady.

References to worship in the first few centuries are rather limited, and, like the New Testament, do not give a clear picture of an established liturgical structure. However, the information available lends helpful insights.[9]

The reformed traditions. Some of the church's great thinkers made their contributions in the 1500s and later. Martin Luther, John Calvin, and other reformers greatly influenced Christianity, but their focus was primarily on redemption theology rather than on a practical explanation of how and why the church should worship. Much of their attention did center on baptism and communion, which are important parts of a church's worship structure. However, the reformers were not united in their ideas on these subjects, and their debates were beyond the understanding of the common man.

Of great value to worship was the emphasis on the priestly function of every believer and the importance of the Bible. Luther used music to proclaim his message, and some of his great hymns are still a vital part of modern liturgy.

Renewal movements (Revivalism). Active renewal movements have appeared throughout church history. Movements usually indicate that people seek to return to a more vibrant, biblical Christianity while risking excommunication, church splits, etc. The established church tends to reject outbursts of religious enthusiasm, revision, or innovative trends. But it should guard against being overly critical of revivalism, realizing that reactionary groups serve a therapeutic function in the body of Christ. Revolting against cold formalism and undue religious domination, restoration movements have helped maintain an alertness and a serious heart for God in the church. Revivalism has been schismatic yet essential in the life of the church. After all, most of our major denominations began this way! Evelyn Underhill wisely comments:

43

Wherever the institutional life stiffens and becomes standardized, there is a (positive) reaction towards that primitive group enthusiasm and prophetic ministry which is described in the New Testament and—even though it sometimes oversteps the bounds of good taste and common sense—is a true part of the church's Godward life.[10]

The pneumatic presence

People involved in primitive Christian worship enjoyed a perceivable presence of Jesus. Early Christians believed that Christ in the person of the Holy Spirit was actually among them. Their gatherings were inspired and blessed by the living Jesus. The Spirit, *pneuma* (Greek), lifted the churches into an awareness of God that transformed the drudgery of Roman existence into the excitement of kingdom living.

Today's church greatly lacks Christ's perceivable presence. The Holy Spirit must be reintroduced to the church. An increasing emphasis must be placed on His work, presence, and activity. He will not shame or embarrass us, but His coming will breathe new life and vitality into our worship services.[11] Dry bones will live again. Wilderness will spring with new life. The miraculous will be apparent and welcome.

The Sacraments. Many Christians participate in the sacramental life of the local church without experiencing God's presence. Although the church has been given only a few ceremonial activities, the Scripture indicates that God will be present in a special way at those events. God in Christ is present in the person of the Holy Spirit, the Pneuma. This pneumatic dimension makes baptism and Communion real to the church.

The charismata. Divine activity characterized the assemblies of early Christians. The gifts or manifestations of the Holy Spirit were frequently displayed in congregational meetings (see 1 Corinthians, chapter 12). They were considered to be more than ecstatic experiences; they were accepted as the logical vehicles of supernatural activity. The Holy Spirit perpetuated the life and ministry of Jesus through manifestations in and through the members of Christ's church. As a result, their worship format had to be flexible. Structure never was so rigid that it ruled out the Holy Spirit's spontaneity and innovation. In fact, this pneumatic appearance gave credence to the worship (see 1 Cor. 14:25).

The prophetic state. Those early meetings had a prophetic aura. The worship was powerful and invigorating, and the minds of the people were inspired to think on a plane more heavenly than earthly. People participated freely in the services (1 Cor. 14:26). Even when they were not doing something, they were still in tune with God's activities and His message for that time.

Tradition must be meaningful

Christianity may have its beginnings in the venerable past, but it must be meaningful to believers now through an alive, active faith. It is not enough to recite ancient creeds, quote church Fathers, defend traditions, or flee to revival activities. G.C. Berkouwer defines true orthodoxy as living, "in continuity with a vibrant past, not indeed a continuity which is a mere thoughtless progression on the trusted paths of tradition."[12]

Our faith is to be guided—not controlled—by the past. The faith of a past generation may have been meaningful for a given time and place, but believers today make a great mistake when they attempt to appropriate a biblical principle or a church tradition without incorporating the active faith that produced it. Belief statements, tenets of the faith, must be meaningful experiences and not just abstract concepts. We must not take doctrines of faith and transform them into sterile dogmas or traditions. We dare not intellectualize the presence of Christ into mere mental acceptance of His existence.

Today's church needs the input of church Fathers and creeds, reformed traditions, and renewal movements. However, that input must be made relevant to today's church through lively religious encounters with God. Real faith is a living relationship with God. Traditions are significant when they connect the God of history with present experiences of today's generation. Leonard Ravenhill wisely commented, "There is a world of difference between knowing the Word of God and knowing the God of the Word."[13]

Fresh encounters with God prepare Christians in every age to meet new situations and continue progressing. To be authentic, these experiences must be grounded in biblical truth. Every church must understand the truth of God revealed throughout history and translate it into faith for today.

God must be free to be and do what He wishes today. His presence and His doctrine cannot be locked into wooden liturgy or into the cement of meaningless dogma. What God means to you will relate directly to the conditions you face. Children must be taught to be learners of God's will for current events—to meet God for themselves. This requires an active faith that joins today's trials and triumphs with the God of history. C. Ellis Nelson summarizes it like this:

> Theology cannot be complete until it is practical theology; that is, until the historical tradition has interacted with the living, human situation.[14]

I do not suggest throwing out the great contributions of the past; rather I urge a constant review, reconsideration, and reevaluation of the church's belief systems. Are New Testament Christians produced by what we believe and do? It is our "duty to resist the suction of ecclesiastical tradition."[15] The sacramental, the evangelical and the charismatic have all become significant parts of the church's heritage, but these endowments from the past must be maintained by dynamic interaction with present events, by continual study of Scripture, and by the reality of the Holy Spirit's presence.

Jesus constantly battled with the leaders of His day over traditions that had become part of the religious system. Washed hands had become more important to them than clean hearts. Jesus' commented on their mistake, "You nicely set aside the commandment of God in order to keep your tradition" (Mark 7:9). On one occasion He told the Sadducees, You are mistaken, not understanding the Scriptures, or the power of God . . . . God is not the God of the dead but of the living" (Matt. 22:29, 32).

Jesus was criticized most frequently for violating Jewish traditional Sabbath observance. The Gospels record six distinct offenses, yet all of the so-called transgressions involved works of mercy which pleased the Father. Today we see hardly any consequence in these offenses, but in that day, religious traditions held Jewish people in a harsh vice that did not allow them to enjoy God.

Human nature imposes recycled "new" restrictions to replace old ones. W.W. Fereday has wisely commented: "It is possible to reject traditions a thousand years old, and yet be slaves to traditions of scarcely fifty years standing."[16] Every generation must realize this tendency.

The same set of Scriptures and traditions used by the Jews were transformed into a new and living way of life for the apostle Paul because of Paul's vital experience with God. When Paul was challenged about the new sect he was promoting, he insisted that "after the way which they call heresy, so worship I the God of my fathers, believing all things which are written in the law and in the prophets" (Acts 24:14 KJV).

Worship will have true substance if Christians keep moving forward with a present-time, spiritual freshness and with constant, vigilant research of Bible truth and historic tradition. The life of a church can be revived and maintained by a proper balance of restored truth and renewed spirit. This argument is not a wild cry in the night. It is the thoughtful evaluation of many who have studied the spiritual life of the church. For instance, Evelyn Underhill in her classic book, *Worship*, tells us:

> The greatest of the dangers [is] . . . the danger that form will smother spirit, ritual action take the place of spontaneous prayer, the outward and visible sign obscure the inward grace.[17]

Ernest F. Scott says:

> There is always the danger that the forms will take the place of the substance. It is almost a law of religious history that a faith originally vital is smothered at last by the ritual which was intended to preserve it.[18]

Judson Cornwall also tells us what to do:

> We go on giving lip service to the words that meant life to our fathers and to the founders of our denominations, often unaware that we have only the liturgy, not the life of these men. We have expressed the words as fact for so long that were unaware that they have become a fable. What can bring us out of our guile back into His grace? Worship![19]

A glorious opportunity

An exciting prospect faces believers today. It is the rejuvenation of the church through renewed worship that is true to God, to the Bible, and to history and that is inspired and enabled by the Holy Spirit. This renewed worship glorifies Jesus Christ and gives people a personal, loving relationship with their heavenly Father. There can be no higher privilege than to be an active participant in such worship.

Reflections

Worship has changed through the centuries. There have been adaptations and adjustments to new circumstances and demands. Worship is not a static entity, but like all living things, it grows in response to environment. Our task now is to ask "What the Spirit says to the Churches" about worship today. —*Leslie Earnshaw*[20]

We have to learn to think historically in order to interpret the Bible. Thinking historically is not the same thing as knowing biblical history: to think historically is to examine the past so that it can be used in a meaningful way for the present. —*C.E. Nelson*[21]

We have lost the art of worship as a result of historical amnesia; the infiltration of rationalism, emotionalism, or entertainment; and the failure to keep balance in all aspects of church life. —*Robert E. Webber*[22]

The tendency of churches has been to start with much enthusiasm and then taper off as the church grows and becomes more "respectable." There is a very real danger in this attitude, however, for it causes the worship climate in a church to swing to the other extreme. No emotion is as unscriptural as excessive, uncontrolled emotion.
—*Evelyn Underhill*[23]

Change can be a frightening thing, especially to older folks. And, since our society regards religion as an area of conservatism, change in this area can be particularly difficult to handle. With everything else in our lives wiggling, many of us lock in on our church customs as a refuge from the turmoil around us. So, when somebody tampers with the way we worship, it shakes some people up. The fear that something essential is being sacrificed and replaced by the latest fad.
—*Chuck Kraft*[24]

7

Treasure New and Old

Every scribe which is instructed unto the kingdom of heaven . . .
bringeth forth out of his treasure things new and old.
—Matthew 13:52 KJV

Followers of Jesus in every generation have added to the rich liturgical heritage of the church. Devout people from every branch of Christendom have filled the church's liturgical storehouse with their genuine spiritual experiences, building a treasury of vast wealth. The storehouse contains all authentic dialogues between God and man, not just a single experience at an isolated time and place. Believers today can view the grand sweep of the church's development through the centuries.

Contributions from past generations lie not so much in methods or symbols as in their experience of reality. Personal encounters with God and treasures of personal devotion are only part of God's dealings with His entire church. It is challenging and inspiring to realize that in spite of theological and liturgical differences, sincere believers in various churches have all met—to some degree—with God in meaningful ways. This is not to say that everything done in every church is necessarily correct. Every person and denomination is limited in its understanding of God and worship, and this is by divine design. A false humility permeates the religious group that feels its approach is the exclusive way. Sects or cults that foster an exclusive mentality among their followers invariably produce an inwardly biased triumphalism that leans toward idolatry and leads to self-destruction.

Sometimes God accommodates the confining limitations of a particular church structure, level, or spirituality; however, the Holy Spirit is working wherever honest Christians sincerely seek to worship the Father in and through the Lord Jesus Christ. Robert Webber strongly affirms this thought:

> Inasmuch as the Holy Spirit has been given to the church, we must acknowledge the illumination of the Holy Spirit in the life of the whole church. If contemporary Christians acknowledge this work of the Spirit, they will not assume an antihistorical stance that rejects what the Spirit has given to the church in the past. Neither will they act as though the Spirit first came to the sixteenth-century Reformers and discount all that

49

precedes them as apostate. Instead, they will affirm the whole church and seek to draw on the resources that have been handed down from every generation of Christian people.[1]

It is encouraging to hear prayer for the unity of the church to fulfill John, chapter 17. All Christians hope to be able to worship the same God together even if they cannot see eye-to-eye on all doctrines.[2] After all, the Bible does declare:

> There is *one* body and *one* Spirit, just as also you were called in *one* hope of your calling; *one* Lord, *one* faith, *one* baptism, *one* God and Father *of all* who is *over all* and *through all* and *in all*. But to each one of us grace was given according to the measure of Christ's gift (Eph 4:4-7, emphasis added).

If there is only one Spirit, one faith, and one baptism, it logically follows that there is only one worship for *all* Christians, even if the form of that worship is not uniform in style or expression.

Jesus and His scribes

Teachers and leaders have the glorious privilege of bringing great riches from the worship treasury of the ages to expectant people today. The treasury holds things new and old—the fresh as well as the familiar—that have ministered to past generations and still are meaningful today.

Before looking at the Psalmic devotional wealth available for today's church, consider Jesus' teaching on "things new and old." Old principles cast light on the present quest for balanced, meaningful worship in today's church. Jesus mystified people with His unique way of combining past, present and future. He maintained a tension between God's past dealings with man and His present and future dealings. He gave Old Testament thoughts and commandments brilliant new insights and applications that astounded people. Jesus taught with authority that sprang from a dynamic relationship with God. The scribes of that day did not have such a consciousness of God (Matt. 7:29).

In His colorful but confusing sermon on the kingdom, Jesus gave a one-verse parable of great significance. The statement not only clarified Jesus' own ministry but also became a guiding principle to all who would lead and feed God's people.

> And He said to them, "Therefore every scribe who has become a disciple of the kingdom of heaven is like a head of a household, who brings forth out of his treasure things new and old" (Matt. 13:52).

The scribe was the educated theologian, the ordained teacher, the religious scholar of the day who answered people's questions. Usually, he was "a Pharisaic teacher of the law."[3] As David Hill comments, "Far from being a mere copyist or secretary, he was an expert in the Law, the authorized rabbi."[4] The scribes were regarded as "the guardians of an infallible tradition."[5]

Jesus gave startling new significance to the old, familiar term *scribe*. The followers of Jesus who understood His teaching about the kingdom of heaven were to be His scribes! (Note Matt. 23:34.) Since the disciples announced that they indeed understood His teaching, Jesus' immediately deputized them as the authorized teachers of His newly established order.[6]

Jesus likened His disciple-scribes to "a householder" (KJV) who brings new and old things out of his "storeroom" (NIV). It has been translated to mean a "rich man" bringing out his treasures (KNOX), or a householder bringing out both "the fresh as well as the familiar" (AMP). Regardless of which application is made, the precious store "brought forth" has a spiritual nature and is to be shared. Link this thought with the following:

> For the mouth speaks out of that which fills the heart. The good man out of his good treasure brings forth what is good; and the evil man out of his evil treasure brings forth what is evil (Matt. 12:34-35).

The good treasure of the kingdom refers to spiritual realities connected with God's own presence as Paul declared:

> But we have this treasure in earthen vessels [our bodies], that the excellency of the power may be of God, and not of us (2 Cor. 4:7 KJV).

Jesus wants His disciples to be well-trained teachers in the affairs of God so they can bring forth precious truths and realities to fill listeners' hearts. Spiritual riches are both new and old, like those delivered by the master teacher Himself. The church's teaching should encompass the best of Judaism and Christianity, "all that is worth knowing."[7] Old truths become significant and useful in a present, appropriating faith. New, present activities of God make the history of God's people come alive and make eternal principles in ancient biblical writings vibrant. A living relationship blends old and new but has no room for meaningless tradition. David Hill makes this accurate statement:

> The "things new and old" are not opposed to one another, or simply added to one another. The new things *are* also the old, as Matthew demonstrates through his Gospel by constant reference to the OT. What was once regarded as old is now new, fresh, relevant and actual, thanks to the coming of Messiah.[8]

Truth is eternal. The Sermon on the Mount illustrates how Jesus' teaching was inherent within the Mosaic Law. Jesus' violent conflict with the Jewish scribes was not over the validity of the Law. Rather, Jesus differed with the scribes' explanation of the written Law. The scribes of Jesus' day promoted certain interpretations of Scripture, but they did not know the living God of the Scriptures!

Today Christian scribes are to make known the "old" mysteries that have always been present in the mind of God (Rom. 16:25; Eph. 1:9; 3:3,4,9) according to the "new" inspiration and application of the Holy Spirit. That way the church enjoys "at our gates . . . all manner of pleasant fruits, new and old" (Song of Sol. 7:13).

Jesus lived in present relationship with God, knowing the "old" treasures of God's past dealings with man. As a result, He could bring fresh interpretation and significance to a "new" generation that needed to meet God. James D.G. Dunn describes Jesus' experience and example:

> With Jesus, in short, we see the freshness of an original mind, a new spirit, taking up old categories and concepts, remoulding them, creating them afresh, using them in a wholly new way in the light of his basic experience of God caring and commanding him and of being bound to God by the closest ties of love and obedience.[9]

Is new wine better than old?

When Jesus changed water into wine at Canna, He did two important things. First, He introduced His power to perform miracles. Second, He gave a sign—a prophetic explanation—depicting how His messianic ministry had replaced the old religious system with one new and better.

At the wedding feast, the miracle wine immediately was judged better than the aged wine! When the master of ceremonies tasted the wine, not knowing its source, his response carried natural and spiritual significance:

> "This is wonderful stuff!" he said. "You're different from most. Usually a host uses the best wine first, and afterwards, when everyone is full and doesn't care, then he brings out the less expensive brands. But you have kept the best for the last!" (John 2:10 LB).

The miracle demonstrated a guiding principle of Christ's messianic ministry. It showed that Jesus does things in a new way. He bypasses traditional, accepted routes that fail to meet the needs of a new generation or fail to conform to God's present desires. The new and miraculous updates the old and traditional. The new way flows from direct relationship with God and not from institutionalized religious systems. Jesus reinforced this concept when he said:

> And no one puts new wine into old wineskins; otherwise the new wine will burst the skins, and it will be spilled out, and the skins ruined. But new wine must be put into fresh wineskins. And no one, after drinking old wine wishes for new; for he says, "The old is good enough" (Luke 5:37-39).

Jesus brought to man a fresh visitation of God that had to be received by responsive, flexible hearts. The new message simply could not be contained in the old, encrusted, traditional frame of mind. New wine demands new wineskins. Attitudes must be open and receptive or the explosive qualities of the fermenting wine of the Spirit will burst the dried-out, stiff, and resistant religious traditions.

Whenever God moves in fresh visitation, the human tendency is to say, "the old is good enough," or even, "the old is better" (Luke 5:39). T.W. Manson comments:

> The fact that wines improve with age was a commonplace in ancient literature. Here it is used to illustrate the power of tradition, established belief and custom in religion. The old ways are congenial; and those who are schooled in them will have nothing to do with new movements. They do not necessarily condemn the new; they just do not want to have

anything to do with it . . . . What our connoisseur says in effect is, "No wine is fit to drink till it is old." Hence no religious belief or practice which has not the sanctity of age is worth following. Jesus here says that a great obstacle to the reception of new revelation is the *pietas* of religious people.[10]

This is true in worship. People's beliefs about how they should approach God rest deeply within their hearts. They settle into unchangeable molds and habits of worship that become comfortable. As William Caird said in 1877, "Every intelligent Christian regards the system of worship followed by himself as the best."[11]

The inclination of religious groups

Man has a penchant to settle into comfortable structures of formalized religion and to neglect the vitality of his religious experience.[12] Paul described this state in its most extreme form as "having a form of godliness, but denying the power thereof" (2 Tim. 3:5). Jesus met people like this in the synagogues and temple. The church fights this tendency in every generation. A.B. Bruce, in his classic book, *The Training of the Twelve*, also sees this continuing process:

> The same thing happens to a greater or less extent every generation; for new wine is always in course of being produced by the eternal vine of truth, demanding in some particulars of belief and practice new bottles for its preservation, and receiving for an answer an order to be content with the old ones.[13]

This does not mean that every new religious movement or doctrine that comes along must be accepted without being tested. Every new surge of religious fervor, with its accompanying "revival phenomena," need not be embraced as authentic or appropriate. Nevertheless, Jesus' teaching warns us to continually recognize our propensity to grasp religious forms and to relax our hold on spiritual devotion and reality.

In religious movements, the first generation always has exuberance and vitality. Prophetic leaders birth new churches as the contemporary church lies in spiritual stagnation. Leaders of the new movement want to right the wrongs, purify the believers, and release the true church to fulfill its destiny in the world. Some biblical truth is presented in dramatic and radical ways with an appeal to "return to the worship of the New Testament church!" The emphasis usually focuses on a personal, satisfying experience with Christ *now*. The movement becomes the custodian of a "present truth."

During the second and third generations, "the flexibility of fresh religious experience begins to harden into set form."[14] Whereas the enthusiastic first generation lived dynamically through their own experience with God, those who follow attempt what is really not possible: to live vicariously through the ministry and message of past generations. As a result, "people find their security in the form, not in the experience of worship."[15]

Illion T. Jones in his well-known book, *A Historical Approach to Evangelical Worship*, suggests that religious reformation through the centuries has been cyclical, alternating between the prophetic and the priestly. He states:

Thus as history goes, reformations in worship are short-lived. The prophets provoke them and then inevitably by a natural process in the history of man's upward climb, the priests take over again. That process is said to result from the weakness of human nature, the weakness of prophetic religion, and the perennial appeal of priestly religion. One generation is unmoved by the high ideals of previous generations or lacks appreciation of their significance, so what once were noble aspirations are ignored, neglected, forgotten, and simply die for lack of support . . . . The enthusiasm and zeal engendered cool perceptibly in transmission from generation to generation, slowly subside, and then stagnate . . . . The high purposes of reformers are too high, too severe, too puritanic, too extreme.[16]

With honest hearts, new leaders attempt to preserve the glorious past of an established group. They formalize the faith and institutionalize their church, as if structure were the ultimate end or objective of the church. Teaching that meant so much to the founding fathers is hallowed and esteemed to the point where none dare challenge, reinterpret, or update it. The past becomes more important than the present.

With less inspired leadership, the church finds it difficult to maintain both spiritual vitality and functional decorum. The path of least resistance seems the easiest and wisest to follow, and organization replaces organism. Personal, spiritual experiences are replaced with teaching about the experiences. Present acts of faith are exchanged for recounting past acts of faith. Tradition becomes traditionalism, and the inspired message becomes a hallowed echo. Forms without spiritual virtue cannot perpetuate faith. Familiarity with mechanical practices of worship breed insensitivity to the Holy Spirit's present activity.

David Watson has confirmed this process. He said:

Often through the history of the church, the pattern has been the same: God breathes into his church fresh life by the renewing power of the Holy Spirit: man likes what he sees, organizes it, regiments it; and the patterns thereof continue for decades, if not for centuries, after the Spirit has quietly made his departure.[17]

In contrast, the local church that is open and responsive to the Spirit finds healthy vitality and excitement. While the order of a worship service requires reverent planning and care, the most inspiring and memorable moments occur when all feel the sovereign touch of God. Finding people with open minds and flexible hearts in an ordered setting, the Spirit comes in and brings inspiration! Stuffiness, dreary predictability, and formality vanishes. Joyful, uplifting worship emerges, and the Holy Spirit ministers to the people.

The Pauline solution

The apostle Paul balanced the new and old. He was a sterling example of the scribe that Jesus described in Matt. 13:52. He taught that the Christian faith is meaningful only when associated with and maintained by an ongoing experience in the Holy Spirit. In the churches he supervised, Paul achieved a dynamic synthesis between doctrinal teaching and pneumatic happening; new, present-day revelations and established traditions; ecstatic, charismatic manifestations and reasonable, proper decorum. He held the new and the old in dynamic tension. The present events of each church were energized by the inspiring hope of Christ's coming. Paul's approach, says James Dunn, has an attractive appeal:

> Perhaps the biggest challenge to twentieth-century Christianity is to take the Pauline exposition seriously, and to start not from what now is by way of tradition and institution, but instead to be open to that experience of God which first launched Christianity and to let that experience, properly safeguarded as Paul insisted, create new expressions of faith, worship and mission at both individual and corporate levels. One thing we may be sure of: the life of the Christian church can go forward only when each generation is able creatively to reinterpret its gospel and its common life out of its own experience of the Spirit and word which first called Christianity into existence.[18]

Any serious study of church renewal has to be anchored in the New Testament churches started under Paul's supervision. They provide the archetype, the model, the paradigm against which new ideas should be compared. Paul had a deep, pastoral concern for God's people. His shepherd's heart, coupled with his responsiveness to the Holy Spirit insured the spread of healthy, growing churches under his apostolic ministry.

Paul's success was not due to an obvious course laid before him, but he depended on daily guidance from the Holy Spirit. Paul clearly understood that Jesus had maintained His authority and view of reality through a continuous personal relationship with the heavenly Father. Jesus' example became Paul's model. Paul encouraged the Spirit within him and nurtured His own relationship with the Father.

Today's churches also prosper under this Pauline approach. Faithful stewardship demands an immediate application of both the old, trusted truths as well as a present cooperation with the Holy Spirit's guidance. God is presenting this glorious opportunity to us today!

Reflections

Every age knows the temptation to forget that the gospel is ever new. We try to contain the new wine of the gospel in old wineskins—outmoded traditions, obsolete philosophies, creaking institutions, old habits . . . . Human nature wants to conserve, but the divine nature is to renew. It seems almost a law that things initially created to aid the gospel eventually become obstacles—old wineskins. Then God has to destroy or abandon them so that the gospel wine can renew man's world once again.

—Howard A. Snyder[19]

Through ecumenical encounter and experience there has come to many of us an appreciation of ways of worship that were at first strange to us and which became, after some usage, means of grace. This is not an aping of each other, or a compromise to find a degree of uniformity. It is the work of the Holy Spirit leading us into the treasure-house of our heritage of worship as Christians.

—Leslie Earnshaw[20]

I am deeply concerned that we all learn all that we can from the great Christians of the past as well as from those living today about ways and means of enriching our worship services and making them more meaningful to all of the participants.

—Robert G. Rayburn[21]

A tradition gets started simply enough . . . . People start a practice because they find meaning in doing it. Others join in the practice . . . the practice gets passed on . . . . it's a tradition. The problem is that any given practice seldom means the same thing to the next generation . . . . those who learn the practice from the originators attach different meanings to that practice . . . . Our kids (and other followers) may learn our tradition, but . . . attach different meanings to them.

—Charles Kraft[22]

. . .the enthusiastic movement is denounced as an innovation, yet claims to be preserving, or to be restoring, the primitive discipline of the Church . . . good Christian people who do not relish an eccentric spirituality find themselves in unwelcome alliance with worldlings who do not relish any spirituality at all . . . . The high that proved too high, the heroic for earth too hard—it is a fugal melody that runs through the centuries.

—Ronald A. Knox[23]

8

Decades of Destiny

Thou knewest not the time of thy visitation.
—Luke 19:44 KJV

Recent events have dramatically affected the contemporary worship scene. Although nearly 2,000 years have passed since the days of the early church, the events of the past four decades have combined to create a spiritual climate reminiscent of Bible days. Serious students see how New Testament principles, lying dormant for a long time, now apply to today's church. Also, the very real potential exists to evangelize the world and to renew the church.

Great new dimensions are particularly evident in worship. Every church is experiencing radical challenge and change. Methodist Pastor David Randolph observed in the mid-1970s that:

> We are in the midst of a worship explosion that is likely to become even more dynamic in the years ahead. Explosion is not too strong a word, for what is happening in liturgy today is bursting forth in new forms of life while at the same time leaving unwanted repercussions in some quarters.[1]

The new openness and responsiveness in Christendom's liturgical renewal can be traced to a number of influences and special pressures. Five primary developments within the past three decades have affected the worship scene and suggest what the focus of church life is becoming.[2]

The Jesus-people movement. Droves of disillusioned, hurting youth during the 1960s turned to the simple good news of Jesus. Starting in California, the movement swept across the country. During this period, ragged youth started coming into our rather comfortable, structured church setting. Some arrived unkempt, uncombed and unshod. I remember one wild fellow with a flowing mane and bare feet who was accompanied by his dog of equally shaggy appearance. Girls came wearing stiff, dirty Levis. My mother, a dignified, godly woman, finally, said to me one day, "Son, I don't know if I can take much more." She expressed my sentiments exactly, but we prayed on.

We decided to keep the doors open to them and found it to be one of the greatest things we ever did. In spite of the problems they presented, their sincere love for Jesus greatly impacted our church as well as other churches that admitted them. They brought something wonderful. We learned a new responsiveness to God and human need.

The hang-loose, guitar-playing generation continues to make its mark on church music and worship. Some of the strongest married couples in our local church came out of that turbulent time.

The prophet pope. The prophetic plea of Pope John XXIII for a contemporary expression of faith and liturgy has profoundly influenced both Catholic and Protestant circles. Pope John used the word *aggiornamento* so often that the word found its way into the dictionaries of the major world languages. This word sounds foreign to the non-Italian ear, but it means "updating" and carries a strong, hopeful evangelical attitude toward the great possibilities open to the church. Vatican Council II adopted aggiornamento as its fundamental theme. Anyone reading *The Documents of Vatican II*[3] must be impressed by the great effort that has been made to enliven the Catholic worship experience. A statement from a Catholic worship booklet illustrates the dramatic suddenness of reform within the church:

> The ordinary Catholic no more looked for changes in the liturgy than he expected a new edition of the Ten Commandments or the election of a board of governors to replace the Pope.[4]

Reverberations of Vatican II liturgical reform have been felt all over the world. Truly the Pope had "opened a window."[5]

The charismatic/pentecostal movement. More than 429 million Christians in the world from nearly every branch of Christendom share a strong, common bond of religious conviction. They all believe the Holy Spirit is active in the church![6] This surging tide of dedicated Christianity has been the religious phenomenon of the 1960s, 1970s, 1980s, and now of the 1990s. It is a grassroots movement that continues to profoundly affect the longstanding worship traditions of Protestant and Catholic churches alike.[7] The astonishing worldwide growth is partially charted in Diagram 3.[8]

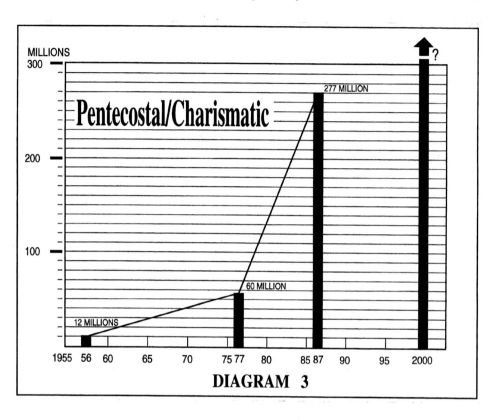

DIAGRAM 3

Many of these people are actively involved with the Holy Spirit. They believe in the rebirth of the *charismata,* or "gifts of the Holy Spirit" mentioned in 1 Corinthians, chapter 12, which includes prophecy, healing, and speaking in tongues. Charismatics who have had a dynamic encounter with the Holy Spirit suddenly find that Jesus, the Bible, and worship become the intense focus of their lives. When these people get together, their meetings usually involve participatory worship with free expression of praise and adoration. One leading charismatic Catholic remarked:

> The charismatic renewal fosters (among other things) a desire for worship. The more the developments of modern society makes people less and less satisfied with performing formal worship out of duty, the more the church needs movements which lead people to a spontaneous, freely chosen worship.[9]

The church-growth movement. A leading expert on contemporary church renewal is Lyle E. Schaller, editor of the excellent *Creative Leadership Series* books. He makes this observation:

From this observer's perspective the most significant development on the American religious scene during the past half century was the emergence of the Charismatic Renewal Movement during the 1960s. In a more recent and shorter time frame the most influential development of the 1970s was the emergence of the church growth movement.[10]

The church-growth movement recognizes Dr. Donald McGavran as its "father" and his classic, *Understanding Church Growth* as its basic text.[11] One of the most exciting concepts to emerge from this movement is the belief that many new churches can and must be started by existing churches, using apostolic church planters![12] The science of church growth analysis has become quite sophisticated, and some of these findings apply to local church worship.

In a chapter he wrote for one of Schaller's books, McGavran, lists four major difficulties in church planting and growth. One problem is liturgical style.[13] He claims liturgical styles keep many would-be sheep out of the fold. Denominations create their own cultures, settling into forms of worship that suit their own people but do not fit the majority of the community.

Many growing churches with less-formal, more expressive, free styles of worship reach and retain larger numbers of people. The trend of the times cannot be ignored. "Among evangelicals," explains Robert Webber of Wheaton College, "there is a growing demand to change the form of worship, to incorporate more variety in the service and to realize a more creative and meaningful expression of worship."[14]

The Media Explosion. The emphasis on worship is reaching an all-time high! Books on church growth, church renewal, and Christian community have flooded the evangelical reading market. Seminars, clinics, and conventions have created an awareness of the church's high calling and the importance of her mission. Television enables everyone to hear and see what other churches are doing, and viewers can observe the various modes of worship being modeled for them. Cassette tapes take new songs and messages around the world and cause all believers to sing the latest songs about Jesus Christ together.

Church life in 1980s and 1990s

The 1960s, 1970s, and 1980s laid groundwork for revitalizing Christ's church. The 1990s hold particular promise for re-emphasizing the importance of worship. *Charisma* magazine ranked praise and worship among the ten most significant trends in the 1980s.[15] One of the greatest contributions that may come out of present renewal activities would be a return to direct, heartfelt, participatory worship.

In the late 1970s, Fuller Theological Seminary conducted a survey of 30 prominent evangelical leaders. They were asked to make projections for the church of the 1980s. Some of the leaders said, "Worship will be the focus of church life in the 1980s." Some participants felt "a more biblical form of worship will develop," and that "worship will become increasingly participatory as lay involvement grows."[16] These predictions seem almost prophetic as we view what is now coming to pass!

Every leader must face this time of revolutionary change in church worship and find answers for people. Henry E. Horn, back in the early 1970s in *Worship In Crisis*,

correctly stated a truth that still rumbles powerfully in our day. He wrote, "the sweep is irresistible. Few congregations can maintain their composure."17
 This is a time of exciting opportunity for the church. The growing desire for new expression in worship should encourage every Christian because it indicates a deep longing by people to know and experience their God in a more gratifying way. Jerry Kerns suggests that "worship arises from the life of the people and expresses that life."18 This explains why dedicated Christians naturally will desire meaningful church services. This is happening NOW! A book from the mid-1980s by Vinson Synan confirms it. He states:

> A major reason for the existence of the Pentecostal/charismatic movements and the new "third wave" movement in the mainline churches is a great hunger for more expressive worship among most Christians. This emotional need is obviously not being satisfied by the liturgies and rituals of the historic churches. In a major study done in Minnesota in 1983, Christians of the mainline churches demonstrated what Martin Marty called a "pick and choose" attitude toward their faith.
>
> About 90 percent of the respondents preferred a "free-form" type of communication with God, in preference to the stylized and ritualized forms of traditional worship and prayer. The majority of the Minnesota respondents were Lutheran and Roman Catholics. The desire for direct and free communication with God who "intervenes in their lives and directs them in their vocations" leads many of them to participate in Pentecostal and charismatic prayer and worship services.
>
> Where the churches are not meeting this need, the people are voting with their feet.19

 Pastors must realize that God has allowed current events to precipitate a great need in people for inspiring and satisfying corporate worship. A primary responsibility of Christian ministers is to lead people in dynamic adoration of God. We dare not be intimidated by a new, searching generation and fail this challenge.
 Like Jesus and Paul, Christian believers nurture spiritual vitality by maintaining a fresh, personal relationship with God. It gives them an appreciation of their religious heritage as well as a sensitivity to the present working of the Holy Spirit. The admonition to the churches of Asia certainly seems appropriate today:

> He who has an ear, let him hear what the Spirit says to the churches (Rev 2:7, 11, 17, 29; 3:6, 13, 22)

Reflections

With the birth and rapid growth of several large "celebration-style" Adventist churches in Oregon and California, and with hundreds of congregations adding celebrative elements to their worship services, the church has been and is being forced to restudy the entire concept of worship to see how much innovation it will allow.

—*Myron Widmer*[20]

The point that needs to be made as these details are worked out by each congregation is that order ought to be the servant of spontaneity, not its enemy. The worshipers who learn and practice the principle will recover a dynamic sense of worship as an offering of praise and thanksgiving by the community of God's people.

—*Robert E. Webber*[21]

Fascinating to observe that we condemn what the Bible expressly commands as part of worship.

—*J. David Newman*[22]

In the past few decades Seventy-day Adventists have learned that carried to extreme, our highly cognitive, decent and orderly services can lead to a silent wasteland of dullness and passivity as devoid of genuine worship as fanaticism. Too often such an atmosphere has put us in touch not with the "still, small voice of God," but merely with the sound of a woman unwrapping a breath mint five pews away.

—*Deanna Davis*[23]

Part III

Challenging Thoughts on Biblical Worship

Mere mortal man can worship and serve the awesome eternal God.

9

A Fresh Look at the Meaning of Worship

Come! Let us throw ourselves at his feet in homage,
let us kneel before the Lord who made us.
—Psalm. 95:6 NEB

The object of a person's deepest respect and veneration receives his worship. The object may be the Lord, a false god, or a thing. It becomes the emotional focus of the worshiper and governs his thoughts and lifestyle in direct proportion to his sincerity. The worshiper acknowledges his dependence on his "god," and stands in awe as he recognizes his god's power and majesty. Keith Miller suggests that worship is "the object of your life's most intense focus."[1]

Worship directed toward the Lord expresses appreciation for who He is, for what He is, and for what He has done. Man expresses his total emotional, mental, spiritual, and physical nature when he reaches upward to God in adoration, praise, and thankfulness. Leslie Earnshaw describes it as "the whole personality engaged in aspiration, intent to seek, to find, and to express a true relationship with God.[2] Anne Ortlund, in her delightful little book, *Up With Worship*, tells us that worship is "admiring God" and that we should "tell God how wonderful He is by every fresh, innovative way you can."[3] David R. Mains shares this insight:

> When I transfer my attention vertically to God and tell Him the value I place on Him because of who He is, I am attributing worth to God, or worshipping.[4]

The definition of the English word *worship* reflects its history, according to Ralph Martin:

> Worship is a noble word. The term comes into our modern speech from the Anglo-Saxon *weorthscipe*. This later developed into worthship, and then into worship. It means, to attribute worth to an object. . . . To worship God is to ascribe to Him supreme worth, for He alone is worthy.[5]

65

A person becomes like the object he worships. A Christian's love relationship with God helps the Christian become like God. Ps. 115:8 says, "Those who make them (heathen gods) will become like them," while Christians "are being transformed into the same image (of the Lord)," according to 2 Cor. 3:18. In a way, it is like a devoted elderly couple who have lived many years together and have developed similar mannerisms. They may even tend to look alike.

Believers change when they worship. They take on the very attributes of whatever or whomever they esteem. The very basis of worship, according to D.C. Benson, is the "interfacing of the nature of our God and our collective being."[6]

Definitions of worship become more sharply focused through personal encounters with God, particularly in corporate worship in a local church. "Definitions may make the experience more meaningful," James F. White wisely comments, "but the experience of Christian worship in one's own life is absolutely necessary to understand the definitions."[7]

A true worshiper

Although the word *worship* does not appear in the narrative in Luke 7:36-50, the heroine of the story clearly illustrates its meaning.

A fallen woman who was touched and blessed by Jesus had chosen His way to be her way. As she thought of Him and all He had done for her, she decided to look for Him to express the deep appreciation that filled her heart. When she learned that Jesus would be dining at the house of Simon the Pharisee, she determined to go there. She realized how irrational it would be to arrive uninvited at a dinner party of one of the city's most illustrious persons. Such a gathering would be no place for an immoral woman to appear!

The sins of her past loomed before her eyes. Rather than discouraging her, they sent her searching through her belongings for a gift suitable to express her deep repentance. Her eyes lit upon the alabaster box, and she knew immediately that this most precious possession would declare the feelings of her heart. The expensive ointment contained in the vial suddenly seemed of little value when compared to the miracle Jesus worked in her life. Grasping the gift, the uninvited woman hurried to the dinner.

Meanwhile, Jesus arrived at Simon's house. No affectionate embrace or kiss greeted the visiting rabbi, and no water was offered for the washing of the visitor's feet. These actions did not go unnoticed by those present, but Jesus offered no protest or comment. We can only wonder why the common courtesies of the day were not performed. Was Simon so excited that he forgot? Some suggest that the oversights were deliberate.

The guests intermingled and conversation flowed. Servants brought the food and drink while the guest's reclined on low couches around the table. Undoubtedly, Simon wished for all to be impressed, and he savored the effect created in having the popular teacher in his home.

Then it happened.

Suddenly she was there, bending over the bare feet of Jesus! The reclining men looked aghast at the immoral woman who not only had broken in upon their revelry but dared approach the honored guest.

Silence fell upon the room as the woman's tears began to drop upon Jesus' dusty feet. The revelation of who He was broke upon her, and the woman's soul released like a fountain. Her copious tears washed the Master's feet, and she added reverent kisses. The perfume of the alabaster jar began to permeate the atmosphere. To everyone's amazement, the woman anointed His feet.

Then, undoing the tresses of her hair, the bowing woman began to wipe dry the feet of Jesus with her crowning glory. The woman and Jesus seemed oblivious to any embarrassment. However, Simon quickly responded by decrying such an emotional display as unnecessary and unwarranted. The woman's very character and motive were questioned. Since he strained to accept Jesus as a prophet, the Pharisee was easily amazed at, and contemptuous of, the sinful woman's acceptance of Him as Savior.

Jesus received the woman's tears, kisses, ointment and the drying of His feet with her hair. The Lord saw in this obeisant woman an expression of worship that would be envied by every succeeding generation and culture. What was unorthodox and improper to the religious Pharisee was completely approved—even preferred—by Jesus.

Many years later, Charles Wesley captured the feelings of that woman (and everyone else who has been touched by the Master) when he wrote the hymn:

> Depth of mercy! Can there be
> Mercy still reserved for me?
> Can my God His wrath forbear
> Me, the chief of sinners, spare?
>
> I have long withstood His grace.
> Long provoked Him to His face.
> Would not hearken to His calls,
> Grieved Him by a thousand falls.
>
> Lord, incline me to repent;
> Let me know my sins lament;
> Now my foul revolt deplore,
> Weep, believe, and sin no more.
>
> Still for me the Savior stands,
> Holding forth His wounded hands;
> God is love! I know, I feel,
> Jesus weeps and loves me still. Amen

A second anointing

Mary, the sister of Lazarus, also anointed the feet of Jesus and wiped them with her hair. She did it in the house of Simon the Leper (John 12: 2-8); Mark's account adds significantly that the fragrant nard was poured on Jesus' head (Mark 14:3-9).[8]

Both women bowed before Jesus, literally bending over so that lips, tears and hair could minister to His feet. Personal vanity was cast aside by the women at the opportunity to express their deep devotion. By using their hair to wipe His feet, they indicated that their greatest "glory" (1 Cor. 11:15) paled to insignificance in His presence.

Each woman had her own reason for worshiping Jesus. The immoral woman acknowledged Him as Savior from her sins. About three years later, Mary bowed before Him as Lord of her life. They represent the two extremes of the spectrum of worship. Worship begins for the individual when he turns in repentance from his sins and acknowledges that God alone can save him. This is beautifully pictured by the first woman. Unlike the unnamed woman, Mary had followed Jesus for a period of time. She knew His teaching and His miracle-working power. She had reflected on His life and message, and in that grand moment of devotion it all climaxed for her as she anointed Him Lord.

The women's stories show how people's revelation of worship is directly affected by the position Jesus occupies in their lives. Worship is an integral part of the total Christian experience and commitment—not something separate. As Christians mature spiritually, the Holy Spirit deepens the revelation within them and keeps worship fresh. Believers cannot stop their spiritual progression without stopping their worship progression.

The root meaning of worship

The Hebrew and Greek words most frequently translated as *worship* in the Bible actually describe the bowing actions of Mary and the unnamed woman. The words refer to the physical act of a worshiper prostrating himself before his deity. A worshiper bows with an inner attitude of devotion and humility. David clearly captured the essence of these words in the invitation:

O come, let us worship and bow down; let us kneel before the LORD our maker. For He is our God . . . and we are the sheep of His hand (Ps. 95:6 KJV).

The prominent Greek word for worship is *proskuneo*.[9] W.E. Vine states in his dictionary that the word means:

To make obeisance, do reverence to (from *pros*, towards, and *kuneo*, to kiss) . . . the most frequent word rendered worship. It is used of an act of homage and reverence.[10]

The New International Dictionary of NT Theology adds this insight:

The basic meaning of *proskyneo*, in the opinion of most scholars, is to kiss . . . . Among the Greeks the vb. is a technical term for the adoration of the gods, meaning to fall down, prostrate oneself, adore on one's knees . . . in order to kiss the earth (i.e., the earth deity) or the image of a god, one had to cast oneself on the ground.[11]

Picture a person falling on his knees or face and kissing someone else's feet, the hem of a garment, or the ground on which a person or deity stands. That is Old Testament worship. The heart attitude is primary, but the concept of worship in the Bible includes appropriate body action. The humility of the total person is involved.

A Fresh Look at the Meaning of Worship

The most-used Hebrew word for worship is *shâchâh*. It means to show reverence, to bow down, to do homage, to prostrate oneself before another. The literal meaning is "a bowing down." Ralph Martin comments that the emphasis is in:

> the way in which an Israelite fittingly thought of his approach to the holy presence of God. He bows himself down in lowly reverence and prostration . . . . The Greek term, used in the Septuagint to translate *shahah*, is *proskunein*, with the same overtone of submissive lowliness and deep respect.[12]

In his book *Worship of Ancient Israel*, A.S. Herbert makes this helpful statement:

> The English noun and verb indicated the response of the soul to the absolute worth of God, and that response will normally include outward, physical expression. The Hebrew word most commonly translated "to worship" . . . emphasizes the physical expression appropriate to one who comes into the presence of the holy majesty of God. He bows himself down, prostrates himself. It is the appropriate action before a leader or a king (Gen. 27:19; 1 Sam. 25:23; 2 Sam. 14:33, 24:20) . . . . It corresponds to the usage (though not its etymological meaning) of the Greek verb *proskuneo* by which it is most frequently translated in the Septuagint. To worship God is quite literally to bow oneself down to the ground before the divine King.[13]

Although bowing was customary in honoring kings and holy men, this fact does not discount the obvious significance of the action in biblical worship.[14] The people of Bible days understood the difference between the bowing that honored men and the homage that exalted God:

1. Mordecai refused to bow to Haman (Esther 3:2).
2. Peter rebuked Cornelius for bowing before him (Acts 10:25).
3. John was rebuked in heaven for bowing before the messenger (Rev. 19:10; 22:9).
4. Jesus' classic use of *proskuneo* in John 4 certainly indicates the spiritual significance now assigned to the root meaning.
5. Satan, of course, knew the implications involved in tempting Jesus to bow before him (Matt. 4:9).
6. The worship of heaven involves constantly repeated bowing (mentioned twenty-four times in Revelation).

Napoleon Bonaparte probably gave one of the best explanations of the difference between honoring a man and worshiping God: "If Socrates would enter the room, we should rise and do him honor," Bonaparte said. "But if Jesus Christ came into the room, we should fall down on our knees and worship him."[15]

Must today's worshiper bow?

Just because ancient Hebrew concepts of worship involved physical homage, do twentieth-century Christians literally need to bow down to truly worship God? Worshipers need not always assume a bowing posture. The Bible directs worshipers to stand at times (see chapter 22). But it is equally important to state that the sincere worshiper will, at suitable times, bow or involve appropriate bodily action in his worship. Although it may not always be convenient or necessary to assume a bowing posture, the prostration of our pride remains an unchanging necessity. The real, inner self must be truly humble before His presence.

> And whoever exalts himself shall be humbled; and whoever humbles himself shall be exalted (Matt. 23:12).

> All of you, clothe yourself with humility toward one another, for *God is opposed to the proud, but gives grace to the humble.* Humble yourselves, therefore, under the mighty hand of God, that He may exalt you at the proper time. (1 Pet. 5:5, 6, emphasis added).

Consider how the actions of Mary and the unnamed woman who kissed the feet of Jesus point to the real heart of *proskynesis* (noun form of *proskyneo*).[16] They allowed their true inner feelings to flow forth in total devotion, and their worship literally became pneuma-psycho-somatic as it involved spirit-soul-body.[17] The essentials of worship are seen in each of their five actions:

- Bowing shows humility, submission, breaking of self-will.
- Weeping shows repentance springing from godly sorrow.
- Wiping shows relinquishment of earthly claims and glory.
- Kissing shows devotion, love, gratefulness, joy.
- Anointing shows homage, recognition, acclamation, awe, sacrifice.

Men continue to search for more meaningful and relevant worship styles, formats, symbols, and architecture. These things certainly are appropriate in their places; however, a serious search to find an adequate theology of worship only leads back to the Greek word proskynesis. It implies the prostration of human pride, the laying low of human will, before the Lord.[18] To approach God in worship, man needs an attitude of genuine humility and dependence. He needs an awareness and conviction of God's greatness. He needs to acknowledge that God is the source of life and blessing. Watchman Nee must have had this in mind when he wrote:

> If we truly intend to be worshippers of God, then a day must come in our history when we realize that merely to know Him as our Father and ourselves as His children is totally inadequate. We need to know God as God and ourselves as His bond-servants. Not until this revelation breaks upon us can we worship Him in truth. Not until we meet God as God can we really bow before Him. Not till then do we realize that we are His subjects. It is this realization that begets worship. But it does not end there. Such a seeing of God not only causes us to fall before Him; it leads us to recognize His ways.[19]

A Fresh Look at the Meaning of Worship

Old Testament examples
Consider the following Old Testament characters who worshiped, bowing low before God:
- *Abraham* worshiped God for demanding the sacrifice of his son (Gen. 22:5).
- *Eliezer* worshiped God for prospering his journey through miraculous guidance (Gen. 24:26, 48, 52).
- *Moses* worshiped on Sinai as God revealed Himself and proclaimed His ways (Exod. 34:8, 9).
- *Joshua* worshiped God as he met the Captain of the Lord's hosts (Josh. 5:14).
- *Gideon* worshiped God gratefully for confirming His will (Judg. 7:13-15).
- *Hannah* and *Elkanah* worshiped God for promising a child (1 Sam. 1:19).
- *Job* worshiped God when deprived of everything (Job 1:20, 21).

The eight people mentioned above worshiped separately, but the Old Testament also mentions eight occasions of corporate or congregational worship where reverential awe was accompanied by physical prostration:
- When Moses and Aaron had told the elders of Israel about God's desire to deliver from Egypt, "then they bowed low and worshiped" (Exod. 4:31).
- While Moses met with God in his tent, "all the people would arise and worship, each at the entrance of his tent" (Exod. 33:10).
- When Moses explained the Passover, "the people bowed low and worshiped" (Exod. 12:27).
- At Solomon's coronation "all the assembly blessed the LORD, the God of their fathers, and bowed their heads, and worshiped the LORD, and did obeisance to the king" (1 Chron. 29:20 RSV).
- When the fire of God fell at the dedication of Solomon's temple all the people "bowed themselves with their faces to the ground upon the pavement, and worshipped, and praised the LORD" (2 Chron. 7:3 KJV).
- Jehoshaphat and all the people, reacting to the prophetic word, "fell before the LORD, worshipping the LORD" (2 Chron. 20:18 KJV).
- All the people worshiped during the time of Hezekiah's revival (2 Chron. 29:28-30).
- The people responded to Ezra's leadership by crying, "Amen, Amen, with lifting up their hands: and they bowed their heads and worshiped the LORD with their faces to the ground" (Neh. 8:6 KJV); also, amazing as it seems, the people confessed and worshiped for a fourth part of a day (9:3).

Examples from Matthew and John
The first account of proskynesis in the New Testament is found in Matthew, chapter 2. Appropriately, the first recorded worshipers are *wise* men. An extraordinary sign in the heavens had arrested the attention of these serious seekers of truth. They recognized that an unusual star testified to the birth of *the* King of the Jews. Kings in their own right, they willingly journeyed through perilous places to find the godly child. At first sight of Him, they fell down and worshiped. The Greek text says literally, "and falling they worshipped him"(M).[20] Their choice gifts, much like the accoutrements of our worship services, were only significant when presented *after* their hearts and postures had rendered true proskynesis.

71

Approximately twenty-five years later, the matured Jesus came to the end of an exhausting forty-day wilderness fast (Matt. 4:4-11). With physical energies depleted, Jesus faced the climax of the most diabolical of all temptations: the glory and power of all kingdoms would be His if He would only "fall down and worship" the devil. Summoning up all remaining physical strength and spiritual reserve, the Son of God avowed Moses' statement that proskynesis belongs only to the LORD God! Satan, unable to stand before such an acclamation, made a hasty retreat.

Matthew continues to use this word to describe the pitiful leper asking for healing (8:2); Jairus seeking life for his daughter (9:18); the awe-struck disciples after seeing Jesus walk on water (14:33); the begging Canaanite woman who would not take "no" for an answer (15:25); the mother and sons with the improper request (20:20); the women beholding the resurrected Jesus (28:9); and the eleven elated disciples when they saw Jesus (28:17).

So many people sought healing and help from Jesus. The miracles recorded in the Bible describe people who first came to worship and then received help. This principle of putting "first things first" should not be ignored. People must not worship only for what they can get from God. They must love and adore Him for what He is.

In the key New Testament text on worship in John, chapter 4, a Samaritan woman argued with the Messiah at a well. Imagine a harlot debating the theology of worship with Jesus! Firmly but kindly, he told the woman that true proskynesis involves more than a holy place for sacred liturgy. He spoke of a communion with God that would be in Spirit and Truth, a Spirit-empowered worship that would transcend hollow religious activities of sectarian groups and truly be acceptable to God.

The Gadarene

The madman of Gadara provides one of the most amazing incidents recorded in the Bible. Possessed by a legion of unclean spirits, the man wandered the uninhabited land like a wild animal. His presence terrified the village folk. However, nothing could hold him. He broke all chains.

All night and all day, among the tombs and in the mountains, he would howl and gash himself with stones (Mark 5:5 JB).

Then he saw Jesus and he felt drawn by an irresistible power greater than the evil spirits within. Running toward Jesus, the madman fell at Christ's feet, offering inward and outward proskynesis to his new-found Lord!

The blind man

In John, chapter 9, Jesus used an unusual agent to heal a man born blind. Jesus mixed His spittle with dust and placed the resultant clay upon the sightless eyes. When the clay was rinsed away later at the pool of Siloam, the man could see. Everyone was astounded, including the man's parents. However, the Pharisees challenged the authenticity of the miracle since it was performed on the Sabbath. Ordinarily the poor man would have been no match for their religious interrogation, but now his argument was flawless—he could see!

The blind man did not even know Jesus. He had never seen Him. Later when Jesus came to him and identified Himself, the man exclaimed, "Lord, I believe!" The Bible text adds: "And he worshiped Him" (John 9:38). Imagine the depth and intensity in this man's proskynesis. His inward-outward response is explained by H. Schönweiss who stated that this "obeisance is nothing less than the outward reflex action of faith: to believe means to adore Jesus, to recognize him as Lord, to render him homage as king."[21]

Proskynesis in Heaven

Proskuneo appears twenty-four times in the Apocalypse. Proskynesis is constantly repeated by the worshipers of heaven (Rev. 4:10, 5:14, 7:11, 11:16; 19:4). Every reference mentions falling down. Adoration seems to be the chief characteristic of the heavenly worship—an adoration that releases a creative power in the *proskunountes* (worshipers) to offer increasingly greater offerings of praise to their king and God.

The worship of the dragon, beast and image is also emphasized (Rev. 13:4, 8, 12, 15; 14:9, 11; 16:2; 19:20; 20:4). Such references indicate that worship in these last days is an issue of major consequence. Unable to conquer Jesus, the devil next seeks the religious devotion of men everywhere, particularly those bearing Christ's name. However, the LORD ultimately triumphs, and—as the overcomers sing—"all nations shall come and worship before thee" (Rev 15:4 KJV).

Reflections

Worship is, in the first place, a complete prostration of the soul before its object; whether the heart of the worshiper be directed toward the vain imaginations of the heathen, or to the one true and living God.

—*Thomas Kimber*[22]

I come to adore His splendour, and fling myself and all that I have at His feet, this is the only possible formula for worship.

—*Evelyn Underhill*[23]

Worship is the adoration of God, the ascription of supreme worth to God, and the manifestation of reverence in the presence of God.

—*Willard L. Speery*[24]

It is the soul's approach to God in wonder, adoration, love and communion . . . the response of the human soul to the brooding tenderness, the matchless love, the pure holiness, and the awesome majesty of God . . . . an experience in which we consciously join our hearts with the Eternal, and the currents of the spirit flow between the human soul and the divine.

—*Edward K. Ziegler*[25]

What is the essence of worship? It is the celebration of God! When we worship God, we celebrate Him: We extol Him, we sound His praises, we boast in Him . . . . As a thoughtful gift is a celebration of a birthday, as a special evening out is a celebration of an anniversary, as a warm eulogy is a celebration of a life—so a worship service is a celebration of God!

—*Ronald Allen and Gordon Borror*[26]

Worship is nothing more than opening one's heart to God and enjoying a relationship of loving communion with him.

—*Bob Sorge*[27]

In Jn. 4:20ff. proskynein seems to have a wholly figurative sense. Yet the act of worship stands in the background. What Jesus says is that there is no one place of worship. The concrete act is lifted up into the sphere of spirit and truth which now controls it. This does not mean a total spiritualizing of worship but the possibility of true worship at all times and in all places.

—*H. Greeven*[28]

10

The Majesty of God

Then when you realize your worthlessness before the Lord,
He will lift you up, encourage and help you.
—James 4:10 LB

The word majesty best describes the transcendent greatness of God. People speak of the "majestic Alps," or "Her Majesty's Navy," but majesty finds its most appropriate use applied to God, for only He is truly regal, lofty, imposing, grand, magnificent, splendid, glorious, noble, and elegant.

> O LORD our God, the majesty and glory of your name fills all the earth and overflows the heavens (Ps. 8:1 LB).

> Bless the LORD, O my soul! O LORD my God, Thou art very great; Thou art clothed with splendor and majesty (Ps. 104:1).

> On the glorious splendor of Thy majesty, And on Thy wonderful works, I will meditate (Ps. 145:5).

Awareness of God's awesome majesty also brings an immediate consciousness of human poverty. The spiritual man humbly bows or prostrates himself *proskuneo* (Greek) before God, laying all that he is before the revelation of his God's greatness.[1] Men may lie or crawl at the feet of a worldly monarch to appease him or win his acceptance, but the biblical concept of prostrating oneself before God does not convey the idea of groveling. Biblical worship rests on the conviction that God is all-glorious, wonderfully perfect, devoted to the care and concerns of His people, and totally worthy of highest praise.

> Thou art worthy, O Lord, to receive glory and honor and power; for thou hast created all things, and for thy pleasure they are and were created (Rev. 4:11 KJV).

A worshiper of almighty God relinquishes human demands. He realizes that, without God's help, he has no merit, dignity, maturity, seniority, or authority. Man cannot approach God on a basis of how much he has, what he knows, or what he deserves. Man is helplessly dependent on God's mercy and grace. "No flesh should glory in His presence" (1 Cor. 1:29 KJV).[2]

This is a gateway to a glorious destiny, not a dismal sentence to mediocrity. Men find self-esteem and self-worth when they focus on God's majesty. Men exist to glorify God by sharing His glory. His glory has been and will be shared in direct proportion to the way men properly worship. Men become like the God they worship. Worshipers of the Lord abandon self-help and human pride.

> For thus says the high and exalted One
> Who lives forever, whose name is Holy,
> "I dwell on a high and holy place,
> And also with the contrite and lowly of spirit
> In order to revive the spirit of the lowly
> And to revive the heart of the contrite (Isa. 57:15).

> For though the LORD is exalted,
> Yet He regards the lowly;
> But the haughty He knows from afar (Ps. 138:6).

Worship, or "worth-ship," is simply recognizing merit in another. Man recognizes and proclaims God's merit when he praises and adores God. Worship allows God to occupy the center of attention and frees man's mind from concentrating on his own merit or personal concerns. Psalmic modes of singing and physical movement fit naturally with heartfelt, genuine, theocentric worship expressions. Pastor Jack Hayford captured this thought well in one of his sermons:

> There is no shame in submitting to the supernatural by both inward sincerity as well as overt, public action. God is my ALL. My reservations are released. I now fully acknowledge the absolute supremacy, the unquestioned authority, and the supremely glorious majesty of the one and only true and living God. It is then that His hand "picks me up" and with trembling flesh I now know that His hand is upon me and I am His messenger.[3]

Seraphs cry, 'Holy, holy, holy'

People have been inspired for centuries by the great worship event Isaiah saw when God called him to the prophetic ministry. King Uzziah's tragic death provided the setting. The king reigned for fifty-two years, and "as long as he sought the LORD, God prospered him" (2 Chron. 26:5). However, as time passed, Uzziah became less dependent on God's help. He built fortress cities and great engines of war. He developed a strong army plus an additional group of elite fighting men. All went well until:

He became strong, his heart was so proud that he acted corruptly, and he was unfaithful to the LORD his God, for he entered the temple of the LORD to burn incense on the altar of incense (2 Chron. 26:16).

The king was stricken with leprosy because he presumed to worship God on his own terms. He even raged at the priests who tried to restrain him from his madness. His rash acts became known throughout Judah, and the leprous king became a graphic symbol of God's judgment on improper worship. As Uzziah died, God summoned Isaiah using a dramatic worship setting that clearly contrasted the glorious splendor of God's majestic holiness with the wretched spiritual state of the fallen king. Isaiah's humility stood in sharp contrast with Uzziah's pride and arrogance.

In the year of King Uzziah's death, I saw the Lord seated high on a lofty throne, while the train of his robes flowed over the temple floor. Seraphs hovered around him, each with six wings—two to cover their faces, two to cover their feet and two to keep them in the air. They kept calling to each other, crying:

"Holy, holy, holy is the Lord of hosts; The whole earth is full of his glory."

The doorway shook to its foundations at the sound of their voices, and smoke began to fill the temple. Then I said, "Alas for me—for I am finished! I am a foul-mouthed man and I live among a foul-mouthed people. For with my own eyes I have seen the King, the Lord of hosts." Then one of the seraphs flew towards me carrying a red-hot coal which he had taken with tongs from the altar. With this he touched my mouth saying, "See, now your guilt shall go and your sin be forgiven!" Then I heard the voice of the Lord, saying: "Whom shall I send? Who will go for us?"

And I said, "Here am I: send me." Then he said, "Go, and say to this people . . ." (Isa. 6:1-9a, PHILLIPS).

A format for dramatic flow

In true worship a dynamic dialogue occurs between God and man. This is sometimes referred to as "the drama of worship." Isaiah's account of heavenly worship is often used to illustrate the potential dramatic flow of a church service. Diagram 4 outlines a sample or model format for the drama based on Isaiah, chapter 6.[4] The Isaiah passage does not explicitly mention every step shown in this drama outline. The outline merely suggests an underlying framework upon which a more comprehensive order of worship can be built.

Two significant facts emerge from the study of the Isaiah paradigm:

1. God initiates the process of worship by impressing the prophet with God's majestic holiness. God reveals. God forgives. God renews. God commissions.

2. Man responds to God's continual initiative, showing his personal incapability to worship properly without divine aid. Man acknowledges . . . man confesses . . . man responds . . . man offers himself.

In other words, in worship we give worth to God because He first gives worth to us through Christ.

THE DRAMA OF WORSHIP
(An Exciting Dialogue Between Man and God.)

God initiates the process.

Man responds to God's initiative.

The Steps in the Dialogue

1. God reveals himself to man.

2. Man acknowledges God with praise, adoration, reverence, awe, wonder.

3. God reveals man's condition to man (sin).

4. Man acknowledges his sin, confessing it to God.

5. God forgives man and cleanses him.

6. Man is now freed to release other burdens to the Lord (through prayers of petition and intercession).

7. God takes those requests and relieves man of the burden.

8. Man responds with gratitude to God.

9. God speaks to renewed man revealing His will and desires.

10. Man responds by submitting himself to God's will offering himself for whatever God desires.

11. God is pleased and seals man's decisions by His Spirit.

12. Man is now a restored, refreshed, commissioned person and he leaves this encounter with God rejoicing and celebrating.

DIAGRAM 4

The dilemma

In a nutshell, the dilemma of worship asks: Is it possible to know the majestic God of the Bible and personally enjoy Him? To know the God of the Bible is both terrifying and appealing. His loftiness or solemnity seems to make God so transcendent and alone, yet the Bible suggests that He is accessible to man. Men must find an approach to God that balances humility and joy. God's majesty requires man's humility, and God's grace releases joy in man. The following famous words from the Westminster Catechism capsulizes the dilemma:

Q. What is the chief end of man?
A. Man's chief end is to glorify God, and to enjoy Him forever.

The worshiping New Testament Christian finds Christ's answer to religion's dilemma and fulfills man's chief end to glorify and enjoy God.

Grace greater than all my sin

King David leaped over foreboding Old Testament concepts of worship into a New Testament understanding. His insights release new dimensions of joy and open deeper relationships with God. Many of David's Psalms are messianic. They speak of a coming Son of God who fulfills God's requirement for justice and righteousness. This Messiah also releases a flow of grace and love that makes knowing God a wonderful experience. Living in one age, David experienced the worship of an "age to come."

The New Testament church draws from David's prophetic insights. Christians energized by the Holy Spirit enjoy Jesus' salvation and learn to come boldly to God's throne, trusting in His mercy and grace.

The author of the book of Hebrews compares the severity of the Old Testament system with the abounding grace of the New Testament approach. Jesus Christ has made the old approach to God "obsolete" (Heb. 8:13). He Himself has becomes the glorious, new, high priest who lives to make intercession for us (7:25). Christ offered Himself as an atoning sacrifice. His act of worship was perfect. It superseded that of all mankind combined. His act was performed once, never to be repeated because it never could be duplicated.[5] The incense of Jesus' worship continues spreading its pleasing aroma before the throne of God. Jesus the Priest and sacrificial Lamb becomes the Leader (*leitourgos*) of our worship (8:1, 2)! Through His death, He opened a new and living way so that the church now approaches God with joyful boldness and confidence through the precious blood of Jesus (10:19, 20).

These thoughts from the book of Hebrews link directly with the thunderous acclamations in the book of Revelation. There God accepts the redeemed and gives them an audience through Christ the Priest and Christ the Lamb.

Worthy is the Lamb that was slain to receive power and riches and wisdom and might and honor and glory and blessing (Rev. 5:12).

To Him who sits on the throne, and to the Lamb, be blessing and honor and glory and dominion forever and ever (Rev. 5:13).

The Spirit brings an overwhelming revelation! The inaccessible, Old Testament God of fire has become the personally involved, New Testament Christ of love, mercy and grace. Christ has paid for man's rebellion and sin in one great sacrificial act of worship. Justice is satisfied and forgiveness granted (Heb. 12:18-29). And now, the church of sainted sinners finds complete access to God through prayer and worship, thanks to Christ the ever-living intercessor and mediator. God sees His people today through Christ's atoning blood. God extends loving grace to men and women, beckoning them to come forward as redeemed sons and daughters to enjoy the bounties of His presence.

Reverential awe characterized Old Testament prayer and worship. Today, New Testament worshipers still must acknowledge God's majesty with great reverence; however, believers have the indwelling Holy Spirit and Jesus Christ to mediate their approach to God. Like a plastic overlay that gives new significance to another transparency, the life of Jesus translates the unbearable judgment of God into loving acceptance. This is why Jude wrote:

> Now to Him who is able to keep you from stumbling, and to make you stand in the presence of His glory blameless with great joy, to the only God our Savior, through Jesus Christ our Lord, be glory, majesty, dominion and authority, before all time and now and forever. Amen (Jude 24, 25).

God retains His majesty yet His grace causes Him to see His redeemed people as perfect and whole through Christ. His people, in turn, see such an amazing love pouring forth from His lofty throne that they find great joy in His presence rather than cringe in fear. Worship is truly authentic and pleases God the Father when it centers on Christ.

Jack Hayford's worship chorus, *Majesty,* has been sung all over the world in many languages. It captures the transfer of emphasis on majesty from the awesome, lofty God to the loving, grace-filled Jesus.

> Majesty, worship His Majesty.
> Unto Jesus be all glory, honor, and praise,
> Majesty, Kingdom authority
> Flows from His throne, unto His own;
> His anthem raise.
> So exalt, lift up on high
> The name of Jesus.
> Magnify, come glorify
> Christ Jesus, the King.
> Majesty, worship His majesty;
> Jesus who died, now glorified,
> King of all kings.[6]

Worship in Spirit and truth requires humility and dependence, even though the natural mind does not see the need for it. Human nature yields to carnal pride even in dedicated Christians. The answer to pride is more of God's grace. Oddly, God supplies the needed grace through difficulties and situations that humble people and make them dependent on Him. Therefore difficulties are blessings in disguise. God knows that unless His people maintain a humble dependence on Him, their ambitions will develop an incompatibility with His will. God wants to bless His people but only if they walk in His ways, according to His principles.

Jesus stressed this very thing when He said, "Blessed are the poor in spirit." (Matt. 5:3). Jesus meant "poor" in the sense that His followers know that they can do no good thing without divine assistance. They are dependent on His power to help them do what God requires them to do.

Serious prayer also compels people to face human pride and genuinely repent before the Lord. Prayer enables them to align themselves properly with the will of God.

As Pastor Paul Y. Cho points out, "No one can sense pride in the presence of a holy God . . . . Brokenness and pride cannot coexist!"[7]

Reflections

If there be one characteristic more than others that contemporary public worship needs to recapture it is this awe before the surpassingly great and gracious God.

—*Henry Sloane Coffin*[8]

I now believe that an awareness of God's transcendence demands that we recover a sense of the majesty of God in our worship services. This will call for a revolution of consciousness whereby we change our perception of God and our habits of relating to Him. And in doing so, we will recover the true spirit of worship which dominated the Church in the New Testament days . . . . This is nothing new, but rather a recovery of our heritage.

—*Robert E. Webber*[9]

In practical terms the dilemma of worship is to know how to unite the solemn and the joyous, remembering that solemn does not mean mournful, for God is not dead and Jesus is the risen Savior, and that joyous is not another word for flippant, for God is holy and Jesus is Lord.

—*Ralph P. Martin*[10]

The transcendent aloneness of God and yet also, paradoxically, His accessibility to man.

—*C.F.D. Moule*[11]

When the heart on its knees moves into God's awesome presence, and hears with fear and wonder things not lawful to utter, the mind falls flat. Words, which were previously its faithful servants, become weak and totally incapable of telling what the heart hears and sees. In that moment, the worshiper can only cry, "Oh!"

—*A.W. Tozer*[12]

We need to know the fear of the Lord—the overwhelming, compelling awe and reverence of a holy God. The fear of the Lord is the beginning of wisdom: It provides the right perspective on God's sovereign rule over all creation; the sense of God's power and perfection that dwarfs mere men and women, that causes them to bow and worship and glory in His amazing grace.

—*Charles Colson*[13]

11

Worship Him, Serve Him!

*Thou shalt worship the Lord thy God,
and him only shalt thou serve.*
—Matthew 4:10 KJV

Many things go together naturally like bread and butter, nuts and bolts, salt and pepper, and male and female. An old song romanced the virtues of "love and marriage" that go together "like a horse and carriage." In Christian thinking, worship and service should go together.

Most American churches call their Sunday morning congregational meetings "Worship Services." They frequently turn out to be neither worship nor service. Those involved in church renewal should rethink the relationship between these two important terms. A misunderstanding of these two words has caused a tragic loss of vitality in the church and accounts for the pathetic condition described by theologian Paul Hoon:

> Something seems to have fatally gone wrong, and one suspects that it has to do not least with the church's worship. The powerlessness of worship to transform life is appalling, and seems to be reducing the church to impotence.[1]

Heart ignites religious duty

Doing things *for* God must not replace the love given *to* God. Love characterizes the worship which the heavenly Father seeks (John 4:23). Duties can complement a person's devotional experience with God but never substitute for it.[2]

Worship of God in its purest sense must precede service to others on God's behalf. Actually, genuine humanitarian service springs from true worship. A worshiper will serve. To expose oneself to the serving heart of God through our adoration will only cause our own attitude to be as His. Religious duty which is ignited by a worshiping heart will be free of selfish ambition and desire for recognition. Clarice Bowman states:

83

Always, when the worship of the living God is made central, it has fired people with moral earnestness, inflamed their ethical zeal, and sent them forth to right wrongs in society.[3]

Christians do not have the option to choose between worship and service. Such a choice would be like a person choosing to keep either his heart or his lungs; both are essential, and a choice is out of the question. Local church programs must balance worship with service such as church attendance, evangelism, and welfare activities.

Through Him then, let us continually offer up a sacrifice of praise to God, that is, the fruit of lips that give thanks to His name. And do not neglect doing good and sharing; for with such sacrifices God is pleased (Heb. 13:15-16).

When Jesus taught on the Ten Commandments, He reduced them to two (Matt. 22:36-40). He did not oversimplify God's laws; instead he showed that God's ultimate intention for His people is to worship God and to serve men.

Worship and service hold each other in balance or "tension" against each other. Vital and energetic forces, qualities, or moods in people not only need equalizing but require full expression. A church held together in such a dynamic tension will resemble the church of Bible days. Unfortunately, men often find it easier to serve God by doing things rather than to worship Him with devotion. This grave error must be challenged. Worship must be done first![4]

Devotion balances lifestyle

When Jesus resisted the devil's temptation by saying, "Thou shalt worship the Lord thy God, and him only shalt thou serve" (Matt. 4:10), He was merely affirming an established principle of Scripture. The Old Testament depicts a union between worship and service. The Ten Commandments warns against worshiping and serving foreign gods (Ex. 20:5). Deuteronomy, Joshua, Judges and the rest of the Old Testament, contain too many significant references to "worship and serve" to ignore. Compare the following:

Deut. 4:19; 5:9; 6:13; 8:19; 11:13,16; 17:3; 26:10; 29:26; 30:17; Josh. 23:7, 16; 2 Chron. 7:19. Comparative references on *serve*: Deut. 17:12; 18:5, 7; 19:9; 20:18; 28:14, 36, 47, 48, 64; 29:18; 30:20; 31:16, 18; Josh. 22:5; 2 Kings 17:33-35.

Service, in the Old Testament sense, includes not only devotional actions in a religious setting, such as sacrifice and incense-burning, but also lifestyle, manner of living, priorities, and goals. Consider the powerful challenge to serve God in Joshua 24:14-16. The word *serve* is used seven times. The message of the book of Deuteronomy can be summarized in the word *remember*. As people remembered and obeyed God's commands, they served the Lord.

And now, Israel, what does the LORD your God require from you, but to fear the Lord your God, to walk in all His ways and love Him and to serve the LORD your God with all

84

your heart and with all your soul, and to keep the LORD's commandments and His statutes which I am commanding you today for your good? (Deut. 10:12-13).

Life of service is sacred

The word *proskuneo* refers to an intense-yet-humble adoration of and brokenness before God with inward and outward expressions (see chapter 9). Another Greek word, *latreuo,* sometimes is translated "worship," but more accurately is translated "service." Thomas Kimber confirms this difference:

> The Greek word (*proskuneo*), rendered "to worship" more than fifty times in the New Testament, literally means to kiss (the feet) or to prostrate one's self before the object of adoration. Another word, *latreuo*—occasionally translated "worship" in the King James Version—more properly signifies service, and is so generally rendered in the revised text.[5]

This distinction is also clarified by C.F.D. Moule, who confirms the connection in Hebrew words as well:

> The modern Christian application of terms such as "divine service" or "a service" to specific acts of public worship may tend to obscure the fact that in its NT context the word "service" does literally mean the work of servants. One of the regular Hebrew words for worship, *aodah,* is derived from the same root as the word for the suffering "servant" or, for that matter, any slave or servant. It is used in Exodus for the hard servitude of the Hebrews under Pharaoh.[6]

The most striking text in the Bible to combine the thought of worship (*proskuneo*) and service (*latreuo*) is in Jesus' response to one of the Devil's temptations. The Devil offered, "all these things will I give thee, if thou wilt fall down and worship me" (Matt. 4:9). Jesus' significant answer: "It is written, 'Thou shalt worship the Lord thy God, and him only shalt thou serve'" (v. 10). William Nicholls explains:

> Here the crucial Greek words are *proskynein* and *latreuein,* the two New Testament words which may be translated "worship." *Proskynein,* here translated "worship," originally referred to the physical action of bowing down, prostrating oneself, before an earthly king. Thus in reference to God it has the connotation of humbling oneself in adoration. It corresponds to *hishtahawah* in the Hebrew Bible, which has the same meaning. *Latreuein,* which came, in later theology, to be the normal technical word for worship, means to serve, with the service of a hired labourer or slave. Significantly, there lies behind it the Hebrew word *abocah,* which is the same root as the noun *ebed*: the Suffering Servant of the Lord, whose part Jesus assumed, is called in Hebrew the *ebed yahweh.*[7]

By His answer, Jesus made it clear that both adoration and service belong only to God. Both are sacred acts. In the deepest sense, the offering of *latreia* or service becomes sanctified to God as an act of sacrificial worship by a humble attitude of

85

proskynesis. Out of deep, reverential worship springs joyous, spontaneous service activities for God.

The close connection between worship and service is underscored by the way translators have handled the last word in Rom. 12:1. Translators of the familiar King James Version chose the word *service* to translate *latreia:*

> I beseech you therefore, brethren, by the mercies of God, that ye present your bodies a living sacrifice, holy, acceptable unto God, which is your reasonable service.

Other versions and translations prefer some form of *worship,* for instance:

> your spiritual worship (RSV); spiritual worship (NIV); the worship offered by mind and heart (NEB); true worship (TEV); an act of intelligent worship (PHILLIPS); worship him (JB); the worship due from you as rational creatures (K); service and spiritual worship (Amp).

By using *offer* and *sacrifices,* the apostle implies that Christian sacrifice is a life of service to God. The more modern translations indicate this service is so significant to God that it can be considered worship (see Rom. 15:16). Technically, "service is the proper sequel to worship."[8] Here we see the genius of Christian living. Believers' lifestyles are forms of adoration of God.

Spiritual sacrifice fills lifestyle

Greek scholars define *latreuin* as "to serve," but look how the word is used in the New Testament. The verb form appears twenty-one times, and the noun appears five times. The book of Hebrews contains more mentions (eight) of the word than any other book.

> Matt. 4:10; Luke 1:74; 2:37; 4:8; John 16:2; Acts 7:7, 42; 24:14; 26:7; 27:23; Rom. 1:9, 25; 9:4; 12:1; Phil. 3:3; 2 Tim. 1:3; Heb. 8:5; 9:1, 6, 9, 14; 10:2; 12:28; 13:10; Rev. 7:15; 22:3.

About half the time *latreuin* refers to a religious duty, function or act that is so much a part of the worship experience it legitimately can be translated "worship" in the devotional sense. Here are seven illustrations from the above list:

1. Luke 2:37—Anna worship-served God night and day with fasting and prayer. Note that "worship is used by LB, PHILLIPS, RSV, TEV, NIV, NEB.

2. Rom. 9:4—The service which belonged to Israel referred to the whole Levitical system of worshiping God.

3. Phil. 3:3—those who worship in the Spirit are the true circumcision. So stated by KJV, LB, PHILLIPS, RSV, TEV, NIV, JB, NEB..

4. 2 Tim. 1:3—Paul's reference to serving God with clear conscience is linked with unceasing, daily prayer. See also Acts 24:14.

5. Heb. 9:1— "Ordinances of divine service" in KJV is translated worship in LB, RSV, TEV, NIV, JB.

6. Heb. 12:28— says "serve God" in the KJV, but the rendering elsewhere is "acceptable worship" (RSV), "worship" (TEV), "worship God acceptably" (NIV), "worship God in the way He finds acceptable" (JB), and "worship him as he would be worshipped" (NEB).

7. Rev. 7:15 and 22:3—The ritual and adoration of God come together in the highest manner possible. Again, other versions use "worship."

The Old Testament order inherently allowed godly men to worship God by serving. The New Testament introduces an entirely new concept of approaching God. Physical, animal sacrifices offered by Levitical priests were replaced by "spiritual sacrifices" (Heb. 13:15). An undying priest in heaven, Jesus, mediates the new sacrificial system. The New Testament Christian can adopt a lifestyle which enables worship to fill every aspect of his life. The Christian's daily life is a living sacrifice (Rom. 12:1). He can worship continuously in Spirit and truth (see 1 Thess. 5:16,17).

Origin of public servants

Another Greek word family in the New Testament text describes service given to men as well as to God. It is *leitourgia, leitourgos,* and *leitourgein*).[9] A close look at the word's fifteen appearances in the New Testament shows similar use as the *latreuein* family words.

In Luke 1:23 and Acts 13:2, the same term describes Zacharias serving in the temple and the Christians at Antioch worshiping God. In secular literature, the term typically refers to service to the state. The English word *liturgy* is derived from the middle Latin *liturgia,* which was taken from the Greek word *leitourgia.* Its two root words mean public (*leitos*) and work (*ergos*). The immediate meaning is "public that works" or "service of the people" or public servant.

Luke 1:23; Acts 13:2; Rom. 13:6; 15:16, 27; 2 Cor. 9:12; Phil. 2:17, 25, 30; Heb 1:7, 14; 8:2, 6; 9:21; 10:11.

Gottesdienst poses problems

German theologians, their writings, and evangelical traditions have influenced Christian thinking world-wide. The German word *gottesdienst,* means "service of God," and has been commonly used for worship, but it has an inherent problem. The word has two parts: "God" clearly is the first half, but "dienst" is not familiar to English-speaking people.

In Germany, every service station is identified with the word. "Service" is the best translation. The word "service," whether in English or German, commonly describes what one person does for someone else or for the public. Accordingly, service stations supply gasoline to the public, catering services supply food, a store's service department helps customers with problems, a secretarial service provides secretaries, and a government Forest Service takes care of national forests. In this light, a church worship service would be expected to supply worship to consumers. This concept neglects religious devotion and worship as acts of service.

Gottesdienst raises practical and academic issues not inherent in the English word *worship*. In English, worship is a general term for reverence, honor, or respect toward an important person or God. In religious terms it means to venerate, adore, and perform religious acts of homage to God. The American mind interprets the basic meaning of *gottesdienst* as people serving God through honoring Him in traditional worship forms or perhaps in doing various service-oriented activities for God. It comes as a surprise to find that various leading German theologians do not think that way, and their churches reflect that mindset.

Who does the serving?

Although *gottesdienst* means "service of God," an uncertainty exists over how to interpret the first part of the word, *gottes*. It can mean either "[our] serving God," or "God's serving [us]." John Reumann explains the problem:

> The German "Gottesdienst" means "service of God," but the tricky question is whether to take the genitive, "Gottes-," "God's service," as an objective or subjective genitive. The former would make God the object of the action in serving; Gottesdienst in this sense would be "serving God" and implies much of what "worship" does—honor, veneration, acts of homage, e.g., in cult. The subjective genitive, however, takes the "Gottes-" part of the compound as the subject of the action of serving, and so the sense is "God's serving us." Worship, on that reading, means when God ministers to men and brings the Good News and his grace into their lives.[10]

German evangelical tradition has understood *gottesdienst* in the second sense, that God is serving mankind, doing something for people that they cannot do for themselves. Thus in the worship service, people experience the saving action of God working through the preaching of the Word, the performance of baptism, and the celebration of the Lord's Supper. God comes and does something to people and for people. People's response should be in obedience, prayer, and confession of faith. The church's service before God, then, "Takes place in the world and especially takes the form of service to the brother."[11] It is obvious that the doctrinal emphasis chosen by a church on this question will affect the manner and form of its worship.

The Lutheran theologian Peter Brunner, in his well-known *Worship in the Name of Jesus*, sets out the two aspects succinctly:

> worship as a service of God to the congregation; worship as the congregation's service before God.[12]

An over-emphasis on God serving man leads man to wait passively to receive what someone else spoon-feeds him. This can be misleading. People must receive from, as well as participate in, God's saving actions.

Christians do not have an either-or choice between divine action and human action. God enjoys reciprocal action and dialogue with His people. Like King David, believers today receive God's presence in their gatherings, and they understand the Lord delights to receive the praises of His people. To truly appropriate this saving presence worshipers must be more than observers or spectators. The gathered saints must faithfully participate in the Word, sacraments, spiritual gifts, and Psalmic forms of worship. When believers assume an active role, God, in turn, ministers and serves His people. Those who experience God's generous presence in worship respond by reaching out to others. Millar Burrows expresses it like this:

> Worship gives power for service . . . . Service completes worship by putting the power to work[13]

Let the way appear
The young man ran scared for good reason. He had deceived his father, conspired with his mother, and defrauded his brother. From the time Jacob grabbed the heel of his twin brother at birth, he had lived up to his name, which means supplanter, deceiver, schemer, and trickster. Sent away hurriedly by anxious parents, Jacob journeyed to a far country seeking asylum—and a wife. For the first time in his life he was alone, really alone. He knew his brother, Esau, was furious with him, and his life was in jeopardy. He usually stayed close to home, so his present journey held frightening possibilities.

The proudly self-reliant man, whose cleverness, strength, and resourcefulness had made him a match for most situations, now found himself reduced to an empty-handed fugitive, an exile. He had been raised to believe in the God of Abraham and Isaac. He knew the stories well, but now—a day's journey from home—Jacob felt exiled not only from home but from heaven as well.

He camped at the place of divine choosing,[14] not realizing what God had in store for him. The lonely and rugged hill of Bethel became shrouded in the darkness of night, and weary Jacob attempted to make himself comfortable.

Soon he was fast asleep, a tired, discouraged man.

> And he dreamed, and behold a ladder set up on the earth, and the top of it reached to heaven: and behold the angels of God ascending and descending on it (Gen. 28:12 KJV).

A shining stairway or ramp ("staircase" LB) stretched upward from the mountain to the very presence of God Himself. Celestial glory lit the atmosphere, and angelic beings were coming and going. Then as God spoke, the earthly fugitive realized he was not an exile from heaven. A cosmic bond tied heaven and earth together. God had put down His ladder in Jacob's life.

Jesus makes this astounding story even more incredible by his interpretation:

> Truly, truly, I say to you [Gk. pl. all of you], you shall see the heavens opened, and the angels of God ascending and descending upon the Son of Man (John 1:51).

Jesus claims to be the ladder. Touching earth, He is the Son of man; touching heaven, He is the Son of God. The only way to reach heaven is through Christ the Ladder. William Nicholls, in his excellent book on worship, *Jacob's Ladder*, comments: "The essence of worship lies in Christ, considered as the true Jacob's Ladder, upon which God's love comes down to earth, and man's response travels back to God."[15]

The secret of the ladder

The sudden appearance of the heavenly ladder must have seemed to Jacob to be God's invitation to come up into His presence. The transcendent God created a direct way to meet with lowly man. With the ladder, God initiated worship. He made a way for men to come before God. Then, Jacob saw angels model the responsive action of a worshiper. The text speaks of the angels ascending first and then descending. Symbolically, the angels showed what must take place in people's lives if they are to be true, successful servants of the Lord. First, having "seen" the heavenly invitation, they ascend the shining staircase through their worship. Then, after being in the presence of God, they descend the ladder back to earth to perform acts of service. First they go up to meet with God; then they can go down to the world with ministry of service.

Another popular interpretation of this event makes the angels conveyers of God's blessing to man and of man's response to God. Angels do perform such work, but it stresses the text to overemphasize angels as intermediaries between God and men when there is only *one* mediator, Jesus Christ (1 Tim. 2:5).

The beloved hymn, *Nearer My God to Thee*, has immortalized Jacob's story. In 1841, at the belated request of her pastor, Sarah F. Adams quickly composed this simple hymn to close the pastor's message about Jacob. Although she wrote hundreds of hymns, only this one is remembered.

The idea that a person can draw close to the living God really is inspiring. As the great ship Titanic prepared to sink, the Rev. John Harper gathered a number of passengers on the deck for prayer, and at his request the band struck up this familiar hymn. Hundreds of voices sang these words as the sea swallowed the Titanic.

A contrasting story tells how President William McKinley lay dying by the hand of an assassin, and he was heard to sing faintly the words of that beautiful hymn. Many other stories could be told of how Jacob's life, presented in this cherished hymn, has inspired people who were discouraged or facing death.

Let the Scripture and hymn inspire you daily to draw near to God through worship (ascending) that will enable you to be a profitable servant of the Lord in the world (descending). Out of discouragement, be drawn upward through Christ the Ladder into God's presence; then, filled with His Spirit and joy of His presence, go forth to serve Him in this present evil world.

Nearer, My God To Thee

Nearer, my God, to Thee,
Nearer to Thee!
E'en though it be a cross

That raiseth me;
Still all my song shall be,
Nearer, my God, to Thee,
Nearer, my God, to Thee,
Nearer to Thee.

Though like the wanderer,
The sun gone down,
Darkness be over me,
My rest a stone;
Yet in my dreams I'd be
Nearer, my God, to Thee,
Nearer, my God, to Thee,
Nearer to Thee.

There let the way appear
Steps unto heav'n;
All that thou sendest me
In mercy giv'n;
Angels to beckon me
Nearer, my God, to Thee,
Nearer, my God, to Thee,
Nearer to Thee.

Then, with my waking thoughts
Bright with thy praise,
Out of my stony griefs,
Bethel I'll raise;
So by my woes to be
Nearer, my God, to Thee,
Nearer, my God, to Thee,
Nearer to Thee. Amen.
—*Sarah F. Adams, 1841*
Based on Gen. 28:10-22

Reflections

We worship God both in humbly paying honage to this one greater than all others and in serving him in the world. Without both characteristics, there is not true worship. For without adoration and homage, worship becomes only a busy organization. Without service, worship is only a group of people performing religious exercises, a holy club.

—*Wendell Willis*[16]

Worship first, service second. Until we have fulfilled the worship requirement, we cannot serve properly. All service must flow out of worship lest it become a substitute for worship. We long ago learned that God will curse a substitute but may bless a supplement . . . it is not an "either/or" situation but "both/and." We will both worship and serve the Lord God; but in that order.

—*Judson Cornwall*[17]

Without doubt the emphasis in Christian teaching today should be on worship. There is little danger that we shall become merely worshipers and neglect the practical implications of the gospel. No one can long worship God in spirit and in truth before the obligation to holy service becomes too strong to resist.

—*A.W. Tozer*[18]

There can be no genuine religion which does not express itself in the active service of God. But it is through worship that man becomes conscious of God, that he brings his own life into relation with the divine life. The power which urges him to acts of practical obedience is communicated by the approach to God in worship.

—*Ernest F. Scott*[19]

Worship, in the last analysis, is the secret of service, and service is an expression of worship.

—*G. Campbell Morgan*[20]

In both the Old and New Testament, worship has the double meaning of serving and prostrating oneself. One worships by KNEELING before the Lord; one also worships by SERVING Him.

—*E. Leroy Lawson*[21]

Part IV

On Earth As It Is In Heaven

At local churches here on earth, as we unite in worship, we simultaneously participate—by the Holy Spirit—in the dynamic, exuberant worship of the hosts of heaven.

- **Chapter 12 Only One Worship**
  We do not worship alone. We participate with the saints above. Local worship services mirror and augment worship in the heavenlies.

- **Chapter 13 The Sights And Sounds Of Heaven**
  Seven dramatic scenes of heavenly worship discovered in the book of Revelation occupy the main focus of Jesus' last message to His church.

12

Only One Worship

*There is one body and one Spirit, just as also
you were called in one hope of your calling; one Lord, one faith, one baptism, one
God and Father of all who is over all and through all
and in all.*
—Ephesians 4:4-6

Early Christians certainly had their minds on heaven. Their apocalyptic hopes constantly fanned the flame of enthusiasm in the early church. They believed that the future order of the kingdom of heaven was projected into the present life of their assemblies.

> We have been given possession of an unshakable kingdom. Let us therefore hold on to the grace that we have been given and use it to worship God in the way that he finds acceptable, in reverence and fear (Heb. 12:28 JB).

> For the kingdom of God is . . . righteousness and peace and joy in the Holy Spirit (Rom. 14:17).

In their meetings, they tasted "the powers of the age to come" (Heb. 6:5). Worship services flowed with vitality explained only by the church's close attention to heaven's adoration. Martyrs died with songs of victory on their lips. In the greatest agony of this earth's woes, they nevertheless endured because of the heavenly vision.

> But being full of the Holy Spirit, he [Stephen] gazed intently into heaven and saw the glory of God, and Jesus standing at the right hand of God; and he said, "Behold, I see the heavens opened up and the Son of Man standing at the right hand of God" (Acts 7:55, 56).

The book of Hebrews strongly taught the early church that their religion and worship were synonymous. The descriptions of the church in Acts and 1 Corinthians and the majestic pictures of heavenly worship in Revelation show that early Christians understood their earthly worship was directly related to celestial worship above. They knew their worship blended with the heavenly choir and rose as one fragrance before the throne of God.

The one worship of heaven and earth

The worship of the church on earth is one with the church in heaven. Since heaven's occupants worship continually, it stands to reason that the exultation of people on earth joins the celestial chorus before God. "The worship of the church on earth is really a participation in and an anticipation of the worship of heaven" says Massey H. Shepherd.[1] Paul H. Hoon links the hope and faith of "the worshiper's present worship in earth as one with the church's worship in heaven."[2]

This is undoubtedly what the writer of Hebrews had in mind when he said:

> But you have come to Mount Zion and to the city of the living God, the heavenly Jerusalem, and to myriads of angels, to the general assembly and church of the firstborn who are enrolled in heaven, and to God, the Judge of all, and to the spirits of righteous men made perfect, and to Jesus, the mediator of a new covenant, and to the sprinkled blood, which speaks better than the blood of Abel (Heb. 12:22-24).

Another remarkable confirmation comes from one of John's heavenly visions:

> And another angel came and stood at the altar, holding a golden censer; and much incense was given to him, that he might add it to the prayers of all the saints upon the golden altar which was before the throne. And the smoke of the incense, with the prayers of the saints, went up before God out of the angel's hand (Rev. 8:3, 4).

Actually, the thought of linking heavenly and earthly worship is not new to liturgical theologians.[3] One ancient example is found in today's Orthodox Church. Timothy Ware states:

> Worship, for the Orthodox Church, is nothing else than 'heaven on earth'. The Holy Liturgy is something that embraces two worlds at once, for both in heaven and on earth the Liturgy is one and the same — one altar, one sacrifice, one presence.[4]

Dr. Ware titled one of his chapters, "Orthodox Worship I: The Earthly Heaven." Below the title he quotes the classic statement of Germanus, Patriarch of Constantinople, who died in A.D. 733: "The church is the earthly heaven in which the heavenly God dwells and moves."[5] Quoting Ware:

> The icons which fill the church serve as a point of meeting between heaven and earth. As each local congregation prays Sunday by Sunday, surrounded by the figures of Christ, the angels, and the saints, these visible images remind the faithful unceasingly of the invisible presence of the whole company of heaven at the Liturgy. The faithful can feel that the walls of the church open out upon eternity, and they are helped to realize that their liturgy on earth is one and the same with the great Liturgy of heaven. The multitudinous icons express visibly the sense of 'heaven on earth.'[6]

This historic church body has maintained a principle of truth. Their application making church buildings represent heaven may seem extreme, but their basic thought is provocative. When people come for worship on Sunday, spiritually weary and worn, they have a right to expect an experience that will lift them into the heavenlies. The average man wants—even craves—this touch of heaven much more than he desires theological arguments. Robert S. Simpson says:

> The worship of God in the common services of our church is the one experience of earth in which a man enters into the triumph and victory of heaven.[7]

Local church services should represent worship in the heavenlies. While the kingdom of heaven has not taken over military and political rule of the nations, divine rule has taken over the hearts of God's people. It is when these kingdom people gather to worship Him that God has promised to be in their midst in special presence. Every local church should epitomize the heavenly church—a joyful, divinely blessed community within the larger, joyless secular community.

Spiritual preparation for heavenly worship
True worship demands not only proper attitudes in worshipers but also an infilling of the Holy Spirit. The quickening and inspiration of the Holy Spirit makes communion alive; consequently, every Christian must make a priority of being led by and filled with the Holy Spirit. The apostle Paul linked the Spirit with worship:

> Be filled with the Spirit, speaking to one another in psalms and hymns and spiritual songs, singing and making melody with your heart to the Lord; always giving thanks for all things in the name of our Lord Jesus Christ to God, even the Father (Eph. 5:18-20).

In heaven, the worshipers' quality and intensity of spirit determines the quality of worship. It does not depend on the sound. Heaven functions in a fourth dimension: the Spiritual, beyond what the natural man understands of time, distance and space. Finite man without the aid of the Holy Spirit cannot comprehend heaven's adoration because it is in a prophetic, infinite realm.

> Now we have received, not the spirit of the world, but the Spirit who is from God, that we might know the things freely given to us by God, which things we also speak, not in words taught by human wisdom, but in those taught by the Spirit, combining spiritual thoughts with spiritual words. But a natural man does not accept the things of the Spirit of God; for they are foolishness to him, and he cannot understand them, because they are spiritually appraised. But he who is spiritual appraises all things, yet he himself is appraised by no man (1 Cor. 2:12-15).

To understand or participate in spiritual worship, people require the help of the Holy Spirit. Like John, Christians today must approach the highest of human activities with open minds and dependence on the Spirit of the Lord. The key thought in Rev. 4:2 tells readers that John was "in the Spirit" (KJV) or, "became in spirit" (M), "came under the (Holy) Spirit's power" (AMP), "was caught up by the Spirit" (NEB); or, more dramatically stated, "the Spirit possessed me" (JB). Jesus said:

> God is Spirit, and those who worship Him must worship in Spirit and truth (John 4:24 ANCHOR).

Christians must not underestimate the importance of the Holy Spirit's help in understanding heavenly things, particularly worship. Jude's advice to pray "in the Holy Spirit" must not be ignored (Jude 20). Paul says Christians "have access in one Spirit to the Father" (Eph 2:18). Seeley D. Kinne adds this timely warning:

> Any attempt to worship this Infinite Great and Almighty One by the feeble powers of man without the quickening guiding power of the Holy Spirit is a great error, which now God is calling on us to see and correct.[8]

God left a record of John's experience as an example of proper preparation for heavenly activity. It is the Spirit that makes our worship one with heaven's.

Today's call to worship

John's revelation stands as a divine invitation to the church to enter a new dimension of spiritual relationship. God placed in the Bible the vision of heavenly worship that gripped and inspired the early church to ignite hearts today as well.

John's account, as it was passed on to the early Christians, contained no great surprises. Of course, the intensity and vastness of the sights and sounds of heaven were truly impressive, but the basic spirituality was already enjoyed by the joyous church of that day. Some Bible scholars suggest that John's vivid, first-hand descriptions are similar to the worship he was accustomed to in the church of the New Testament times.[9]

A.W. Tozer has described worship as "the missing jewel in the evangelical church."[10] It is time to restore this gem to its crowning position. Heaven itself, the highest example of all that is right in worship, issues a timeless command with insistent tone to this present generation:

> Give Praise . . . Worship God! (Rev. 19:5, 10).

Reflections

When we worship together as a community of living Christians, we do not worship alone, we worship "with all the company of heaven."

—*Marianne H. Micks[11]*

Indeed, the church is to be a worshiping community par excellence, called to join the heavenly throng. In worship, the earthly church is lifted into the heavens and joins the eternal chorus in praise of God's character and loving action toward his creatures.

—*Robert E. Webber[12]*

Very early, there had emerged the thought that the Church's worship was the antitype of a more glorious worship above, and that the strains of both were blended together as they rose to the throne of God.

—*Alexander B. Macdonald[13]*

Whatever Christian worship is offered on earth is linked with that which is beyond the veil, where Christ stands as our representative before the heavenly throne . . . . the worshiping church is already united with the whole company of heaven: Christians have already come to mount Sion and are there at worship with the angels in festal array and the whole community of the first born.

—*C.F.D. Moule[14]*

One Vast Brotherhood, in which Saints on Earth, and Spirits of the Redeemed, and Infinite Hosts of Angels, are in Sweet and Mystic Communion Around the Throne of God, Forever and Ever and Ever.

—*Henry H. Halley[15]*

Come, we who love the Lord,
And let our joys be known;
Join in a song of sweet accord,
And thus surround the throne.

—*Isaac Watts, 1709*

101

13

Sights and Sounds of Heaven

*And I heard, as it were, the voice of a great multitude
and as the sound of many waters
and as the sound of mighty peals of thunder saying,
Hallelujah! For the Lord our God, the Almighty, reigns.*
—Revelation 19:6

My wife and I had escaped to the beach for a few days. We needed some rest and time for contemplation. Pastoral concerns and a church building project weighed heavily on my mind, but I was plagued by a question. In other critical times, God had given me answers to prayer and insights as I took solitary "prayer walks," so it seemed right to take a stroll on the beach.

At sunset, ocean waves rolled in and reflected the last rays of the sun in luminescent splendor. A constant din of sound surrounded me. A few sea birds wheeled above the waters. I thought of John's visions of heavenly worship in the book of Revelation. I had read and meditated on renewal of worship in today's church, yet I did not understand how the church could develop a theology of worship that would unify and inspire people. The question had puzzled me many years. As I walked along the lonely beach, I received the answer.

In gratitude, I began to praise the Lord devotionally. Then a second question crowded into my mind: "Why would God allow the aged Bishop John to be taken from shepherding the flock to be exiled on the forsaken island of Patmos in the Aegean Sea?"

I looked above the waves. Beautiful streaks of crimson light set the sky ablaze. My spirit began to soar like a gull. As I worshiped, the sights and sounds embracing me washed out the cares of this life and lifted the burdens of the church. Suddenly I realized why God had allowed John to be put on a small island surrounded by ocean sights and sounds. The severe natural setting was a blessing in disguise! For John, the island meant release from earthly entanglements. After the initial shock of loneliness had passed, he realized that the Lord had arranged a rendezvous with him completely free from pastoral distractions.

As his soul poured out, earthly ties and burdens broke loose. The island's solitude prepared his mind and readied his worshiping heart to receive the sights and sounds

103

of heaven. The last of the original apostles was to see, hear, and record worship in its highest form for the benefit of future generations.

As I stood on the beach, my spiritual eyes opened to see that no theology of worship or liturgical reform takes place in the church without leaders as well as people undergoing the preparatory, purifying work of a personal "Patmos experience." I do not mean that everyone must relinquish earthly interest. I do mean that every worshiper must be humbled for the Holy Spirit to be quickened!

Also, heavenly praise should be mirrored in churches on earth. "Thy will be done on earth as it is in heaven," Jesus prayed (Matt. 6:10). Praise on earth should prepare believers for heavenly praise sessions, and any practical, relevant worship theology must be shaped and influenced by heaven's worship, as recorded by John. John's view of heaven adds new dimensions to the Lord's Prayer. His description of apocalyptic adoration seems overwhelming, yet his observations provide some of the most significant information available on the subject.

In the Revelation account, a voice rang out like a trumpet, and the weary exile looked up. Suddenly, John was captured by a divine afflatus! As his body slept in trance, the inner man soared upward on spiritual eagle wings to the very presence of God. John saw seven scenes of heavenly worship showing how the inhabitants of heaven make His praise glorious! (I suggest Handel's "Hallelujah Chorus" as appropriate background music for the rest of this chapter!)

Scene 1: Holy! holy! holy!
Rev. 4:8-11

John saw God in His glory, enthroned as omnipotent Creator in the midst of dazzling color and empyrean splendor.

> Flashes of lightning were coming from the throne, and the sound of peals of thunder, and in front of the throne there were seven flaming lamps burning, the seven Spirits of God (Rev. 4:5 JB).

It was a magnificent sight! God deliberately showed Himself and His throne to John first because all things in heaven focus upon and revolve around the royal seat. John carefully recorded that sight as his first entry in the account! Then, four strange-yet-familiar figures caught his eye. They surrounded their heavenly Sovereign with devotion.

Four personalities, best described as "four living creatures" were "ceaselessly saying" (literal Greek meaning) or declaring the holiness of God. This may mean that they were in a singing chant. The NEB says "without a pause they sang," and the JB says "they never stopped singing."

A holy awe permeated the scene as the creatures responded purely to the essence of all that God is—holy! Three times they said it with uninhibited feeling. His presence pulled this insight from their inner beings. It was as the psalmist said, "Deep calleth unto deep" (Ps. 42:7). The three declarations also signify the tri-unity of God's nature and how that nature extends across past, present, and future.

Twenty-four elders joined the living creatures. They fell down before the Creator-God (the JB uses the word *prostrate*), and together they gave highest acclaim as they said ("cried" NEB):

> You are our Lord and our God, you are worthy of glory and honor and power, because you made all the universe and it was only by your will that everything was made and exists (Rev. 4:11 JB).

Scene 2: Worthy is the Lamb!
Rev. 5:6-14

Although Jesus is not mentioned in chapter 4, He suddenly appears in chapter 5 as the conquering Lion and the helpless Lamb. Jesus is seen as a lamb standing "as it had been slain" (KJV), or more literally, "as having been slain" (M). The NEB says, "A lamb with the marks of slaughter upon him," and the LB states that "on the Lamb were wounds that once had caused His death" (Rev. 5:6).

The Lamb is the living Jesus radiant in His glory! The wounds that caused His death gleam as the proof of His saviorhood. The last verse of the hymn *Crown Him with Many Crowns* describes majestically those glorious wounds:

Crown Him the Lord of love!
Behold His hands and side,
Those wounds, yet visible above,
In beauty glorified:
All hail, Redeemer, hail!
For Thou has died for me:
Thy praise and glory shall not fail
Thro'out eternity. Amen.

Because of His death, Jesus was entitled as the Lamb of God (John 1:29) to break open the book of destiny and allow God's historical purposes to climax. The precious body and blood of the Lamb appear as the very heart and bosom of God the Father, and as such, are positioned "in the midst of the throne." At first, only the omnipotent, Father-Creator-God was worshiped, but now the atoning, Triumphant-Savior-Son receives worship as well.

Heaven reverberates with the passionate and extravagant worship of the heavenly hosts. Cries of "Worthy is the Lamb!" roll through the heavenlies in ever-swelling tones. The words of this great hymn by J. Mountain express in a small measure the sights and sounds of this celestial scene:

'Tis the church triumphant singing
Worthy the Lamb;
Heaven throughout with praises ringing
Worthy the Lamb.
Thrones and powers before Him bending,
Odours sweet with voice ascending,
Swell the chorus never-ending

Worthy the Lamb!

Every kindred, tongue and nation,
Worthy the Lamb;
Join to sing the great salvation,
Worthy the Lamb.
Loud as mighty thunders roaring,
Floods of mighty waters pouring,
Prostrate at His feet adoring,
Worthy the Lamb!

Harps and songs forever sounding
Worthy the Lamb;
Mighty Grace o'er sin abounding
Worthy the Lamb.
By His blood He dearly bought us;
Wand'rings from the fold He sought us,
And to glory safely brought us:
Worthy the Lamb!

Sing with blest anticipation
Worthy the Lamb;
Through the vale of tribulation,
Worthy the Lamb.
Sweetest notes, all notes excelling,
On the theme for ever dwelling,
Still untold, though ever telling,
Worthy the Lamb!

In the heavenly scene, John felt the familiar, living presence of Jesus; however, the reality was amplified beyond his human experience of the Last Supper and beyond eucharistic celebrations of early New Testament churches. John saw the uninhibited, eternal vitality and power of Jesus' body and blood in heaven. He viewed the archetype—the original—and was compelled to a higher appreciation and understanding as he viewed the Fountainhead from whom all blessings flow to the church.

The living presence of Christ is essential in Christian worship services. Without Him the church is nothing. John's second heavenly scene shows the Lord of redemption proclaiming His living blood and body. The scene pictured in Revelation, chapter 5, acknowledges Christ's earthly act of redemption in the same way the early church's worship did by focusing on Christ's body and blood.[1]

John stands in heaven awestruck by the redemptive scene unfolding before him. A tide of worship surges from a grateful creation toward the God of all grace. In return, unlimited blessings and spiritual life flow from Him. God and man reciprocate in living worship.

As the song swells, the atmosphere comes alive with an unfolding revelation of God, Christ, and the people of God. In such a setting the body and blood become a living experience. Redeemed people magnify God!

The ancient desire of God for a kingdom of worshiping priests mentioned in Exod. 19:6 finds fulfillment in Rev. 5:10. Music from harps enhance the singing. Then John hears "the sound of an immense number of angels . . . shouting" (JB) hurrahs to the Lamb. Finally, the song of the redemption climaxes when the voices of "all the living things in creation" (JB) add their acclaim to God and the lamb with, in St. Augustine's words, an "insatiable satisfaction."[2]

> And the four Living Beings keep saying, "Amen!" And the twenty-four Elders fell down and worshiped Him (Rev. 5:14 JB).

Scene 3: Victory!
Rev. 7:9-12, 15

In this scene John sees the white-robed overcomers standing before the throne. It is "a vast throng" (NEB), "beyond man's power to number" (PHILLIPS), and they shout victoriously of the saving power of God and the Lamb (Rev. 7:9). Why such excitement? They are the triumphant followers of Jesus who come out of the Great Tribulation. Washed in the blood of the Lamb! With joy they stand before God's throne blessing His name and waving palm branches:

> They shall never again feel hunger or thirst, the sun shall not beat on them nor any scorching heat, because the Lamb who is at the heart of the throne will be their shepherd and will guide them to the springs of the water of life; and God will wipe all tears from their eyes (Rev. 7:16-17 NEB).

The waving palm branches are reminiscent of Jesus' triumphal entry into Jerusalem. Undoubtedly these heavenly overcomers were doing more than just holding the branches. The same electric excitement that John saw years before on the Jericho road leading into Jerusalem, he now sees in heaven springing from clear understanding. Jesus gratefully accepted the joyous acclaim of His disciples.

> And some of the Pharisees in the multitude said to Him, 'Teacher, rebuke your disciples.' And He answered and said, 'I tell you, if these become silent, the stones will cry out!' (Luke 19:39-40).

God delights in enthusiastic, exuberant worshipers, whether in heaven or on earth. In Jesus' triumphal entry:

> The great multitude . . . when they heard that Jesus was coming to Jerusalem took the branches of the palm trees, and went out to meet Him, and began to cry out (i.e. shout), 'Hosanna!' (John 12:12, 13).

Crowds of people carpeted the road with their cloaks, and some cut branches from the trees to spread in his path. Then the crowd that went ahead and others that came behind raised the shout: 'Hosanna in the heaven!' (Matt. 21:8, 9 NEB).

And now, as he was approaching the downward slope of the Mount of Olives, the whole group of disciples joyfully began to praise God at the top of their voices for all the miracles they had seen (Luke 19:37 JB).

The prophetic cry of that earthly multitude was "glory in the highest heaven" (NEB). This is wonderfully fulfilled as Christ is praised by the overcomers of Revelation, chapter 7.

Scene 4: The Lord reigns!
Rev. 11:15-18

The sounding of the trumpet by the seventh and last angel releases loud, shouting voices which announce that worldly kingdoms have fully "passed into the possession" of the living God (Rev. 11:15 GDSP). This new revelation elicits a response from the twenty-four elders who "prostrated themselves and touched the ground with their foreheads worshiping God" (v. 16 JB).

Back in the old days, churches commonly had an "Amen corner." The preacher was encouraged by the shouts of "Amen!" as he waxed eloquent on some point. These twenty-four elders are the most enthusiastic "ameners." They shout, sing, play their guitars (i.e., harps), throw down their crowns and prostrate themselves in worship!

In fact, it seems hard to keep up with their actions. Although they possess thrones, they constantly fall from their thrones to give enthusiastic endorsement and worship. It is as though the ever-unfolding wonders of God's nature elicit an unending reaction of adoration. His marvels continuously occupy the rapt attention of worshipers throughout eternity!

Scene 5: 144,000 singing harpists
Rev. 14:1-3

Here is thunderous singing of the highest magnitude. With no inhibitions to limit purity of content or strength of expression, the vast throng exalts the God of the past, present, and future.

A voice from heaven . . . louder than water in full flood, or heavy, heavy thunder . . . . It was the singing of a choir accompanied by harps (Rev. 14:2 LB).

Imagine a choir of 144,000 singers! I have felt the power in meetings where several thousand people sang as a choir. Once I sang a capella with 4,000 other men in a seminar gathering. It was incredibly moving. Think of that "new" song issuing from so many mouths—and accompanied by strings!

Scene 6: The song of Moses and the Lamb
Rev. 15:2-4

The overcomers again take up the harps of God as they accompany themselves in song, fulfilling the highest and noblest intentions of both Old and New Testaments. These are not mere believers, but those who have "come off victorious" (Rev. 15:2) over ever-diabolical efforts to destroy them.

Moses' song immediately recalls Exodus, chapter 15, set to music to describe how God—at the last moment—delivered Israel from Egypt's cavalry (v. 3). With one great stroke, God ended forever the grip that Egypt held on His people. They overcame the enemy by the power of God! It climaxed Israel's exodus from Egyptian bondage.

The "song of the Lamb" (v. 3) can be linked with Rev. 5:9-10. The ringing victorious testimony tells how the Son of God, through the Cross, made possible our exodus from sin and its bondage. John's description of these overcoming saints and the recounting of their triumphant song has been a strength to believers through the ages. In heaven and on earth the saints sing joyfully of their victory through God and His Son.

Scene 7: The four hallelujahs
Rev. 19:1-10

With the momentum of a great river, the theme of worship flows continuously through the pages of the Bible. It starts like a trickling stream with the patriarchs in Genesis. They struggled to know and fellowship with the true God. The stream grows wider and deeper as it passes through the Law and the Prophets. By the time it reaches the zealous, adoring early church in the New Testament, the river surges forcefully with clear direction.

Later, as spiritual decline led the church into the dark ages, the mighty river hid underground. Today, the joyful sound has broken above ground again! The mighty current of praise once more surges ahead, catching people in its influence.

In the seventh scene, the great river rolls in full, glorious strength. It is the highest, grandest expression heaven's occupants can bring—the climax of the ages! Like great peals of joyful thunder, majestic praise fills the heavenlies!

> After this I heard what sounded like the roar of a vast throng in heaven and they were shouting: Hallelujah! . . . Hallelujah! . . . Hallelujah! . . . Hallelujah! (Rev. 19:1-10 NEB).

Four times a grand "hallelujah!" fulminates through the creation of God. This expressive word meaning "praise the Lord!" is universal. It is pronounced the same in all human languages. Although a popular word in Old Testament Psalms and much-used by Christian hymn writers, this word is not used anywhere in the New Testament except in Revelation, chapter 19.

How fitting that it appears here—four times in consecutive shouts of acclamation. Twice the great multitude cries out their exultation because the "great harlot," symbolic of all that is false and corrupt in religion, has been brought to judgment. The elders and creatures add their hallelujah! Then, a divine directive issues from the throne—a command that has echoed through each generation of saints and demands a response from the church today:

> Give praise to our God, all you His bond-servants, you who fear Him, the small and the great (Rev. 19:5).

All in heaven respond to this word! God is praised for His greatness, and, the highest intention of God now happens: Christ and the church become one! The marriage of the Lamb and His bride has come. All divine activities with the people of God are culminated, and the joy of the redeemed breaks forth in unrestrained, thunderous praise!

> Alleluia! . . . Alleluia! . . . Amen, Alleluia! . . . Praise our God . . . Alleluia! . . . Exult and shout for joy and do him homage . . . . It is God you must worship . . . . It is God you must worship (NEB).

Today it is time again to make His praise glorious. The church here on earth once again should emulate heaven's ways.

An important lesson
The awestruck John still fettered with unrefined human emotions, made the mistake—in heaven—of falling before a man to worship him while still in the presence of the Almighty:

> And I fell at his feet to worship him. And he said unto me, See thou do it not: I am thy fellow servant, and of thy brethren that have the testimony of Jesus: worship God: for the testimony of Jesus is the spirit of prophecy (Rev. 19:10 KJV).

John's mistake stands as a prophetic warning to the church of succeeding ages. If the beloved John—so close to Jesus that he laid his head on Jesus' bosom, the author of five books of the New Testament, the last of the original apostles, the esteemed bishop of the church at Ephesus—could make such a mistake in his worship, surely it is possible for the church today to be misguided in its worship. The fact that John repeats his mistake in Rev. 22:8 reinforces the idea that it is meant as a flashing caution light, warning the church to guard the purity of its worship.
The atmosphere of heaven was overwhelming in magnitude and impression, and John's action was undoubtedly an excited, unintentional response rather than a deliberate act of misguided devotion. From his experience this simple truth is evident: We may worship *with* the saints in heaven, but we cannot worship the saints in heaven.[3]

The lingering sound
Celestial sounds must have lingered in John's mind and lifted him into realms of inspiration. The holy aura around the aged apostle still lingers over his book. The hope that such worship might be renewed in the church continues to inspire men today. Basilea Schlink spent several weeks in a small house on the island of Patmos.

Her time of solitary prayer moved her deeply and produced the inspiring book, *Patmos: When the Heavens Opened*. In addition to her colorful insights on heaven's worship, she describes her visit to the traditional place of John's revelation:

> Often I would climb up the steep donkey path leading to the grotto, which since the first centuries of Christianity has been recognized as the historical site where the apostle John received the Revelation of Jesus Christ. [Today it is enclosed by a grate. An icon depicting the event can be found above the historic spot.] The events of long ago are still captured in the atmosphere of the grotto. Upon entering, I could immediately sense the presence of God . . . and I was constrained to kneel down at this site . . . . In the past I had visited many places that were of significance for the kingdom of God and I had been blessed by the great deeds God had performed there in the lives of godly men long ago. But at this holy site my heart trembled, overwhelmed by the awe-inspiring event that had taken place here.[4]

John's descriptions of worship add excitement to the revelations of heaven and to the prominence worship occupies there. The sights and sounds haunt readers' minds and create homesickness for the Lord and His adoring hosts. Whoever reads the book of Revelation can easily identify with John Bunyan as he dreamed of Pilgrim entering the Celestial City:

> Now, just as the gates were opened to let in the men, I looked in after them, and behold, the City shone like the sun; the streets also were paved with gold; and in them walked many men with crowns on their heads, palms in their hands, and golden harps to sing praises withal. There were also of them that had wings, and they answered one another without intermission, saying, "Holy, holy, holy is the Lord!" and, after that they shut up the gates, which when I had seen I wished myself among them.[5]

Reflections

Surely that which occupies the total time and energies of heaven must be a fitting pattern for earth.
                —Paul E. Billheimer[6]

The seer John . . . sought to set forth his depictions of the heavenly scene and the celestial worship by projecting on to his canvas the forms and patterns which belonged to his knowledge of the worship of the Church on earth.
                —Ralph P. Martin[7]

As a whole it constitutes a majestic epic. Its spirit never can be caught, and its visions never can be understood, by a mind which moves only in the sphere of sober prose. Here celestial music is sounding, choirs of angels are singing, and "harpers harping with their harps," and we hear the hymns of the redeemed in glory.
                —Charles R. Erdman[8]

Worshipers all have to be taught how to worship. We may have gone to church for years and yet never developed our worshiping muscles! Let none of us assume we know how. In fact, scenes of heaven in the book of Revelation seem so foreign to us we probably know much less than we think we know.
                —Anne Ortlund[9]

There the singers are playing the most glorious music on their harps as they raise their voices in song before the throne. And the sound of this heavenly music is so enthralling that in the other spheres of heaven everyone who hears the vibrant chords of the harps and the jubilant voices is overwhelmed with delight. In their anthems the singers worship God and His perfect ways.
                —Basilea Schlink[10]

Set before us in the book of Revelation is a glorious example worthy of our emulation. I am keenly anticipating that day when our worship around the throne will be free from all hindrances and shackles of self-consciousness! Heaven is noisy and passionate in its demonstration of praise and worship to God. God himself is fiercely and passionately emotional, and he responds to us accordingly! We will never go wrong in using the heavenly prototype of worship as a pattern today. As we gain insight into the heavenly worship, we can then pray that we experience worship "in earth as it is in heaven."
                –Bob Sorge[11]

Part V

David's Revelation

David, having discovered the joy of total-person involvement in worship, now summons all people to join him in enthusiastic, Psalmic praise.

- Chapter 14 **The Magnificent Obsession**
  David had a consuming desire to glorify God with his whole being and to make Jerusalem the worship capital of the world.

- Chapter 15 **The Order of Temple Worship**
  Based on his understanding that "God is enthroned on the praises of Israel," David initiated a new, twenty-four-hour-a-day approach to worship on Mount Zion. Later, his new order of worship was incorporated into Solomon's temple and every period of revival that followed.

14

The Magnificent Obsession

But as for me, my joy is my nearness to God;
In Thee, Lord Jehovah! I take refuge,
that I may tell of all that Thou hast done.
—Psalm 73:28 DEWITT

A daring, ambitious plan gripped King David's heart: He would make Jerusalem the worship center of the world! His mind swirled with the audacity of the new idea. If God was behind this plan, a worship system that had roots stretching back five hundred years to Moses would be revamped!

David's yearning to build a temple for God in Jerusalem was not a token afterthought of the benevolent eastern monarch; rather, it was the consuming ambition of a man who sought to exalt his God before all nations and to establish Jerusalem as the religious capital of the earth (2 Samuel, chapter 7). The books of Kings and Chronicles, coupled with many psalms, show that David was imbued with a passion to worship God and to share his vision of the true God with all mankind (1 Chron. 16:23-31).

Expressing his heart's cry for God and Jerusalem, David wrote and sang a stream of prophetic songs such as:

> Great is the LORD, and greatly to be praised,
> In the city of our God, His holy mountain.
> Beautiful in elevation, the joy of the whole earth,
> Is Mount Zion in the far north,
> The City of the great King (Psalm 48:1, 2).

> There is a river whose streams make glad the city of God,
> The holy dwelling places of the Most High.
> God is in the midst of her, she will not be moved (Psalm 46:4, 5).

David's preparation

From boyhood, David loved to worship. His sensitive nature and musical genius found inspiration and fulfillment in expressions toward God. As a lad watching his father's sheep, he saw music calm nervous flocks. Like other boys, he fashioned reed flutes and crude stringed instruments and experimented with enchanting sounds; however, David and his music were destined for greatness.[1]

The singing shepherd boy became so well known that he was invited to come to the King's palace to play the harp (1 Sam. 16:14-23). King Saul's wild antics had terrified his servants and advisors. At times evil spirits came upon him, driving him mad. Nothing seemed to help, and everyone feared for his life. His attendants were desperate. Finally, some advisors recommended soothing music, and David, son of Jesse, "a skillful musician," (16:18) was brought to the court. His stay at the palace was short-lived. He soon found it necessary to run for his life. The mad king made David the scapegoat for the king's many troubles and pursued him relentlessly. The book of 1 Samuel tells the exciting story.

During these harsh times, the fugitive learned secrets of inspired prayer and worship. David experienced new dimensions of faith and understanding and found strength in the presence of God. Only the crucible of suffering could produce the Psalmic masterpieces of lament attributed to David such as Psalm, chapter 40. Charles Spurgeon aptly said, "David's griefs made him eloquent in holy psalmody."[2]

David's qualification

The Bible calls David "a man after God's own heart" (1 Sam. 13:14; Acts 13:22). No other person in the Bible receives this tribute. He could have been honored like this because he:

• Respected God's name and anointing.
• Sought to do God's will.
• Had a truly repentant heart.
• Was dependent on God's help.

However, his heart for worship was his finest qualification. He originally received the distinction in a worship setting. Saul had just transgressed in his sacrificial offerings and disregarded directions from the prophet Samuel (1 Sam. 13:8-14). David became the Lord's Anointed because he was sensitive to God's wishes and desires, he obeyed the Lord's commandments, and he expressed his love and devotion in a pleasing way to God.

David became a great world leader and one of history's most famous figures. He was a brave warrior, a shrewd politician, a great military leader, and a famous king. However, his greatest accomplishment lies in the magnificent worship system he constructed for Israel. The hymnal he wrote to preserve his reforms guides the church in worship renewal today. It occupies the central portion of the Bible: the book of Psalms.

David's assignment

As he prospered, David developed a burning desire to build a house of God that would be a center of prayer and worship for all people. The idea pleased the Lord, but God told David to let Solomon build it later. David's personal ambition met a disheartening response (2 Sam. 7:4-16; 1 Chron. 22:8).

God disqualified David from building the temple. Instead, God gave plans to David for the physical structure and for the order of worship in the building. David prepared the material and workmen for the construction project, but he relished his most important task of training the priesthood in the exuberant worship God enjoys. The blueprint for the building came by divine revelation. Bible students usually study the pattern that came to Moses for the tabernacle of his day, but few investigate the same prophetic inspiration that came to David for the temple. Not only did David "see" the structural layout, but he also received a plan to maintain God's presence in the building. He clearly understood the temple would be an empty shell without God. He also knew God would not choose to inhabit the building simply because He needed a place to stay. God's life-long dealings with David culminated in the disclosure of patterns for the material and spiritual order in the temple:

> Then David gave to Solomon his son the pattern of the porch . . . and the pattern of *all that he had by the spirit,* of the courts of the house of the Lord . . . also for the courses of the priests and the Levites, and for all the work of the service of the house of the LORD . . . . . All this, said David, *the Lord made me understand in writing by his hand upon me,* even all the works of this pattern (1 Chron. 28:11-19 KJV, emphasis added).

The New English Bible words verse nineteen:

> "All this was drafted by the LORD's own hand," said David; "my part was to consider the detailed working out of the plan."

David's first step

Before the temple could be built, the ark of the covenant must be brought back to Jerusalem. David considered the ark's return an obvious, essential move. Moses' workmen had built the gold-encased chest—approximately 2' x 2' x 5'—nearly 500 years earlier (Exod. 37:1-9). God manifested His glory over the ark, making it Israel's most precious possession. The heart of their national worship system centered on the ark. Captured once by Philistines, the missing ark had indicted a generation of Israelites for spiritual apathy. The glory of God had departed and "Ichabod" had been written over the people and their land (1 Sam. 4:21).

The heathen captors must have laughed at the sight of the small, fragile box placed at the feet of the massive idol Dagon. In their light-hearted mood they made a tragic mistake. They left the ark overnight in the heathen sanctuary. The next morning, to their surprise, the idol had fallen on its face—the posture of worship—before the ark. Restoring the idol to its place, they left Dagon alone again with the ark. The next morning the shocked people in the city of Ashdod saw their god dismembered, broken before Israel's ark (1 Sam. 5:4). With great haste they sent the ark out of their country on a new oxcart (6:11). The ark was returned to Kiriath-Jearim (7:1) where it remained for twenty years.

Finally, David decided to gather the people and bring the ark to Jerusalem (2 Sam. 6; 1 Chronicles, chapter 13). Singers and musicians led the celebration in procession (1 Chron. 13:8). Abruptly, the festive worship halted when Uzza, one of the priests, slumped to the ground dead (2 Sam. 6:7; 1 Chron. 13:10). The stunned king and his people watched terrified. The man carelessly and irreverently had touched the ark! King David's fear quickly turned to anger. Was not his intense praise and worship sincere and genuine? Why had God done such a thing?

For three months David sought the Lord while the ark remained stored at the house of Obed-Edom, a Levite. Then David realized that, in spite of their sincerity, he and the priests had not done things the way God had prescribed (1 Chron. 15:13). The Levites were to carry the ark on their shoulders—not on an oxcart, Philistine-style! This insight proved again that David was a man after God's own heart. David's next attempt to return the ark succeeded gloriously. Singers and musicians gave their best efforts, outdone only by the king himself who danced joyfully before the ark.

And David was dancing before the LORD with all his might ("without restraint," NEB; "whirling around," JB) (1 Chron. 15:28, ANCHOR).

So all Israel transported the ark of the covenant of Yahweh with shouts of joy accompanying the sounding of the horn, the trumpets and the cymbals, and the music of the harps and zithers (1 Chron. 15:28, ANCHOR).

David's tabernacle

Before bringing back the ark, David pondered a daring plan. He wanted to place the ark in a special tent, and surround it with an atmosphere of constant worship and praise in Jerusalem.[3] This would involve a radical move and a revolutionary approach to worship. Logically, the ark should go back to its ancient, time-honored shelter, the Tabernacle of Moses. At that time, the old tent was at Gibeon, five miles from Jerusalem (1 Chron. 16:39; 21:28-30; 2 Chron. 1:3-6, 13). Under the leadership of Zadok, priests offered routine sacrifices there, and people recognized the old tent as the worship center of Israel.

However, David decided to bring the ark to Jerusalem and install it temporarily (until the temple was built) in the Tabernacle of David (2 Sam. 6:17; 1 Chron. 16:1; 2 Chron. 5:5)—a tent bearing his name and given equal importance with the tent bearing Moses' name.[4] Practical concerns with governing the land, plus David's deep prophetic feelings toward Jerusalem, influenced his decision to bring the ark to Jerusalem and to leave the old tabernacle where it stood.

Commentators offer various reasons for not returning the ark to Gibeon. Keil-Delitzsch conjecture in their commentary that "one of the principal motives for allowing the existing separation of the ark from the tabernacle to continue, may have been that . . . two high priests had arisen."[5] Zadok officiated at Gibeon, but Abiathar had faithfully served David as high priest and spiritual advisor during the years they both lived in the wilderness running from King Saul. Deposing either priest from his office would be difficult, so maintaining two centers retained both men equitably.

David may have considered bringing the Tabernacle of Moses to Jerusalem, but after hundreds of years "it had gone to decay and was not fit to be removed," according to Matthew Henry.[6] Also, David would have faced inevitable protests from the Gibeonites.[7] Above all, David realized that bringing the ancient tent to Jerusalem would only perpetuate a system of worship that needed renewal and updating. Moses' tabernacle represented the old, established way of doing things and could pose a threat to David's innovations.

The ark of the covenant, the center of the Mosaic sanctuary, could be brought to Jerusalem. Its presence and symbolic significance could easily be part of the transition period David envisioned. The best of the Mosaic covenant could join the Davidic revelation.

Politically, wise King David wanted to "make the capital of his kingdom the central point of the worship of the whole congregation of Israel."[8] The presence of the ark would reinforce the authority and legitimacy of the kingdom's organization and administration.

The land had two great centers of religion in David's time: Gibeon and Jerusalem. Although priests continued to function at the ancient Tabernacle of Moses, the emphasis shifted to the Tabernacle of David. Regular burnt offerings and peace offerings continued to take place (apparently only at Gibeon after the initial installation), but a new dimension of joyful celebration was introduced.

While the temple remained unbuilt, new priestly functions of song and musicianship maintained and enhanced the presence of God among the people as well as began making Jerusalem the joy of the whole earth.

> And he appointed some of the Levites as ministers before the ark of the LORD, even to *celebrate* and to *thank* and *praise* the LORD God of Israel . . . with musical instruments, harps, lyres . . . loud-sounding cymbals, and Benaiah and Jahaziel the priests blew trumpets continually before the ark of the covenant of God. Then on that day David first assigned Asaph and his relatives to give thanks to the LORD . . . . So he left Asaph and his relatives there before the ark of the covenant of the LORD, to minister before the ark continually, as every day's work required (1 Chron. 16:4-7, 37, emphasis added).

The new worship patterns were not new to David, but they had not been established in the religious life of Israel. They were compatible with Israel's heritage but required a new exercise of faith by the people and by the priests.

David's nine ways of worship

David's concept of worship is simple and workable. It revolves around total, fervent adoration of God. Spontaneity, exuberance, excitement, youthfulness, and celebration—all accompanied by body actions—characterize Psalmic worship. The Psalms say much about the heart, the center of affection, because true worship originates deep within. Common, human reactions quickened by the Holy Spirit express these honest feelings for God. Voices, hands, and even body posture can demonstrate enthusiasm for God. "We cannot avoid the realities of emotion if we are to have a genuine worship," David Randolph said.[9]

Many Christians have faced the enthusiastic language of Psalms with hesitation. In an interview with *Pastoral Renewal,* James I. Packer made the following admission:

> The other things that threw me [about the Psalms] was that they are simply so exuberant. The way that we are conditioned into by much of our culture, both Christian and secular, means that we are not really prepared for the kind of uninhibited expression of ourselves

119

before God that the Psalms model for us. And as long as a person feels that the psalmists were rather uncivilized fellows, because they expressed themselves so wholeheartedly, even fiercely, he will find it hard to identify with them. That was a problem for me at that time. I am happy to say that as the years go by I feel more in tune with the Psalms.[10]

Diagram five shows nine ways to express worship. Giving token references from the Psalms, the diagram lists human reactions common to everyone. Whenever people gather for enjoyable, public, group experiences, all of these positions and expressions occur. For instance, people chant, shout, and sing at football games and join without reservation in clapping, waving banners, and using noisemakers. They may stand, jump, or fall in the excitement!

David and his singing priests in the Psalms simply say that godly people should be as excited about God as they are about worldly things! The gatherings of God's people should be more like celebrations than funerals. David wanted to lift people out of the straitjacket of excessive formalism that characterizes priestly religion.

Somehow David discovered the secret of enjoying God with his entire being. These nine ways of expressing heartfelt worship were so meaningful to him that he wanted other people to enjoy them. As a result, he pitched a tent on Mount Zion, brought the ark of the covenant, and surrounded it with a singing, prophetic priesthood to worship 24 hours a day. Later, Solomon merely moved the procedure into the temple.

NINE WAYS OF PSALMIC WORSHIP

VOICE		HANDS		POSTURE	
1. Speak!	34:1	4. Lift!	63:4	7. Stand!	134:1
2. Sing!	47:6	5. Play Inst.!	33:2,3	8. Bow!	95:6
3. Shout!	27:6	6. Clap!	47:1	9. Dance!	149:3

DIAGRAM 5

Reflections

The most valuable thing the Psalms do for me is to express the same delight in God which made David dance.

—*C.S. Lewis[11]*

Can you believe, actually believe that King David danced up and down the streets when he brought the ark of the Lord into Jerusalem? (question accompanied by pictures of dancers in their Presbyterian church!)

—*Marilee Zdenek and Marge Champion[12]*

The whole person, with all his senses, with both mind and body, needs to be involved in genuine worship.

—*Jerry Kerns[13]*

The whole history of worship might be written around the fascinating and difficult question of the relation between the outward and the inward; and that something is undoubtedly lost (whatever corresponding gains there by be) when such external expression as, let us say, corporate movement form no part of worship.

—*C.F.D. Moule[14]*

As we march back into the history of the nation Israel, we find that worship there was an active event. And talk about physical! Why, there was dancing, clapping, processioning, singing, shouting, and all the rest. Even in her apostasy, Israel seems to have been more alive in the worship of the Lord than most contemporary Christian churches . . . . For as these people were alive in the Lord, they certainly held nothing back in manifesting their praise and worship to God in very physical ways.

—*Peter Gillquist[15]*

15

The Order of Temple Worship

*It was in the days of David and Asaph that the custom began
of having choir directors to lead the choirs in hymns of praise
and thanks to God.*
—Nehemiah 12:46 LB

The temple was the world's most magnificent building! Mechanical details had been meticulously handled. The splendid, shining house of prayer and worship brought glory to God and inspired awe in other nations. No effort had been spared to fulfill David's vision:

* The house of God had been built according to divine blueprint.
* Trained priests stood ready to minister in music and prophecy.
* The ark of God rested in the Holy Place of the temple.
* Lavish sacrifices had been offered.

Upon completion, the people waited for the crowning event of dedication. They looked for God to come and accept their sacrifice! The usual fortnightly contingent of sanctified priests was not sufficient (1 Chronicles, chapter 24). The comment in 2 Chron. 5:11 indicates, "The festival was so great, that not merely the course appointed to perform the service of that week, but also all the courses had sanctified themselves and cooperated in the celebration."[1]

Trained musicians made a lavish display of harmonious sound, and suddenly, the glory of the Lord filled the temple. Two accounts of the event are given, but one offers a special insight as to why God came to His temple:

And all the Levitical singers, Asaph, Heman, Jeduthun, and their sons and kinsmen, clothed in fine linen, with cymbals, harps, and lyres, standing east of the altar, and with them one hundred and twenty priests blowing trumpets *in unison* when the trumpeters and the singers were to make themselves heard with *one voice* to praise and to glorify the LORD, and when they lifted up their voice accompanied by trumpets and cymbals and instruments of music, and *when they praised the* LORD saying, "He indeed is good for His lovingkindness is everlasting," *then* the house, the house of the LORD, was filled with a cloud (2 Chron 5:12-13, emphasis added. See also 1 Kings 8:10, 11).

The glory of God was revealed when every singer and musician "together as one man, sang with one voice to praise."[2] All the priests made aggressive, enthusiastic efforts to praise God with all their strength and hearts.

The dwelling of His presence

Every creature has its element or its own set of proper living conditions—its comfort zone. Fish swim in water, birds fly in the air, and animals occupy the land. Man exists best when an envelope of gases surrounds the planet. In his ingenuity, man has made ways to occupy the domains of fish, birds, and animals, yet in every domain, man must have an air supply.

God also exists best in a certain environment. An atmosphere of praise and worship best exercises God's majesty and attributes. David understood this very well, capsulizing the thought as follows:

> Yet Thou art holy, O Thou who art enthroned upon the praises of Israel (Ps. 22:3).

The verb *yawshab* (*inhabit* in the King James Version) literally means to sit down, to dwell, to remain. Modern versions appropriately translate the word as *enthroned* in this verse. The character of the person affects how it is translated. For a judge it could be translated *seated* in court. In this Psalm, it is appropriate to think of Almighty God, King of the universe, sitting upon a throne.

A host usually ushers guests to the best seat in the house. Welcome guests should be made comfortable. In congregational church services, God's people invite the Lord of Glory to come. God does not need a frail human chair, yet an atmosphere of praise extends welcome to Him. He greatly delights to be in the midst of His praising creation. As Jack Hayford says, "the King of the universe makes His throne to descend in the place where people praise Him."[3]

Imagine the Lord seated, enthroned upon the praise of worshiping churches! His power emanates and His directives come from His throne. This explains why wonderful things happen and spiritual gifts operate in an atmosphere of praise and worship!

When Solomon dedicated the temple, ministering priests and Levites—in unity—deliberately invoked God's presence through praise. A building filled with an atmosphere of praise provided an avenue for God's great visitation. Worship brought the earthly house of God into harmony with the atmosphere around heaven's throne. Heaven did not come down; people of praise entered the heavenlies! Frances Metcalfe expresses this thought:

> The Bible reveals that God's direct presence and His shekinah glory are manifested on earth only when His people provide for Him an atmosphere of pure and fervent praise, similar to that high praise which continually surrounds His throne, in which He dwells. Our God lives and moves in the midst of *praise*. So pure, so exalted, so holy is His nature, that any other atmosphere is unfitting and dishonoring to the great God and King of Heaven.[4]

The chicken or the egg

Who originates worship? God or man? If God responds to man's praise, then man could get the impression that man initiates worship and that God is at the mercy of man's whims. A heavy religious emphasis on "serving God" also gives the impression that what man does is of primary importance. This may seem as confusing as the old question, "Which came first, the chicken or the egg?"

Jesus clearly declared that God originates worship! This truth must not be lost.

> No man can come to me, except the Father which hath sent me draw him . . . . Every man therefore that hath heard, and hath learned of the Father, cometh unto me (John 6:44-45 KJV).

Christian worship depends on God revealing Himself through the Lord Jesus Christ to man. Man simply responds to the revelation. Man cannot initiate suitable worship. He cannot fully comprehend his own inner workings, let alone the wonder of God. Paul declares in Rom. 11:36, "For from Him and through Him and to Him are all things," and although the immediate context of the verse is not worship, the principle applies to worship.

The book of Psalms confirms that God initiates worship in the following:

22:25a	From Thee comes my praise in the great assembly. (Thou dost inspire my praise. NEB).
27:8	When Thou didst say, "Seek My face," my heart said to Thee, "Thy face, O LORD, I shall seek".
30:11, 12	Thou has turned for me my mourning into dancing; Thou has loosed my sackcloth and girded me with gladness; that [to the end that] my soul may sing praise to Thee, and not be silent.
36:9	For with Thee is the fountain of life; (Life's own fountain is within thy presence, MOF) In Thy Light we see light.
80:18b	Revive us, and we will call upon Thy name.

God comes to sinful, uninterested men and women to reveal His grace. God's tender, merciful dealing with man shows divine mercy at its best. After accepting God's salvation, man can become a worshiper. Raymond Abba describes it clearly:

> Worship . . . begins not from our end but from God's; it springs from the divine initiative in redemption. We come to God because God, in Jesus Christ, has come to us: we love Him because He first loved us.[5]

God actually makes man capable of worship by revealing His grace to Him. Douglas Horton says, "Worship is a response [by man] to an experience originally brought to him."[6] Evelyn Underhill comments that worship is:
- a distinct response to a distinct revelation.[7]
- the result of, and the response to, God's prevenient act and pressure.[8]
- a willed response to God's inciting action: a humble and costly cooperation with His grace.[9]

Dynamic, corporate worship requires that people know God is actively interested in them and that He initiates loving actions toward them. People also must know that He has accepted them in His presence by His mercy. Response follows revelation. Both are required! "In a high sense worship includes both the revelation and the response."[10] This is clearly seen in the Revelation accounts of worship in Heaven as "God speaking to his creatures and his creatures making decent reply to him."[11]

A stern warning by H. Grady Davis is timely here:

> He does not need our consent to be God. But he is my God only when I acknowledge him as my God. Though all creation worships him, he is the church's God only when the church acknowledges him to be its Lord.[12]

The law of His presence

Just as clouds bring rain, worship brings the outpouring of the Holy Spirit. The Bible often uses rain to symbolize God's blessing and presence. A natural phenomenon pictures a spiritual truth (see 1 Cor. 15:46).

The Principle. Evaporation occurs when the rays of the sun pour down on the surface of oceans and other bodies of water. Heated surface water undergoes a change; it passes from a liquid into a vapor. The sun draws the moisture upward into the earth's atmosphere, where it gathers into clouds. The clouds then move over land and, as temperatures cool, empty themselves as rain, snow, or sleet. Falling rain eventually finds its way back into streams and rivers that return to replenish the ocean's water supply. Diagram 6 depicts the hydrologic cycle.

The following Bible verse shows that the ancient book teaches things about rain that modern weather scientists only recently have come to understand:

> For He [God] draws up the drops of water, they distill rain from the mist, which the clouds pour down, they drip upon man abundantly. Can anyone understand the spreading of the clouds, the thundering of His pavilion? (Job 36:27-29).

The following references reinforce the principle: Psalm 147:7, 8; Prov. 11:25; Eccl. 1:7, 11:3; Amos 5:8, 9:6.

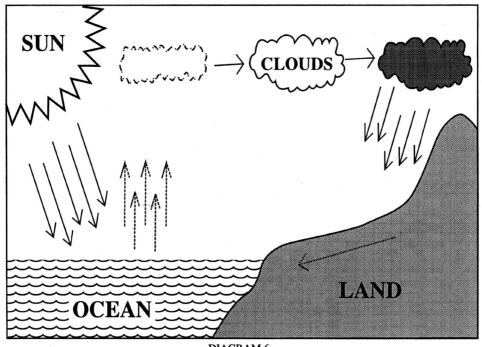

DIAGRAM 6

The Application. Churches can make spiritual rain by applying this principle in congregational worship. I call this concept, "The Law of His Presence." It is the unfailing way of bringing God's presence to His people. Here is the spiritual application of nature's hydrologic cycle:

- The Water   = Mankind
- The Sun's Rays   = The dealings of God with mankind
- Evaporation   = The worship-response of God's people, aided by the Spirit
- Precipitation   = The outpouring of God's Spirit.

First, God deals with the hearts of people. Then, men and women respond to God, losing their identity in wholehearted seeking of the Almighty. God's people pour themselves UP in prayer and adoration just as water vapor rises in evaporation. God, in turn, pours DOWN His great presence on His people like rain. A "dry" heart—or a "dry" church—can initiate a downpour of the Spirit by responding to God's invitation to worship. Individuals and churches can seed the clouds with praise (see Hos. 6:3, 10:12; Joel 2:23; Zech. 10:1; James 5:7).

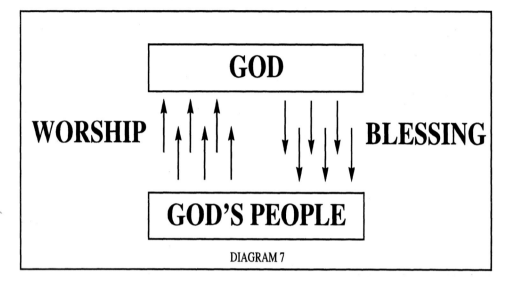

DIAGRAM 7

Thoughts that shaped David's concept of worship

As David made preparations for the temple, key ideas directed his thinking.

Sacrifice. David came to realize that God desired praise sacrifices more than animal sacrifices. Spiritually leaping over the intervening years, David adopted a New Testament mentality of true sacrifice.

Will I eat the flesh of bulls, or drink the blood of goats? Offer unto God thanksgiving; and pay thy vows unto the most High: And call upon me in the day of trouble: I will deliver thee, and thou shalt glorify me (Ps. 50:13-15 KJV).

For thou desirest not sacrifice; else would I give it: thou delightest not in burnt offering. The sacrifices of God are a broken spirit: a broken and a contrite heart, O God, thou wilt not despise. O Lord, open thou my lips; and my mouth shall shew forth thy praise (Ps. 51:16, 17, 15 KJV).

By him therefore let us offer the sacrifice of praise to God continually, that is, the fruit of our lips giving thanks to his name (Heb. 13:15 KJV).

The methods of praise and worship. David had a conviction that God had prophetically revealed to him how to praise the Lord. "The command was from the Lord" to institute new methods of worship, according to 2 Chron. 29:25. The command came through the prophets David and Nathan. Psalmic declarations such as "praise his name in the dance" (Ps. 149:3), and "lift up your hands in the sanctuary" (Ps. 134:2), and "Clap your hands all ye people" (Ps. 47:1), are instructions by the Spirit of God on how to praise Him.

The importance of order. David was convinced by God that enthusiastic, emotional worship in and of itself was not enough. It had to be done in order. The attempt to bring back the ark without considering how God wanted it done had ended abruptly with a dead priest and frustrated people (2 Sam. 6:7; 1 Chron. 13:10). David had learned that things must be done properly in God's way (1 Chron. 15:13). The New Testament confirms the need for order (1 Cor. 14:40).

Form and corporate worship. David worshiped God fervently, yet he also caught a higher vision of corporate worship. He understood that people often think more clearly when alone and that some problems are better faced alone; however, he also found, as H.S. Coffin has stated, "we worship best in a devout assembly."[13] Coffin quotes Luther as saying:

> At home in my own house there's no warmth or vigor in me; but in the church, when the multitude is gathered together, a fire is kindled in my heart, and it breaks its way through.

David wished to share with Israel and the world the exhilaration of worshiping the great God of heaven and earth. By joining his praise with the praise of others, both he and the congregation were built up, and collectively they glorified the Lord in a grand way. David saw God enthroned upon congregational praise: "O thou that inhabitest the praises of Israel" (Ps. 22:3 KJV).

For a congregation to employ the fervent, enthusiastic modes David envisioned, he knew it would need a form or structure to follow. J.W. Pearce cleverly describes this ordered approach to God as "God's table manners." He concludes that just as some sort of table manners have value when dining, the church needs reasonable guidelines for its congregational worship.[14]

If God receives greatest glory in corporate worship, then the framework for corporate worship is very important. David approached this challenge with much prayer, perhaps feeling much as Edward K. Ziegler who wrote:

> It is our high privilege so to order the conditions and atmosphere of the worship experience that the people of our churches, entirely forgetting us, may through the programs we have planned and our unobtrusive guidance, come into the presence of God.[15]

The order of temple worship
The Tabernacle of David was erected at Jerusalem to house the ark of the covenant. While the Tabernacle of Moses still stood at Gibeon, David initiated a new Levitical system at Jerusalem. He introduced musical instruments and psalm-singing in the daily, twenty-four-hour effort to surround the ark of God with the praises of Israel.

THE ORDER OF TEMPLE WORSHIP

KEY VERSE: 2 CH 29:25

"He then stationed the Levites in the house of the Lord with cymbals, with harps, and with lyres, according to the command of DAVID and of GAD the king's seer, and of NATHAN the prophet; for the command was FROM THE LORD THROUGH HIS PROPHETS."

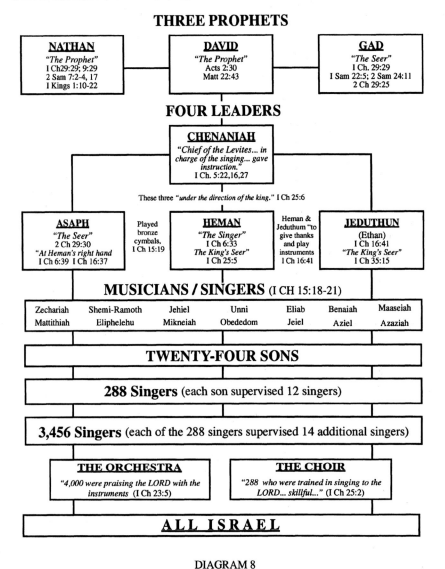

THREE PROPHETS

NATHAN	DAVID	GAD
"The Prophet"	*"The Prophet"*	*"The Seer"*
I Ch 29:29; 9:29	Acts 2:30	I Ch. 29:29
2 Sam 7:2-4, 17	Matt 22:43	I Sam 22:5; 2 Sam 24:11
I Kings 1:10-22		2 Ch 29:25

FOUR LEADERS

CHENANIAH
"Chief of the Levites... in charge of the singing... gave instruction."
I Ch. 5:22,16,27

These three *"under the direction of the king."* I Ch 25:6

ASAPH	Played	HEMAN	Heman &	JEDUTHUN
"The Seer"	bronze	*"The Singer"*	Jeduthum "to	(Ethan)
2 Ch 29:30	cymbals,	I Ch 6:33	give thanks	I Ch 16:41
"At Heman's right hand"	I Ch 15:19	*The King's Seer"*	and play	*"The King's Seer"*
I Ch 6:39 I Ch 16:37		I Ch 25:5	instruments	I Ch 35:15
			I Ch 16:41	

MUSICIANS / SINGERS (I CH 15:18-21)

Zechariah	Shemi-Ramoth	Jehiel	Unni	Eliab	Benaiah	Maaseiah
Mattithiah	Eliphelehu	Mikneiah	Obededom	Jeiel	Aziel	Azaziah

TWENTY-FOUR SONS

288 Singers (each son supervised 12 singers)

3,456 Singers (each of the 288 singers supervised 14 additional singers)

THE ORCHESTRA	THE CHOIR
"4,000 were praising the LORD with the instruments (I Ch 23:5)	*"288 who were trained in singing to the LORD... skillful..."* (I Ch 25:2)

ALL ISRAEL

DIAGRAM 8

From the 38,000 Levites who were thirty years of age and older, David appointed 4,000 to sing and play instruments (1 Chron. 15:16-22). Diagram 8 shows the structure of worship Solomon instituted in the temple in obedience to his father David (2 Chron. 8:14).

The three prophets. The diagram lists three prophets who delivered the command from the Lord about temple worship: Nathan, David, and Gad (2 Chron. 29:25). God adhered to his own principle by establishing the new direction "by the mouth of two or three witnesses" (Deut. 19:15 KJV).

The four leaders. Chenaniah was the chief musician. His name, which means Yahweh establishes, indicates the prophetic burden of responsibility that he carried. Asaph, Heman, and Ethan (Jeduthun) were the leading choir directors, coming respectively from the clans of Gershon, Kohath, and Merari (the three sons of Levi). They also had remarkable prophetic abilities (2 Chron. 35:15) which blended well with the playing of musical instruments (1 Chron. 25:1-3, 5-6). The prophetic gifts in these men point to the close association between prophecy and worship. The presence of God manifested during worship produces what might be called a prophetic state. This aura or atmosphere must have delighted the heart of David.

Twenty-four courses. Two hundred eighty-eight skilled musicians were divided into twenty-four *courses* or groups to facilitate the ministry of music. The courses were divided according to the number of the sons of Asaph, 4; Heman, 14; Jeduthun-Ethan, 6. The ministry of song and instrument was performed entirely by the Levites. David Blomgren gives this insight:

> The later Psalms, especially beginning with Psalm 92, seem to place a definite emphasis upon the participation of all the people in song. This suggests that Psalm-singing by the congregation must have developed some time after the temple worship patterns had been already established by the Levitical singers. The worshippers first began to interject single words of acclamation, and then eventually entire refrains were repeated.[16]

Restoration during revival periods

Solomon's reign started gloriously as the humble king led his people in prayer, and singers and musicians filled God's house with praise. However, when Solomon died, the nation fitfully divided into two kingdoms. Their histories relate directly to the good or the evil of the kings in power at a given time. All nineteen of northern Israel's kings were evil, and idolatry abounded during their reigns. Finally, Assyria overran the nation. The southern kingdom of Judah also had some ungodly kings, but fortunately four good kings brought religious revival to the nation. During each of the four revivals, the king and priests reinstituted Davidic worship. Paul E. Billheimer summarized Davidic worship:

> Although God is omnipresent, He is not everywhere present in benign influence. Where there is joyful praise, there He is dynamically and benevolently active.[17]

Jehoshaphat. During the reign of the good King Jehoshaphat, a massive army from Moab, Ammon, and Mount Seir marched against Judah. The Jews gathered for fasting and prayer about the matter, and the king led in penitent prayer. Suddenly, the Spirit of the Lord came upon Jahaziel, one of Asaph's descendants, who prophesied:

> "You need not fight in this battle; station yourselves, stand and see the salvation of the LORD on your behalf, O Judah and Jerusalem." Do not fear or be dismayed; tomorrow go out to face them, for the LORD is with you (2 Chron. 20:17).

The king and people dropped to the ground in worship as the Levites (some Kohathites and some Korahites) stood up and loudly praised the Lord. The next day, Jehoshaphat urged the people to trust God and believe His prophets (v. 20).

After consultation, the king gave an unprecedented directive: send the Levitical singers and musicians out in front of the army. It must have been a rather tense situation as the white-robed priests began to march straight toward the enemy. The singing chant which so captured the message of Davidic worship began:

> Praise the LORD! For His mercy endureth forever! (v. 21 KJV).

Soon the message gripped the soldiers as well as the priests. As the voices grew stronger, the sound carried to the camp of the enemy, undoubtedly surprising the troops. Chanting priests leading the soldiers? God came on the scene and routed the enemy.

The point here is that King Jehoshaphat, at the time of his great need, employed the great revelation of David to his advantage. The God enthroned on the praises of Israel once again displayed His awesome presence as His people worshiped Him.

Joash. To dethrone the wicked Queen Athaliah, the priest Jehoiada gathered faithful Levites throughout Judah. According to a prearranged plan, they crowned young Joash king. He then led the people in renewing their covenant with God "that they should be the Lord's people" (2 Chron. 23:16).

The spiritual revival of Judah during Joash's reign was due to the restored authority of the Levitical priesthood—not only to offer burnt offerings according to the Mosaic Law, but also to incorporate "rejoicing and singing according to the order of David" (v. 18).

Hezekiah. The revival under Hezekiah clearly involved Davidic worship. 2 Chronicles 29,(vv. 25-30 , emphasis added):

> He then stationed the Levites in the house of the LORD with cymbals, with harps, and with lyres, *according to the command of David and of Gad the king's seer, and of Nathan the prophet; for the command was from the LORD through His prophets.*
>
> And the Levites stood with the *musical instruments of David*, and the priests *with the trumpets.*
>
> Then Hezekiah gave the order to offer the burnt offering on the altar. When the burnt offering began, *the song of the LORD also began with the trumpets, accompanied by the instruments of David*, king of Israel.
>
> While the whole assembly *worshiped, the singers also sang and the trumpets sounded*; all this continued until the burnt offering was finished.

Now at the completion of the burnt offerings, the king and all who were present with him *bowed down and worshiped*.

Moreover, King Hezekiah and the officials ordered *the Levites to sing praises to the* LORD *with the words of David and Asaph the seer. So they sang praises with joy, and bowed down and worshiped* (2 Chron. 29:25-30, emphasis added. See 31:2).

Josiah. King Josiah began to seek the Lord at the age of sixteen, and when he was twenty, he began to purge Judah and Jerusalem of idolatry. The Book of the Law was discovered by workmen repairing the temple, and the king began immediately to rectify every wrong which he knew existed in the domain. A great Passover feast was called and:

The singers, the sons of Asaph, were also at their stations *according to the command of David, Asaph, Heman, and Jeduthun the king's seer.* (2 Chron. 35:15, emphasis added).

Once again Davidic worship played a role in spiritual renewal. The recognition of David's command indicates that his approach to worship was indeed by divine revelation.

Rebuilding the temple. When Cyrus, king of Persia, issued his decree permitting the Jews to return and rebuild the temple, 42,360 returned, including "200 singing men and women" (Ezra 2:65). At the laying of the temple foundation:

the priests stood in their apparel with *trumpets*, and the Levites, *the sons of Asaph, with cymbals, to praise the* LORD *according to the directions of King David of Israel.*

And they sang, praising and giving thanks to the LORD, saying, "For He is good, for His lovingkindness is upon Israel forever." And all the people shouted with a great shout when they praised the LORD because the foundation of the house of the LORD was laid (Ezra 3:10, 11, emphasis added).

Reading law. When Ezra, the priest, brought the Law of Moses to the people, they responded in Davidic revival fashion.

And Ezra opened the book in the sight of all the people for he was standing above all the people; and when he opened it, *all the people stood up.* Then Ezra *blessed the* LORD the great God. And all the people *answered, "Amen, Amen!" while lifting up their hands*: then they *bowed low* and *worshiped the* LORD *with their faces to the ground* (Neh. 8:5, 6, emphasis added).

Dedicating the wall. When the time came to dedicate the wall rebuilt around Jerusalem, Nehemiah searched for all the Levites to have them attend the ceremony. The singers were assembled (Neh. 12:28), and two great choirs were appointed (v. 31) to circle the city, walking on the walls. The two choirs (lit. thanksgiving choirs) gathered at the Valley Gate and proceeded in different directions. The two groups were identical, each having a choir, secular leaders, lay leaders, seven priests, and eight

Levites. They had with them "the musical instruments of David the man of God" (v. 36), and the heads of the Levites were there to "praise and give thanks, as prescribed by David the man of God, division corresponding to division" (v. 24).

Verse 42 says, "the singers sang," but this does not do justice to their efforts. The *Anchor Bible* comments, "The singers . . . sang vociferously. Literally 'the singers made heard.' The meaning is that the vocal and instrumental music resounded throughout the area".

> For they performed the worship of their God and the service of purification, together with *the singers* and the gate-keepers in accordance with *the command of David and of his son Solomon.*

> For in the days of *David* and *Asaph*, in ancient times, there were *leaders of the singers, songs of praise and hymns of thanksgiving to God* (Neh. 12:45-46, emphasis added).

Reflections

God gave to King David such a revelation of the importance and power of praise upon earth that, following the heavenly pattern, he set aside and dedicated an army of four thousand Levites whose sole occupation was to praise the Lord (I Ch. 23:5). They did nothing else. One of the last official acts of King David before his death was the organization of a formal program of praise. Each morning and each evening a contingent of these four thousand Levites engaged in this service.

—Paul E. Billheimer[18]

It is in the process of being worshipped that God communicates His presence to men.

—C.S. Lewis[19]

When God's people begin to praise and worship Him using the Biblical methods He gives, the Power of His presence comes among His people in an even greater measure.

—Graham Truscott[20]

Whenever His people gather and worship Him, God promises He will make His presence known in their midst. On the other hand, where God's people consistently neglect true spiritual worship, His manifest presence is rarely experienced.

—Ralph Mahoney[21]

The Old Testament writers were extremely proficient at attributing worth to God. They diligently practiced the art of worshipping and I am sure their entire concept of God was vastly expanded as a result. How often the Twentieth-century mind looks at that ancient Judaic heritage with false superiority. 'Their concept of the God-head was not as developed as ours is today,' we self-righteously exclaim. Yet most Christians are barely able to offer rudimentary private prayers of praise, much less to participate in worship on a congregational level.

—David R. Mains[22]

135

Part VI

Nine Psalmic Worship Forms for Today's Church

We should share in David's discovery! Why should the total involvement of biblical Psalmic worship involving voices, hands, and body posture be reduced today to an unemotional, non-expressive worship? Let us restore the nine worship forms of the Psalms.

- Chapter 16 **Speak!**
- Chapter 17 **Sing!**
- Chapter 18 **Shout!**

People of every generation have discovered the wonder and power of lifting their voices in acclamation to the true and living God.

- Chapter 19 **Lift!**
- Chapter 20 **Play Instruments!**
- Chapter 21 **Clap!**

The expressive power of the hands finds greatest fulfillment in the magnification of God.

- Chapter 22 **Stand!**
- Chapter 23 **Bow!**
- Chapter 24 **Dance!**

The body should not be kept on ice while the inner spirit rejoices warmly and appreciates the Lord.

16

Speak!
First use of the voice

*With one voice glorify the God and Father
of our Lord Jesus Christ.*
—Romans 15:6

The human tongue releases spiritual power. Words spoken in faith can declare the purpose of God and affirm man's agreement with it. Spoken words also may praise almighty God. "My mouth shall speak the praise of the Lord" (Ps. 145:21). Thoughts and emotions lay hidden or concealed in the inner man until words express them. Jesus referred to this principle when He said to the Pharisees:

> O generation of vipers, how can ye, being evil, speak good things? For out of the abundance of the heart the mouth speaketh. A good man out of the good treasure of the heart bringeth forth good things: and an evil man out of the evil treasure bringeth forth evil things (Matt. 12:34, 35 KJV).

A sinner receives Christ's salvation not only by believing in his heart but also by speaking words with his mouth.

> The word is nigh thee, even in thy mouth, and in thy heart: that is, the word of faith, which we preach; that if thou shalt confess with thy mouth the Lord Jesus [i.e., Jesus as Lord], and shalt believe in thine heart that God hath raised him from the dead, thou shalt be saved. For with the heart man believeth unto righteousness; and with the mouth confession is made unto salvation (Rom. 10:8-10 KJV).

The spoken testimony of the early church had an explosive impact on first-century society. Jesus' followers faithfully witnessed for Him (Acts 1:8). Their words led some of them straight to martyrdom (Acts 7:59-8:2). The words "Jesus Christ is Lord" will be spoken ultimately by all men either in this life or, under less pleasant circumstances, in the life to come (Phil. 2:11).

Power in expression

God creates things with His words. He speaks and makes something out of nothing. The Word of God brought the world and all it contains into existence:

> By the word of the Lord were the heavens made; and all the host of them by the breath of his mouth (Ps. 33:6 KJV).

Genesis, chapter 1, preserves the story of how God created the world and the surrounding universe. He simply declared His thought in words, and things came to pass.

> And God said, Let there be light (v. 3).
> And God said, Let there be a firmament (v. 6).
> And God said, Let the waters under the heaven be gathered (v. 9).
> And God said, Let the earth bring forth (v. 11).
> And God said, Let there be lights (v. 14).

God did not just wish the universe into being. He *spoke* it into being! Men's and women's words also have life-giving power! A congregation of voices worshiping together releases even greater spiritual strength.

Words convey ideas or thoughts from one person to another. An idea must be expressed or verbalized for it to be fulfilled. In the beginning, God had glorious thoughts He wanted to express. He communicated His thoughts to men, speaking directly to them and indirectly through prophets. God had men preserve His Word, writing it down. Then Jesus came among men as the tangible, literal expression of God's thoughts; hence, He has the name: "The Word." Jesus conveyed God's thoughts to man by His teaching and by His exemplary lifestyle.

> In the beginning was the Word [God's idea or thought], and the Word was with God, and the Word was God. The same was in the beginning with God . . . . And the Word was made flesh [or, expressed], and dwelt among us (John 1:1, 2, 14).

The following five quotations from the book of Proverbs show how the tongue can release inner spiritual power:

* The mouth of a righteous man is a well of life (10:11).
* A man shall be satisfied with good by the fruit of his mouth (12:14).
* The tongue of the wise is health (12:18).
* A wholesome tongue is a tree of life (15:4).
* Death and life are in the power of the tongue: and they that love it shall eat the fruit thereof (18:21).

The Bible abounds with stories of men and women who used their voices in faith to declare the purpose and will of God. Moses' words destroyed the gods of Egypt; Joshua's word made the sun stand still; Jesus' words healed the sick, and so did His followers'.

Verbalize your prayers

Most references to prayer and worship in the Bible describe verbalized prayer and worship. Sometimes people assume—because of personal inclinations—that prayer or worship should be silent or "in the heart." Prayer certainly should involve the heart (feelings), and people can pray silently; however, the great bulk of Bible references indicate that prayer should be verbal!

When teaching His disciples to pray, Jesus said:

When you pray, say . . . (Luke 11:2).

The early church prayed vocally and collectively:

And when they heard this, they lifted their voice to God with one accord, and said . . . (Acts 4:24).

References from the book of Psalms speak of prayer and mention the associated use of the mouth.[1] The same principle applies to using the voice in worship.

- I cried unto the Lord with my voice (3:4).
- My voice shalt thou hear in the morning, O Lord (5:3).
- thou heardest the voice of my supplications when I cried unto thee (31:22).
- Hear my prayer, O God; give ear to the words of my mouth (54:2).
- I cried unto him with my mouth, and he was extolled with my tongue (66:17).

The voice puts power in spiritual exercise. Praying out loud enhances personal prayer time; and audible worship increases dynamism. Christians who worship out loud can revolutionize their own spiritual vitality as well as that of the church!

Develop a worship vocabulary

Most people have difficulty knowing what to say to human dignitaries, let alone to God. People who meet the Queen of England or the President of the United States receive special coaching. They learn what to say and how to say it. By reading the Bible—particularly the Psalms—Christians interact with words inspired by God and uttered by people just like themselves.[2] The Bible gives believers words to say. It directs or coaches them as they develop a worship vocabulary.

The Psalms contain statements actually prescribed for use in worship. More than twenty verses have word combinations worshipers can adopt. Many additional verses teach believers how to pray by example.

Consider this simple, wonderful prayer: "O LORD, open my lips, that my mouth may declare Thy praise" (Psalm 51:15). This prayer appeals to God for aid to properly vocalize praise. The words emphasize *speaking*, but they also ask for God's help to maintain right attitudes. Judson Cornwall, a leading Charismatic worship teacher, states:

Worship, of course, begins as an attitude, but worship is more than a mere attitude; it is an attitude positively expressed to God, and it is the expressing of that attitude that so

141

often gives us difficulty, for it is our deepest thoughts and strongest feelings that defy true expression with our limited vocabulary.[3]

The following list does not include all Psalmic worship expressions, but it will help studious worshipers get started. Believers can *speak* these statements in prayer and worship times. The quotations below come from the New American Standard version:

When Thou didst say, "Seek My face," my heart said to Thee, "Thy face, O LORD, I shall seek" (27:8).

But as for me, I trust in Thee, O LORD, I say, "Thou art my God" (31:14).

All my bones will say, "LORD, who is like Thee, Who delivers the afflicted from him who is too strong for him. And the afflicted and the needy from him who robs him?" (35:10).

And let them say continually, "The LORD be magnified, Who delights in the prosperity of His servant" (35:27).

Let those who love Thy salvation say continually, "The LORD be magnified!" (40:16).

I will say to God my rock, "Why hast Thou forgotten me? Why do I go mourning because of the oppression of the enemy?" (42:9).

Say to God, "How awesome are Thy works!" (66:3).

Let all who seek Thee rejoice and be glad in Thee; and let those who love Thy salvation say continually, "Let God be magnified" (70:4).

"All my springs of joy are in you" (87:7).

He will cry to Me, "Thou art my Father, My God, and the rock of my salvation" (89:26).

And let all the people say, "Amen" (106:48).

Also see: Ps. 91:2; 96:10; 116:4; 118:2, 3, 4; 124:1-5; 140:6-11; and 142:5-7.

The congregational voice of worship

The Bible clearly states that God desires people to use their voices in prayer and worship. "My mouth will speak the praise of the LORD" (Ps. 145:21). The truth applies not only to praise spoken privately, but also to congregational prayer, praise, and worship. The private challenge pales before the awesome idea of *speaking* praise with others in a church service. Suddenly all the praise passages in the Psalms come to life!

I will greatly praise the Lord with my mouth; Yes, I will praise Him among the multitude (Ps. 109:30 NKJV, see also, 35:18; 111:1).

Nothing else compares to the power of a corporate worship experience enfolding the believer. Responding to God in vocal praise with other people is the highest group activity!

Ways people can speak in a worship service include:

- Vocalizing praise
- Reading Scripture
- Saying "Amen!"
- Reciting creeds
- Making short declarations
- Repeating the Lord's Prayer
- Declaring benedictions

Vocalizing praise. Local churches can weave Psalmic expressions tastefully into their worship patterns. Leaders must allow time for assembled believers to express praise words audibly to God in prayer and worship.

Reading Scripture. The voice has been used in public worship for centuries in public readings of Scripture. The apostle Paul directed Timothy to do it. Ralph P. Martin calls Paul's written instruction "the first historical allusion to the use of the Scriptures in the church's liturgy."[4]

Until I come, give attention to the public reading of Scripture, to exhortation and teaching (1 Tim. 4:13).

Paul tells the Thessalonians "to have this letter read to all the brethren" (1 Thess. 5:27), and a statement in Colossians indicates that he fully expected local leaders to circulate and read his epistles in public convocations:

And when this letter is read among you, have it also read in the church of the Laodiceans; and you, for your part read my letter that is coming from Laodicea (Col. 4:16).

Primitive cultures need the Scriptures read publicly because few people own printed Bibles. Western churches benefit from the practice, too, even though most members own Bibles. Believers may carry many different Bible versions to church but still can enjoy lifting their voices together to declare the Word of God if the church provides pew Bibles or prints the text in the bulletin or on overhead transparencies. Attempting to read from different versions simultaneously in public causes confusion.

Saying "Amen!" Speaking with their voices, church members participate in and affirm what happens during a worship service. "And let all the people say, 'Amen.' Praise the LORD!" (Ps. 106:48). To endorse truth with an enthusiastic "Amen!", members of congregations must clearly understand what is being said and done in the assembly. The apostle Paul emphasized the need for clear understanding in 1 Cor. 14:16. Gordon D. Fee, in his highly acclaimed commentary on 1 Corinthians, discusses this verse. He says Amen was "borrowed from the Hebrew, meaning 'that which is sure and valid.'" Corporate worship customarily included "wholehearted response to and endorsement of the words of another."[5] James Dunn comments on the same text:

> The 'Amen' which the congregation utters after a prayer or prophecy is not just a formal liturgical assent; it indicates rather the importance Paul attaches to the community's members being able to understand and to give assent to what is said in its worship.[6]

When the priests read the Law to Israel, all the people responded "Amen!" (Deut. 27:11-26). When a congregation says Amen, they are saying a united "Yes!" to God,[7] agreeing with and praising the acts and ways of God. When Ezra blessed the Lord, all the people endorsed his words enthusiastically by lifting their hands and proclaiming a double Amen (Neh. 8:6).

In some churches, only the enthusiastic members who approve what the preacher has said will shout Amen. Some churches say Amen only as "a unison congregational response at the end of prayer," according to Presbyterian Robert G. Rayburn.[8] Serious thought should be given to the use of Amen and how churches can meaningfully employ it.

Reciting creeds. Early church fathers contributed great creedal statements of faith which became rocks upon which the church anchored its faith. Creeds simplified and codified the basics of Christian belief. Teaching people the creeds successfully challenged, resisted, and overcame the rampant heresies of the day (particularly concerning the deity and humanity of Christ). Creeds made the message of the church clear. As people voiced the creeds, the tenants of the Christian faith were inculcated more deeply into their minds.[9] Boldly reciting a creedal statement of faith encourages believers to stand with each other!

Making short declarations. Short declarations or hortatory exclamations add excitement to the church worship experience. Churches have used the following expressions since the early New Testament times:
- Jesus Is Lord! (1 Cor. 12:3; Rom. 10:9).
- Come Quickly Lord Jesus! or, Maranatha! (1 Cor. 16:22).
- He Is Risen! (Mark 16:6).

Preachers can have their congregations repeat key words or phrases of a sermon in unison. It can focus attention effectively on a truth and reinforce and personalize people's beliefs.

Repeating the Lord's Prayer. Called by many "the most prayed prayer in the world," the Lord's Prayer lends itself dramatically to audible, unified, congregational speech (Matt. 6:9-13; Luke 11:2-4).

Jesus summarized His best understanding of the heavenly Father in this prayer. He taught what the Father is like, capturing vibrant concepts of prayer and sheathing them in simple statements. Jesus responded spontaneously to a disciple's question on how to pray with this concise, dynamic paragraph of three sentences. In a way, Jesus did for prayer what Einstein did for science when he formulated the theory of relativity, $E=MC^2$. The scientific genius of man packed the mighty forces of the natural universe into a simple equation. Into three sentences, with sixty-six words

144

(KJV), Jesus reduced all that men need to know about almighty God and how to make prayers acceptable to Him. G. Campbell Morgan says:

> He gathered together the things with which they were most familiar and placed them in such perfect relation to each other as to reveal as never before the whole plane of prayer. To pray that prayer intelligently is to have nothing else to pray for. It may be broken up, each petition may be taken separately and expressed in other ways, but in itself it is inclusive and exhaustive.[10]

Jesus gave the pattern prayer. It was not so much an academic exercise in semantics as it was an explosion of spiritual reality pouring forth from His lips. Under the inspiration of the Spirit, He shared what had become the strength of His life. Murray states, "it was borne out of the prayer [life] of our Lord Jesus. he had been praying, and therefore was able to give that glorious answer."[11]

People of a church who use the Lord's Prayer as a format for daily prayers will pray according to the will of God, and the united congregational voice repeating those majestic words will have great significance.[12]

Declaring benedictions. Usually, the pastor will dismiss the congregation at the conclusion of the worship service. It would be novel and exciting to have everyone recite in unison the benediction, adapting the wording to mean "us." A number of the closing words of the epistles could be applied in this way. For example:

- The grace of the Lord Jesus be with us all. Amen (Rev. 22:21).
- Now to Him who is able to keep us from stumbling, and to make us stand in the presence of His glory blameless with great joy, to the only God our Savior, through Jesus Christ our Lord, be glory, majesty, dominion and authority, before all time and now and forever. Amen (Jude 24, 25).

Reflections

God is to be praised with the voice, and the heart should go therewith in holy exultation.
—*Charles H. Spurgeon*[13]

It is important to remember that the utterance of the words, together with appropriate actions, was believed to have power. They are not merely pious reflections, but effective words through which Israel's "soul" was conveyed to God, and His energy in judgment and renewal was released into Israel's soul and through that into the world of nature and man.
—*A.S. Herbert*[14]

It is so important that we watch what comes out of our mouths. Our mouths are the way we cast our vote. When we praise the Lord, we are casting our vote for God and against the Devil. This moves us into a tremendous place of spiritual victory.
—*Terry Law*[15]

Unfortunately multitudes of believers have come to regard the word Amen as the minister's way of indicating that he has finished with his prayer. This is not what the word is to indicate at all. It would be best if the minister leading the corporate worship did not use the word when he finished his prayers but let the congregation use it to indicate their hearty agreement with and fellowship in the offering up of the praise and petitions of his prayer.
—*Robert G. Rayburn*[16]

I would warn those who are cultured, quiet, self-possessed, poised and sophisticated, that if they are embarrassed in church when some happy Christian says "Amen!" they may actually be in need of some spiritual enlightenment. The worshiping saints of God in the body of Christ have often been a little bit noisy.
—*A. W. Tozer*[17]

17

Sing!
Second use of the voice

I will sing to the LORD as long as I live;
I will sing praise to my God while I have my being.
—Psalm 104:33

The church has much to sing about. The Lord has done great things for His people. The everlasting joy of God vibrates in their hearts, and they share the song of the Eternal One as He sings through them!

In the beginning, when God said, "Let there be light," the song of God rang throughout creation. Scientists now have discovered a phonetic value for every ray of light, which means the light of the sun and stars speeds through sidereal space as a singing sound. The morning stars sang together in the beginning of creation, according to Job 38:7. God Himself probably sang joyfully as He created things!

Human beings have a remarkable capacity to sing. They have been equipped physically to sing a wider range of notes than most other creatures. They also receive motivation and inspiration through a special relationship with God. After a robin or meadowlark swells his breast with air, the intense little bird emits less than a dozen token tones using all his strength to praise the Almighty. This choice comment, many years old, lingers in my mind:

> "Not only is inanimate nature full of music," says an eminent writer, "but God has wonderfully organized the human voice, so that in the plainest throat and lungs there are fourteen direct muscles which can make over sixteen thousand different sounds. Now, there are thirty indirect muscles which can make, it has been estimated, more than one hundred and seventy-three millions of sounds. Now, I say when God has so constructed the human voice, and when He has filled the whole earth with harmony, and when He recognized it in the ancient temple, I have a right to come to the conclusion that God loves music."[1]

A singing people

The history of God's singing people unfolds throughout the Bible. In Old Testament times, song and worship were inseparably linked to the joy of the Lord. When Pharaoh was finally overthrown at the Red Sea, "then sang Moses and the children of Israel" (Exod. 15:1). Moses cried out, "Sing ye to the Lord, for he hath triumphed gloriously." This set an exuberant example for coming generations in Israel as well as the church. King David's psalms picked up the theme and amplified it in numerous, encouraging hymns calling people to "come before his presence with singing."

Moses wisely preserved the ways and dealings of almighty God in song. The song enabled Israel to maintain its historic consciousness of God by singing the story from generation to generation (Deut. 31:19, 22, 30; 32:44). The magnificent Song of Deborah commemorates the great victory over Sisera in a similar, unforgettable fashion (Judges, chapter 5).

David's Psalter served, in a sense, as the premier theology book of the Hebrew Scriptures; however, it does not present systematized, dry dogma. It presents concepts and short stories clothed in singable melodies. This glorious musical synthesis of all Old Testament teachings makes the Psalter into a singing sword of truth.[2]

The Lord Himself sings the most amazing song of all over His beloved people: "He will joy over thee with singing" (Zeph. 3:17). The same Lord, through the prophets, challenges people to sing praise joyfully to Him (Isa. 12:5; 42:10; Jer. 20:13; Zech. 2:10).

The singing church

One still night over the hills of Judea, a shining angelic chorus introduced the Christian era dramatically with a glorious song: "Glory to God in the highest, and on earth peace, good will toward men" (Luke 2:14). Singing not only introduced Christ's birth but also ushered Him to His death. At the close of Jesus' ministry, just before He left the fellowship of His last Passover meal, He joined His disciples in singing a hymn (Matt. 26:30).

The early church's worship involved vibrant singing. Paul and Silas, badly wounded and lacerated by cruel scourging, sang praises to God at midnight in the Philippian jail (Acts 16:25). The apostle Paul told the Ephesian and Colossian churches that "psalms and hymns and spiritual songs" would encourage and edify the Christians (Eph. 5:19; Col. 3:16).

Contrary to what many Christians think, the church has not always had great congregational singing. Until about 450 years ago, common people in the church did not sing at all. Only priests or specially selected choirs produced music. The entire service—including songs—was in Latin, which common people did not understand.

Then came the Protestant Reformation in Europe. Martin Luther, the renowned leader of this spiritual renewal, was a talented musician and an excellent singer. God used him as an instrument to restore congregational singing to the church. Luther accomplished more by setting all Germany singing than he did by preaching. In 1524, Luther published the first Protestant hymnal in Wittenberg, Germany, with four of the eight hymns written by Luther himself. He continued to write hymns and became known as "the Nightingale of Wittenberg." The Book of Life comments:

Within twenty years after the first hymnal was issued, at least 17 collections of hymns by Luther and his associates had been printed. Protestant Germany became a veritable "sea of song." In this way the great Reformer has come to be known as the father of congregational singing, which under his leadership rapidly grew in popularity.[3]

God continued to raise up inspired hymn writers, and they became like musical cheerleaders to the church. For instance, Isaac Watts lived in England almost two hundred years after Martin Luther. The Reformed church of his day had grown more and more strict, allowing only rhyming versions of the Psalms to be sung. And even these were sung in a most distressing way. A church clerk read aloud one line at a time, and the people would follow by singing that line. Watts desired to correct this uncomfortable approach and began writing hymns which did not just lift lines of Scripture for song lyrics but were sound theologically. Many people responded enthusiastically. All together, he wrote more than six hundred hymns, the most famous being "When I Survey the Wondrous Cross".

Charles Wesley, considered by some to be the greatest of all hymn writers, was converted in 1738. One year later, he wrote the beautiful hymn, "O For a Thousand Tongues to Sing". Then with a pen "tipped with flame," he proceeded to write more than 6,000 hymns. Who can measure the impact of such songs during times of spiritual renewal? Ian Paisley has said, "Revivals in the church are borne in song and lead to singing."[4]

Every converted sinner still exclaims: "He [the Lord] hath put a new song in my mouth" (Psalm 40:3). Singing will continue in heaven as the redeemed sing "a new song before the throne" (Rev. 14:3). Scripture says of the church triumphant in heaven, "they sing the song of Moses, the servant of God, and the song of the Lamb" (Rev. 15:3). The Lord's redeemed will carry on the grand tradition, making a joyful song unto the Lord our God!

God wants His people to sing! Eighty-five places in the Bible exhort the church to sing praise to the Lord. Singing is mentioned more than seventy times in Psalms alone, and in one verse the church is told four times to sing praises:

Sing praises to God, sing praises! Sing praises to our King, sing praises! (Ps. 47:6).

The New Testament says to "sing with the spirit, and . . . with understanding" (1 Cor. 14:15). Christ, in the person of the Holy Spirit, sings in the congregation (Heb. 2:12; Ps. 22:22). James tells cheerful saints to sing psalms (James 5:13). Paul exhorts the church at Rome to sing to His name (Rom. 15:9; Ps. 18:49).

Mortals join the mighty chorus which the morning stars began; Father love is reigning o'er us, brother love binds man to man. Ever singing, march we onward, Victors in the midst of strife; Joyful music lifts us sunward in the triumph song of life.[5]

Of all the scriptural modes of worship, singing is mentioned and practiced most. Singing also is the most acceptable form of Psalmic worship to most people. More than fifty times the book of Psalms urges the church to sing unto God.[6] Here are five samples:

- Sing for the honour of his name: make his praise glorious (66:2).
- Sing unto God, sing praises to his name (68:4).
- O come, let us sing unto the Lord (95:1).
- Sing unto him, sing psalms unto him (105:2).
- Sing unto the Lord a new song (149:1).

Examples of Bible songs

In the Psalter the praises of God's people resound more clearly than elsewhere, yet the songs of Israel certainly were not confined to the book of Psalms. Songs appear in practically every book of the Bible, and certainly throughout the Old Testament. Many of the materials of the Old Testament, such as the story of creation in Genesis 1:1-2:4a, were shaped by liturgical use. With today's abundance of Bible versions and printed information, it is hard to imagine the difficulty ancient Israel faced in its attempts to remember and communicate God's Word. To help people recall their divine heritage, Israel put the Word to music, and the people sang and chanted its message from one generation to another. Eleven Old Testament psalms not in the Psalter and two from the New Testament are listed below. Most commentators would agree these passages were set to music:

- Song of the Sea (Exod. 15:1-18, 21): to exalt the Lord for victory at the Red Sea.
- Song of Moses (Deut. 31:30-32:44): to remind them of their faithful God.
- Song of Deborah (Judg. 5:1-31): to celebrate victory over Sisera.
- Song of Hannah (1 Sam. 2:1-10): to give thanks for God's mercy.
- Song of David (2 Sam. 22:2-51): to give thanks for God preserving him.
- Song of Judah (Isa. 12:4-6): to give thanks to the Lord.
- Song of Hezekiah (Isa. 38:9-20): to memorialize his healing.
- Song of Jeremiah (Jer. 15:15-18; 17:14-18; 18:19-23; Lam. 3, 5): to sing lament.
- Song of Jonah (Jonah 2:1-9): to thank God for saving him.
- Song of Habakkuk (Hab. 3:2-19): to praise God for ultimate victory.
- Song of Mary (Luke 1:46-55): The "Magnificat."
- Song of Zacharias (Luke 1:67-79): The "Benedictus."

The experience of song

Songs and music powerfully impact people. Religious song moves people to experience God and spiritual devotion. The following statements by an English playwright, a theologian, a prisoner, and a preacher illustrate the effect:

George Bernard Shaw sat on the platform with various dignitaries and famous people; an American clergyman, Joseph Fort Newton, sat beside him. They were attending a great Jubilee Service in London's Royal Albert Hall at the conclusion of World War I. During the service, the audience rose and sang Isaac Watt's hymn, "O God, Our Help in Ages Past." After they finished, Shaw, moved by the chorus of thousands, leaned over to Newton and said, "I'd rather have written that hymn than all my silly plays." For a moment George Bernard Shaw got a glimpse of a [shining, spiritual] mountain. His commitment to rationalism would not allow him to climb it, perhaps, but he knew it was there.[7]

Sing! Second use of the voice

Jonathan Edwards (1703-1758), a theologian, philosopher, psychologist, scientist, metaphysician, college president and powerful Calvinistic preacher, was the principal figure in the Great Awakening. Basically, he was a mystic who yearned for an intensely intimate communion with God, as this excerpt from his personal narrative reveals:

> Before, I used to be uncommonly terrified with thunder, and to be struck with terror when I saw a thunder-storm rising; but now, on the contrary, it rejoiced me. I felt God, if I may so speak, at the first appearance of a thunder storm; and used to take the opportunity, at such times, to fix myself in order to view the clouds, and see the lightnings play, and hear the majestic and awful voice of God's thunder, which oftentimes was exceedingly entertaining, leading me to sweet contemplations of my great and glorious God. While thus engaged, it always seemed natural for me to sing, or chant forth my meditations; or, to speak my thoughts in soliloquies with a singing voice.[8]

Howard Rutledge spent almost seven years in a prison in North Vietnam—five of them in solitary confinement. On Sundays, before he was imprisoned, he had worked or played hard and had no time for church. For years his wife Phyllis had encouraged him to join the family at church, but he was too busy, too preoccupied to spend one or two short hours a week thinking about the really important things.

In prison he changed. "When one is dying from starvation," he said, "a bowl of sewer greens is a gift from God. Before every meal during my captivity, I offered a prayer of thanks . . . . But in prison, grace was not a routine endured out of habit, guilt, or pressure. To thank God for life seemed the natural thing to do."[9]

He had no pastor, no Sunday-school teacher, no Bible, no hymn book, and no community of believers to guide and sustain him. He and other prisoners tried desperately to remember portions of Scripture and the hymns they sang in church. Scripture and hymns made it possible for Rutledge to conquer the enemy and overcome the power of death that surrounded him. His story follows:

> I tried desperately to recall snatches of Scripture, sermons, the gospel choruses from childhood, and the hymns we sang in church. The first three dozen songs were relatively easy. Every day I'd try to recall another verse or a new song. One night there was a huge thunderstorm—it was the season of the monsoon rains—and a bolt of lightning knocked out the lights and plunged the entire prison into darkness. I had been going over hymn tunes in my mind and stopped to lie down and sleep when the rains began to fall. The darkened prison echoed with wave after wave of water. Suddenly, I was humming my thirty-seventh song, one I had entirely forgotten since childhood

Showers of blessings,
Showers of blessing we need!
Mercy drops round us are falling,
But for the showers we plead.

I no sooner had recalled those words than another song popped into my mind, the theme song of a radio program my mother listened to when I was a kid.

> Heavenly sunshine, heavenly sunshine
> Flooding my soul with glory divine.
> Heavenly sunshine, heavenly sunshine.
> Hallelujah! Jesus is mine!

Charles R. Swindoll, one of the most famous preachers in America, believes in singing, and says so emphatically:

> I love to sing! Of greater importance, I love to sing with others. I can think of no more glorious sound than a body of people who love their Lord, singing and making melody in their hearts. Whether the voices are blending together in harmonious a cappella or accompanied by a grand pipe organ or even a full orchestra, there is no sound on earth more heavenly than the sound of singing saints. As my minister of music has often said, 'If you don't love to sing, then why in the world would you ever want to go to heaven.'[10]

Psalms and hymns and spiritual songs

A worshiping church requires music and song. Some church leaders have even suggested that liturgy stands on a foundation of singing, and without it the vital force is gone.[11] Christianity would not be the same without the "psalms and hymns and spiritual songs" that make up the warp and woof of its spirituality.

The historical stream. A wide variety of musical expressions have poured into the powerful stream of music running through church history. The list includes: Gregorian chants, Huguenot psalms, Lutheran chorales, Scottish Covenantor psalms, Negro spirituals, Anglo-Saxon revivalist hymns. The list extends right to the present day Christian rock and charismatic choruses. Jim Bock, general editor for *Hymns for the Family of God*, makes the following observation:

> For two thousand years, Christians have been a singing people. From early chants to sung Scriptures; from versified Psalms to original words and music written in our own time, our musical heritage is as varied as it is long. Different musical styles have spoken the eternal truths of God's Word.

Then he adds this insight:

> The great advantage we have over our forefathers is being able to enjoy the richness of the past together with the creativity of the present.[12]

The Holy Spirit instigates this creativity just as He has in past centuries and in other cultures. The Spirit endeavors to keep the worship of God's people fresh and relevant as they maintain the historic faith and meet emotional needs in emerging generations. Wayne Lukens draws this historical perspective: "The reformers were quick to graft the pop-music idioms of their day into their religious music. Luther recognized that the German people not only needed the Bible in their own language but also craved religious music in their own language."[13] The following paragraph from the Preface of *The Mennonite Hymnal* explains this inherent flexibility and adaptability, this living-rather-than-static nature of Christian song:

> Moreover, this stream of music is as something alive, discarding the unusable, adaptive to new circumstances, creative in meeting needs as they may exist. Church music has not been contained in rigid, unyielding forms or patterns, but in different ways has supplied musical expression for the church in its developing life and worship. Hymnology, too, as a significant part of the musical heritage of the church, has not been locked in the closed canon of an ancient and unchanging tradition, but has been alive and growing, dynamically ministering to a living and growing Christendom.[14]

Donald P. Hustad writes: "Throughout the history of the Christian church each period of spiritual renewal has been accompanied by an outburst of new Christian song." He then adds this insight, "If we keep this fact in mind, a look at the contemporary scene is encouraging."[15] The historical development of song and music holds great interest, but that information has been thoroughly covered by other sources.[16]

The three musical terms. The New Testament lists three types of songs to be sung in churches: "psalms (*psalmoi*), hymns (*humnoi*), and spiritual songs (*hodais pneumatikais*)." Two different New Testament books use the same three terms in identical expressions. Listed below are the two references followed by two closely associated verses:

- Speaking to one another in *psalms and hymns and spiritual songs, singing* and making melody with your heart to the Lord (Eph. 5:19, emphasis added).
- Let the word of Christ richly dwell within you, with all wisdom teaching and admonishing one another with *psalms and hymns and spiritual songs, singing* with thankfulness in your hearts to God (Col. 3:16, emphasis added).
- I shall *sing* with the *spirit* and I shall *sing* with the mind also (1 Cor. 14:15, emphasis added).
- What is the outcome then, brethren? When you assemble, each one has a *psalm*, has a teaching, has a revelation, has a tongue, has an interpretation. Let all things be done for edification (1 Cor. 14:26, emphasis added).

Bible scholars agree that these three words merit more than passive interest, but disagree on the meaning of the terms. On the one hand some feel that it is "doubtful whether firm distinctives . . . can be drawn."[17] For instance, Gerhard Delling believes that "such identifications must remain hypothetical,"[18] and Ronald Allen thinks "These verses are probably not referring to specific kinds of songs . . . but the idea of balance seems indicated."[19]

I believe that this triad of musical terms does identify and differentiate the musical forms used in the New Testament churches. "It is extremely significant," says Jack Hayford, "that two epistles issue explicit directives to sing 'psalms, hymns and

153

spiritual songs.'"[20] Robert Rayburn also agrees that it is significant that three types of song are mentioned rather than one alone.[21] Don P. Hustad's states:

> And what were "psalms and hymns and spiritual songs"? It is little short of amazing that the Apostle delineates three different *genre* of music for worship, mentioning them in two different letters to young churches. We must believe that they were contrasting—in origin, in subject matter, and possibly even in performance. This is substantiated by Egon Wellesz, one of the leading authorities on the music of this period.[22]

Some commentators think that Paul was "emphasizing the rich variety in Christian song"[23] or describing "the full range of singing which the Spirit prompts."[24] These thoughts are good, but the appearance of identical terms in two New Testament books compels me to conclude that the three words represent three forms which can be defined distinctly yet are strongly interrelated and can overlap at times with good results. David Blomgren comments that they are not "options,"[25] and the church must agree. A balanced, biblical worship program ought to have a pleasing blend of all three.

Psalms. Mentioned first, this term refers to Scripture set to music. When believers sing Psalms, they sing the inspired words of God! These songs are directed to God and glorify Him and His Word by declaring His greatness. The importance of Psalmic forms is underscored by Psalms being mentioned first. Generally speaking, Psalms refer to the Hebrew Psalter but conceivably can include all songs of Scripture and "songs in the character, spirit, or manner of Old Testament Psalms."[26] Hustad proposes that Psalms "no doubt included all the psalms and canticles that were common to Jewish worship, in the tabernacle, the temple, and the synagogue."[27] Of the ten times that the Greek noun *psalmos* appears in the New Testament text, five times it refers to Old Testament Psalms and the balance to the New Testament Pauline application.[28] The verb form occurs four times in the New Testament.[29]

Hymns. Whereas Psalms use divinely inspired words from Scripture, hymns are composed by people. Authors write hymns to make statements of faith and theology set in contemporary patterns of music. Hymns can be sung to or about God, and they can be light or heavy, but they must subscribe to and express a sound, orthodox, biblical theology. For example, they must affirm the faith of Jesus Christ (Jude 3) and testify of Him. A broad category, hymns allow saints to make expanded, more descriptive statements of their theology than is possible in Scripture portions alone.

Though they are songs of praise which glorify God and His ways, they are also directed towards man and bear a strong horizontal thrust. "This is in basic contrast to psalms which intend God as the primary and exclusive recipient of songs of praise."[30] Jack Hayford feels that "hymns are songs of testimony, triumph, exaltation, adoration and celebration . . . the subject is God—His grace, His works, His purpose, His people, His power, His glory or His person."[31] Such hymns may be written to promote human responsiveness to God.[32]

Spiritual songs. No one laboriously composes and massages these songs into acceptable form. The Holy Spirit inspires these songs spontaneously. They are conceived while the Spirit moves upon the singer, who is in an ecstatic state. Flowing

154

extemporaneously from the hearts of people who are experiencing God, spiritual songs rise over the congregation and form an invisible cloud of His presence.

I like to translate *Hodais pneumatikais* as Pneumatic odes with a capital P.[33] Until the Holy Spirit was sent by Jesus to fill His church, prophetic happenings in congregational meetings did not involve more than just a chosen few. Now, pneumatic Christians—people of the Spirit, prophetic people—fill New Testament churches.[34] The presence of the Holy Spirit in and among His people creates a "magnetic field of the Holy Spirit" in local congregational meetings.

The word *spiritual* does not mean a song is necessarily light and joyful. Some commentators question whether spiritual applies only to *songs,* saying that the word characterizes all three, very general types of songs. Other commentators contend that spiritual is synonymous with sacred, giving songs a general, higher classification than ordinary songs.[35] Instead, Jack Hayford calls this category "a distinct music form unique to the church."[36] The code that unlocks the mystery appears in other New Testament passages where the use of *pneuma* cognates clearly imply the activity of the Holy Spirit. Both chapters 12 and 14 of the book of 1 Corinthians open with a form of the word *pneumatikos* to introduce discussions of Holy Spirit-enabled manifestations. Also, the expression "sing with the Spirit" is contrasted with "sing with the understanding" (14:15). The evidence points to this being a Spirit-inspired, Spirit-enabled song. God considerately added this special way for each Christian to express his or her own very personal worship to God.

We may sing Psalms composed by God, hymns composed by others, and our own personal new songs. Spirit enablement produces a wonderful, intimate freedom in all three types of New Testament song.[37]

Summary

Ideal Psalmic worship will pleasingly balance three types of singing:

• **Psalms**	The Written Bible	The **Word** of God in Scripture portions
• **Hymns**	Sound Theological Tradition	The **Ways** of God through human composition
• **Spiritual songs**	An Immediate Presence	The **Awareness** of God by inspired expressions

155

Reflections

O for a thousand tongues to sing, My Great Redeemer's praise, The glories of my God and King, The triumphs of His grace.

—Charles Wesley, 1739

Ultimately, worship will be our ETERNAL PURPOSE in heaven, and singing will be a great part of his eternal purpose.

—Dick Eastman[38]

The church has always sung . . . whether on the high mountain of victory and celebration or through the valley of persecution and despair . . . still the church has sung with great fervor.

—Ralph Carmichael[39]

It is regretted that the niceties of modern singing frighten our congregation from joining lustily in the hymns. For our part we delight in full bursts of praise, and had rather discover the ruggedness of a want of musical training than miss the heartiness of universal congregational song. The gentility which lisps the tune in wellbred whispers, or leaves the singing altogether to the choir, is very like a mockery of worship. The gods of Greece and Rome may be worshipped well enough with classical music, but Jehovah can only be adored with the heart and that music is the best for his service which gives the heart most play.

—Charles H. Spurgeon[40]

Sing lustily, and with a good courage. Beware of singing as if you were half dead, or half asleep; but lift up your voice with strength. Be no more afraid of your voice now, nor more ashamed of its being heard, than when you sung the songs of Satan . . . . Above all, sing spiritually. Have an eye to God in every word you sing. Aim at pleasing Him more than yourself, or any other creature. In order to this, attend strictly to the sense of what you sing; and see that your heart is not carried away with the sound, but offered to God continually; so shall your singing be such as the Lord will approve of here, and reward when he cometh in the clouds of heaven.

—John Wesley[41]

A spiritual song is a spontaneous song prompted by the Holy Spirit. It should be part of every Christian's daily worship and walk with God. This is one of the ways in which we build ourselves up in the Holy Spirit . . . . Having learned this great secret of spiritual song, we should carry it into the congregation when we are all assembled together.

—James L. Beall[42]

18

Shout!
Third use of the voice

The people shouted with a loud shout,
and the sound was heard far away.
—Ezra 3:13

Shouts fill the air whenever people worship the Lord God Almighty in Psalmic style. Done appropriately, a shout pleases God and excites knowledgeable worshipers. Shouting fully releases a person's voice. In each of the three categories of Psalmic worship, one mode is more strenuous, dramatic, or demonstrative, making it more controversial, needing explanation.

- The full release of voice   —   **Shout!**
- The full release of hands   —   **Clap!**
- The full release of posture   —   **Dance!**

The more sophisticated students of worship use the word *acclamation* instead of shouting, but the meaning remains "to call or cry out loudly and vigorously."[1] The Bible and church history abound with stories of people who released their enthusiasm for God with impressive vocal outbursts. For instance, in St. Jerome's day (the post-apostolic church), the sound of the Amen often "seemed like a crack of thunder."[2] Sounds best described as roaring or peals of thunder punctuate four heavenly worship scenes in the book of Revelation!

On the early American frontier, campmeeting time was as robust as the people who came. They all liked to sing, and one favorite song celebrated Satan's defeat. Imagine those boisterous days when saints sang enthusiastically, ending eighteen stanzas with the rousing refrain:

Shout, shout, we're gaining ground,
Hallelujah!
We'll shout old Satan's kingdom down,
Hallelujah![3]

157

Shouting in the Old Testament

The following examples show several Old Testament characters shouted to or for God. God's people, on occasion, were bold in demonstrating their feelings for Him in full-throated, roaring approbation or joy.

Rejoicing in God. Balaam declared God's blessings on Israel, stating that "The LORD his God is with him, and the shout (jubilation) of a king is among them" (Num. 23:21). Keil and Delitzsch make this comment: "The 'shout of a king' in Israel is the rejoicing of Israel at the fact that Jehovah dwells and rules as King in the midst of it (cf. Exod. 15:18; Deut. 33:5)."[4]

This opening reference holds the key to the entire subject. When Israel was faithful to the divine call and continued in covenant fellowship with the Lord, the people stood strong against the world's influence. And when the nation's confidence in God was strong, joyful shouting and jubilation characterized its worship!

Destroying Jericho's walls. The city of Jericho stood like an angry sentinel guarding the gateway into the Promised Land. In a theophany, God appeared to the awestruck Joshua with an astounding battle plan to take the stubborn city! Obeying the plan, Israel marched silently around the outer perimeter of the walls once each day, and then seven times on the seventh day. During the last march around the city, the people shouted. The plan worked. The walls fell flat as the people shouted (Josh. 6:5, 20).

Bringing back the ark. King David brought back the ark of God to Jerusalem at last. He installed it temporarily in a special tent. It would wait there until the temple was built to receive it. Priestly singers and musicians had surrounded the ark in the magnificent procession. The King danced for joy and all the people shouted (1 Chron. 15:28).

Routing the enemy. When Jeroboam's massive Israelite army drew up in battle formation against King Abijah's Judean force of half the size, the frightening outcome was a foregone conclusion. However, Abijah feared the Lord, and he expressed his faith in a bold move. Standing before the enemy and his own troops, he loudly announced Judah's belief in God's covenant with David and warned his erring brothers not to fight against God Himself in this situation (2 Chron. 13:5).

Suddenly, Israel attacked from the rear in an unexpected ambush. Then, Judah "cried to the LORD, and the priests blew the trumpets" (v. 14). Their prayerful cry stirred up such an excited confidence in God among them that they raised a mighty shout ("war cry") and at that moment that the Lord routed Israel (v. 15). Their shout was not one of fear, but acclamation. Verse 18 says they conquered "because they trusted in the LORD." When they shouted, they routed.

Making an oath. Challenged by the prophet Azariah, King Asa led Judah in repentance and reform. The people "made an oath to the LORD with a loud voice, with shouting, with trumpets and with horns" (2 Chron. 15:14, 15).

Laying temple foundations. The people "shouted with a great shout" when the foundation of the temple was laid. Verse 11 says the shout occurred "when they praised the LORD" (Ezra 3:11-13).

Bringing forth the top stone. Zerubbabel, the discouraged political leader of the Jews, saw his task of rebuilding the temple of God like a great mountain. The prophet challenged him saying this would be accomplished by the Spirit of God, and that he

158

would actually bring forth the top stone that would climax the whole project, shouting "Grace, grace to it!" (Zech. 4:7).

Shouting in Psalms

The King James Version contains eight references to *shout* in the Psalms. It lists an additional eight references, similar in meaning, under *joyful noise,* or a loud noise. Other versions of the Bible boost the total to forty-one verses that advocate shouting. Five or more Bible versions use the word shout in the following nine Psalms. The initial reference is given from the King James Version:

- 32:11   Be glad in the LORD, and rejoice, ye righteous: and shout for joy, all ye that are upright in heart.
- 35:27   Let them shout for joy, and be glad, that favour my righteous cause. ("Let them shout with delight, 'Great is the Lord,'" LB.)
- 47:1   O clap your hands, all ye people; shout unto God with the voice of triumph. ("Shout to God with loud songs of joy," RSV.)
- 71:23   My lips shall greatly rejoice when I sing unto thee. ("My lips will shout for joy when I sing praises to Thee," NAS, RSV.)
- 81:1   Sing aloud unto God our strength: make a joyful noise unto the God of Jacob. ("Shout for joy to the God of Jacob!" RSV; "Shout joyfully," NAS.)
- 95:1   O come, let us sing unto the LORD: let us make a joyful noise to the rock of our salvation. ("let us cheer in honor of the Rock," ML; "shout in triumph," RHM; "shout joyfully," NAS.)
- 95:2   Let us come before His presence with thanksgiving, and make a joyful noise unto Him with psalms. ("shout aloud to him," RHM; "shout joyfully to Him with psalms," NAS.)
- 132:9   Let thy priests be clothed with righteousness; and let thy saints shout for joy. ("may your people shout for joy," TEV.)
- 132:16   I will also clothe her priests with salvation: and her saints shall shout aloud for joy. ("shout for joy," RSV.)

Why shout?

The church certainly does not shout because God is hard of hearing. Judson Cornwall states: "It is not that God desires the volume or puts a premium on noise, but that man needs the release of his pent-up joyful emotions that shouting can bring him."[5] Worshipers can feel emotions for God so strongly that they can and should express their feelings audibly in shouting. Emotional excitement in worship should not seem strange. Old Testament characters mentioned above and King David's Psalms make pretty good company for today's worshipers who shout.

Society subtly encourages people to enjoy and express their emotions in all types of secular situations but not in religious worship. The Bible challenges that assumption, teaching that God's people can be as excited about Him as any crowd cheering a team at a football game. At a game, people who shout understand the rules, love the game, and support a team they wish to cheer on. The Bible says Christians

159

can have the same emotional excitement rise within them as they realize the power, majesty, and victory of their God and they can express these emotions in shouts of praise that honestly convey their inner feelings.

C. Peter Wagner's comments about Pentecostals in Latin America cast light on this subject:

> Even in times of prayer, the noise level is high. Simultaneous prayer is common practice. When it comes time for talking to God, everybody in the room talks to Him, and the noise rises to a loud roar. The exuberant worshipers do not feel particularly inhibited about their own voice levels either, and some actually shout while they are praying.
>
> Is this unspiritual? Hardly. Hundreds of people addressing God together must be some sort of a highly spiritual exercise. Does it aid worship? Yes. It has many beneficial effects on the type of people who are doing it. *It produces a sense of high drama, it nourishes the emotions, and it makes the presence of God more real to them.* Anthropologist Eugene Nida has observed that this even helps people to pray, since it brings prayer from the semi-professional level found in many churches to the level of the common person (emphasis added).[6]

In the highest sense, acclamations or shouts to God pay homage to Him as King. But it is more than a passive acknowledgement or a perfunctory vocalization of a religious belief. Worshipers utter powerful statements in the presence of the Lord. Their statements affirm the present dominion of the Lord and legally bind the congregation to the rule of God. As Peter Brunner puts it, "the throne-power of the triune God manifests itself in these acclamations in the church's worship."[7] God releases His presence among worshipers as their emotions focus on Him and His kingdom.

The book of Revelation roars with creation's response to the revelation of God Almighty. Certainly the church should expect worshipers to make periodic, loud statements that express assurance in Christ's victory over Satan. The church should shout its applause to the living Lord. The church must express its belief in God and do it powerfully! In Psalmic, Spirit-inspired worship, believers should expect their emotions to blend with those in heaven, creating a cosmic acclamation of the King of Kings and Lord of Lords. Latin American Pentecostals may leap to their feet several times during a service, throwing their arms upward to God, shouting with great feeling, "Gloria a Dios!" Witnessing such services is exhilarating to me.

Old Testament scholar A.S. Herbert wrote:

> Israel's worship was distinctly vocal in character; it is to shout exultantly. It was normally accompanied with such instruments as produced a vigorous and loud noise. But the shout or cry of praise reinforced by loud instrumental noise is not an end in itself, nor is it merely expressive of strong religious emotion. The purpose of the praise cry (tehillah) or the ringing cry (rinnah) is to convey the life-soul of the worshiper to God.[8]

160

I repeat Herbert's last line: "The purpose of the praise cry . . . is to convey the life-soul of the worshiper to God." With a shout, a worshiper identifies his life with the life of God. He is like a man who watches prizefighters on television and gets emotionally involved in the activity. He may be a "couch potato" miles from the actual fight, yet he identifies so closely with one fighter that he twists in his seat, throws punches, groans and shouts with excitement! Likewise, it is reasonable to believe that praise and worship of the church can identify with God so intimately that believers' emotional expressions and feelings can literally "convey" them into God's felt presence.

At a conference I attended, a leader told the 1,200 assembled ministers that he wanted everyone to shout victoriously unto God with all their might after he said the name Jesus. Then he proceeded to make strong, affirmative statements about God, His victory, and His power. After about five sentences, he said the wonderful name of Jesus, and voices shouted with a volume and intensity equal to cheers heard in any athletic stadium. Wow! It was one of the most powerful shouts I ever heard. We "conveyed" ourselves to God!

The triumphal entry
All four Gospels record Jesus' Triumphal Entry into Jerusalem. Riding on the colt of an ass, He approached the city. The throngs again and again broke into shouts of praise: "HOSANNA to the Son of David! BLESSED IS HE WHO COMES IN THE NAME OF THE LORD; HOSANNA in the highest!" (Matt. 21:9). Much of their excitement probably had roots in national aspirations to free themselves from Roman oppression. Some in the crowd shouted because of miracles they knew He had done. Nevertheless, the enthusiasm and excitement for Jesus warmed the heart of God.

Some Pharisees observed this fanatical behavior and said to Him, "Teacher, rebuke your disciples!" (Luke 19:39). Jesus' response: "I tell you, if these become silent, the stones will cry out!" (Luke 19:40).

When Jesus entered the temple, children began shouting, "Hosanna to the Son of David!" (Matt. 21:15). The chief priests and scribes were incensed and demanded their silence. Jesus quoted Psalm 8:2 in response, implying that Psalmic-style praise was perfectly appropriate for the occasion.

Shouting in heaven
Spectacular prophetic visions in the book of Revelation show powerful worship offered ceaselessly before God's throne. Significantly, worshipers shout in four of the seven scenes covered previously in chapter 13. Intense worship precedes and propels the prophetic drama. Functioning prophecy depends on an active worship environment. Local church worship leaders should pay attention to this connection. This could be the most valuable truth for the church today from the book of Revelation. The four scenes from Revelation with shouting are as follows:

Angels declare. In scene number two, a "loud voice" of multiplied angels (more than 100 million) declare: "Worthy is the Lamb that was slain to receive power and riches and wisdom and might and honor and glory and blessing!" Then, all creatures everywhere join the angelic throng "exclaiming" (LB) or "crying out" (AMP): "To Him who sits on the throne, and the Lamb, be blessing and honor and glory and dominion forever and ever" (Rev. 5:12-13).

Vast crowd from all nations. The third scene of Revelation pictures "a vast crowd, too great to count, from all the nations and provinces and languages, standing in front of the throne and before the Lamb" (7:9 LB). Worshipers were "crying out with a loud voice" (7:10 RSV) or "shouting with a mighty shout" (LB): "Salvation to our God who sits on the throne, and to the Lamb" (NAS). These worshipers are the persecuted saints who come out of great tribulation. Resplendent in shining white robes cleansed by the blood of the Lamb, they unashamedly lift their voices in unrestrained, clamorous praise of their God! There is no shout more triumphant than the martyrs' shout of victory!

Roaring waterfall. In scene five, John hears "a sound from heaven like the roaring of a great waterfall or the rolling of mighty thunder" (Rev. 14:2 LB). One hundred forty-four thousand followers of the Lamb of God, inscribed with the name of God, sing joyously. The mighty voice John hears sounds like thunder accompanied by harps. It is the highest fulfillment of passages such as:

> I will also praise Thee with a harp,
> Even Thy truth, O my God;
> To Thee I will sing praises with the lyre,
> O Thou Holy One of Israel.
> My lips will shout for joy when I sing praises to Thee;
> And my soul, which Thou has redeemed (Ps. 71:22).

> Sing for joy to God our strength;
> Shout joyfully to the God of Jacob.
> Raise a song, strike the timbrel
> The sweet sounding lyre with the harp (Ps. 81:1, 2).

Voice from the throne. In scene seven, the mighty "four-fold Hallelujah" bursts forth (Rev. 19:1, 3, 4, 6). Although "hallelujah" appears nowhere else in the New Testament, the word's appearance here more than makes up for its absence elsewhere! First, a mighty multitude shouts, then shouts again, followed by the twenty-four elders and the living creatures who lift their voices. Then a voice calls the multitude to worship. The voice rings out from the throne itself: "Give praise to our God, all you His bond-servants, you who fear Him, the small and the great" (v. 5). The great multitude receives the divine charge with enthusiasm, and a thunderous response of unrestrained praise roars forth! The Amplified words the fourth hallelujah as follows:

> After that I heard what sounded like the shout of a vast throng, like the boom of many pounding waves and like the roar of terrific and mighty thunderpeals, exclaiming, Hallelujah—Praise the Lord! For now the Lord our God the Omnipotent—the All-Ruler—reigns! Let us rejoice—and shout for joy—exulting and triumphant! Let us celebrate and ascribe to Him glory and honor.

Why should all the shouting be saved for the future? Why not shout now? Preaching this message to my church, I had the people shout various statements from the Psalms with me several times. Then I had them stand and shout three times with ever-increasing volume: "Hallelujah! For the Lord our God, the Almighty, reigns!" With these Scriptures in their minds, the people "thundered" the words. It was glorious!

Reflections

Well over 300 times God's Word instructs His people to praise Him! Indeed, (if frequency has any relationship whatsoever to importance) praise, joyfulness, thanksgiving, song, rejoicing—even shouting—must be an attitude of life God considers highly significant, and in which His Church, both in our corporate worship and in our personal daily lives, is often deficient.

—John W. Peterson and Norman Johnson[9]

The Lord does not delight in our solemnity.

—Marilee Zdenek and Marge Champion[10]

It is to be feared that the church of the present day, through a craving for excessive propriety, is growing too artificial; so that enquirers' cries and believers' shouts would be silenced if they were heard in our assemblies. This may be better than boisterous fanaticism, but there is as much danger in the one direction as the other. For our part, we are touched to the heart by a little sacred excess, and when godly men in their joy o'erleap the narrow bounds of decorum. We do not, like michael, Saul's daughter, eye them with a sneering heart.

—Charles H. Spurgeon[11]

This may be hard for some to admit, but when we are truly worshiping and adoring the God of all grace and of all love and of all mercy and of all truth, we may not be quiet enough to please everyone.

—A.W. Tozer[12]

The Bible seems to emphasize volume when it mentions music and praise. There are very few scriptures, among the 850 I have discovered that refer to music, that suggest we play or sing quietly. But there are some that COMMAND us to play or sing loudly. "Sing unto him a new song; play skillfully with a loud (powerful, great, intensified) NOISE (clamor, acclamation of joy, battle cry, clangor of trumpets, alarm, joy, jubilee, shouting, joyful sounding signal, sound of tempest, crying out)" Ps. 33:3 (Emphasis is mine).

—LaMarr Boschman[13]

It happened in Zion of old, and it happens in spiritual Zion today. When the Majesty and Greatness of the Presence of God is in the midst of His people, His people cry out their praises and worship to Him.

—Graham Truscott[14]

164

19

Lift!
First use of the hands

Let us lift up our heart with our hands unto God in the heavens.
—Lamentations 3:41 KJV

Crude art forms in the catacombs of Rome have long been a source of wonder and intrigue. The subterranean cemeteries were the cradles of Christian art. They provided the only opportunities for artistic expression of the early church's faith in Christ and hope of eternal life. In that era of persecution, Christian artistry or slogans could be displayed only in the underground chambers of the dead—nowhere else.

Exaggerations and misconceptions grew around historical accounts of the catacombs. Actually, Christians did not live there during times of persecution and did not commonly resort there for worship. The foul-smelling air of the tombs would have made living there impossible for anyone. Some teachers have suggested that Christian activity taking place underground escaped the attention of the Roman government. On the contrary, Walter Lowrie in his book, *Art in the Early Church*, points out, "Roman Law, which permitted the slaughter of Christian martyrs, protected their tombs."[1] Lowrie supplies this interesting information:

> We know now that the total length of the subterranean galleries is something like five hundred and fifty miles, and that they were made expressly for Christian burial. Not for Christian assemblies certainly, for the galleries were barely a yard wide, and the chambers to which they led were not often large enough to contain fifty people.[2]

Early artists depicted the Christian message of hope of eternal life and resurrection of the dead. Powerful expressions of faith contrasted sharply with the pessimism and gloom surrounding heathen death. Early Christians did not want to be buried with non-Christians; hence, the catacombs became the decorated burial place of Roman Christians who knew that life would ultimately conquer death.

The reappearance of two art forms

The two most popular art figures to resurface from the catacombs are the sign of the fish and uplifted hands and arms. The latter figure (known as the orant[e] or orans) has reappeared in Western society as a symbol of worship—both in printed material and as standard practice wherever enthusiastic Christians gather for worship. Early Christians drew large numbers of human figures with upraised arms and hands. Why? Theodor Filthaut offers the commonly accepted reason:

> Ancient Christian art knew the picture of the orante as an image of the church at prayer . . . . The orante posture is a prayer-attitude that was well known everywhere in antiquity, and that is explicitly mentioned in the Scriptures.[3]

Walter Lowrie adds this thought:

> The orant in the catacombs is evidently praying for HIMSELF, supplicating God for deliverance or giving thanks to him for it. In any case the attitude of the orant expresses faith, for prayer is an expression of faith.[4]

The art in the catacombs assure Christians today that lifting hands to God was part of the worship experience of the first-century church.

Lifting hands in the New Testament

The New Testament holds four references on uplifted hands; two are exhortations and two are descriptions. The disciples saw Jesus for the last time as He ascended with His hands lifted to the Father.

> And he led them out as far as to Bethany, and he lifted up his hands, and blessed them, And it came to pass, while he blessed them, he was parted from them, and carried up into heaven (Luke 24:50, 51 KJV).

Paul admonished Timothy to lead worship with upraised hands.

> Therefore I want the men in every place to pray, lifting up holy hands, without wrath and dissension (1 Tim. 2:8).

Paul did not leave this directive only for leaders to follow when they pronounce blessings or benedictions. Everyone who follows Paul's advice benefits from it. He undoubtedly taught new churches he established to pray this way. He took an ancient Jewish prayer posture and adopted it for gentile Christian worship ("men pray *everywhere*," KJV, emphasis added). The single direct reference in 1 Timothy reinforces the fact that upraised arms and hands in prayer were commonplace in the early church, making written instructions not necessary.[5]

The Scripture that exhorts believers to "lift up the hands which hang down" (Heb. 12:12) may be a charge to exercise faith in God by joining prayer with the time-honored practice of using outstretched hands. Positive actions, gestures, and postures dispel gloom clouds. Peter Gillquist testifies:

Having now experienced this sort of intercessory prayer, it constantly amazes me how this physical involvement in prayer actually bolsters our faith as we pray.[6]

A mighty angel in Revelation comes from heaven "wrapped in a cloud, with a rainbow over his head; his face was like the sun, and his legs were pillars of fire" (Rev. 10:1 JB). With his right foot on the sea and the left foot on the earth, the majestic messenger lifts up his right hand to God (v. 5) and swears that there will now be no more delay in bringing the fulfillment of all God's promises. The angel raises his hand to signal that he speaks in God's name and with God's delegated authority.

Lifting the hands in covenant or oath

In a courtroom, a witness takes the stand, places one hand on the Bible, lifts the other hand, and swears an oath to tell the truth. By raising his hand, the witness pledges that his testimony will be accurate. The action lends credence to his testimony.

God Himself raises His hand to make oaths and covenants. He legally swears to covenant with His people. He obligates Himself to His people publicly and on the record!

> For I lift up my hand to heaven, and say, I live for ever (Deut. 32:40, KJV; see Exod. 6:8, NIV; also Ezek. 20:6, 15, 28, 42; 36:7).

> And I will bring you to the land I swore with uplifted hand to give to Abraham, to Isaac and to Jacob (Exod. 6:8, NIV).

In Dan. 12:7, a man in linen lifts both hands to indicate double affirmation. Abraham used similar action in Gen. 14:22. The king of Sodom tried to wheel and deal for the war booty recently taken, but Abram wanted no alliance with the ungodly man. Abram declared, "I have lift[ed] up mine hand unto the LORD, the most high God, the possessor of heaven and earth" (KJV). Abram knew that his source of supply was God alone; hence, he unashamedly lifted up his hand *to* and *before* God and renounced any claim on the spoils of war.

Christians reaffirm their covenant with God by lifting their hands in worship. With raised hands, they declare their commitment to God openly, bluntly and without shame and place all horizontal relationships in secondary positions. The lifting of hands avows obedience. It shows a willingness and readiness to do God's will.

> And I shall *lift up my hands* to Thy commandments, Which I love; and I will meditate on Thy statutes (Ps. 119:48, emphasis added).

Believers should use their hands in prayer as naturally as they use their tongue.[7] The tongue verbalizes and articulates a person's thoughts. Raised hands give thoughts and words additional impetus. Hands stretched toward God release the whole person to express a greater degree of sincerity and intensity. Charles Wesley caught the heart-meaning of the lifting up of the hands when he wrote:

Father, I stretch my hands to Thee,
No other help I know;
If Thou withdraw Thyself from me,
Ah! whither shall I go?

When circumstances get desperate, human emotion generates serious prayer. When things have reached a breaking point, no one needs to be told the appropriate posture for prayer! Inward longings become passionate desires that lead easily to energetic expressions like outstretched hands. Charles Spurgeon comments:

> Uplifted hands have ever been a form of devout posture, and are intended to signify a reaching upward towards God, a readiness, an eagerness to receive the blessing sought after. We stretch out empty hands, for we are beggars; we lift them up, for we seek heavenly supplies; we lift them towards the mercy seat of Jesus, for there our expectation dwells.[8]

Gestures and body actions in worship express a desire for God. J.J. von Allmen, a noted Reformed worship authority, says: "Gesture [which includes lifting hands] is the suitable attitude implemented and intensified . . . a very personal action which reacts upon the one who performs it . . . . To give up gestures is to weaken the intensity of the encounter between God and His people."[9]

Supplication in the Old Testament

Moses, David, Solomon, and Ezra lifted their hands uninhibited.

Moses. In Israel's first battle with a heathen nation, the Amalekites attacked Israel (Exod. 17:8-16). The enemy chose to assail stragglers at the rear or outer fringes of the camp (Deut. 25:18). Moses sent a detachment of choice men under Joshua's leadership to engage the enemy. Moses himself retired to the summit of a hill with Aaron and Hur. There he lifted the rod of God heavenward in his hands. Israel's troops received special strength from God while Moses' hands were upraised, so when Moses tired, Aaron and Hur held up his hands until the victory was complete.

In Egypt, Moses had stretched out his hand with the rod to bring judgment.[10] He also had ended the plague of thunder and hail by stretching out his hands to God (Exod. 9:29, 33); however, the battle with Amalek was more than just another military skirmish. It was a prototype of all future conflicts between the people of God and their physical and spiritual adversaries. It revealed a perpetual concept. It showed how God's people in every generation can win over their enemies by prevailing prayer and praise.

The mindless lifting of a staff had not secured victory for Israel's warriors. By raising his hands, Moses expressed total dependence on God and offered praise. Standing on the mountain, Moses was more than a standard bearer or a psychological symbol of victory. His raised hands holding the rod of God were a prophetic sign as well as a literal intercession to God for Israel. His hands symbolized the power of dynamic prayer and praise.

God responded by supplying supernatural aid to His people. *The Torah*, a Jewish commentary, makes the following comment:

Lift! First use of the hands

Ancient Near Eastern armies went into battle behind standards symbolizing their gods, hence the picture of Moses, his hands upraised and supported by Aaron and Hur, presents a symbolic standard which is to remind the people that God is fighting for them.[11]

After the battle, Moses:

- Memorialized the occasion by documenting the victory in a book.
- Built an altar, calling it Adonai-nissi, "The Lord is my banner."
- Coined a watchword expression for Israel to remember the lesson.

The statement intended for repetition is not easily recognized in English Bibles. The words in Exod. 17:16 were given to remind Israel in the future that their God would always respond whenever they would humbly lift their hearts and hands to the throne of God. The New International Version gives one of the best wordings of the verse as follows:

> Moses built an altar and called it The LORD is my Banner. He said, *"For hands were lifted up to the throne of the LORD. The LORD will be at war against the Amalekites from generation to generation"* (emphasis added).

Keil/Delitzsch makes this interesting comment on the coined watchword:

> The words can hardly be understood in any other sense than "the hand lifted up to the throne of Jehovah in heaven, war to the Lord," etc.; and thus understood, they can only contain an admonition to Israel to follow the example of Moses and wage war against Amalek with the hands lifted up to the throne of Jehovah.[12]

David. David's sincere, fervent prayer and worship could not be contained by emotionless, conversational tones. He employed energetic speech. As he lifted his voice, David also lifted his hands. Standing, he involved his posture in meaningful, spiritual activity. He stretched his soul to reach out to God in a natural, correct way.

On an airline flight, Pastor Lloyd Ogilvie of Hollywood Presbyterian Church opened his Bible to study. A fellow passenger noticed his practice of lifting hands in prayer and praise. In response to inspiring thoughts, he raised his hands to God. The woman seated beside him noticed his hands go up a few times and asked, "Are you well? I notice that you stretch a lot."[13]

The first time I really studied lifting hands to God, I was so stirred by the Scriptures that I would raise my hands (when alone) whenever I could. My office was adjacent to the sanctuary; and whenever I walked through the church building, I found my hands in the air praising the Lord!

David and other psalmists had this to say about lifting hands in supplication 'to" or "toward" God (that is, stretching out in the direction of God's presence):

> Hear the voice of my supplications when I cry to Thee for help, When I *lift up my hands* toward Thy holy sanctuary (Ps. 28:2, emphasis added).

169

When I was in distress, I sought the Lord; at night I *stretched out untiring hands* and my soul refused to be comforted (Ps. 77:2, NIV emphasis added).

My eye has wasted away because of affliction; I have called upon Thee every day, O LORD; I have *spread out my hands* to Thee (Ps. 88:9, emphasis added).

May my prayer be counted as incense before thee; The *lifting up of my hands* as the evening offering (Ps. 141:2, emphasis added).

I stretch out my hands to Thee; My soul longs for Thee, as a parched land (Ps. 143:6, emphasis added).

David considered the lifting of the hands a normal part of prayer and worship. He found lifting hands:
*   Helped them give fuller expression to intense feelings.
*   Lifted their souls to God and brought their emotions directly to Him.
*   Enabled them to surrender themselves to God's will.

In Psalms, David pictures a child crying and stretching its hands toward its mother, just as afflicted children of God reach toward their heavenly Father. A crying voice, weeping eyes, outstretched hands, and a broken heart characterized David's prayer and worship.

"It is remarkable that this attitude of prayer," says Theodor Filthaut, "in spite of explicit apostolic prescription, could have become so much neglected by Christians. And yet, how wonderfully suited it is to Christian prayer!"[14]

Solomon. At the temple dedication, King Solomon led the people in prayer. Realizing the importance of the occasion, he stood on a special scaffold or platform built specially for this occasion and he lifted his hands. In an intense, emotion-charged moment, the great king humbled himself publicly before God and man.

And Solomon stood before the altar of the LORD in the presence of all the congregation of Israel, and *spread forth his hands toward heaven* (1 Kings 8:22, emphasis added).

What prayer and supplication soever be made by any man, or by all thy people Israel, which shall know every man the plague of his own heart, and *spread forth his hands toward his house* (1 Kings 8:38, emphasis added).

And it was so, that when Solomon had made an end of praying all this prayer and supplication unto the LORD, he arose from before the altar of the LORD, from kneeling on his knees with *his hands spread up to heaven* (1 Kings 8:54, emphasis added).

Solomon did what came naturally to him as well as emulating the examples of Moses, his father David, and other men of prayer. Solomon also referred to God stretching out His arm on behalf of His people (1 Kings 8:42).

Ezra. When Ezra heard of mixed marriages taking place between Israelites and foreigners, he was appalled. His intense prayer of contrition was accompanied by lifted hands.

> But at the evening offering I arose from my humiliation, even with my garment and my robe torn, and I fell on my knees and *stretched out my hands* to the LORD my God; and I said, "O my God, I am ashamed." (Ezra 9:5, emphasis added).

Lifting hands in blessing and praise

To *bless* God means to give, impart, or transfer something to Him that was not in His possession. It is easy to believe that God can bless people. He has much to give and the ability to bestow His gifts whenever He desires. God blesses His people by putting Himself, His presence, upon them, thereby imparting prosperity, health, etc. For example, the Old Testament priesthood spoke and acted on behalf of God.[15]

> And Aaron lifted up his hand toward the people, and blessed them (Lev. 9:22).

Parents bless their children, giving them gifts or doing something for them. Through the gift or action, parents transfer part of themselves to their children and renew or strengthen a bond of affection.

God's people have valuable gifts and actions they can give to God. They can bless the Lord in worship and praise by proclaiming to Him their high appreciation for all He is and has done. Their humble-yet-fervent acknowledgement of His greatness—the transfer of their pride, esteem, and thankfulness—from themselves to Him. Worship, in its basic definition, proclaims God's worth. His people bless Him by genuinely expressing such feelings to Him. It is startlingly simple and hard to believe. David, in the wilderness of Judea, declared:

> Thus will I bless thee while I live: *I will lift up my hands* in thy name (Ps. 63:4, emphasis added).

The Levitical watchman in the temple, on duty to maintain the twenty-four-hour-per-day praise of God, sang:

> *Lift up your hands* in the sanctuary, and bless the LORD (Ps. 134.2, emphasis added).

The energetic worship mentioned in Nehemiah confirms this principle:

> And Ezra blessed the LORD, the great God. And all the people answered; Amen, Amen; with *lifting up their hands*: and they bowed their heads, and worshiped the LORD with their faces to the ground (Neh. 8:6, emphasis added).

171

Lifting the hands in thanksgiving and praise

The Hebrew word for hand is *yâd*, which is incorporated into one of the Hebrew words for praise or thanksgiving, *yâdâh*. This word appears nearly one hundred times in the Hebrew text, but its root significance is obscure to the casual English reader. It is translated thirty-six times as give thanks[16] and sixty-one times as praise. Yâdâh means:

- To stretch out the hand.
- To worship or revere with raised or extended hands.
- To give thanks to God accompanied by uplifted hands.

One example of its use is in Psalm, chapter 107. The following chorus appears four times: "Let them *give thanks* to the LORD for His lovingkindness" (vv. 8, 15, 21, 31). Yâdâh authenticates the stretching out of hands in worship.

An additional confirmation comes from another Hebrew word, *tôwdâh,* appearing more than twenty times in the Hebrew Scriptures.[17] It means:

- Thanksgiving.
- To extend the hands in thanksgiving, a thank offering.

The sacrifice of praise as an act of faith is implicit in the meaning of Ps. 50:23: "He who offers a sacrifice of thanksgiving honors Me."

Summary

Psalmic worship for today's church should include the lifting of the hands because it:

- Reaffirms the covenant!
- Intensifies my prayer and supplication!
- Signifies the surrender of my will!
- Lifts up my soul!
- Blesses the Lord!
- Brings the sacrifice of thanksgiving!

Jeremiah's statement in Lam. 3:41 capsulizes what the church must now do: "Lift up its heart and hands toward God in heaven."

172

Reflections

The raising of one's hands in prayer or in praise to God then is neither a new phenomenon developed within churches bent toward the emotional nor is it a holdover from the pre-Christian era. Rather, this practice is thoroughly biblical, having been practiced in the worship patterns of the Old Testament period, and carried on into the New Testament era—and therefore into the Christian era.

—Ronald Allen and Gordon Borror[18]

In our case, not only do we raise our hands, we even spread them out, and, taking our model from the Lord's passion, even in prayer we confess to Christ.

—Tertullian, Latin church father[19]

Usually when we are conducting our "song and praise service" we will ask the people to raise their hands as they sing a song . . . to give testimony that the song being sung applies to them; it is like casting a vote by lifting our hand—an Amen! Other times we will ask the people to raise their hands as an act of surrender to the Lord. We are saying, in effect, "I mean this with all my heart . . . ." the universal sign of surrender. " . . . I am surrendering my will and heart to you, O God."

—James Lee Beall[20]

"Hands" are the symbols of supplication. Outstretched hands stand for an appeal for help. It is the silent yet eloquent attitude of a helpless soul standing before God, appealing for mercy and grace.

—E.M. Bounds[21]

At a given signal, usually by the pastor, the entire group raises hands to heaven and, with uplifted faces, enters into adoration and praise. This is not a subjective thing, an attempt to "work up" an ecstatic emotionalism for the sake of the thrill. But the objective thrust of the united praise and worship of him who alone is worthy often results in an inundation of the Holy Spirit's presence—which is nothing short of heavenly, for it echoes the praises of the celestial throng around the throne.

—Paul E. Billheimer[22]

One objection I often hear about raising hands is that it will make non-Christians uncomfortable. In certain sectors of North America that may be true . . . . On the other hand, many southern California churches that raise hands have learned to practice it in a way that seems to be culturally acceptable to a wide range of people. In fact, these churches seem to have the nonchurched present in larger numbers than the churches that do not raise hands.

—Barry Liesch[23]

173

20

Play Instruments!
Second use of the hands

And 4,000 were praising the LORD with the instruments
which David made for giving praise.
—1 Chronicles 23:5

Adding musical instruments to corporate or individual worship enriches the worship experience. Individuals often sit privately in the Lord's presence and sing spontaneous songs of praise while playing basic chords on the piano or guitar. It can be one of the most spiritually helpful things a person can do.

The Hebrew word zâmar means to touch or play the strings. It appears three dozen times in the book of Psalms and has "the sense of singing praise to the accompaniment of musical instruments."[1] The King James Version usually translates it as sing forth praises.[2]

With their voices, worshipers express love and appreciation from their hearts to the Lord, but adding music creates a sublime dimension unattainable by any other means. Psalm 71:22 says "I will also praise Thee with a harp, even Thy truth, O my God; To Thee I will sing praise [zâmar] with the lyre, O Thou Holy One of Israel." And David enthusiastically endorses this spontaneous song: "I will sing a new song to Thee, O God; upon a harp of ten strings I will sing praises [zâmar] to Thee."

Most verses that use zâmar refer to worship in a congregational setting. For instance, David declares: "I will offer in His tent sacrifices with shouts of joy: I will sing, yes, I will sing praises [zâmar] to the LORD" (Ps. 27:6). When an entire congregation brings its personal devotional songs into the higher level of spontaneous, congregational singing, the resulting harmony of many voices is truly uplifting especially if an orchestra joins in. Such spontaneous songs of praise may not be musical masterpieces—or even meaningful—to others but these songs of praise will be deeply satisfying to the worshiper and to the Lord.

Instrumental accompaniment has a soothing, liberating, peaceful effect. David sang and played his harp for King Saul. The music relieved the raging Saul, causing the evil spirit to depart (1 Sam. 16:23). Also, Elisha was challenged to prophesy in a very hostile, unbelieving setting. Needing God's presence, he called for a minstrel, a

Levitical priest who could sing and play the psalms of David. As the harpist played, the hand of the Lord came on Elisha!

The manifesto of Psalm 150

Scholars subdivide the book of Psalms into five sections or books. Book One ends with chapter 41; two with 72; three with 89; four with 106; and five with 150. Each of the five interior books ends with climactic praise, but Psalm 150 outdoes them all. It closes the entire book of Psalms with a summons to all mankind to praise Him in all places for all things. Psalm, chapter 150, makes the greatest endorsement for Psalmic worship. It commands God's people to employ the full capacity of human musicianship in stringed, wind, and percussion instruments in unrestrained acclamation of the Lord God! It becomes a veritable manifesto pointing the direction that the church must take in worship. Here is a colorful translation:

> Hallelujah! Jehovah!
> Hallelujah God in his holy place!
> Hallelujah him through the heavens which he rules!
> Hallelujah God for his sovereignty!
> Hallelujah him in the overwhelmingness of his grandeur!
> Hallelujah him with the blast of trumpets!
> Hallelujah him with harps and bass violins!
> Hallelujah him with (bouncing) tambourines and dance!
> Hallelujah him with stringed instruments, with flutes,
> Hallelujah him with ringing castanets!
> Hallelujah him with cymbals crashing joyfully!
> Let every thing that has a breath hallelujah Jehovah!
> Hallelujah Jehovah![3]

The passage tells believers:
- Where to praise the Lord: in His sanctuary and throughout the expanse of the universe (v. 1).
- Why the Lord is praised: because of the great things He has done and because of His own greatness (v. 2)
- How to praise the Lord: with full orchestral sound and dancing (vv. 3-5).
- Every breathing (living) person is to praise (hallelujah![4]) the Lord.

The church resembles a mighty pipe organ. Every person's windpipe is not only a personal breathing tube but also is a "pipe" in the church's pipe organ. The pipes range from small piccolos to the great pipes larger than a man. Together, the pipes create a thunderous, glorious expression of praise!

Would David be comfortable?

In March, 1985, our local church's music department really entered the computer age. I could not believe my eyes! Five minutes before starting the morning service, I saw the lighted screen face of a computer smiling at me on the platform. My oldest daughter, Sharon, the choir director, and her husband John, the orchestra director, were beaming like excited little children. "The computer is going to play the synthesizer this morning!" they said. I had not even adjusted to the synthesizer yet—let alone a computer in the orchestra to play the synthesizer! Sharon had programmed the computer to play the choir accompaniment, but it still was somewhat mystical to have the keyboard perform without human fingers as she directed the choir.

I couldn't help but wonder, "What would David think if he were here now?" The prolific inventor of instruments and composer of odes and psalms would probably be as fascinated and excited as anyone! Judging from his own words, if David were pastoring a Christian church today, he would be making the most joyful sounds he could by the most sophisticated means possible!

Instruments in the time of David

The instruments David introduced and used were crude by modern standards. Drawings in Bible encyclopedias show eight or ten versions of ancient harps, some crude drums, simple flutes and horns, and castanets.[5] Many churches of the world still use these instruments. In Nigerian village churches, people worship God enthusiastically, and their main accompaniment comes from crude percussion instruments such as drums. Some people just beat sticks together. Their intensity and volume more than compensates for what they lack in sophisticated equipment. I was moved to tears when I saw it.

People do invent ways to offer praise to God. King David searched for and found a variety of ways. He assigned 4,000 Levitical musicians to praise God on instruments specifically made "for giving praise" (1 Chron. 23:5).

Sometimes the zeal for innovation can go too far. People really can get carried away with some worship expression that is personally satisfying, yet offensive—even bizarre—to others. Many years ago my father was an army band leader. Once, he brought home an old, discarded glockenspiel. My younger brother immediately confiscated this instrument for use in the small, mission-type church he attended in Monterey, California. The congregation already had an orchestra of sorts. They had a guitarist and a dilapidated piano, played by whoever was available. The most interesting musician was an older man who played his harmonica. Unfortunately, the poor fellow was hard of hearing and invariably out-of-sync with the others.

However, things changed when my brother brought the glockenspiel to church. The sharp, piercing, metal tones produced by the energetically wielded wooden mallet were overpowering not only to the congregation but also to the harmonica player who had to cover an ear with one of his hands! So the glockenspiel had to go. Musical things can get out of hand.

David coupled his quest for musical expression with a sense of excellence. He insisted that the Levitical musicians be "trained in singing," and "skillful with musical instruments" (1 Chron. 25:7; 2 Chron. 34:12), and "play skillfully with a shout of joy" (Ps. 33:3b).

David initiated a very sophisticated musical program for Israel (1 Chronicles, chapter 15). The worship system was given by divine revelation along with the pattern for Solomon's temple, and David was very diligent in following through with the plan

(1 Chron. 28:11-19). He did not simply express his wishes but made a command concerning the musicianship of praise (2 Chron. 8:14). God gave prophetic insight to David, Gad, and Nathan. Even later, under Hezekiah, the people knew what was expected because of the command "from the LORD through His prophets" (2 Chron. 29:25). During the time of Zerubbabel, when they laid the foundation of the restored temple, the Levites ministered with trumpets and cymbals "to praise the LORD according to the directions of King David of Israel" (Ezra 3:10). In revivals in Judah, when the kingdom was divided, priests always reinstituted Psalmic worship methods with the instruments of David.[6]

The Chronicles present a priestly perspective of Israel's history during the period of the kings. They report how David's instructions for Psalmic worship were implemented in the Tabernacle of David and Temple of Solomon. Musical instruments are mentioned in twenty verses of Psalms[7], but the Chronicles show what occurred, including prophecy on musical instruments (1 Chron. 25:2-3).[8] Specific instructions called for:

- Musicians to play lyres, harps, and cymbals (1 Chron. 25:1).
- Asaph, Heman and Jeduthun to direct the musicians (v. 6).
- The song to the Lord to be played by trumpets accompanied by the instruments of David (2 Chron. 29:25-27).

Instruments in the New Testament church

The New Testament says very little about musical instruments in the church. Although the New Testament gives no specific teaching—pro or con—on the subject, the Scripture carries a perceivable tenor that validates the use of musical instruments, climaxing with instruments in heaven.

Church leaders have hotly debated the issue throughout the church age. Controversy has challenged the types of instruments used. For instance, Calvin believed pipe organs were of the devil; however, other groups insist that pipe organs are the only appropriate instruments for congregational worship. The Salvation Army has always used bands. Today an increasing number of churches use orchestras. Christians who had a hard time accepting guitars in church now contend with drum sets. And what about electronic keyboards?

Jesus referred to Jewish folk music when He mentioned flutes and dancing (Matt. 11:16, 17; Luke 15:25). Paul used musical instruments to illustrate certain points. For instance, clanging cymbals describe lives without love (1 Cor. 13:1), and uncertain bugle, flute, or harp sounds are like confused prophetic utterances (1 Cor. 14:7, 8).

Paul's use of psallo (Gk.) in Eph. 5:19 is taken by some commentators as a possible reference to the use of stringed instruments. For instance, Markus Barth says:

> If . . . the original meaning of *psallo* is in mind, that is, "to pluck or twang a string" (in particular the bowstrings of a musical instrument), then Ephesians 5:19 encourages the use of fiddles, harps, and other instruments.[9]

The book of Revelation records the use of harps (5:8; 14:2; 15:2) and trumpets (8:2, 6, 13; 9:14) in heaven. It also states that the sound of harpists, musicians, flute players, and trumpeters will be heard no longer in Babylon (18:22). Many see these references confirming the use of instruments in church services; however, others reject such an idea claiming that apocalyptic symbolism is not acceptable proof. Whether literal or symbolic, instruments used in heavenly worship extend the great praise of the Lord initiated in the great manifesto of Psalm, chapter 150.

The Cross as filter

Christians should not follow every Old Testament teaching. The following procedure should be used to analyze teachings that may be appropriate:

First, ask, "Is this particular subject of the Old Testament valid for today?" Then search for the answer in the New Testament.

As you search the Scriptures ask, "Do we find replacement, abolishment, or spiritual application of this Old Testament order in the New Testament church?"

Finally, "Has the death, burial, and resurrection of Jesus Christ in any way affected, changed, or abolished the Old Testament item under consideration?"

The Cross acts as a filter for New Testament standards. If an Old Testament teaching can stand the scrutiny of Christ's redemptive act and apostolic teaching, it can be used safely in today's church. Nowhere does the New Testament indicate that the worship and praise characterizing the Psalms (including the use of instruments) is to be depreciated, diluted, or discontinued.

So how far do we go?

Just how far should a church go in promoting musical instruments in the worship experience? Is a million-dollar pipe organ warranted?[10] Are all those guitars really necessary? Should a church have an orchestra—and where should it be used? How often should the piano in the sanctuary be tuned up?

A variety of instruments and music that is relevant to both the message and the culture may be used. How can the concept of Psalmic instrumentation be employed in such a way that is culturally relevant, better enabling the local church to worship God dynamically and reach today's generation evangelistically? This passage by Peter Wagner asks the most appropriate question:

> One of the most unreal things I saw when I was first being introduced to Latin American Pentecostalism was an orchestra of about 500 members with the basic instruments being guitars, mandolins, and accordions. Not a pipe organ in the place! But a pipe organ never sounded like those 500 instruments.
>
> Some will respond that they prefer a pipe organ in church any time. I would agree, as long as pipe organs are producing culturally-relevant liturgies that align people to the church and to Jesus Christ. To many Latin Americans, guitars and accordions are more attractive than pipe organs. It would be extremely difficult to classify one more "biblical" than the other. A more important question is: Which sounds better to our people?[11]

Instruments are prophetic of creation

When a musician plays an instrument in a church service, it is an enactment of a prophetic parable of what will happen at the end of the age. In Rom. 8:19-21, Paul speaks of creation being held in bondage until the manifestation of the sons of God. He is saying that nature itself in the age to come will be transformed, just as His people will be. In fact, nature will be changed and glorified because the church will be changed first! All creation wishes to join in unrestrained praise of almighty God.

When a musician in a church service takes inanimate objects (plastic, wood, wire, metal) and causes them to make sounds to the glory of God, he prophetically portends how the church will be the instrument of God that will release all creation to an unrestrained praise of God. Using inanimate objects now in the praising of God points to the coming eternity when bondages and restraints will no longer exist.

Reflections

Although there is very little to be found in archeological findings in Hebrew history concerning musical instruments, other surrounding nations supply a reasonable measure of information. The Hebrew nation, following the strict letter of the law which forbad the making of any form of images or sculpture strictly refrained from such in contrast to other nations. Whatever may have been the exact description of the instruments of Bible times, enough information shows that they fell into the same basic categories as mentioned in Psalm 150. That is, stringed, wind, and percussion instruments.

—Kevin Conner[12]

Instruments of all types are returning to the church. The congregation is no longer being entertained by choirs, or vocalists, who have little relationship themselves with the God of whom they are singing. Instead the believers are experiencing the anointing of God in a fresh new way.

—A.L. and Joyce Gill[13]

We may say that instrumental music was an integral part of worship in the Old Testament. In the New Testament Church, it was not. There are two main reasons for this situation. First, the early Church was more influenced by synagogue than Temple. And there were no instruments used in synagogue worship except the shophar which was not really regarded as a musical instrument. Second, it was mainly the special circumstance of the early Church that caused instrumental and even vocal music to be de-emphasized, but it was not prohibited on scriptural or theological grounds.

—Frank Longino[14]

Those of us who use musical instruments in praise must be careful not to become too dependent upon those instruments so that when the music stops, the praise and worship immediately cease! Our praise should ascend to God even when no instruments are readily available. But God has ordained that musical instruments be used to help facilitate our praises. He has created us with musical sensitivities that immediately respond to good musicianship, and he has shown us that the proper response to music should take the form of praise.

—Bob Sorge[15]

It is an interesting example of historical irony that some churches which use no modern hymns but only the psalms in their worship are at the same time opposed to the use of musical instruments.

—Millar Burrows[16]

181

21

Clap!
Third use of the hands

Come everyone, and clap for joy!
—Psalm 47:1 LB

At the nominating convention that picked Bill Clinton to run for president of the United States, thousands of exhilarated delegates sustained a roar of adulation with a clap-until-your-hands-hurt applause. By repeatedly striking the palms of their hands against one another, the delegates thundered their resounding, joyous approval, appreciation, encouragement, and backing for the young man and his platform. Clapping was their normal, natural response.

People "caught up" in a cause or an occasion commonly express their pent-up emotions by clapping. Audiences enraptured by Luciano Pavarotti, the great Italian tenor, regularly stand clapping furiously, and some even shouting, as the singer bows graciously and exits. The audience wants—even demands—more! Then, the big man, mops his perspiring face and returns to the platform smiling from ear to ear. "Ah," he might say to himself, "they love me. They enjoy my voice—they demand an encore!" So he sings again, renewed by their grand attention. The response of adoring fans compels him back to sing again. The audience has inspired the man with the magnificent voice to return and perform once more.

Everyone has applauded at athletic events, speeches, children's program performances, etc., and some privileged people have received applause. Applause has animating power. Without applause, a performance or event is like an unfinished painting, like a business deal without final payment, like a sail hanging limp in calm air. Appreciation must be given and received, and the abrupt, sharp sound of clapping hands is a universally accepted way of doing it.

Religious clapping
Clapping may be expected at speeches and other events, but is it ever really appropriate in a worship service? This question is best answered by the following question! Since God and His acts are more worthy of applause than anyone or

anything else, why shouldn't this normal, natural response be part of a worship experience?

But does the Bible teach clapping? This increasingly popular worship form has only a single direct reference in the entire Bible! However, the following two poetic references depict nature applauding God and His triumphant ways:

- Let the rivers clap their hands (Ps. 98:8).
- The trees of the field will clap their hands (Isa. 55:12).

To picture the natural world in great jubilation for God, Isaiah and the psalmist show rivers and trees praising the Lord with clapping, but only one verse urges people to clap their praise to God. This singular statement is such a powerful exhortation that it does not need to be repeated elsewhere:

Clap your hands, all people! Shout to God with loud songs of joy! (Ps. 47:1, RSV).

This call to enthusiastic worship opens a vibrant, popular psalm. Sung frequently in Israel, it clearly accented clapping as an authentic mode of worship expression. Dedicated to the theme, "The Lord Shall Subdue All Nations," this psalm is poetically grand, practically expedient, and prophetically accurate. The two simple lines of this key verse dramatically call for—even demand—the most intense, glorious, clamorous, acclamation of praise to God for His majestic rule over the earth and its inhabitants.

The meaning of clapping

Definitions of clapping from Hebrew lexicons and the English dictionary provide the following reasons for clapping in a worship service:

- To express approval or appreciation.
- To applaud.
- To greet or encourage.
- To show joy, a token of rejoicing.
- To express triumph.
- To pledge oneself as collateral.

If people can direct their heartfelt emotions to God with their voices, they also can find fulfillment in clapping unto God in appreciation for all He is and has done. True worship inspires the triumphant feeling described in the book of Revelation, and triumphant emotions commonly trigger clapping.

Striking hands was part of business in Old Testament times. Like a handshake, striking hands with someone signified a pledge. It committed the two parties as collateral in a business arrangement (Job 17:3; Prov. 6:1; 11:15; 17:18; 22:26)."[1] Clapping in congregational worship can be considered a spiritual application of this concept. It can signify reaffirmation of the covenant between God and man, a renewal of fellowship similar to the breaking of bread at the Communion table.

Clap! Third use of the hands

Appropriate warning

Admittedly, some clapping in churches these days simply keeps time with music rhythms. Bob Sorge, in his book *Exploring Worship*, comments:

> It is important that we link the clapping of hands with a heart that ascends unto the Lord, because the clapping of hands without a heart involvement is really very empty. In studying Hebrew forms of praise, one does not get the impression that this "clapping of hands" was intended to be a "keeping of the beat." It was intended, rather, as just another form of making a "joyful noise" unto the Lord.[2]

Choruses accompanied by clapping might be characterized as simplistic praise, but they are appropriate and necessary. From deep veneration in believers' hearts the Spirit often triggers spontaneous clapping and triumphant shouting to God throughout the congregation. It is powerful!

The frivolous approach to clapping that sometimes appears in charismatic and other groups is a legitimate concern. They may clap when leaders ask them to praise the Lord. Their actions seem to equate heartless, shallow clapping with meaningful praise. After experiencing deeper dimensions of worship, many do not find satisfaction in simplistic clapping!

The controversial and well-known old-time Pentecostal Kenneth Hagin has warned, "We've just gotten clap-happy in charismatic circles." He laments, according to Ken Walker, "that many congregations are prone to clap at all the wrong times."[3] Emotional highs and noisy activity cannot replace heartfelt waiting on God. Brief bursts of physical noisemaking cannot substitute for the sincerity, purity, and depth of praise. The church needs good teaching to maintain a proper, balanced approach on this subject.

Reflections

Clap your hands, all ye people;
Shout unto God with a voice of triumph!
Clap your hands, all ye people;
Shout unto God with a voice of praise!
Hosanna! Hosanna!
Shout unto God with a voice of triumph!
Praise Him! Praise Him!
Shout unto God with a voice of praise!

—*Jimmy Owens*[4]

Sing and clap your hands
Sing your praise to the Lord (3X)!
Clap your hands
And sing to the Lord!

—*Sharon L. Dermer*[5]

Clap your hands, as men transported with pleasure, that cannot contain themselves.

—*Matthew Henry*[6]

The name of Jesus has often made lame men leap as a hart, and has made sad men clap their hands for joy.

—*Charles H. Spurgeon*[7]

At the Billy Graham Greater Los Angeles Crusade of 1985, tens of thousands in the crowd began to applaud as people came forward to profess salvation. Billy Graham was taken aback. He tried to stop the audience from applauding but could not. He seemingly did not know what to make of it. Then he said something to the effect, "You Californians are different." To the Californians their clapping was a means of affirming those making a decision for Christ, a way of praising God for answered prayer.

—*Barry Liesch*[8]

22

Stand!
First use of posture

I praise him with my whole body.
— Psalm 28:7 NEB

No chairs, benches or other furniture offered seating for priests in the Tabernacle of Moses or the Temple of Solomon. Priests stood when they blessed the Lord and lifted up holy hands (Ps. 134:1-2; 135:1-2). Even the night watch stood. The nightly vigil needed wide-awake praisers who used the quiet hours to good advantage just like the angelic hosts in heaven who praise and magnify God day and night (Rev. 4:8). Even at night, priests were to fill the sacred precincts ministering to the Lord and His people.[1]

The first time I saw people stand a long time to worship, I was amazed. With lifted hands, they praised God fervently as they stood for five minutes . . . fifteen minutes . . . thirty minutes . . . finally stopping after an hour. As an ordained minister I was accustomed to spiritual exercise, but that was glorious! Such long worship services exhilarate worshipers but bore churchgoers.

When the Spirit of God moves, people stand to worship longer because services tend to run longer. Ladies standing in modern high-heeled shoes sense discomfort. Perhaps God's original suggestion to Moses is the simple solution (Exod. 3:5).

Some people in the United States and other developed countries question the importance of standing since most of their churches have padded seating. In fact, the carpeted floors of some churches provide more comfort than the seats in foreign mission churches they sponsor! People naturally question the importance of standing because sitting is easier. Churches never will eliminate their seating, but they can honor the ministry of standing in congregational worship.

Definition of "stand"
A standing person assumes an upright position, supporting himself in an erect or nearly erect position on his feet. Standing indicates that he is alert, aware, and ready to act. It also signifies honor, respect, and reverence. The challenge to "stand up and be

counted," means that a person must make up his mind about a given issue and act on it.

While the West Point football team is on the field playing, the entire corps of cadets stands to show their total commitment and support for their team and school. The united action of so many young people generates awesome energy and enthusiasm!

At the first public presentation of Handel's *Messiah*, the king of England reverently stood acknowledging his subordinate relationship to the supreme King of the universe. The king's action started the custom, still in effect today, of audiences standing during the "Hallelujah Chorus." The congregation of Saint Augustine in the seventh century stood and listened while he sat and preached to them. They had no pews in their church!

The Eastern custom of standing

In the synagogue of Jesus' day, "the people stood during prayer with their faces turned to Jerusalem."[2] In His own teaching on prayer, Jesus assumed that standing to pray was customary because He said, "And when ye stand praying . . ." (Mark 11:25). One commentator explains:

> And He Himself prayed standing; not that the evangelists state it explicitly, any more than they tell us of other things that they took for granted. It was everyone's custom to pray standing with hands raised, and so Jesus did the same.[3]

Standing for prayer, worship, or public reading of Scripture does more than just change a person's posture. "Standing has a purpose over and above that of mere utility," says Theodor Filthaut, "It is also an expression of an inner spiritual process."[4] Standing reflects religious conviction.

Jesus habitually attended a local synagogue meeting on the Sabbath.[5] Services usually involved psalm-singing, prayer, and the reading and study of Scripture. (The sacrificial and priestly functions of Hebrew worship did not take place in synagogues but continued in the temple in Jerusalem.) After returning to His home synagogue in Nazareth, Jesus was asked to read the Scripture and give commentary as a visiting rabbi. He "stood up to read" (Luke 4:16). After He read, "he closed the book, and he gave it again to the minister, and sat down." Jesus' action conformed to the custom of His day, but undoubtedly reflected His own deep esteem for Scripture. It was "an act of humility, to be exact, an action of respect for the Word of God; He stood in order to give honour to that word."[6]

Old Testament illustrations

When God came down on Mount Sinai, the fiery spectacle overwhelmed the frightened Israelites. They saw the lightning and thunder and heard the trumpet blasts. "When the people saw it, they trembled and *stood* at a distance" (Exod. 20:18, 21, emphasis added). The Israelites stood in a combination of terror, respect and awe. Who could casually sit through such an experience?

On another occasion, God's presence came to the tabernacle and God spoke "face to face" with Moses. Meanwhile, the people stood at their tent doors and worshiped (Exod. 33:8-11).

When Aaron and his sons were consecrated to the priesthood, the people stood to await God's manifestation. Suddenly, the fire of God fell, consuming the sacrifice. "And when all the people saw it, they shouted and fell on their faces" (Lev. 9:24).

God commanded Israel to perform a strange ceremony after they entered the Promised Land. He ordered half of the tribes to stand on Mount Gerizim and the other half on Mount Ebal. As the Levites read the law of cursings and blessings to the assembled tribes, they shouted "Amen!" (Deut. 27:12). In this case, standing in the assembly demonstrated commitment to God's will. The people stood in the same type of gathering when Ezra taught God's Law. They stood while they were taught (Neh. 8:7; 9:3).

The priests were to "*stand* before the LORD to serve Him and to bless His name" (Deut. 10:8; 17:12; 18:5, 7). Elijah described his ministry for God with a similar expression: ". . . before whom I stand . . ." (1 Kings 17:1). His successor, Elisha, adopted the saying, too (2 Kings 3:14; 5:16).

At the dedication of Solomon's temple, the people stood as the king gave them a prophetic blessing (2 Chron. 6:3). Also, "all Israel stood" during the priests' ministry and during the offering of sacrifices (2 Chron. 7:6).

Fear swept through Judah as a great army of several nations massed to invade the country. King Jehoshaphat stood in the house of the Lord and prayed fervently with his frightened people. In his prayer, he claimed the divine promise: "If . . . we *stand* before this house . . . and cry unto thee . . . then thou wilt hear and help" (2 Chron 20:9 KJV, emphasis added). But they did more than just recite God's command! "And all Judah *stood* before the LORD, with their little ones, their wives, and their children" 2 Chron. 20:13 KJV, emphasis added). The final victory came when the singers began to praise the Lord! It is carefully noted that the Kohathite Levites "*stood up* to praise the LORD God of Israel with a loud voice" (2 Chron. 20:19 KJV, emphasis added).

When King Josiah made covenant between Israel and God, he had the people stand as a sign of human surrender to God's will (2 Chron. 34:32).

The sculptured olive wood cherubim in the Most Holy Place of Solomon's temple symbolized God's creatures showing deference to God. These massive statues (with an approximate wingspread of fifteen feet) "*stood* on their feet" in the presence of God (2 Chron. 3:13, emphasis added). The heavenly creatures set an example for others to stand in God's presence! The following references show the Levites standing for worship:

And (the Levites were) to *stand* every morning to thank and praise the LORD, and likewise at evening (1 Chron. 23:30, emphasis added).

And the Levites . . . *stood up* to praise the LORD God of Israel with a loud voice on high (2 Chron. 20:19, emphasis added).

And the Levites *stood* with the instruments of David, and the priests with the trumpets (2 Chron 29:26, emphasis added)

Then the Levites . . . said, *stand up* and bless the LORD your God for ever and ever: and blessed by thy glorious name, which is exalted above all blessing and praise (Neh. 9:5, emphasis added).

Behold, bless ye the LORD, all ye servants of the LORD, which by night *stand* in the house of the LORD (Ps. 134:1, emphasis added).

Ye that *stand* in the house of the LORD, in the courts of the house of our God, Praise the LORD; for the LORD is good: sing praises unto his name; for it is pleasant (Ps. 135:2, 3, emphasis added).

Standing in the church

"Stand up! Stand up for Jesus! Ye soldiers of the Cross . . . ."[7] For many years this stirring hymn has challenged the church to fight spiritual warfare. The hymn prods Christians to make inward, personal decisions, but standing physically in a church worship service outwardly demonstrates an inner attitude. It should mean the individual unashamedly declares his faith in Christ and commits himself to the fellowship of the saints.

When the church stands for prayer, Bible reading, etc., it should "embody the idea of reverence."[8] Christians should demonstrate attitudes of deep respect, careful attention, and loving obedience.

Theodor Filthaut, a distinguished French Catholic theologian, says about standing:

Standing expresses primarily the redemption, the fundamental reality of Christian existence. By standing erect the believer affirms that he is no longer a bound slave, but a redeemed and free man, a son or daughter of God, one who has risen to eternal life with God. In the early church for a time it was forbidden to pray kneeling during the season of Easter. In those days Christians took the standing position very seriously as a witness to belief in Resurrection.[9]

A person standing on his or her feet is *ready* for sudden surprises. The Israelites in Egypt ate the Passover in haste, ready to move out at Moses' command (Exod. 12:11). A person standing erect before his superior reports he is ready and willing to do whatever is commanded. Christians should be like the happy servants of Solomon who, the Queen of Sheba noted, "stand continually before thee" (1 Kings 10:8). King Jesus is like Solomon to today's church. When believers happily minister before Him and do His will with ready hearts, even the people of the world will acknowledge the beauty of God's kingdom.

Practically speaking, people sing better in worship if they stand. They do not feel inhibited. Changing posture adds variety and maintains alertness.

Standing erect affirms a person's freedom from sin's bondage. It also prophetically points to the coming resurrection of the human body. Ezekiel prophesied the Word of the Lord to Israel's valley of dry bones. The Spirit of God blew with creative power, "and they lived, and *stood* upon their feet, an exceedingly great army" (Ezek. 37:10, emphasis added).

Stand! First use of posture

The prophet Daniel lost his strength as God's vision came to him. "And, behold, a hand touched me, which set me upon my knees and upon the palms of my hands. And he said unto me . . . *stand* upright . . . And when he had spoken this word unto me, I stood trembling" (Dan. 10:10, 11, emphasis added). Standing belongs in worship because it speaks so eloquently of resurrection life!

In summary
The church stands to the Lord and before the Lord! On the basis of Scripture given in this chapter, one has every right to stand as an enthusiastic act of worship to the living God. Entering the house of God, you stand as:

- An act of reverence.
- An affirmation of freedom through Christ and authority in Christ.
- A testimony of faith in Christ and His church.
- A sign of eager readiness to do His bidding.
- An obedient action of faith to the Bible's teaching.
- A prophetic declaration of our resurrection life!

Reflections

At the conclusion of all the Scriptures let the Gospel be read, as the seal of all the Scriptures; and let the people listen to it standing up on their feet, because it is the glad things of the salvation of all men.

—Cannons of Addai, 3rd cent.[10]

According to Basil, in his fourth-century treatise on the Holy Spirit, we stand up to pray on Sunday "because that day is in some way the image of the future age." Standing is an active posture. It is the posture of one who has been resurrected.

—Marianne H. Micks[11]

I stand amazed in the presence of Jesus the Nazarene, and wonder how He could love me, A sinner condem'd unclean. How marvelous! how wonderful! And my song shall ever be: How marvelous! how wonderful is my Saviour's love for me!

—Charles H. Gabriel, from the hymn "My Saviour's Love"

Standing was by far the most common form of physical action in the early Church, especially to receive the bread and wine. In fact the Council of Nicaea forbade anyone to kneel on Sunday, the Lord's day, and at the Eastertide, because only standing could declare the Christian's faith in the victory of the Resurrection.

—Paul W. Hoon[12]

One thing that reduces yawns in Pentecostal churches is the need to keep moving. Worshipers stand up and sit down so frequently that no one settles back enough to get sleepy. Lifting hands up and down also keeps the pulse beating.

—C. Peter Wagner[13]

23

Bow!
Second use of posture

Come, let us worship and bow down;
Let us kneel before the LORD our Maker.
—Psalm 95:6

Captains of industry, more than 2,000 politicians, and other notables gathered for the annual Leadership Luncheon in the main ballroom of the Washington Hilton in January, 1991. The Persian Gulf War had begun two weeks earlier.

Charles Stanley, the Atlanta pastor and television luminary, was the main speaker. He preached from James 5:16: "The prayer of a righteous man is powerful and effective." He preached eloquently and fervently about the need for America to humble itself before God as Elijah and Solomon and others had.

Near the end of his message, he crept out on a limb. Without raising his voice he mused, "What would happen today if 2,000 people got on their knees, humbled themselves before God, and cried out for forgiveness?" He dropped a few more hints and gradually the crowd realized he was serious. He was talking about *them* getting on their knees—in their Brooks Brothers suits. He allowed that some might not be physically able, but for the rest he said, "Unless God does something in this nation, we are going to be humiliated in some fashion, at some time. I want to ask you if you'll join me on my knees and pray until whenever the moderator thinks the time is over." With that, he turned and dropped from sight. End of sermon.

The ballroom got quiet. Gradually, chairs began shuffling, and before long most of the crowd had followed his lead. A sober, reverent mood filled the room.[1]

Is kneeling out of style?
Kneeling takes place less and less in churches. It's almost a lost art! Today's fast-paced society sees kneeling as uncomfortable, unflattering, and unnecessary. Every Christian knows that God hears prayer from any posture, so why kneel, bow, or be uncomfortable? Furthermore, no Scripture *commands* people to kneel when they pray.

193

Bowing involves bodily action

Of all the body movements that complement religious experience, bowing is the most significant and widely recognized. The most common Old Testament word for worship *shâchâh* means a literal bowing down. This humble action was the most natural approach to the holy presence of God and formed the root idea of worship. Serious disciples of Christ emulate the many kneeling, bowing saints seen in the Bible.

People usually associate bowing with kneeling, but bowing can take seven different forms:

- Bending both knees
- Bowing the head while standing
- Bowing the upper part of the body while in a standing position (like a bulrush)
- Bending over double in a standing position
- Stooping with one knee bent
- Prostrating oneself in a spread-eagle position on the ground
- Kneeling on both knees with the body prostrated (bent forward) and arms extended on the ground.

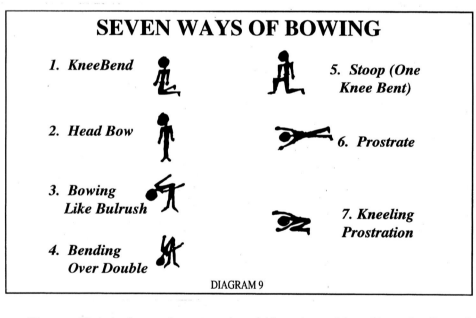

SEVEN WAYS OF BOWING

1. KneeBend

2. Head Bow

3. Bowing Like Bulrush

4. Bending Over Double

5. Stoop (One Knee Bent)

6. Prostrate

7. Kneeling Prostration

DIAGRAM 9

Western Christianity tends to associate faith and worship with an intellectual pursuit rather than an activity. In reality, faith and worship involve bodily actions as well as the mind and spirit. The church definitely needs to harmonize its liturgical feeling and the kinetic expression of that feeling. To restrict emotional involvement and body movements renders worship sterile. Worship should be "an avenue through which the whole of man can celebrate."[2] Luther commented that God gave man five senses, with which to worship, and using less shows sheer ingratitude.[3]

No one should seek to tack body movements onto worship. "Worship itself is action."[4] An emotionally involved person finds bodily expression perfectly natural. When a person bows, G.W. Bromiley explains, "the gesture is expressive of humility, need, respect, submission, and adoration."[5]

Psalmic worship allows Christians to be themselves, and allows their normal performance to glorify God and demonstrate feelings toward Him. The Holy Spirit uses the bodily forms of Psalmic worship as meaningful ways for people to relate to God.

Particularly important, kneeling enhances spiritual life. John Wesley's advice was to "always kneel during the public prayer."[6] The motto of the Welsh Revival was: "Bend the church, and save the people." Unfortunately, some churches find kneeling awkward or unnecessary. H. Asmussen has said:

> It is curious to note that the kneeling of the congregation or of certain members of it is regarded as wrong in almost all Evangelical Churches. And yet there are thousands of faithful who long to have the right to kneel. We have become enslaved to a false shame, a shame which is rooted in the fact that we no longer dare to confess openly our faith.[7]

Peter Wagner makes a contrasting comment about Chilean Christians:

> In Chile the Methodist Pentecostals have even designed a unique kind of pew to allow for another motion—kneeling to pray. Crowded conditions push the pews so close together that there would not be room enough to kneel, if it weren't for the movable backs on the benches. When the signal is given, the congregation kneels and everyone pushes on the back of the bench ahead of him.[8]

Upon your knees

A marble cutter, with chisel and hammer, was shaping a stone into a statue. A preacher looking on said, "I wish I could make such changing blows on stony hearts." The workman answered, "Maybe you could, if you worked like me—on your knees!"

Many identify the beautiful picture of praying hands as the true symbol of prayer. Actually, bent knees comes closer to reality though it's more difficult to picture in an endearing way! James, the Lord's brother, was a classic example. The godly man lead the Jerusalem church until A.D. 61 when he was stoned to death. According to Hegesippus, quoted by Eusebius:

> He was in the habit of entering alone into the temple, and was frequently found upon his knees begging forgiveness for the people, so that his knees became hard like those of a camel, in consequence of his constantly bending them in his worship of God.[9]

Kneeling does four things

Gives you the right perspective. Kneeling is a deliberate act of submission and openly avows God's superiority. It expresses humility and subjugation to the will of God. It makes a person totally vulnerability and puts him in a position of surrender. No one can retaliate from this position. When a person kneels, he cuts himself down to insignificance! Theodor Filthaut explains kneeling as follows:

> Kneeling, a man makes himself small. He does not want to announce his greatness, but his abasement. In the true sense, man need kneel only to God. In this way he acknowledges God as the Lord of his life, as the supremely great and infinitely powerful One, and at the same time as the Creator who has called him out of nothing. Kneeling can even go the length of complete prostration upon the ground.[10]

Encourages you to be straightforward with God. Kneeling helps worshipers be more honest and conversational with God. Sometimes people pray as if they are preaching to God, but the Lord is not interested in speeches and orations. He does want people's love and conversation!

Enables you to concentrate better. The less the mind is distracted, the better the prayer. Kneeling before the Lord in sincerity and simplicity helps keep thoughts more clear. Spiritual things come into focus, and the will of God becomes more apparent. Kneeling helps calm the anxious mind.

Empowers you to serve. This beautiful sonnet on prayer by Archbishop Trench captures the change so beautifully:

> Lord, what a change within us one short hour
> Spent in thy presence will avail to make!
> What heavy burdens from our bosoms take;
> What parched grounds refresh, as with a shower!
> We kneel, and all around us seem to lower;
> We rise, and all the distance and the near
> Stand forth in sunny outline, brave and clear!
> We kneel, how weak! We rise, how full of power![11]

Old Testament examples

The Old Testament offers numerous illustrations of individuals and groups kneeling, prostrating themselves, falling down, or bowing low. The human form in bent posture best portrays reverential fear and dependence. The following examples illustrate that bowing was a common posture of prayer or worship:

- As Jacob approached death, he worshiped by bowing (Gen. 47:31).
- Moses bowed low as God passed before Him (Exod. 34:8; also Deut. 9:18).
- Gideon gratefully "fell to his knees" as God confirmed his plan (Judg. 7:15).
- David frequently bowed before God (Ps. 5:7; 45:11).
- Solomon unashamedly knelt before all Israel (1 Kings 8:54; 2 Chron. 6:13).

- King Jehoshaphat feared for his nation as a massive army gathered against him; leading the people in penitent prayer, he "bowed his head with his face to the ground" (2 Chron. 20:18).
- As Hezekiah rededicated the temple, he "bowed down" (2 Chron. 29:29).
- It is said of Daniel that "he kneeled upon his knees three times a day, and prayed, and gave thanks before his God" (Dan. 6:10).
- In great consternation over his people's sins, Ezra fell on his knees and prayed an impassioned prayer (Ezra 9:5). Later, he worshiped with Israel by bowing low with his face to the ground (Neh. 8:6).

The following individuals "fell on their face" prostrating themselves on the ground so their eyes faced down: Abraham (Gen. 17:3), Eliezer (Gen. 24:52), Manoah and his wife (Judg. 13:20), Ezekiel (Ezek. 1:28), and Daniel (Dan. 8:17). Also note Exod. 4:31; 12:27; Lev. 9:24; and 2 Chron. 7:3.

Helene Lubienska de Lenval makes the following observation:

> Certainly in the whole of biblical and Christian tradition prostration is the action most expressive of submission to God; none other signifies so well man's complete abasement before almighty power and divinity.[12]

New Testament examples

- Christ "knelt down and began to pray" His great prayer of agony in Gethsemane (Luke 22:41).
- Stephen, the church's first martyr, "kneeled down" as the angry mob hurled stones (Acts 7:60).
- When Dorcas died, the church called for Peter to come. Alone with her body, Peter "kneeled down and prayed" and restored her to life (Acts 9:40).
- Paul the apostle called together the Ephesian church elders, then unashamedly "kneeled down and prayed" with them all (Acts 20:36). He also "kneeled down on the shore, and prayed" with the Christian men, women and children of Tyre (Acts 21:5).
- The elders in heaven are constantly "falling down" in worship (Rev. 4:10; 5:8, 14; 7:11; 11:16; 19:4).

Paul states, "I bow my knees unto the Father of our Lord Jesus Christ" (Eph. 3:14), and also foretells that "every knee should [or must eventually] bow" (Phil. 2:10).

The heart of it

Subordinate to almighty God, believers bow their knees and acclaim "Jesus is Lord!" This is the heart of worship, and as Martin Luther said, "Where worship is offered from the heart, there follows quite properly also that outward bowing, bending, kneeling, and adoration with the body."[13]

Reflections

To kneel is a universal, symbolic act in all religions and offers a variety of meanings. It may express meditation, humility, contrition, sorrow, repentance, or the complete giving over of self.
                                                                    —*Margaret Fisk Taylor*[14]

The first element in worship is adoration. The Hebrews expressed this by their posture and not alone by their word. For they prostrated themselves before God. O come, let us worship and bow down; let us kneel before the Lord our Maker. They did not come with an easy familiarity into the presence of God, but were aware of his greatness and majesty, and came with a sense of privilege to this house.
                                                                              —*H.H. Rowley*[15]

Kneeling is a way of saying; "I fully understand who's Boss here. Far be it from me to try to manipulate you or play games with you. I'm well aware of my status in this relationship, and I deeply appreciate you taking time to interact with me."
                                                                            —*Dean Merrill*[16]

Because the risen Lord is really present, because the last things have their beginning in worship service, it behooves the congregation to drop to its knees even now before the King of kings and the Lord of lords, as it lauds and glorifies Him in its words.
                                                                          —*Peter Brunner*[17]

"He kneeled down and prayed." Note those words. Kneeling in prayer was Paul's favorite attitude, the fitting posture of an earnest, humble suppliant. Humility and intensity are in such a position in prayer before Almighty God. It is the proper attitude of man before God, of a sinner before a saviour, and of a beggar before his benefactor.
                                                                            —*E.M. Bounds*[18]

24

Dance!
Third use of posture

and a time to dance.
—Ecclesiastes 3:4

On the cover of the usually conservative *Presbyterian Life* magazine three young women were pictured "dancing before the Lord." The caption on the April, 1972, issue read, "Church dance: restoring an ancient tradition." Led by a pastor trained in drama and modern dance, Westminster Church in San Diego sought to demonstrate "that new and dramatic innovations in the church . . . can be ways of serving God that are both earnest and happy."[1] This church found their dance program united younger and older generations as well as enhanced their mutual worship experience. Religious dance was becoming acceptable in mainline Protestant churches.

Although religious dance always has been in the church, the past twenty years have seen an astounding proliferation of dance activities in churches worldwide. Dancing in the church today covers the entire spectrum from individual expressions of ecstatic joy to elaborate, choreographed, musical, dramatic productions. Dance seems like a new way to worship God only because the form has been neglected so long.

Nothing is more personal than one's manner of worship, so innovative approaches naturally raise suspicion, questions, and even antagonism. Religious dance certainly does that! Regardless of the formidable arguments presented for or against, the church will always have dancing children.

Our present objective

The vast amount of literature available on religious dance surprises the uninitiated.[2] Opinions run the gamut from a blissful, simplistic naivete that will experiment with any form of dramatic art to an unwillingness even to consider the importance of body expression for worship enhancement. Every local church will deal with the question: Does Psalmic worship in today's church include religious dancing? The subject is deceptively complicated, and it is doubtful any one solution can be found satisfactory to all.

David danced in worship and advocated, in the Psalms, that worshipers praise God in the dance. Today a pastor must ask himself two questions: "What does the Bible teach on this subject?" and, "How can religious dance benefit my church?"

Helpful definitions

Several definitions of dance provide a broad perspective. From *Random House Dictionary*:

> (1) to move one's feet, or body, or both, rhythmically in a pattern of steps, esp. to the accompaniment of music. (2) to leap, skip, etc., as from excitement or emotion; move nimbly or quickly. (3) to bob up and down.[3]

Margaret Taylor, a significant leader in religious dance for a number of years, gives this concise statement: "I define *dance* as moving in rhythm with a pattern of expression."[4] Debbie Roberts, in her enthusiastic book, *Rejoice*, says:

> Dance can be complex or simple. Dance combines thoughts of the heart and motor coordination to bring forth a structure of movement. As this structure takes form, it is called pattern movement or dance . . . . Dance has pattern and order just as music does.[5]

The International Standard Bible Encyclopedia defines dancing:

> Dancing, that is, the expression of joy by rhythmical movement of the limbs to musical accompaniment, is scarcely ever mentioned in the Bible as social amusement. Dancing can be grouped under two heads: the dance of public rejoicing and the dance which was more or less an act of worship.[6]

The power of kinetic expression

One of the most startling illustrations of dance I have encountered is the following account given by Rev. Richard Wurmbrand, who for fourteen years was a prisoner of the communists:

> Alone in my cell, cold, hungry and in rags, I danced for joy every night. The idea came to me with boyhood memories of watching dancing dervishes. I had been moved past understanding by their ecstasy, the grave beauty of these Moslem monks, their grace of movement, as they whirled and called out their name for God, "Allah!" Later I learned that many others—Jews, Pentecostals, early Christians, people in the Bible like David and Miriam, altar-boys in Seville Cathedral celebrating Easter, even today, also danced for God. Words alone have never been able to say what man feels in the nearness of divinity. Sometimes I was so filled with joy that I felt I would burst if I did not give it expression. I remembered the words of Jesus, "Blessed are you when men come to hate you, when they exclude you from their company and reproach you and cast out your name as evil on account of the Son of Man. Rejoice in that day and leap for joy!" I told myself, "I've carried out only half this command. I've rejoiced, but that is not enough. Jesus clearly says that we must also leap."

Dance! Third use of posture

When next the guard peered through the spy-hole, he saw me springing about my cell. His orders must have been to distract anyone who showed signs of breakdown, for he padded off and returned with some food from the staff room: a hunk of bread, some cheese and sugar. As I took them I remembered how the verse in St. Luke went on: "Rejoice in that day and leap for joy—for behold your reward is great." It was a very large piece of bread: more than a week's ration.

I rarely allowed a night to pass without dancing, from then on; although I was never paid for it again, I made up songs and sang them softly to myself and danced to my own music. The guards became used to it. I did not break the silence, and they had seen many strange things in these subterranean cells. Friends to whom I spoke later of dancing in prison asked, "What for? What use was it?" It was not something useful. It was a manifestation of joy like the dance of David, a holy sacrifice offered before the altar of the Lord. I did not mind if my captors thought I was mad, for I had discovered a beauty in Christ which I had not known before.[7]

In every possible situation, Christians have experienced the joy of Jesus which no man can take from them. Saint Francis of Assisi was known among his contemporaries as "The Dancing Fool" because he always danced and smiled in his outdoor worship. On many occasions I have gone into our church sanctuary alone and danced before the Lord just for the sheer exhilaration of His joy in my heart.

In a cartoon from the comic strip *Peanuts,* Charlie Brown's beagle jumps up and down, his floppy ears flying out behind him. A benign smile fills his face, and his eyes close in satisfaction. As he leaps, Snoopy says: "If you can't dance, at least do a happy hop!"

The use of body movement, or kinetic expression, has been argued by liturgical theologians and common worshipers alike. Such discussions cover more than dance, but since dancing is the most strenuous and energetic, it naturally draws the most attention, especially from people hesitant to participate in bodily worship. Yet, worship always requires *some* action of the body. Just standing or singing in a church service is kinetic expression. Closing the eyes or bowing the head also is a mild form.

Actions in worship can be symbolic but in a sense they "express man at his deepest level."[8] Sincere Christians from different backgrounds agree on the importance of bodily participation in the worship of almighty God. The following statements illustrate the same concern:

Man . . . responds to him [God] best not by a simple movement of the mind; but by a rich and complex action, in which his whole nature is concerned . . . . He is framed for an existence which includes not only thought and speech, but gesture and manual action; and when he turns Godward, his life here will not be fully representative of his nature, nor will his act of worship be complete, unless all these forms of expression find a place in it . . . . therefore those artistic creations, those musical sounds and rhythmic movements which so deeply satisfy the human need for expressive action, must all come in. (Evelyn Underhill).[9]

201

The body is put on ice until you leave most worship settings . . . . mainline churches do not have such movement anymore (D.C. Benson).[10]

As believers we need to return the physical to our worship services. We have become so "mental" in our worship that it's no longer worship. It is private thought or meditation. We worship God as whole people and our wholeness includes the physical. I believe that the church that has the courage to gain back the physical acts of worship will soon discover that their people will be alive and active in the Lord in a way they never thought possible (Peter E. Gillquist).[11]

Dancing in the Old Testament

According to the *Encyclopedia Judaica*, eleven verb forms describe dancing in the Bible.[12] Almost all references to dancing in the Old Testament refer to occasions of worship. Even welcoming returning armies, the dancing maidens acclaimed God's victory in holy war.[13] My first discovery of this prolific use of dance in the Hebrew Old Testament and culture came some years ago while reading this surprising statement in *David's Harp*:

> The ancient Hebrews must have danced on every possible occasion. We find countless passages in the Bible mentioning dance in the daily life of the people. Biblical Hebrew has no less than twelve verbs to express the act of dancing. When we add to these the many terms found in rabbinic literature, we can only conclude that no other ancient language possesses such a wealth of expressions describing its various aspects.[14]

For further research of the Hebrew, diagram 10, prepared by David Fischer, offers a guide to Bible references.[15] The Hebrew and Greek words listed are words whose root meanings involve forms of the dance (taken from Strong's Concordance); in the translation of these words into English, definitions are often broadened, and words such as "joy", "rejoicing", etc., are used. Some references are underlined, which indicates a clear, important reference.

Many words for dance are related generically while the common root is not always perceptible in the English translation. A scholarly approach should not lead one to a simplistic application of words based simply on their twentieth-century definitions. In a few centuries, word definitions commonly change. Approach such study cautiously.

HEBREW WORDS FOR DANCE

1. Gul; Gil: (Gool; Gheel): to spin round (under the influence of any violent emotion), i.e. usually rejoice, or (as cringing) fear: be glad, joy, be joyful, rejoice; to go in a circle

Psalms 2:11; 9:14; 13:4, 5; 14:7; 16:9; 21:1; 31:7; 32:11; 35:9; 43:4; 48:11; 51:8; 53:6; 89:16; 96:11; 97:1, 8; 118:24; 149:2; Isaiah 9:3; 16:10; 25:9; 29:19; 35:1, 2; 41:16; 49:13; 61:10;65:18, 19; 66:10; 1 Chronicles 16:31; Job 3:22; Proverbs 2:14; 23:24, 25; 24:17; Song of Solomon 1:4; Jeremiah 48:33; Joel 1:16; 2:21, 23; Hosea 9:1; 10:5; Habakkuk 1:15; 3:18; Zephaniah 3:17; Zechariah 9:9; 10:7.

2. Chul; Chil: (Chool; Cheel): to twist or whirl (in a circular or spiral manner), i.e. specifically to dance, to turn round, to dance in a circle; also to writhe in pain, especially of childbirth, to travail.

Deuteronomy 2:25; Job 15:20; Psalms 29:9; 55:4; Isaiah 13:8; 23:4; 26:17, 18; 54:1; 66:7-9; Jeremiah 4:19; Ezekiel 30:16; Joel 2:6; Micah 4:19; Judges 21:21, 23

Machol = a (round) dance, dancing, chorus. (from Chul above).

Psalms 30:11; 149:3; 150:4 Jeremiah 31:4, 13; Lamentations 5:15

Macholah = a dance company or chorus, dances (fem. of Machol).

Exodus 15:20; 32:19; Judges 11:34; 21:21; 1 Samuel 18:6; 21:11; 29:5; 1 Kings 19:16; Song of Solomon 6:13

3. Karar: to dance (whirl); to go or move in a circle.

2 Samuel 6:14

4. Rekad: to stamp, to spring about (wildly or for joy), dance, jump, leap, skip.

Psalms 29:6; 114:4,6; 1 Chronicles 15:29; Job 21:11; Ecclesiastes 3:4; Isaiah 13:21; Joel 2:5; Nahum 3:2

5. Dalag: to spring or leap.

2 Samuel 22:30; Psalms 18:29; Isaiah 35:6; Song of Solomon 2:8; Zephaniah 1:9

6. Pazaz: to leap, to bound, to be light, agile; (associated with root "to separate and purify metals from dross, by means of fire; to solidify as if by refining, be made strong.").

Genesis 49:24; 2 Samuel 6:16

7. Chagag: to move in a circle, specifically to march in a sacred procession, to observe a festival, celebrate (from the idea of leaping and dancing in sacred dances), keep a solemn feast; by implication to be giddy or drunken.

1 Samuel 30:16; Exodus 5:1; Leviticus 23:14; Psalms 42:4; Exodus 12:14, 17; 23:14; Deuteronomy 16:15 (A derivative of this word is the main Hebrew word for "feast.")

DIAGRAM 10

On one extreme, some scholars propose that many Bible texts were created to express moments in movement through song, actions, or dance rather than to simply provide texts for teaching and preaching. One leading exponent of this approach says:

> Dance lives at the heart of the Hebrew Scriptures; there is scarcely a chapter that does not have at least an indirect relationship to dance . . . the Bible as it was originally composed is not and never was intended to be simply philosophical theses or theological reflections about God. It is far more a "language event" . . . . That is, the form of a biblical passage indicates that it is often more like a happening than theory, more like a worship service than philosophy, more like a dance than a dissertation.[16]

Explicit dance passages occur in the Hebrew Scriptures. The contemporary rebirth of sacred dance in many churches and synagogues is easily traced to such passages as 2 Samuel, chapter 6, and Psalm, chapter 149. The following ten references best evidence the qualities of Hebrew dancing:

> And Miriam the prophetess, Aaron's sister, took the timbrel in her hand, and all the women went out after her with timbrels and with dancing (Exod. 15:20).

> The women came out of all the cities of Israel, singing and dancing, to meet King Saul, with tambourines, with joy and with musical instruments (1 Sam. 18:6).

> Is this not David, of whom they sing in the dances (1 Sam. 29:5).

> And David was dancing before the LORD with all his might, and David was wearing a linen ephod . . . . Then it happened as the ark of the LORD came into the city of David that Michal the daughter of Saul looked out of the window and saw King David leaping and dancing before the LORD; and she despised him in her heart (2 Sam. 6:14, 16).

> Thou hast turned for me my mourning into dancing: Thou hast loosed my sackcloth and girded me with gladness (Ps. 30:11).

> Let them praise His name with dancing (Ps. 149:3).

> Praise Him with timbrel and dancing (Ps. 150:4).

> and a time to dance (Eccl. 3:4).

> Again you shall take up your tambourines, and go forth to the dances of the merrymakers . . . the virgin shall rejoice in the dance (Jer. 31:4, 13).

Dances of the Old Testament could be referred to as the processional dance, the encircling dance, and the ecstatic dance.[17] Debbie Roberts has prepared a table of twelve different dances based on Old Testament references.[18] Dancing was part of the Hebrew culture. The degree to which today's local church should carry over this worship mode is open to debate because no one has a clear understanding of the styles used in Old Testament cultural and religious dancing. Could this mode of worship be a cultural experience as opposed to a spiritual one?[19]

Dancing in the New Testament

Marilyn Daniels, a strong advocate of religious dance, says simply: "The New Testament has no direct reference to religious dance."[20] Jesus did refer to dance but not in a worship sense (Matt. 11:16, 17; Luke 7:32; 15:25). He did tell those persecuted for righteousness to "leap" for joy (Luke 6:23).

The strongest argument presented for dance in the New Testament is based on the Greek word *agalliao*, translated "rejoice" in English Bibles. The lexicons make a strong argument for the word to be translated "dance," or "leap for joy." The noun form is found five times (Luke 1:14, 44; Acts 2:46; Heb. 1:9) and the verb form eleven times (Matt. 5:12; Luke 1:47; 10:21; John 5:35; 8:56; Acts 2:26; 16:34; 1 Pet. 1:6; 4:13). The word clearly means exultation, extreme joy, celebration; to gush, leap, spring up, to jump for joy.

Certainly New Testament believers were happy people. William Tyndale, in his prologue to the New Testament, catches this spirit of joy when he defines gospel in the Old English vernacular:

> Euangelio (that we cal gospel) is a Greke word, and signyfyth good, mery, glad and joyfull tydings, that maketh a mannes hert glad, and maketh hym synge, daunce, and leepe for ioye.

Because the New Testament does not advocate—or even mention—congregational religious dance, arguments have developed to explain this void! For instance, David Watson, author of the well-known *I Believe in the Church*, says, "it was never written about as it was never a problem in the early church." He advocates dance, believing that the apostle Paul (when he spoke of singing psalms) would suggest that both the musical instruments and dance would accompany the psalm-singing.[21] When Susan Fay, a liturgical dance teacher at Wheaton College, was asked how she justifies dance from a biblical point of view, she replied:

> I hate to segment the Bible into the Old and New Testament and act as if the Old Testament doesn't count any more. Dance is certainly a natural part of worship in the Old Testament. It was never censured so I think we can take it as exemplary.[22]

The basic biblical argument in favor of religious dance states: *because the New Testament text is silent, the silence implies that God gives tacit approval.*

Not everyone can be so liberal. A contrasting approach, strongly taken by many churches, is that of James Beall, pastor of Bethesda Christian Church in Sterling Heights, Michigan. He says:

> Our rule of procedure is: We embrace the truths of the Old Testament which are carried into the New Testament by the apostles and prophets. We stand upon their Scriptural foundation. We are instructed to sing Psalms, lift holy hands without wrath and doubting, and glorify God, but we are not instructed to dance. If ministers and congregations want to become involved in congregational dancing, that is their prerogative but they do not have sound Scriptural ground to stand upon and to biblically exhort others to do the same.[23]

Invariably, scholars who search for the roots of worship will dig into the church Fathers for appropriate quotes and verification. Statements by Chrysostom, Ambrose, Augustine, etc., though very interesting, are too scanty for any solid discussion. Their statements and the development of dance in church history is covered well in other sources.[24]

Contemporary use of dance in worship
Dancing in today's church takes several forms:
* The performance of religious dance.
* The congregational-participation dance.
* Ecstatic "dancing in the Spirit."

The performance of religious dance. Performance dance includes a wide range of activities from major stage productions with pageantry and choreography to a young person simply "signing" the words of a song.[25]

In dance and actions, young people in our church dramatized the parable of the sower and seed. In this type of dance, the church observes the presentation and vicariously experiences the message as it is being performed. People who dance in this manner make it a ministry and seek to convey a message as surely as if they were preaching. David Watson explains the benefit:

> There is little doubt that dance today is a perfectly valid form of praise and worship, especially in a generation that is increasingly word-resistant and that responds quickly to the language of movement. The Spirit of God is a Spirit of movement, and the formal and static nature of much of the worship of the church today does not help to communicate the reality of the living God and the vitality of those who have come alive in him.[26]

Performance can become exhibitionism, which is shameful. It happens so subtly. Congregational worship should emphasize total church participation. Dancers in front expressing their own feelings through artistic gestures may find personal satisfaction in a worship service, but they also can distract people endeavoring to personally adore God. On the other hand, certain lively choruses can be enhanced by an energetic worship-dance team. For instance, the large Verbo Church in Guatemala City has banner-waving youth dancing up and down the aisles during certain types of songs. They generate great enthusiasm.

A musical production seems ideal for people in performance ministry as well as for those who watch and vicariously participate. Regular church attenders and visitors come mentally prepared to relate to the message through the artistic medium. The setting creates no distractions, and a communication objective is beautifully achieved.

The congregational-participation dance. Many churches see that passages in the Old Testament need a congregational fulfillment, so leaders urge the entire church to participate in happy expressions of dancing before the Lord. Corporate exhibitions of praise and worship bring individuals and congregations to high levels of excitement. It is quite a joyful experience. As an example, Peter Wagner describes the Methodist Pentecostals in Chile:

> Spiritual dancing introduces a kind of motion into the worship services that the newcomer considers unusual at first, but later finds to be quite enchanting. Ordinarily during congregational singing or during a choir number, several individuals will begin dancing right in their pews, moving their arms and bodies with varying degrees of gracefulness. Some will find their way to the aisles or to open spaces at the back or front of the church. I once saw what must be the most unusual sign ever posted on the wall of a church: 'dancing on the stairs prohibited.' This was just another indication that not only order, but also physical safety is a concern of Pentecostal brethren.[27]

This type of dancing has no set form. Several churches in the San Francisco Bay area have racially mixed congregations. They cater to the racial mixture by encouraging corporate productions as well as individual efforts that reflect ethnic styles. I have seen happy folks dancing or shuffling in what were—to me—unbelievable ways. At least I could not duplicate them. Regardless of individual preferences, the bottom line still remains: good fruit will come from meaningful worship.

Ecstatic 'dancing in the Spirit.' This type of dancing has consistently been a trademark of revival-meeting ecstasy. Depending on the denomination, revival music often has been accompanied by dancing. Sometimes a person may dance alone, or several may dance together. Campmeetings of the past were characterized by enthusiasm, which sometimes broke out as people danced up and down the aisles. Smith Wigglesworth, one of the old-time Pentecostal pioneers, gave a cautionary word about these things:

> You can dance, if you will do it at the right time. So many things are commendable when all the people are in the Spirit. Many things are very foolish if the people round about you are not in the Spirit. We must be careful not to have a good time at the expense of somebody else. When you have a good time you must see that the spiritual conditions in the place lend themselves to help you and that the people are falling in line with you. Then you will find it always a blessing.[28]

To be excited and enraptured with God and His glory is truly exhilarating. Billy Bray, a converted Cornish tin miner in the early 1800s, became a literal folk hero because of his love and enthusiasm for God. Billy probably was the "dancingest" Christian that ever lived. He said:

> Bless the Lord! Well, I dance sometimes. Why shouldn't I dance as well as David? David, you say, was a king; well, bless the Lord! I am a King's son! I have as good a right to dance as David had. Bless the Lord! I get very happy at times; my soul gets full of the glory, and then I dance too! I was home in my changer t'other day, and I got so happy that I danced, and the glory came streaming down upon my soul, and it made me dance so lustily that my heels went down through the planchen (floor boards).[29]

Some appropriate guidelines

Here are a few guidelines:
1. Bodily expression in worship should not be discounted, but it should not be done in a lewd and sensual manner.
2. The biblical base does not seem to be established for a literal transfer of Old Testament happenings into the New Testament church service, especially when we talk of a Hebrew cultural-spiritual experience such as dancing maidens greeting the returning armies.
3. Worship should be geared to involve the whole congregation and not just supply a channel for a few artists to find personal satisfaction. Individual performance must enhance, not detract from, corporate worship satisfaction. The congregation should follow the directions of the worship leader.
4. The worship of the local church should have a reasonable explanation from Scripture.
5. Local churches should ask themselves, "Where will this form of worship lead us?" and
6. "Will this form of worship bring any reproach?" and
7. "Are those who lead worship properly attired?"
8. If a church learns to live on performance and entertainment, true worship in Spirit and truth will soon be lost. The form of worship must glorify God and edify people.
9. A balanced use of religious dance can be an edifying experience for today's church. Although the New Testament does not advocate dancing, it seems that as with musical instruments, clapping, etc. (which also are not mentioned in the New Testament, yet are permitted in churches that refuse dancing), it is nevertheless a natural way for people to joyfully participate in the worship of God.
10. This subject needs to be viewed with tolerance. It is possible for every church to maintain an acceptable form of worship—and teach it firmly to its own people—without being hostile or antagonistic to other groups.

In the final analysis, each church must be responsible for the spiritual fruit and practical results that come from whatever approach is espoused.

Reflections

The universal language of symbolic movement is one of the rare religious arts which finds response in all who witness it, from the oldest to the youngest, the most spiritually sensitive to the seemingly insensitive, the most vigorous to those in need of health. The experience of religious insight that the congregation feels in the interpretations of a symbolic dance choir has a spiritual reality which draws everyone together into a spiritual union.

—*Margaret Fisk Taylor*[30]

No area of communication is more dependent on symbolic expression than is religious experience. The close connection between religious feeling and expressive movement, the dance, has been coeval with the history of man.

—*Marilyn Daniels*[31]

If worship be the response of the whole man, it must be in outward expression as well as inward intention. This is especially true of man as the bible presents him—an animated body energized by spirit. Further, and again, in the biblical understanding of man, he is essentially a member of a society, and in his worship specifically a member of the people of God, and worshipping community. It is that total community that gives depth and meaning to the individual life. Worship therefore must include recognized public acts and words through which and whom God is known to approach His people. It is by such criteria that the media of worship must be constantly tested.

—*A.S. Herbert*[32]

Dancing is not a profane thing that one might introduce as if by force into the sanctuaries of our churches. It does not enter into the temples of prayer as a stranger, but rather as a daughter of God. Song is the joy of the voice; dancing is the joy of the body. Together, singing and dancing, both created by God, must, like all his other creatures, praise the Lord . . . . It is thus that God himself, in his word that manifests itself to us in Psalm 150, demands that we dance for his praise. Not as a concession made to the weakness of man does he ask for dancing, but as a valid means of praising him. Who dances for God, then, accomplishes his will.

—*Lucien Deiss and Gloria Weyman*[33]

Part VII

Psalmic Worship
in the New Testament

The following five chapters present solid arguments for believing that Psalmic worship was a vital part of the early church and should occur in today's churches.

- Chapter 25 **Universal Appeal and Acceptance of the Psalms**
  The vibrant, pulsing life of the Psalms makes it a favored source of inspiration for all Christians.

- Chapter 26 **Sound Biblical Hermeneutics**
  Five key principles from hermeneutics confirm that the worship modes of Psalms are appropriate for church life today.

- Chapter 27 **Davidic Theology of the New Testament**
  The Psalmic writings of David and the Davidic Covenant strongly influenced and shaped the emerging theology of the New Testament church.

- Chapter 28 **Psalmic Praise in the New Testament**
  Upon comparing the praise in the Psalms with praise in the New Testament, we discover an undeniable sameness. Does worship differ from praise?

- Chapter 29 **The Celebrative Nature of the Early Church**
  From sterile synagogue to celebrative church! The worship of the new Jewish Christians could not be contained in Judaism's old wineskins.

25

Universal Appeal
and Acceptance of the Psalms

Jesus answered them, "Yes. Did you never read this,
'Out of the mouths of little children, yea, of infants,
you have perfect praise'?"
—Matthew 21:16 w

This is the first of five chapters contending that Psalmic worship, in methodology and theology, is an essential part of New Testament Christianity and should be used in today's church renewal. Support for this proposition comes in the next five chapters. Each chapter explains one of the following five arguments:
- The appeal and acceptance of the Psalms.
- Sound principles of biblical hermeneutics.
- Davidic theology of the New Testament.
- Psalmic praise in the New Testament.
- The celebrative nature of the early church.

First of five arguments:
The lasting appeal and universal acceptance of the psalms and their message clearly justify Psalmic worship in today's church.

A profound religious experience permeates David's writings. An irresistible, magnetic spiritual intensity pulses through the book. The living words are poetically grand and attract people in every generation. Behind the hymns and prayers are real people who experienced a vivid relationship with God, which is what every believer wants.

An overarching awareness of God weaves through the writings. The book's appeal centers in this "God consciousness" evident in every chapter. Readers easily relate to the gamut of human feelings expressed in lamentation and in jubilation, but the awareness of an immediate, involved God encourages—even enthralls—readers. "Thus every Psalm," as Leslie S. M'Caw writes it, "becomes a draught from the very fountain of life."[1]

Psalms seems like a New Testament book. Readers sense an affinity with the writers of Psalms more than with other Old Testament authors and books. That helps

213

explain why the Psalms are often printed in New Testament editions. Most Christians easily accept the New Testament and Psalms as appropriate for today. Samuel Terrien comments:

> Here is to be found religion so pure, so deeply spiritual, that without the least sense of obtrusion we can place it alongside the profoundest ideas and the loftiest heights of aspiration in the words of Jesus or Paul.[2]

Christians throughout the church age have quoted, prayed, read, and declared the Psalms as a vital part of their present experience in God. As early Christians burned at the stake or faced lions in the Roman arena, they sang undaunted, "I will bless the Lord at all times; his praise shall continually be in my mouth" (Ps. 34:1). John Huss recited Ps. 31:1 as he went to the stake, and so did Jerome of Prague a year later. Savanarola was left unharmed in A.D.1498 so that he could write his confession to the church; instead he composed a meditation on Psalms, chapters 31 and 41. Martin Luther was fascinated with the Psalter and called it a Bible in miniature. The Huguenots put the Psalms to music. Through a century of persecution, European Protestants typically met death singing Ps. 118:24, "This is the day . . ." The Catholic leader, Thomas More quoted Ps. 51:1 at his execution. The Puritans sang the psalms as they arrived in the New World. The famous "Bay Psalm Book," *The Whole Book of Psalms*, was the first book published in the American colonies.

The universal appeal of the Psalms is clearly seen throughout the church world. "No other book of hymns and prayers has been used for so long a time and by so many diverse men and women."[3] Andrew W. Blackwood says:

> This is the supreme book of praise in the history of corporate religion, the only book of sacred song which the students of English at Princeton and Oxford rank among the masterpieces of world literature. Here is the most important book in the Old Testament, at least for the student of public worship.[4]

Psalms is not just about God. It is about David and others like him who have a relationship with God. Although certainly emotional, the Psalms are spiritual and liturgical, having what Elmer A. Leslie calls "the poetic rhythm of spiritual exaltation."[5] The force of a musical poetry sweeps prayerful readers heavenward and causes souls to repent and congregations to rejoice. Behind it all lay the inspired piety and genius of the psalmists. God used them to create wonderful words for summoning His people to worship His majesty.

Whoever argues that the Psalms are not meant for today's church has to show proof from the New Testament. Christ and His apostles treated the Psalms (including the expressive forms) as appropriate for their day. The Christian church has consistently followed their tradition.

The problem today does not lie in the acceptability of Psalmic worship. Rather, the problem lies in finding the same God-consciousness and sincerity as the psalmists had. Those attitudes are prerequisites for such worship.

If Christians accept the Psalms on a par with the New Testament, they should accept worship forms contained and explained in the Psalms. All sects of the Christian church commonly quote expressions of jubilant worship from the Psalms, particularly when exhorting people to worship. Why do they only read and quote? *Doing* those things they have been reading about for years also is appropriate!

Jesus and the apostles accepted the Psalms as God's Word and so does the church today. However, for some reason, today's churches tend to take all the exuberant expressions of praise and interpret them only as singing. Is it right to read Ps. 66:1 and 81:1, which command worshipers to shout joyfully, yet never actually shout joyfully? To read clear biblical statements requiring action without actually doing such action fosters disbelief in the congregation.

Consider the clear references on musical instruments used in the praise of God. Also notice the various Hebrew words used for praise, some of which indicate the lifting of hands and dancing before the Lord. Some psalms specifically mention bowing and prostration. Also, this question is inescapable: "Why do we urge each other to sing 'a new song unto the Lord' when we sing the same songs Sunday after Sunday?"

Young Christians have a right to rise up and ask, "Why don't we do what we say we believe? It's embarrassing to profess a religious belief without doing what you confess. If Christians are to obey other instructional teachings of the Bible, then why not Psalmic worship, especially since Psalms is generally accepted by the universal church on a par with New Testament books?"

Consider two final, significant questions. First, "If God permitted, even encouraged, the entire person to be involved in worship in the Old Testament, why would he forbid it in the New?" and second, "Is it logical for the Psalms to call all nations to Davidic praise and then have the whole idea dropped by the early church as it evangelized those nations?" It does seem unlikely.

Reflections

The influence of the Psalms on Christian hymnody must never be overlooked. The fact that the Psalter was the principal hymnbook for the church for the first thousand years of its existence simply cannot be ignored.

—*Robert G. Rayburn*[6]

After studying the biblical accounts revealing how our God was praised at the beginning of time, in the Old Testament, in Jesus' earthly ministry, in the early church, and foreseeing how we will worship in Heaven, does your heart cry out with mine, "Oh, God, reveal to your church how we may praise You acceptably today!"?

—*Larry Lea*[7]

I earnestly believe it is the desire of God's heart today that all of His children enter into the ministry of Davidic praise and worship. David did. The apostles did. And all over the world today, the church of Jesus Christ is being drawn to adore God in this way.

—*Anne Murchison*[8]

The Father is renewing His people, seeking those who are willing to worship Him in Spirit and truth. One of the ways He is doing this is by restoring a Biblical form of worship in His church. He is drawing us into an intense, intimate and expressive worship—worship earmarked not only by outward expressions of worship such as bowing, kneeling, lifting of the hands, but worship which causes us to come before Him with a renewed expectancy.

—*John Wimber*[9]

If all the copies of the Old Testament were lost or destroyed, any scholar who could remember the text of the Psalms would have at his disposal the essential materials for an Old Testament theology; for the Psalter is, in a sense, the first of all Old Testament theologies.

—*G.W. Anderson*[10]

The reason for this continued vitality of the psalms is that their words are directed to God, they are prayers and appeals to Him . . . . they retain those fundamental aspects of man's appeal to God which remains constant over all boundaries and through all changes in patterns of prayer.

—*Claus Westermann*[11]

26

Sound Biblical Hermeneutics

*Be diligent to present yourself approved to God as a workman
who does not need to be ashamed,
handling accurately the word of truth.*
—2 Timothy 2:15

Second of five arguments:
**Sound principles of biblical hermeneutics confirm that Psalmic worship was
practiced by New Testament Christians and is appropriate for the church today.**

The thoughts of God come to man through the Bible. To communicate His thoughts, God put them in words. The science and art of interpreting God's words to understand His thoughts is called hermeneutics. Over the years, scholars have attempted to establish hermeneutical guidelines and rules for interpretation. These rules attempt to answer the following three basic questions: (1) What has God said? (2) What did God mean in what He said?, and (3) What does this mean to me today?

Over the years, countless interpreters have developed and refined dozens of hermeneutical principles. This chapter examines five major principles.

Seek the literal sense
Principle 1: *Interpret the Bible literally.* The Bible should be interpreted according to its literal sense. Since the Bible is a work of literature, the methods of literary scholarship apply to any complete study of the Bible.[1]

"Whenever we read a book, an essay, or a poem," says Bernard Ramm, "we presume the literal sense in the document until the nature of the literature may force us to another level."[2] Sound interpreters first seek the ordinary meaning of words. Their desire must be to identify "the most natural, clear, evident meaning."[3] This is a safe, sane approach that guards the integrity of the Scripture, protects the scholar from excessive imagination, and allows for reasonable applications. David L. Cooper of the Biblical Research Society calls the following the "The Golden Rule of Interpretation":

217

When the plain sense of Scripture makes common sense, seek no other sense; therefore take every word at its primary, ordinary, usual, literal meaning, unless the facts of the immediate context, studied in the light of related passages and axiomatic and fundamental truths, indicate clearly otherwise.[4]

Looking for the literal sense involves other rules such as seeking to find the genre or literary mold of the writing. The book of Psalms is Hebrew poetry, much of which was put to music. Does that make exhortations like "praise the Lord," "shout unto God," and "praise Him in the dance," merely poetic imagery? Are these statements simply figurative and not literal commands to obey?

From the start, the entire Christian church has acknowledged Psalms as poetic, understanding that statements on forms of worship are to be taken literally. For instance, when David says, "So I will bless Thee as long as I live; I will lift up my hands in Thy name" (Ps. 63:4), he certainly meant that he would literally, physically lift his hands. The early church took these statements literally because Paul told Timothy, "I want the men in every place to pray, lifting up holy hands" (1 Tim. 2:8). This is reasonable.

Leland Ryken has a common-sense rule to determine if a poetic statement is to be interpreted figuratively. He says to interpret as figurative any statement that does not make sense at a literal level in its context.[5] The Davidic forms of worship (speaking, singing, shouting, lifting hands, playing instruments, clapping, standing, bowing and dancing) make perfect sense literally, even though they may appear in poetic literature.

Psalmic worship styles pleased Jesus. His disciples were literally "praising God joyfully with loud voices," shouting in the best Davidic tradition, when they were criticized by Pharisees. Jesus rebuked the Pharisees saying, "I tell you, if these become silent, the stones will cry out!" (Luke 19:40). The stones—foundation stones of the New Testament church—*were* crying out!

Retain context

Principle 2: *Consider every verse contextually*. The context of each verse is the entire book of Scripture. Examine the context: the immediate passage as a whole and the book as a whole.[6] This is what is meant by "Scripture interprets Scripture."[7] No doctrine should run contrary to the tenor of the whole body of Scripture. The bulk of Scripture controls the interpretation of any single or obscure passage. Vague passages must fall in line with the plain.

Consider the context of two extreme forms of psalmic expressions: clapping hands and shouting. "O Clap your hands, all peoples; Shout to God with the voice of joy" (Ps. 47:1) or "cries of joy" (NIV). These exuberant worship forms show up not only in Psalms but also in the revivals in Judah under the monarchy and during the rebuilding of the temple. Israel shouted when the people marched around Jericho (Josh. 6:10). Shouting and jubilation filled Israelite festivals. Jesus Himself confirmed shouting as an authentic worship form when he rebuked the chief priest and scribes for criticizing the children who were crying out in the temple, "Hosanna to the Son of David!" (Matt. 21:15). Jesus quoted Ps. 8:2 in defense of the children's shouts. Paul unashamedly said, "we cry out, 'Abba! Father!'" (Rom. 8:15), referring to the

Davidic statement, "He will cry to me, 'Thou art my Father'" (Ps. 89:26). And jubilant shouts of the redeemed give the book of Revelation its climax. When the voice from the throne urges, "Give praise to our God," the heavenly congregation responds with a roar of praise that sounds like thunder! (Rev. 19:5, 6).

The Bible depicts the people of God in Old and New Testaments as responsive, demonstrative worshipers. The New Testament does not provide much doctrinal explanation, but it does describe people actually worshiping in the Psalmic emotional-physical modes considered normal and appropriate. The New Testament does not need detailed explanations on how to worship simply because the subject is so adequately covered in the Psalms.

Bernard Ramm suggests this rule: "We may take direct application from all of those incidents that the Bible directly censures or approves."[8] Believers learn from the faith of Abraham, the obedience of Moses, the loyalty of Elijah, and the love of John the Apostle. The worship of David can be added to the list in harmony with this hermeneutic principle. God still approves of the fervent, demonstrative worship described throughout the Bible. The book of Psalms fulfills what J. Edwin Hartill calls "The Full Mention Principle", which states:

> God declares His full mind upon any subject vital to our spiritual life. Somewhere in the Word, God gathers together the scattered fragments that have to do with a particular truth, and puts them into one exhaustive statement. That is His full mind concerning that truth.[9]

Luke records that the disciples "were continually in the temple, praising God" (Luke 24:53). He did not explain doctrine or methods; he simply recorded in general terms what is already understood by psalmic worshipers. When Paul says, "Rejoice in the Lord always; again I will say rejoice!" (Phil. 4:4), he does not find it necessary to explain something so much a part of the worship schema of the Psalms.

Scattered New Testament references simply allude to a subject fully explained in Psalms. Milton S. Terry explains a verifying principle:

> The obscure or doubtful passages are to be explained by what is plain and simple. A subject may be only incidentally noticed in one place, but be treated with extensive fullness in another.[10]

Hartill's principle called "The Direct Statement Principle" bluntly says, "God says what He means, and means what He says."[11] Apply this principle to statements on worship in the Psalms. Remember the early Reformers' primary rule of hermeneutics: *Sacra Scriptura sui interpres* (Sacred Scripture is its own interpreter). No interpretation can produce conflict with what is clearly taught elsewhere in Scripture. The worship behavior of New Testament believers and the wondrous praise of the book of Revelation merely illustrate the principles already given by the psalmists.

Read passionately

Principle 3: *Read the Bible experientially.* This rule is good, but sometimes it is subject to extreme applications. R.C. Sproul suggests "that as we read the Bible, we ought to get passionately and personally involved in what we read."[12] Christians ought to read experientially, particularly during responsive readings of the Psalms in church services. The very purpose for using Scripture in congregational meetings it to incite a greater emotional response among the congregation in worship. Passively reading the following call to worship is not the same as appropriating it and actually doing it.

O Come, let us sing for joy to the LORD; Let us shout joyfully to the rock of our salvation. Let us come before His presence with thanksgiving; Let us shout joyfully to Him with psalms (Ps. 95:1, 2).

Just as the author of Hebrews says:

Through Him then, let us continually offer up a sacrifice of praise to God, that is, the fruit of lips that give thanks to His name (Heb. 13:15).

People have a tendency to talk about God, but the book of Psalms draws the believer into direct dialogue with God. The Bible and the God of the Bible are meant to be experienced.

Apply it to everyone

Principle 4: *Apply Scripture universally, unless told not to.* Every teaching of Scripture applies to every person, unless the Bible itself limits the audience. All Scripture should be received as normative by all people in all societies of all time. The audience may be limited only by the context of the passage or the larger context of teaching elsewhere in the Bible.

The following principle stated by J. Robertson McQuilkin holds great practical value.[13] The Bible interpreter must answer the question: Is the message of the passage to people of all time, or is it to some specific person or group that does not include me? New Testament writers' comments on Old Testament teachings clearly identify concepts and practices that have been abolished, replaced, or updated. The writers also comment on whether Old Testament information should be taken literally, spiritually, or symbolically.

This concept can be condensed into the following basic hermeneutical question: "Has the death, burial, and resurrection of Jesus Christ in any way affected, changed, or abolished the Old Testament idea under consideration?" For example, the message of faith from the Abrahamic covenant continues on in the church (Gal. 3:9). On the other hand, circumcision from the Abrahamic covenant ceased to have religious significance at the Cross and is not demanded today by God (Gal. 5:6; 6:15).

Consider the Mosaic covenant. Levitical dietary laws, that prohibit eating unclean animals, are no longer in effect (Mark 7:29; Acts 10:15; Col. 2:16). However, the New Testament clearly endorses the moral laws in the Ten Commandments.

Nothing in the New Testament halts the worship emphasis of Psalms. In fact, such worship is the rightful spiritual inheritance of all nations. The Psalms frequently summon the nations to praise the Lord. The following psalm validates universal Psalmic worship:

> O God, in mercy bless us; let your face beam with joy as you look down at us. Send us around the world with the news of your saving power and your eternal plan for all mankind. How everyone throughout the earth will praise the Lord! How glad the nations will be, singing for joy because you are their King and will give true justice to their people! Praise God, O world! May all the people of the earth give thanks to you . . . people from remotest lands will worship him (Ps. 67:1-7 LB).

God issues a powerful, prophetic call for the Gentiles to join Israel in worship in the following:

> Praise the LORD, all nations; Laud Him, all peoples! For His lovingkindness is great toward us, And the truth of the LORD is everlasting, Praise the LORD! (Ps. 117:1-2).

Paul understood God's desire for a universal—and perpetual—audience for worship. He used the verse above to prove the Gentiles may glorify God in Rom. 15:9-12. He also included quotations from Ps. 18:49 and Deut. 32:43 to prove that the Gentile Romans can worship now with believing Israelites:

> and for the Gentiles to glorify God for His mercy; as it is written, "THEREFORE I WILL GIVE PRAISE TO THEE AMONG THE GENTILES, AND I WILL SING TO THY NAME." And again he says, "REJOICE, O GENTILES, WITH HIS PEOPLE." And again, "PRAISE THE LORD ALL YOU GENTILES, AND LET ALL THE PEOPLES PRAISE HIM."

David and Paul clearly intended to include believers from all nations in the Scriptural praise of almighty God. McQuilkin says:

> We must take the psalms, the teachings of Christ, and the teachings of the epistles as universal in their application and normative for us today because that is the way the early apostles took those teachings.[14]

Although Mosaic, Levitical elements stopped at the Cross, Psalmic elements of worship continue now and carry into eternity. Jesus sang psalms (Matt. 26:30), and He continues to sing in the midst of the church's worship (Heb. 2:12). Nothing in the New Testament depreciates, dilutes, or discontinues the worship and praise that characterizes the Psalms. The Gospels, Acts, Epistles, and the Revelation seem charged with statements about the joy of the Lord. The sacred New Testament record seems to have been conceived and birthed in the spirit that inspired the Psalms. This Psalmic factor runs through the Bible and determines whether a church is dead or alive today.[15] The overcomers of Revelation, chapter 15, combine the best of both

Testaments (the song of Moses and the song of the Lamb) to present a universal paean of praise to the God of all ages and all nations:

> Great and marvelous are Thy works, O LORD God, the Almighty; Righteous and true are Thy ways, Thou King of the Nations. Who will not fear, O LORD, and glorify Thy name? For Thou alone art holy; For all the nations will come and worship before Thee, For Thy righteous acts have been revealed (Rev. 15:3, 4; Ref. Ps. 86:9).

See the movement of God

Principle 5: *View revelation progressively.* Revelation is progressive in the sense that God brings man up from spiritual and theological infancy to maturity.[16] God initiated the movement to reveal Himself. He started revealing truth about Himself and His ways in Genesis and brought the movement to a climax in Christ, who revealed the Father incarnate (John 14:8-9). God's movement through history is recorded in the various covenants or agreements He made with man. Every Scripture has historical and covenantal settings that determine its relationship to other Scriptures.

Historical and theological themes develop in logical sequences in the Bible. The development of most themes can be traced from Genesis to Revelation. Under each successive covenant, themes pick up more detail and amplification. The principle of progressive revelation can be very important to interpreters who see the Bible as one book with one author.

Kevin J. Conner and Ken Malmin in their book, *Interpreting the Scriptures* explain a unique principle they developed called "The Chronometrical Principle."[17] They propose that God has divided and arranged time into a series of ages, times, and seasons, which are successive, each age making way for another. Each age is characterized by one of God's covenants. The Bible interpreter's job is to determine what is abolished in each age and what carries over into another.

Principle five actually combines elements of various principles which recognize that God has dealt with man in terms of dispensations, covenants, ethnic division, and cultural and historical settings.[18] Interpreters must make honest attempts to place their studies in proper relationship to the total Bible mosaic.

In the current messianic or church age, the indwelling Holy Spirit enables people to worship. The Holy Spirit did not dwell in people during any other dispensation. The church age extends from the Cross to the second coming of Christ. During this time, the forms and signs of the Abrahamic and Mosaic covenants are of no literal importance to the worship of the church.

In contrast, the Davidic covenant is very much in effect. God is revealing and using the key of David (Rev. 3:7). Christ is on the heavenly throne of David as king and also as the high priest of the Melchizedek priesthood (Heb. 6:20). The Davidic or Psalmic worship forms continue through this period because no Scriptural evidence calls for them to be dropped. They continue now (and in heaven) as channels through which the Holy Spirit ministers His grace and gifts to the church.

Reflections

This is the primary and basic need of hermeneutics: to ascertain what God has said in Sacred Scripture; to determine the meaning of the Word of God. There is no profit to us if God has spoken and we do not know what He has said. Therefore it is our responsibility to determine the meaning of what God has given to us in Sacred Scripture.

—Bernard Ramm[19]

Scripture itself must determine whom God would have believe and obey a given teaching. If the context itself does not make that clear, appeal may be made to other passages. But in the end, external criteria may not be imposed on Scripture to disallow its applicability to contemporary life.

—J. Robertson McQuilkin[20]

My habitual procedure in the study of this subject is to examine the New Testament interpretation of the Old Testament exegetically, to consider each instance of Old Testament quotation, allusion or application in its immediate New Testament context. This procedure, I am sure, is basic and indispensable. But when it has been followed, the occasion arises to stand back at some distance and view the whole picture—in particular, to consider the dominant motifs which recur throughout the biblical literature and bind the two Testaments together.

—F.F. Bruce[21]

Christian worship should be biblically based. The substance of Christian worship should be biblical. This principle is today shared by Roman Catholic and Protestant alike. This substance should reflect the whole of the Bible and not just select portions of it. Moreover, worship should be representative of the whole of biblical faith—faith of the Bible, critically and prayerfully understood. Worship is not biblical, however, when it simply quotes the Bible. Worship is wholly biblical when the God who spoke through the Bible speaks again.

—David J. Randolph[22]

27

Davidic Theology
of the New Testament

"What do you think about the Christ, whose son is He?"
They said to Him, "The son of David."
—Matthew 22:42

Third of five arguments:
An unmistakable foundation of Davidic theology in the New Testament undergirds and authenticates Psalmic worship for today's church.

David's writings and the covenant God made with him strongly influenced the emerging theology of the New Testament church. The Jews and the early church gave high esteem to David and the prophecies concerning him. This chapter looks at the following seven areas that illustrate the pervading esteem.
* Jesus' use of Psalms.
* Expectations in the Gospels.
* Psalmic quotations in the New Testament
* Covenant comparisons.
* David the King-Messiah.
* A Priest upon His Throne.
* The priesthood of Melchizedek.

Jesus' use of Psalms
Jesus avidly read and memorized the Psalms. He frequently used them in ministry. He sang Psalms with His disciples (Mark 14:26). The Psalms became liturgical food for His inner life, the foundation for His devout piety and walk with God. He absorbed them into His very mental nature, and they helped guide Him in His quest to do the Father's will (Luke 24:44).[1]

His intense prayer in Gethsemane fulfilled the repeated cry "Why are you in despair, O my soul?" (Ps. 42:5, 6, 11 and 43:5).[2] On the cross, Jesus quoted Ps. 22:1 ("My God, My God . . .") and Ps. 31:5 ("Into Thy hand . . .").

When children cried out in the temple, "Hosanna to the Son of David," the chief priests and the scribes became indignant and challenged Jesus to do something about it. Jesus' surprising answer shows an insight that could originate only from a worshipful heart. He said, "Out of the mouths of children and infants You have made (provided) perfect praise" (Matt. 21:16 AMP; Ps. 8:2).

The Gospels contain other illustrations that verify the loving obsession Jesus had with David and his psalming associates. Jesus' manner of personal, spontaneous celebration followed the style modeled in the Psalms. After all, He accepted the boisterous Davidic behavior of the children and His own disciples!

Expectations in the Gospels

New Testament writers show links between the early church and Old Testament characters like Abraham and Moses, but Jesus' messianic ministry has more direct ties to David. Christ comes as a Davidic king to reign on a Davidic throne over a Davidic people.

Jesus was born in the city of David (Luke 2:4). He is called "the Son of David" by His genealogy (Matt. 1:1), by blind men (Matt. 20:30, 31), by children (Matt. 21:15), by multitudes (Matt. 21:9), and by the Syrophoenician woman (Matt. 15:22). The multitudes of Jesus' day expected the Messiah to be the Son of David (Matt. 12:23), and all that Jesus did was evaluated on that basis. The Pharisees believed that the Messiah would be the Son of David (Matt. 22:42). The Book of Revelation says that Jesus has the key of David (3:7), that Jesus is the Root of David (5:5), and that He is the Root and Offspring of David (22:16).

Certain prophetic psalms give clear-cut predictions about the Cross and the Resurrection. Psalm, chapter 22, is so exact in its description, it appears to be history instead of prophecy! Spurgeon called it "The Psalm of the Cross," and made this observation:

> It may have been actually repeated word by word by our Lord when hanging on the tree; it would be too bold to say that it was so, but even a casual reader may see that it might have been. It begins with, "My God, my God, why has thou forsaken me?" and ends, according to some, in the original with "It is finished."[3]

Psalmic quotations in the New Testament

Jesus and the early church frequently used the Psalms. The New Testament writers quote the Psalms more frequently than any other Old Testament books. Stanley A. Ellisen estimates that "of the 360 quotations and allusions to the Old Testament in the New, nearly one-third (112) come from the Psalms."[4] Eighty times, the New Testament quotes between four and five dozen portions of Psalms.[5]

Jesus and His followers considered the Psalms a vital, significant part of their belief and worship. There is no reason to accept the prophetic passages and ignore the modes of free Davidic worship expression.

Covenant comparisons

New Testament writings draw heavily from the story of Abraham and the covenant God made with him. Abraham's faith, the sign of circumcision, the promised seed, and the promised land carry significance for the New Testament believer. Moses' writings and leadership in Israel also lay down important foundations for the church; however, the Davidic covenant is more foundational to the New Testament than covenants with Abraham or Moses. Neither Abraham nor Moses find as close association with messianic destiny as David. It is true that the Messiah was to be "the seed of Abraham" (Gen. 22:18; Gal. 3:16) and "a prophet like Moses" (Deut. 18:15; John 5:45; Acts 3:22; 7:37), but these descriptions of the Messiah rise to significance only in the light of God's Word to David.

Jesus never claimed an association with David. He did not personally publicize His greatest claim but left that for others (Isa. 42:2; Matt. 12:16, 19). The early church directly declared that Jesus was the living king-messiah on David's throne. Early apostolic leaders found inspiration and revelation in God's promise to David, the Davidic Covenant, and David's writings. This importance should not be overlooked, according to F.F. Bruce:

> If the theology of the New Testament writers has been influenced by the divine covenants made with Abraham and later with his descendants in Moses' day, it has been manifestly influenced also by the covenant which Yahweh established with David and his house.[6]

Church leaders in that day proclaimed that the Tabernacle of David and David's kingdom had been restored spiritually. These revolutionary ideas stimulated strong emotions that could be satisfied only through the dynamic worship modes of David. The way David is mentioned and quoted (sometimes anonymously) brings the man and his ministry to special, undeniable prominence.

The Davidic King-Messiah

The idea of their Messiah sitting on the royal throne, fulfilling the Davidic covenant, caught the fancy of the Jewish people. Hard times had fallen on the Jews when Jesus arrived on the scene. Like a liberty bell, the message of God's kingdom rang throughout the Holy Land: the kingdom of heaven is at hand! The people's hope for the Messiah's appearance had reached a fever pitch. The Jews looked for a political and military kingdom to replace the harsh Roman oppression. They wanted utopia. Most people hardly considered a spiritual fulfillment of the Davidic covenant. Only later, after the Holy Spirit came to the church, did the truth become apparent.

The Davidic covenant promised a descendant of David would always sit on David's throne as long as the people remained true to the teachings of God.[7] Here is one of many passages stating God's promise:

> The LORD has sworn to David, A truth from which He will not turn back; "Of the fruit of your body I will set upon your throne. "If your sons will keep my Covenant, And My testimony which I will teach them, Their sons also shall sit upon your throne forever" (Ps. 132:11, 12).

> Other references: 2 Sam. 7:8, 12, 13, 16; 1 Kings 2:4; 6:12; 8:25; 9:4, 5; 1 Chron. 17:11-14; Ps. 89:3, 4, 29-37; 132:11; Isa. 7:13, 14; 9:6, 7; Jer. 33:14-22.

Unfortunately, some of Judah's kings had been idolatrous and rebelled against God. Wickedness under King Manesseh (2 Kings 21:11-15) had become so great that God brought judgment on Judah. An unbroken line of David's descendants had occupied the throne until the reign of Zedekiah, who was the last to rule over Judah. The natural kingdom came to an end. The earthly throne, the Davidic crown, and the royal heredity was history. Unrealized by the Jews, the eternal, spiritual nature of God's promise to David continued to move forward.

The apostles proclaimed Jesus Christ as heir to David's throne. They taught as fact that He now reigns over His people from that throne.[8] All future theological developments in the New Testament rest on this foundation. The messianic aspect of the Davidic Covenant becomes the New Covenant of the Lord Jesus Christ. Kevin Conner summarizes the situation:

> The glory of the Davidic Covenant becomes apparent when we realize that it finds its true fulfillment in David's son, Messiah Jesus, and in the New Covenant. It is the New Testament writers who take these . . . things in the Davidic Covenant and apply them to Christ and His church. Hence, that which was natural, national and material in the Davidic Covenant is found to be everlasting only in and through the spiritual, the heavenly and eternal in the New Covenant in Christ and the church.[9]

The New Testament opens with a four-book review of the life and ministry of Jesus the Messiah. The Gospels begin with genealogies that establish His royal descent. They record His amazing fulfillment of hundreds of Old Testament messianic predictions. [10]Eyewitness accounts of His death, burial, resurrection, and ascension verify His right to the Davidic throne.

On earth, Jesus ruled under the divine mandate given to David's kingdom, and he used it to cast down Satan, heal the sick and proclaim the Gospel. He understood that after His ascension, the kingdom would fill the earth. His announcements of the kingdom of God cannot be understood apart from terms of the Davidic covenant.

Throughout the Acts of the Apostles, the church boldly used Jesus' resurrection to confirm His legitimate right to Davidic kingship. Three major events following Christ's resurrection made strong use of Davidic theology:

Peter's first sermon points to David. After introducing the Christian era as led by the Holy Spirit, Peter uttered his key thought: Jesus Christ was raised from the dead and now sits on David's throne in heaven (Acts 2:30-36). In the heart of his sermon, Peter quotes from the Psalms four times, twice referring to the resurrection (Ps. 16:8-11, 25-28, 31) and twice referring to the Davidic throne (Ps. 132:11; 89:3, 4; 110:1, 31, 34, 35). Incidentally, one of these passages, Ps. 110:1, is the most-quoted Old Testament portion in the New Testament! George Eldon Ladd clearly worded the following summary:

> The exaltation of Jesus to the right hand of God means nothing less than his enthronement as messianic King . . . . Peter means to say that Jesus has entered in upon a new stage of his messianic mission. He has now been enthroned as messianic King . . . . Because of the resurrection and ascension of Jesus, Peter transfers the messianic Davidic throne from Jerusalem to God's right hand in heaven. Jesus has now been enthroned as

the Davidic Messiah on the throne of David, and is awaiting the final consummation of his messianic reign.[11]

Paul's first recorded sermon points to David. The first message Paul preached to the gentiles also contained Davidic emphasis. Paul maintained that the resurrected Jesus is a descendant of David (Acts 13:23), the begotten Son of God according to David (v. 33), and that Jesus has been given "the holy and sure blessings of David" (v. 34).[12] He quotes from Ps. 89:20; 2:7; Isa. 55:3; Ps. 16:10, and Hab. 1:5.

The first recorded apostolic council of the early church looks to David. This historic conference admitted believing Gentiles into the body of Christ without requiring them to be circumcised or keep the Law of Moses (Acts, chapter 15). It was held at Jerusalem by the recognized, Jewish, Christian leaders. This issue almost divided the church despite Paul's testimonies about God's miraculous work among converted gentiles.

To settle the controversy, the apostle James arose and quoted the Greek version of Amos 9:11-12 by divine insight. Amos had delivered the unusual prophecy at a time of natural prosperity and spiritual apostasy in Israel. It foretold the restoration of the Tabernacle of David. The restoration of the royal dynasty would, in turn, restore God's people and bring the Gentile nations under the name of the Lord.

James used the passage as a proof-text to allow converted Gentiles into the church without undue legalistic requirements. The expression *Tabernacle of David* was interpreted in that context. With Jesus Christ on the heavenly (Davidic) throne, the Davidic dynasty (the house or tabernacle) was restored, and the Davidic Covenant was fulfilled. The tabernacle refers to the dynasty or house of David and all it involves, including worship. The dynasty had failed through apostasy. The descendants of Judah had foundered without a king. James reaffirmed that the nationalistic promise is fulfilled in the new Israel of God comprised of all believers in Jesus Christ, both Jew and Gentile.

The assembled leaders agreed with this concept. King Jesus, already on His throne, was proclaimed Messiah-King. The elders and apostles easily saw James' logic in picking up the rest of Amos' prophecy. It referred to a gathering of Gentiles under the name of the Lord. James and the elders interpreted the prophecy to mean that converted Gentiles could come into the church. Fulfillment of the Davidic covenant was broad enough to include all nations. God had opened a door to the Gentiles because the house of David was restored through the resurrected Jesus, the Messiah. James' interpretation was considered a cardinal teaching of the emerging Jewish Christian church.

The restoration of David's tabernacle was a brush with a broad stroke. It meant Christ was spiritually enthroned in heaven and the promises of the Davidic Covenant were fulfilled. In line with His announcements through the Hebrew Scriptures, God began blessing all people through the Davidic priesthood of Jesus.[13] The Davidic Covenant invited all nations to join the covenant people in faith in Christ. It gave the Gentiles an open door to salvation and to Psalmic worship.

The apostle Paul thought that as the Gentiles enter, they should use the scripturally approved method to praise and worship God! In Rom. 15:9-13, he urged converted Roman Christians to join their hearts in Psalmic praise. Choosing three exhortations from the Old Testament, Paul states that this is how all nations may "glorify Him for His mercy." In verse 11, he quotes:

Praise the LORD, all nations; laud Him, all peoples! (Psa. 117:1).

The two Hebrew words used in the quotation and their definitions are :

Hâlal: To laud, to boast, to celebrate, to be joyfully excited, to be explosive in enthusiastic praise, to extol God's greatness, to acclaim His exploits.

Shâbach: To shout joyfully, to laud, to commend, to address in a loud tone, to praise in an exclamatory fashion.

(See more on Hebrew praise words in chapter 28.)

A priest upon His throne
Aware of biblical prophecy, the Jews had watched and waited for a man to restore the Davidic throne. Mystery shrouded his arrival. They knew he would be a descendant of David, but no one knew when he would appear. The promised Messiah or Christ was to be like a branch (shoot, twig, or sprout) springing out of a dead stump.

Then a shoot will spring from the stem of Jesse, and a branch from his roots will bear fruit . . . . Then it will come about in that day that the nations will resort to the root of Jesse (Isa. 11:1, 10).

The dead stump in Isaiah, like the fallen Tabernacle of David in Amos, symbolized the devastated house or dynasty of David. E.W. Hengstenberg, in his classic study, *Christology of the Old Testament*, contends that the cut-off trunk and the deteriorated Tabernacle of David communicate the same concept through different images. He states:

The very expression "tabernacle" suggests the idea of a sunken condition of the house of David. The prophet sees the proud palace of David changed into a humble tabernacle, everywhere in ruins and perforated. The same idea is expressed by a different image, in Is. xi.1.[14]

The coming, royal, Davidic descendant later will be called *Branch* by the prophet Zechariah, a nickname that ties Him directly to the line of prophecies already given by Isaiah and Jeremiah:
- In that day the *Branch* of the Lord . . . (Isa. 4:2, emphasis added).
- a *shoot* will spring from the *stem* of Jesse and a *branch* from his roots (11:1, emphasis added).
- the nations will resort to the *root* of Jesse (11:10, emphasis added).
- Like a tender *shoot*, and like a *root* (53:2, emphasis added).

- I shall raise up for David a righteous *branch* . . . will reign as king (Jer. 23:5, emphasis added).
- I will cause a righteous *Branch* of David to spring forth (Jer. 33:15, 16, emphasis added)

A prophecy in Zechariah says the coming Messiah will fulfill prophecies about the Branch. This Branch will not only be a king but also will be a priest (Zech. 6:9-15). The coming Messiah will be a worship leader, which is the primary task of a high priest.

Zechariah's account begins with messengers arriving in Jerusalem from the Jewish exiles in Babylon. The messengers had brought silver and gold for rebuilding the temple. Zechariah is commanded to take gold and silver from them and make crowns (plural in the Hebrew) for Joshua, the high priest. Gold symbolizes the king's office and silver symbolizes the priestly office. One man can wear only one crown, so the one crown finally constructed must have combined the two metals creatively.

E.B. Pusey suggests, "the silver might have formed a circlet in the crown of gold,"[15] and C.F. Keil comments that "The plural *ataroth* denotes here one single splendid crown, consisting of several gold and silver twists wound together, or rising one above another."[16]

No high priest ever had been a king, too. Two Israelite kings had attempted to perform priestly functions and were severely judged: King Saul when he offered sacrifice (1 Sam. 13:9) and King Uzziah when he attempted to offer incense (2 Chron. 26:18). Still, Zechariah goes to Joshua the high priest and, placing the ornate crown upon his head, prophetically declares that One who is already a high priest will be made a king as well. Joshua is not the One, but he symbolically receives the Davidic, Messianic crown. For that moment, he cooperated in a dramatic, prophetic parable that pictured the intent of the messianic mission.

The heir to the Davidic throne also would be a priest—a King-Priest! The Amplified words (and interprets) the statement Zechariah declares over Joshua as follows:

> Thus says the Lord of hosts: [You, Joshua] behold (look at, keep in sight, watch) the Man [the Messiah] whose name is the Branch, for He shall grow up in His place and He shall build the [true] temple of the Lord.

> Yes, [you are building a temple of the Lord, but] it is He Who shall build the [true] temple of the Lord, and He shall bear the honor and glory [as of the only begotten of the Father], and shall sit and rule upon His throne. And He shall be a *Priest upon His throne,* and the counsel of peace shall be between the two [offices—Priest and King] (Zech. 6:12, 13).

Joshua stands before the prophet representing the coming Messiah whose name would be *Tsemach* meaning the Branch, the Sprouting One. Tsemach would be "a man who would sit upon His throne as both ruler and priest, that is to say would combine both royalty and priesthood in his person and rank."[17]

After the ceremony, the crown was kept in the temple as a memorial for exiles who contributed to the temple's construction and as proof of God's intent and promise.[18] The exiles also symbolized the distant nations that would help build His temple. Zechariah's prophecies, like those of Amos, predicts the New Testament church comprised of Jew and Gentile. F.F. Bruce summarizes this conclusion:

> Just as the promise to build a house for David was fully realized not in Solomon but in Christ, so the prediction that David's son would build a house for God was consummated not in Solomon's temple but in the new temple of Christ's body in which His people "are built . . . for a dwelling place of God in the Spirit" (Eph. 2:22).[19]

This story from Zechariah is foundational to New Testament theology. Jesus Christ is the Branch (Romans 15:12). That means He is not only a Davidic king but also a Davidic priest. The Davidic priesthood of Christ, the Branch, confirms the use of Psalmic worship in the church.

The Melchizedek priesthood

In Psalm, chapter 110, David prophesied the Messiah would be like Melchizedek. Melchizedek was a mysterious character who had a kingly and a priestly nature. He lived in Abraham's time. David reached back a thousand years to refer to Melchizedek. The strange character from the book of Genesis was not mentioned again in Scripture until the book of Hebrews picked up his name and the even stranger prophecy from Psalms.

Hebrews is the key doctrinal worship book in the New Testament and supplies major theological underpinnings for Jesus' office of priest.[20] Introducing the Messiah as king in the following verses 1 and 2, David also proclaims Him a priest in verse 4:

> The LORD says to my Lord: "Sit at My right hand, Until I make Thine enemies a footstool for Thy feet." The LORD will stretch forth *Thy strong scepter* from Zion, saying, "Rule in the midst of Thine enemies."

> The LORD has sworn and will not change His mind, *"Thou art a priest forever* According to the order of Melchizedek" (Ps. 110:1, 2, 4, emphasis added).

Like David, the writer of Hebrews has prophetic insight that transforms the brief account in Genesis into a glorious picture of the ascended Jesus acting as the "worship leader" in heaven. The modern title fits old covenant high priests who led worship through their sacrificial ministry, and the title fits Jesus' present heavenly function as well.

> We have such a high priest, who has taken His seat at the right hand of the throne of the Majesty in the heavens, *a minister* in the sanctuary, and in the true tabernacle, which the Lord pitched, not man (Heb. 8:1-3, emphasis added).

As a minister, "He abides a priest perpetually," (Heb. 7:3) and He "holds His priesthood permanently" (7:24). The Old Testament high priest was "appointed to offer both gifts and sacrifices" for himself and others. The statement is then made "that this high priest (Jesus) also has something to offer."

However, Jesus made only *one* sacrifice. Heb. 7:27 says, "this He did once for all when He offered up Himself."[21] Through His great sacrifice on the cross, Jesus obtained eternal redemption for His people. Now, He no longer needs to shed blood or repeat His sacrifice. Jesus, "who through the eternal Spirit offered Himself without blemish to God" (9:14), offered a sacrifice so perfect and complete that it never needs to be repeated. His death on the cross also became the one perfect act of worship in all of history. It was so perfect that it became the mediatorial vehicle that makes Christians' prayers and worship acceptable to God!

Now, as the Davidic high priest, He mediates between God and man. He sits enthroned at the right hand of God (10:12), "a great priest over the house of God" (10:21). We are encouraged to draw near to God through this heavenly intercessor (7:25). The Book of Hebrews closes with a good Psalmic exhortation (13:15):

> Through Him then, let us continually offer up a sacrifice of praise to God, that is the fruit of lips that give thanks to His name.

Believers offer this method of worship in the name of the Lord Jesus Christ, and their inadequate offerings suddenly become acceptable as Jesus presents them to the Father. Worshipers of the Father, in turn, become priests. Peter calls Christians "a royal priesthood, to offer up spiritual sacrifices acceptable to God through Jesus Christ" (1 Peter 2:5). Thus the church becomes "kings and priests" or a "kingdom of priests" (Rev. 1:6; 5:10), fulfilling God's desire expressed in Exod. 19:6, "and you shall be to Me a kingdom of priests and a holy nation."

Revelation, chapter 5, best describes Jesus' Melchizedek activity in heaven. There He appears as the lamb of God "standing, as if slain" in the midst of heaven's throne room. The New English Bible words the expression, "a lamb with the marks of slaughter upon him," and the Living Bible reads, "on the lamb were wounds that once had caused his death."

Because of His sacrificial death on the cross, Jesus is worthy to receive acclamation from all creation. Elders and living creatures prostrate themselves before the Lamb. Harps play. Singers sing a new song. A great shout fills the heavens:

> Worthy is the Lamb that was slain to receive power and riches and wisdom and might and honor and glory and blessing (Rev. 5:12).

It sounds like Psalmic worship! Voices, hands, and posture combine in the action, and the Melchizedek priesthood worships. Praise is given to the Lamb (the only worship leader capable of soliciting such a response), and the true "Minister of the sanctuary" passes all glory on to the Father.

Reflections

Jesus of Nazareth, crucified by men, said the apostles, has been highly exalted by God. Great David's greater Son reigns, more gloriously than great David himself ever did, as Prophet and Priest and King; but He bears this triple dignity as the Servant of Yahweh who crowned His service by "pouring out his soul to death."

—F.F. Bruce[22]

The subject is THE PRIEST-KING. None of the kings of Israel united these two offices, though some endeavoured to do so. Although David performed some acts which appeared to verge upon the priestly, yet he was no priest, but the tribe of Judah . . . . The Priest-King here spoken of is David's Lord, a mysterious personage typified by Melchizedek, and looked for by the Jews as the Messiah. He is none other than the apostle and high priest of our profession, Jesus of Nazareth, the King of the Jews.

—Charles H. Spurgeon[23]

This David . . . declared that the ultimate Priest should be One like Melchizedek . . . . It is certainly an arresting fact that this was the Psalm [110] which our Lord made use of when He was attempting to bring the rulers of His time to a recognition that the Messiah would be the Son of God.

—G. Campbell Morgan[24]

The believer-priests of the New Testament are to offer, not animal sacrifices as did the Aaronic priest, but the sacrifices of praise. The Rabbis had a saying, "in the future time all sacrifices shall cease; but praises shall not cease."

—Kenneth S. Wuest[25]

28

Psalmic Praise
in the New Testament

Enter into His gates with thanksgiving [tôwdâh]
And into His courts with praise [tehillâh].
Be thankful [yâdâh] to Him, and bless [bârak] His name.
—Psalm 100:4

Fourth of five arguments:
Psalmic praise explains the enthusiasm, power, and success of the New Testament church. It flowed through the people like a mighty, spiritual undercurrent supporting and sustaining all they did. The New Testament text yields profuse evidence of the Hebraic forms of praise in the early church's doctrinal teaching and real-life situations.

A theme of praise flows like a river through the entire Bible, yet much of it has been largely overlooked.[1] Leah, one of Jacob's two wives, uttered the first recorded praise when her son, Judah, was born. The theme climaxes with heaven's voice summoning all servants to "Praise our God!" (Rev. 19:5). The tragic oversight of such a massive content of praise, says Paul E. Billheimer, is "to the shame and defeat of the church."[2] Fortunately, efforts by local churches and denominations are correcting the neglect as worship renewal sweeps through Christendom. Seminars, symposiums, and new worship-oriented magazines and books all play a part in this constructive appraisal.[3] More and more of God's people these days are lifting their hearts, hands, and voices in enthusiastic praise to the living God.
Information in this chapter will:
* Stress the importance of both personal and corporate worship.
* Reexamine the definition of worship and the possible differences and similarities between praise and worship.
* Introduce the seven major Hebrew praise words.
* Present the New Testament references which prove that the early church joyfully carried on the Davidic tradition of Psalmic praise.

Importance of personal and corporate worship

Public, congregational worship reflects the way individuals express their worship and praise to God.[4] Meaningful congregational worship services flow out of personal lives of devotion to God. It is the only thing a person can do now that carries over into eternity! No one ever should minimize the importance of maintaining a personal life of worship. Jim Hayford stresses, "praise is a way of life. As worshippers, we never leave the living presence of God. To think of worship as something that can happen only in a sanctuary or with musical accompaniment is to horribly limit our understanding of why we even exist . . . . Worship is a moment-to-moment reality as people learn to recognize God's presence constantly with them."[5]

The Christian's personal life should be an act of worship. The Bible urges, "present your bodies a living and holy sacrifice, acceptable to God, which is your spiritual service of worship" (Rom. 12:1). Personal worship is important; however, corporate worship occupies the focus of this book. Healthy personal spiritual development requires both.

Worship glorifies God

The words *worship* and *praise* have come to mean the same thing. The word worship came from the cumbersome word *worth-ship*. It meant that people acknowledged God's true worth and assigned it to Him. Its roots stretch back into the days of Shakespeare.

As time passed, the French word *gloire* came to compete with the Anglo-Saxon word *worth* to convey the idea of having a right opinion about God and properly acknowledging His attributes. Popular opinion came to favor the French word.[6]

Consequently, believers normally speak of glorifying God rather than worth-ifying Him. Linguistically, the *worship* of God now means the same thing as *praising* God or *glorifying* His name. They all occur by our having a right opinion of God and then acknowledging His worth and perfection.

The following words by John R. W. Stott ring true in every worshiper's heart: "Christians believe that true worship is the highest and noblest activity of which man, by the grace of God, is capable."[7] All real, biblical worship rests on this foundational concept. It guides the efforts of Christians wishing to experience "true worship."

Does worship differ from praise?

Finding and describing differences between praise and worship challenges the best Bible scholars. It is not easy. It resembles the difficulty in differentiating the human body from the soul. They overlap, intertwine, fuse, and bond together, defying attempts to come up with an all-inclusive statement.

The preceding chapters (particularly 9 and 10) hold a number of definitions and statements about worship, yet it seems impossible to produce a comprehensive definition of worship that is satisfactory to all. As Barry Liesch has said:

> Christian worship has so many aspects to it that it is futile to expect a single definition to embrace the subject adequately.[8]

Bob Sorge makes a similar comment:

> Many have struggled with finding an adequate definition of worship. Praise is not hard to define, but worship is another matter. No one definition seems to adequately express the fullness of worship—perhaps because worship is a divine encounter and so is as infinite in its depth as God Himself.[9]

Even original Greek and Hebrew words do not draw a line between praise and worship. They offer no neat, clear-cut statement distinguishing between the two words. Contemporary definitions tend to be more sophisticated than those of the Hebrew *shâchâh* or the Greek *proskuneo*. Perhaps the ancient people understood the awe of God better than today's Christians, because their words simply meant to bow down in total humility before almighty God.

The Gospel of Christ adds insights of love, grace, thanksgiving, mercy, forgiveness, the ministry of the Holy Spirit, and of our heavenly high priest, Jesus. These concepts enhance and enlarge the worshiper's understanding, but they must not obscure the profound simplicity of the ancient practice of prostration before His Majesty.

Four approaches
The following four quotations reflect much of today's thinking about the comparison of praise and worship. First, a rather simplistic comparison includes prayer as well:

> Prayer is the occupation of the soul with its needs.
> Praise is the occupation of the soul with its blessings.
> Worship is the occupation of the soul with God Himself.[10]

Second, Vivian Hibbert suggests the following distinction:

> Praise: When I say "thank you" to God for what He has done.
> Worship: When I thank and adore Him for what He Himself is.

Third, Judy Christie-McAllister in *Worship Leader* magazine offers a thoughtful perspective:

> I see worship as intimacy with God. We often hear the terms "praise and worship" spoken in one phrase. Praise and worship are two different things. Praise is what we do because of who God is and what God has done for us. Worship is when He comes and fellowships with us because of our praise. The Scriptures talk about the rocks crying out, the morning stars singing and the trees of the field clapping their hands. His creation—the rocks and trees and stars—don't have a relationship with Him, but they praise Him. Only those that have a relationship with God, those that can be intimate with Him, that are made in His likeness, can worship Him. Worship is a response to His presence because of an intimacy that only comes with relationship.[11]

A fourth comparison comes from Jim Hayford's book, *Contending for the Authentic:*

PRAISE: An expression of approval, esteem or commendation. We praise God for who He is . . . not what He has done.

WORSHIP: An attitude of our innermost being directed towards God. We distinguish between praise as an act or physical expression and worship as a frame of mind.[12]

Personal conclusions

Today's generation likes simple, quick directions and solutions. Folks in the computer age like to put words on the screen and click on the answer. That's so simple. Praise and worship do not disclose themselves to the searching heart that easily. After all, this is the highest occupation a human being is capable of. The glorious, many-faceted activity defies minute analysis.

On a subject like tennis, a person can read books and learn the basic concepts. He can watch tennis matches and vicariously project himself into them, but watching tennis does not actually put him on the court, holding the racket, and responding to the ball hurtling toward him like a missile! Likewise, someone may develop an accurate verbal description of interacting with God in worship, but it would not make him a worshiper. Human emotions, feelings, and attitudes interact amazingly with the Spirit of God.

Knowing how inadequate mere definitions are, I attempted in diagram 11 to present a more visual summary. Perhaps seeing the various synonyms for worship categorized like this can reduce this complex subject to at least a more understandable approach.

Definitions are necessary. Somehow *facts* must enter people's minds so that *faith* takes hold in their hearts and allows *feelings* of actual experience. But God must help. The easy, verbal compartmentalization of the most glorious activity known to man can be so sterile. As men seek the God they love, they need His Spirit to translate words into reality.

Facts and rules in the mind must fade into the actual activity so worshipers can carry out basic movements and postures routinely without destroying the flow of enjoyment that springs from spontaneity and interaction.

CORPORATE WORSHIP

Corporate worship occurs when the gathered church, seeking to glorify God, publicly offers heartfelt acknowledgment of His supreme worthiness as almighty God. Ranging from grand, declarative, jubilant statements to deeply personal devotional love and appreciation, the church rejoices in God. Using appropriate physical and vocal expressions, they glorify the Father, through the Name and Person of the Lord Jesus Christ, enabled and inspired by the Holy Spirit.

PRAISE
(Laudatory Worship)

Voices and actions declare in extravagant, joyful fashion how wonderful God is. This praise conveys heartfelt gratitude and thanksgiving for all that He has done and will do for us. It tells God what He means to us and to all of creation. It enthusiastically expresses our warm approval, admiration, and commendation of God.

THE HIGHEST PRAISE
(Devotional Worship)

In deep reverence, awe, wonder, and adoration our innermost beings pour out directly to God. Here we minister to God for who He is not just for what He has done for us. We love Him with a deep devotion and admiration that truly causes praise to be worship in the best sense of the word.

Celebration: *To observe God's greatness with festivity and excitement; to express delight; to make proclamation; to sing praises and make music.*

Acclamation: *To shout or salute Him with enthusiastic approval, acceptance or welcome; to acclaim God's exploits.*

Laudation: *To applaud, compliment, acclaim, commend; to boast excitedly; to speak well of, congratulate; to magnify God with our whole being.*

Confession: *To admit, acknowledge, avow our shortcomings; to recognize, affirm, and state God's deity, attributes, and works.*

Thanksgiving: *To bless, render thanks; to remember joyfully He is the source of all our blessings.*

Gratefulness: *To express appreciation and gratitude; to acknowledge that God is the origin of power and prosperity and even, at times, of difficulty; to "bubble" with praise.*

Glorification: *To give honor and high praise to God; to extol or praise lavishly the glory or excellence of God; to eulogize.*

Esteem: *To regard with favor; to respect and place the highest value on.*

Adoration: *To express our deep love to God for His divinity.*

Wonderment: *To be astonished, awe-struck, or surprised by the marvel of His presence.*

Reverence: *To fear God with genuine sincerity; to honor and respect profoundly.*

Humility: *To bow low in humble recognition of His total supremacy; to give place to.*

Exaltation: *To elevate or raise God to the highest position in our feelings and attitudes.*

Love: *To enjoy God; to experience intense affection and warm feeling for God and Jesus Christ; to rejoice, to delight in God.*

Awe: *To sense the awful majesty of God, an emotion of mingled reverence, dread, and wonder—a respect tinged with fear.*

Veneration: *To regard with respect or reverence; to esteem the worth of.*

Relationship: *To experience association or kinship; to cry with understanding, "Abba! Father!" to respond in love to God because of His love toward me.*

DIAGRAM 11

Synonymous terms

The Scripture strongly emphasizes a number of varied, enthusiastic ways to magnify God. The more I review the references and definitions, the less I am convinced any significant difference exists between praise and worship. I conclude that praise and worship are synonymous terms, with praise emphasizing the public acclamation of God, and worship emphasizing intimate, personal, devotional communication.

If all the praise passages in the Bible were eliminated from the discussion of worship, hardly any Scripture would remain to explain worship. In some references in the next section, several praise words may appear in the same verse. The subtle differences of emphasis are all variations of the same great activity: Worship!

Revelation, chapter 19, describes one of the greatest worship scenes of all times. A voice cries out, "Give praise to our God!" The responsive, thunderous sounds of God's redeemed could certainly be called praise, but who would argue that it is not worship? It is in that context John is told to "Worship God!" (v. 10 NIV).

Because Jesus declared we must worship in Spirit and truth, some people tend to feel that authentic worship is more ethereal, personal, or invisible. Admittedly, real worship is not always outwardly expressed or visible to others. It *can* be personal and spiritual, silent and in solitude, intimate, and not always observable by others. A good heart attitude *sometimes* strikes emotional fire as the Christian sings an old hymn, or bows in contrition, or stands with hands raised in adoration—simple, undramatic, pure worship.

A person need not be militant, aggressive, or boisterous to qualify as a worshiper, but neither should he be hesitant about or hostile toward the celebrative praise and worship that dominates the Scripture references. An unemotional or unfeeling worshiper should not be discouraged. If his heart is right, he will bless God and be blessed by God. Sometimes believers need the experience of a simple, straightforward intellectual worship that acknowledges God without feeling. Settle the matter: God can be worshiped an infinite number of ways!

Perhaps the total picture of the church's relationship with God is one great activity rather than two. Imagine worship as a circle with concentric rings. The most personal, fulfilling experience lies at the heart of the circle. This would represent the highest quality of devotion, the most directly communicative, and the most deeply spiritual experience of worship. But the outer rings moving concentrically into the heart of worship, also represent worship, even if they are called the public praise of God. This is why I labeled the two columns of diagram 11 as I did.

I cannot prove biblically that all praise is not worship or that all worship is not praise. Some expression is meant to be laudatory in the sense that it is bold, public, militant, and outspoken. Nevertheless, it is correctly called worship. Also, I believe a person can praise the Lord silently.

Diagram 11 lists ingredients of worship but does not say how worship can be accomplished. Many books attempt a "how-to" approach to worship that is self-defeating. Worship involves forms and modes, but the mechanical aspects of worship are merely expressions of inner, spiritual feelings and experiences. Believers must follow the exhortations of the Psalms as they worship, but they also should realize that trying to manufacture genuine, exciting worship apart from faith and the activity of the Spirit is not possible. David Watson gives some good advice on this point:

The church that is seeking for renewal in its worship must first seek for renewal in its experience of the Holy Spirit. Liturgical revision may be a helpful aid to worship, but it can never be a substitute for a fresh effusion of the Spirit's power.[13]

Seven key Hebrew words for *praise*

More than fifty different words in the Hebrew Scriptures denote praise. The words are not all translated "praise," but they all describe the action of praising God.[14] Some words appear only once while others appear more than sixty times. The following section contains the seven key words.

A helpful way to visualize all the Hebrew and Greek words which translate as "praise" in the English King James Version is to refer to "praise" in *Young's Analytical Concordance*. On pages 766 and 767, look under "praise," "to praise," "to give or sing praises," and "(worthy) to be praised."[15] Four columns of tightly, minutely printed quotes (over 200 occurrences taken from a dozen different Hebrew and Greek words) are neatly arranged under the various original words that are translated "praise."The seven key Hebrew words are easily identified in this setting.[16] If each of these Hebrew and Greek words are researched further to find additional English words used in their translation in other Scriptures, the concept of praise in the Bible becomes a factor of far-reaching consequence!

The following list of words can be studied in depth using the numbering system established by *Strong's Exhaustive Concordance*.[17] The words are arranged below to proceed from the most-used to the least. This list does not mention every Scripture where the word appears, but a few good references for each Hebrew word illustrate the meaning. Footnotes provide additional references and resources.[18]

One helpful resource book, *The New Englishman's Concordance*,[19] includes the lexical number from *Strong's Concordance* for each word in the Hebrew word listings. Students can easily look up a Hebrew word and benefit from the information given. In contrast to *Strong's* or *Young's*, *New Englishmen's* lists all the places that a Hebrew word occurs in the Old Testament and how it is translated in the King James Version. The references are categorized according to word use (such as, infinitive, imperative, etc.).

The following definitions have vitality. Clearly, praise is demonstrative! Ronald B. Allen, professor of Hebrew Scripture at Western Seminary, describes the corporate context for the seven words under consideration:

> By "praise," the psalmists have in mind a specific type of response to God that is *vocal* and *public* in nature. In the mind of the psalmists, there is no thought of "silent praise" or of "quiet, personal praise."Praise is a biblical word, and needs to be defined biblically. There are a score of words in the Psalms that may each be translated by "praise," but they all have these two things in common: Biblical praise is done aloud, and is done in the presence of others.[20]

1. hâlal, *haw-lal´* S.C. 1984. Appearing about 121 times in the Old Testament,[21] *hâlal* comes from a primitive root meaning to be clear, to be brilliant, primarily used of a clear, sharp tone or sound.[22] The idea is "to shine, to give light"; hence, to make a show, to boast, even to be clamorously foolish or to rave. Most of the time it is translated by some form of praise. Summary thoughts:

- To laud, to boast
- To celebrate with rejoicing
- To make illustrious, glorious (as done with a loud voice)[23]
- To make a show
- To be clamorously foolish; to rave[24]
- To be joyfully excited
- To praise God explosively and enthusiastically
- To acclaim God's exploits
- To boast excitedly[25]
- To recognize, affirm, and state God's deity[26]

This celebrative word could easily be applied to several of the nine Psalmic ways of worship, especially in the use of the voice. The *Theological Wordbook of the Old Testament* brings out, "this praise of Jehovah was especially, though by no means uniquely, congregational . . . . Such praise was an essential element of formal public worship."[27]

Note that Ps. 117:1 opens with "Praise [*hâlal*] the LORD, all nations," the expression used by the apostle Paul in Rom. 15:11 to show how converted Gentiles can glorify God.

Terry Law makes this contemporary application of *hâlal*:

> This word connotes a tremendous explosion of enthusiasm in the act of praising. It is what a person does when his favorite sports team has won the victory in the last fifteen seconds of the game . . . . We are to boast of God's exploits and extol His greatness with such enthusiasm and excitement that others would think it foolish.[28]

Hallelujah, considered by some to be "the premier word for praise,"[29] is actually a compound term, coupling *hâlal* with *Jah*, the name of God. The grand climax of the entire book of Psalms, chapter 150, uses *hâlal* in every verse, beginning and ending this glorious worship manifesto with a resounding *hallelujah!*

In the following example, *hâlal* is translated as praise:

> PRAISE the LORD!
> Praise, O servants of the LORD.
> Praise the name of the LORD.
>
> From the rising of the sun to its setting
> The name of the LORD is to be praised (Ps. 113:1, 3).

2. yâdâh, *yaw-daw´* S.C. 3034. Used more than ninety times in the Old Testament, this word has the Hebrew word for hand, *yâd*, incorporated in it. Therefore, the root meaning suggests the use of the hands being extended or held out. It possibly implies the action of pointing, throwing, casting, or shooting. More

information on this word is given at the end of chapter 19, where lifting hands is discussed in detail.[30] Summary thoughts:
* To stretch out the hand, confess[31]
* To worship or revere with raised or extended hands
* To thank God, accompanied by uplifted hands
* To give public acknowledgment[32]
* To express one's public proclamation or declaration (confession) of God's attributes and His works[33]

A chorus-like refrain appears twice in Psalm, chapter 67: "Let the peoples praise [*yâdâh*] Thee, O God; Let all the peoples praise [*yâdâh*] Thee."

The most dramatic use of *yâdâh* appears in 2 Chronicles, chapter 20. A massive army from three nations is marching against Judah. Good King Jehoshaphat calls the people to fasting and prayer. Suddenly a Levitical priest prophesies not to fear or plan to fight. Some Levites respond by praising [*hâlal*] the Lord loudly in appreciation for His direction.

The next day, the king did something that had never been done before. "He (Jehoshaphat) appointed those who should sing to the Lord, and who should praise [*hâlal*] the beauty of holiness, as they went out before the army saying:

Praise [*yâdâh*] the LORD, For His mercy endures forever (2 Chron. 20:21 NKJV).

This expression of confidence in God put the enemy in utter confusion. The enemy soldiers annihilated themselves! It is possible the priests sang with raised hands Ps. 107:1 which has the theme: "The LORD Delivers Men from Manifold Troubles."

3. bârak, *baw-rak´* S.C. 1288. Appearing more than 300 times in Hebrew Scripture, *bârak* appears about seventy-five times to denote praise to God. This word comes from a primitive root meaning to kneel (possibly related to *berek*, a knee), "implying all for which men kneel before him [God]."[34] In regard to worship, it implies humility while simultaneously blessing God as an act of adoration. Summary thoughts:
* To kneel, to bless, to salute[35]
* To remember joyfully He is the source of all your blessing
* To invoke God, to praise, to celebrate, to adore[36]
* To acknowledge openly that God is the origin of power and prosperity
* To bless, declare blessed[37]

Although the King James only translates *bârak* twice as praise (Judg. 5:2 and Ps. 72:15), the New International Version consistently translates it praise. The King James prefers to translate the word with some form of bless (several columns of Old Testament references are listed in *Strong's*).[38] I have already made some comments on "bless" in chapter 19, which deals with the lifting of hands, and those thoughts are appropriate in the context of this word as well.

Psalm, chapter 103, provides one of the best illustrations of bless as the translation of *bârak*. The chapter opens with David fervently admonishing his own soul to "Bless the LORD!" Then, after enumerating many of God's blessings he closes the chapter with an admonition to angels and all His works to join with David in blessing the Lord. The translators do not use kneel in chapter 103, but the three times it is used elsewhere in the King James are significant. The first such use of *bârak* occurs when Eliezer arrives in the city of Nahor and he makes "the camels kneel [*bârak*] down" (Gen. 24:11). Also, Solomon "knelt [*bârak*] on his knees in the presence of all the assembly of Israel, and spread out his hands toward heaven" (2 Chron. 6:13). Finally, we are told to "kneel [*bârak*] before the Lord our maker" (Ps.. 95:6). The humility and brokenness inherent in the action of kneeling (Gesinius says, "The primary notion lies in breaking, breaking down."[39]) was discussed in chapter 23 of this book. Joyful enthusiasm seems wedded to brokenness, humility, and acknowledgment in this word that is best visualized by kneeling camels and a kneeling King Solomon. Also, recall that the Old Testament English word *worship* is invariably the translation of *shâchâh*, meaning prostration before God.

4. t^ehillâh, teh-hil-law´ S.C. 8416. Used nearly sixty times in the Old Testament, this noun is only translated in the King James as "praise" but certainly refers to singing. *T^ehillâh* is clearly derived from *hâlal*, so this word must indicate dynamic song. To say it is the simple singing of a hymn is not enough. This word means extravagant laudation. Summary thoughts, put in verb form:

* To sing enthusiastically
* To laud
* To sing praises extravagantly
* To celebrate with song[40]
* To sing our Hallals[41]
* To make psalms of praise[42]

The Bible gives more than 300 mandates to sing praise. One of the most popular is Ps. 22:3. The wording in the King James takes on new meaning when one realizes that our fourth Hebrew word is used: "But thou art holy, O thou that inhabitest the praises [*t^ehillâh*] of Israel.[43] Ps. 100:4 translates *t^ehillâh* as praise: "Enter His gates with thanksgiving, And His courts with praise [*t^ehillâh*]."

5. zâmar, zaw-mar´ S.C. 2167. Appearing more than forty times in the Hebrew Scriptures, *zâmar* is both one of the key praise words and a musical term.[44] The root idea is that of striking or plucking with the fingers which came to mean the touching of the strings of a musical instrument, or to play upon the instrument. Instrumental music is to be accompanied by the voice. This praise involves instrumental worship.[45] Israel learned to lift both voices and instruments to praise God. The word is only used in poetry and almost exclusively the psalms; singing may not always apply when *zâmar* occurs.[46] Summary thoughts:

* To sing, to praise
* To pluck or twang the strings of an instrument
* To make joyful expressions of music
* To make music in praise of God[47]
* To celebrate with song and music[48]
* To sing in set composition of words and music[49]

zâmar is sometimes used with other praise words:

Sing [*zâmar*] unto the Lord, O ye saints of His, and give thanks [*yâdâh*] at the remembrance of His holiness (Ps. 30:4).

Praise [*yâdâh*] the Lord with the harp; sing [*zâmar*] unto Him with the psaltry and an instrument of ten strings (Ps. 33:2, 3).

Note the use of this word with three others in 2 Samuel:

Therefore I will give thanks [*yâdâh*] unto Thee, O LORD, among the heathen, and I will sing [*zâmar*] praises [*tehillâh*] unto Thy name (2 Sam. 22:50).

6. tôwdâh, *to-daw´* S.C. 8426. Used thirty-two times in the Old Testament, this cognate noun is derived from *yâdâh*[50] and involves the extension of the hand; such action implies avowal, adoration, or sacrifice. Translated twice as confession and six times as praise(s), *tôwdâh* usually is rendered thanksgiving in the NAS. Summary thoughts:

- To give thanks
- To extend the hands in thanksgiving
- To offer a thank-offering
- To make a sacrifice of praise as an act of faith
- To render praise
- To make confession (Josh. 7:19, Ezra 10:11)

Psalm 95:2 exhorts worshipers to "come before His presence with thanksgiving [*tôwdâh*]."Psalm 50:23 stresses making a sacrifice of praise as an act of faith: "He who offers a sacrifice of thanksgiving [*tôwdâh*] honors Me."At the dedication of the wall of Jerusalem, Nehemiah described two companies of people who gave thanks. The NAS calls these groups choirs and thanksgiving choirs in the margin; mentioned in Neh. 12:31, 38, 40, *tôwdâh* is the word so translated. Also note Ps. 50:23 (KJV), which says, "Whoso offereth praise [*tôwdâh*] glorifieth me."

7. shâbach, *shaw-bakh´* S.C. 7623. Translated five times as praise out of eleven occurrences, this word comes from a primitive root meaning to address in a loud tone; figuratively, it can mean to pacify with words. Summary thoughts:

- To shout
- To address in a loud tone
- To laud, to commend, to speak well of
- To exclaim praise, to proclaim with a loud voice
- To triumph, to glory in praise
- To boast in the Lord[51]
- To adulate, adore in a loud tone

This exclamatory form of praise is used four times in Psalms (63:3; 117:1; 145:4; 147:12). Note that 117:1 summons "all ye peoples" to *shâbach* the Lord.

A corresponding word from the Chaldean language [*shebach*] makes an interesting appearance three times in the book of Daniel (2:23; 4:34,37). Daniel declares his praise of God with this word, and then the humbled Nebuchadnezzar praises [*shebach*] God for the restoration of his sanity.

New Testament validates Psalmic worship

The following references from the five main sections of the New Testament endorse the concept that Psalmic praise and worship styles were part of the lives of the early Christians and should be equally important to us today. It is easy to imagine the Christian assemblies of that day employing the seven Hebrew words of praise! References are taken from the New American Standard.

The Gospels:

Matt. 2:2, 11; 4:10; 5:3-10, 12; 9:8, 18; 11:25; 14:19, 33; 15:22, 31, 36; 20:20, 30; 21:9, 15, 16; 23:39; 26:30, 39; 28:9, 17.

Mark 2:12; 5:22, 23; 6:41; 8:6, 7; 11:25; 14:26, 36.

Luke 1:14, 46, 47, 64; 2:13, 14, 20, 38; 4:8; 10:20, 21; 13:13; 17:15; 18:43; 19:37, 40; 23:47; 24:52, 53.

John 4:21, 22, 23.

The Acts:

Acts 1:14; 2:47; 3:8; 4:24; 5:41; 7:60; 8:8, 39; 9:40; 12:5; 13:2, 48, 52; 16:25, 34; 20:36, 37; 21:5, 20; 24:14.

The Pauline Epistles:

Rom. 5:11; 8:15; 10:9; 11:36; 12:1, 11, 12; 15:6, 9-11; 16:27.

1 Cor. 14:15, 16, 17, 26.

2 Cor. 1:20; 4:15; 6:10; 7:4, 7, 9, 13, 16; 8:2; 9:11, 12; 13:9, 11.

Eph. 1:5, 6, 12, 14, 16; 3:14, 21; 5:4, 19, 20.

Phil. 1:3, 4, 11, 18; 2:11, 17, 18, 28; 3:1, 3; 4:4, 6, 10, 20.

Col. 1:3, 11, 12, 24; 3:16, 17; 4:2.

1 Thess. 1:2, 6; 2:13; 3:9, 10; 5:16-18.

2 Thess. 1:3; 2:13.

1 Tim. 1:17; 2:1, 8.

Philem. 4.

Heb. 1:6; 2:12; 5:7; 7:25; 11:21; 13:15.

James 3:9; 5:13.

246

1 Pet. 1:6, 8; 2:5, 9; 4:13, 16.

Jude 20, 24, 25.

The Revelation:
Rev. 1:6; 4:10, 11; 5:8-14; 7:10, 11; 8:4; 11:15, 16, 17; 12:12; 14:2, 3, 7; 15:2-4; 18:20; 19:1-7, 10; 20:6; 22:9.

Reflections

Worship is the corporate body of gathered believers making a united offering to God . . . . No experience in life so broadens a man's horizon and so stretches his heart and soul as this experience of offering himself with others in true worship.

—J. Winston Pearce[52]

If the highest function of angelic hosts is praise, it follows logically that the highest functions of the human spirit must also be praise.

—Paul E. Billheimer[53]

Praise is the duty and delight, the ultimate vocation of the human community; indeed of all creation. Yes, all life is aimed toward God and finally exists for the sake of God. Praise articulates and embodies our capacity to yield, submit, and abandon ourselves in trust and gratitude to the One whose we are. Praise is not only a human requirement and a human need, it is also a human delight. We have a resilient hunger to move beyond self, to return our energy and worth to the One from whom it has been granted. In our return to that One, we find our deepest joy. That is what it means to "glorify God and enjoy God forever."

—Walter Brueggemann[54]

It is plain that these expressions of praise played a large part in the service of primitive Christianity. They are thus important for the basing of the Christian ethic: when those who are not Christians see your renewed manner of life they will be moved by it (to become Christians and) to join the choir of those who sing praises, in the membership of the Church. Hence Paul establishes the general rule: so fashion your manner of life that (by Jews, and Greeks, and the Church of God everywhere) praise will be offered to God."

—D. Gerhart Delling[55]

Though nothing can add to God's essential glory, yet praise exalts him in the eyes of others. When we praise God, we spread his fame and renown, we display the trophies of his excellency. Praising God is one of the highest and purest acts of religion. In prayer we act like men; in praise we act like angels.

—Charles H. Spurgeon[56]

29

The Celebrative Nature
of the Early Church

*Rejoice always; pray without ceasing; in everything give thanks;
for this is God's will for you in Christ Jesus.
Do not quench the Spirit; do not despise prophetic utterances.*
—1 Thessalonians 5:16-20

Fifth of five arguments:
Sterile synagogues of New Testament times could not contain the celebrative worship of joyous Christians. Therefore synagogues had minimal influence on worship in early church gatherings.

The celebrative worship of King David's time had been lost by Jesus' day. Synagogue meetings had degenerated to low spiritual levels. Psalmic worship had depended upon the endorsement of leaders who shared a joyful enthusiasm for God. It was true then, and it is true today.

The Davidic dynasty began to fail in political and military strength as religious fervor waned. The prophet Amos had predicted that the Tabernacle of David would fall upon hard times (Amos 9:11), and the prophecy certainly came to pass. The prophetic touch upon David and his appointed singers and musicians had not passed automatically to the next generation. The ancient axiom holds true: Every generation must personally meet and experience God in a fresh, living way! (See Chapter 7).

Periodic revivals during the kings of Judah (discussed in Chapter 15) saw the return of the Jews to Psalmic worship. However, invariably the priestly, sacerdotal aspects of corporate religious life squeezed out the prophetic, dynamic influence that had characterized David. Finally taken into captivity, the Jews lost their confidence and joy. It was difficult for them to sing and rejoice as prisoners in a foreign land (Psalm, chapter 137). The collapse of the Jewish religious state, the captivity, and the scattering of the people made them think more of religious survival than of sustaining vigorous worship programs. Their solution was to build the synagogue system.

No one knows exactly how and when the synagogue originated in the centuries before Christ, but it clearly became the vehicle by which the Jews maintained their religious and societal unity.[1] Dispersed among the nations, the Jews would gather locally for study of the Torah and prayers. By meeting in small halls or auditoriums they maintained tight bonds with each other and with their traditions.

The synagogue system also maintained a strong tie with Moses—but not the active experience of Davidic/Psalmic worship forms. The Psalms were indeed read and prayed, and the hope of a messianic king was kept alive, but the services became more perfunctory observances than jubilant congregational celebrations. Thus, the many synagogues scattered throughout the Roman Empire became spiritual frontier forts that served as points of contact for the dispersed people.

The Jews gathered, read, and prayed. They remembered the God of history and prayed for His kingdom to come. But there was little present excitement and prophetic action. The synagogue was more of a forum than a place of inspiring worship. Although the temple was still the focus of Jewish religion and national aspiration, "the synagogue had already become the center of Jewish worship, life, and thought, wherever there were Jews, by the time of Jesus."[2] This would explain why Jesus habitually attended the Sabbath meetings in the synagogues, and why Paul invariably made the local synagogue his first stop in a new area. They took the message where the potentially receptive people gathered.

Early Christians adopted some of the synagogue format for their church gatherings. Several things carried over such as prayer, Scripture reading, singing, and exposition. Even the eldership system and the term *synagogue* were used.[3] However, the synagogue did not have a eucharistic Communion service, as frequently pointed out by Christian commentators.[4]

The difference between the synagogue and the church lay not so much in pattern as in experience. The new-found joy of the Christians increasingly found enthusiastic expression in psalms, hymns, and spiritual songs (Eph. 5:19; Col. 3:16), prophetic manifestations (1 Corinthians, chapter 14), and spiritual gifts (1 Corinthians, chapter 12). Praying "in the Spirit" increased the vitality of the gatherings immeasurably (Jude 20; Rom. 8:26). Intense concentration on Jesus and the activity of His Spirit lifted Christian gatherings to a dynamic worship dimension unknown in the Jewish synagogue. Christians were joyfully Christocentric in their worship and not merely performing token acknowledgment of a grieving Savior at a staid Communion table. They celebrated!

Neither Gentiles nor Jewish Christians in the church of Bible days related well to the Jewish synagogue structure. Early Christians quickly developed a unique system of worship that was fluid and flexible, easily adapting their format to Psalmic worship forms that provided the best format for spontaneous, joyful worship. Illion T. Jones, a highly respected worship commentator, makes this observation:

> Every element of Christian worship was affected by the impact of the Holy Spirit upon the Christians. The enthusiasm, the spontaneous outburst of spiritual power put new vitality into their singing, their prayers, their giving, their preaching, their testimony, and all their relations with one another . . . . It contained a new ingredient of a different quality and force . . . "spontaneity."[5]

The Celebrative Nature of the Early Church

Ernest F. Scott, in *The Nature of the Early Church*, recognizes that Christian services were modeled on the synagogue, with Scripture, prayer, and hymns; however, these activities were given "a Christian coloring." He states:

> Christian worship had thus a root of its own. It was not merely an outgrowth of Jewish worship but sprang out of the new convictions which had taken possession of the church.[6]

The principle Jesus had so carefully explained in the parable of the wineskins had indeed come to pass (Luke 5:37,38). The joyful new wine eventually caused Christians to leave the synagogue and gather wherever possible as the new people of God—the church.

Reflections

The violent arguments, riots, and persecutions which resulted from the testimony of Christians in the synagogues certainly make it all but impossible to believe that Christians succeeded in modifying the worship procedures of this institution.

—Illion T. Jones[7]

The New Testament writings are marked by an unrivalled freshness, vigour, and power . . . . we may be certain that in this high strain they also worshipped. Within them dwelt a surging life of a new thought and emotion; the most astounding things had happened to them; a deep thankfulness and an irrepressible joy possessed them; and their worship came from them much as its full-throated song comes from the bird—as the simple, spontaneous, over-flowing expression of an exuberant life that must of necessity have outlet . . . . we do not begin really to understand their worship until we approach it thus, from within.

—Alexander B. Macdonald[8]

But if the first Christians attended the Synagogue . . . and continued to worship according to the liturgy of the Synagogue . . . How much of that liturgy, if any, did they take with them into the distinctively Christian gatherings . . . when anathemas and hostile public opinion prevented them from joining in the worship of their Jewish friends and founders?

—C.W. Dugmore[9]

The worshipers were filled with a sense of the nearness and certainty of the Kingdom. They were able in some measure to anticipate it. In this meeting of the brotherhood they escaped from the world and were caught up for an hour into the coming age. The worship was thus ecstatic in its character, and the distinctive feature of it was the exercise of the charismata, or spiritual gifts.

—Ernest F. Scott[10]

It has been taken for granted for a long time by New Testament scholars that the early Christians had formed their worship under the influence of the synagogue. This . . . cannot be proved, in spite of the striking similarities between the synagogue and the Early Church . . . . is it any wonder that the early Christians did not adopt the order of worship of the synagogue, since the gentile churches were opposed to the theology of the synagogue, and they would hardly have adopted the most important part of its life, namely its order of worship.

—Dietrich Ritschl[11]

Part VIII

Christ is Actually Present in Our Corporate Worship Times

Christ is truly present in the person of the Holy Spirit. The dynamic, prophetic activity of the Holy Spirit in corporate worship, sacraments, and prayer is encouraged and enhanced in the Psalmic worship forms.

- Chapter 30 **The Spirit of Jesus Among Us**
  Christ is really here and now among us, leading our worship!

- Chapter 31 **The Sacraments**
  Christ is re-presented in the Sacraments of the church, causing the church to become sacramental in nature and expression.

- Chapter 32 **The Local Church as a House of Prayer**
  A great continuing worship program is more dependent on a disciplined, praying people than any other factor.

- Chapter 33 **Gathering the Called-Out Ones**
  Today's worship renewal depends on the nineteen vital New Testament worship service ingredients.

30

The Spirit of Jesus Among Us

And lo, I am with you all the days [perpetually, uniformly and on every occasion], to the (very) close and consummation of the age. Amen—so let it be.
—Matthew 28:20 AMP

Sketchy accounts in the New Testament of the church's first services seem to portray an unstructured, unorganized approach to worship, yet so much was accomplished. Belief in God's present working power permeates the written record. From its inception, worship was enthusiastic, God-inspired, Spirit-filled. It broke forth and was maintained not by observing routine, mechanical ceremonies but by people and their leaders allowing the Holy Spirit to make God intensely real in actual experience.[1] The story of the Spirit-filled early church staggers the modern mind. Illion Jones captures the feeling of that time. He comments:

> It was as though sunshine had broken upon the world, as indeed it did, in the Lord Jesus Christ, and the new worship was the simple, glad, thankful, happy experience of those who had received to their hearts the wonder of the gospel of the love of God in Jesus Christ. Everything was simple, spontaneous, inspirational, pentecostal and, in the deepest sense of the word, evangelical.[2]

The followers of Jesus were pneumatic. The word *pneumatic* is derived from *pneuma* (Greek), which means Spirit. They were the new Israel of God anointed with the actual presence of the Holy Spirit. Caught up in the initial outburst of pneumatic enthusiasm and under the inspiration of the Holy Spirit, Peter quoted Joel's prophecy that foresaw this new era of the Holy Spirit:

> And it shall come to pass in the last days, saith God, I will pour out of my Spirit upon all flesh; and your sons and your daughters shall prophesy, and your young men shall see visions, and your old men shall dream dreams: And on my servants and on my handmaidens I will pour out in those days of my Spirit; and they shall prophesy (Acts 2:17, 18 KJV).

255

The author of Acts quoted Joel's prophecy to give "his readers the key to the right understanding of the history of primitive Christianity."[3] The text also reveals the key to worship: the active, abiding presence of God's Spirit and the people's responsiveness to Him. Jesus had "bequeathed the Spirit as his crowning gift to his people,"[4] and this sentiment pulsed through the lives and writings of early believers.

I am sending forth the promise of My Father upon you; but you are to stay in the city until you are clothed with power from on high (Luke 24:49).

You shall receive power when the Holy Spirit has come upon you (Acts 1:8).

Are you so foolish? Having begun by the Spirit, are you now being perfected by the flesh? (Gal. 3:3).

Because you are sons, God has sent forth the Spirit of His Son into our hearts, crying, Abba! Father! (Gal. 4:6).

The early Christians correlated the Holy Spirit with the person of Jesus. In fact, they perceived the Spirit's presence in the church to be the very presence of Jesus in a new, personal way. This idea escapes many modern Christians. It is missing in their theological thoughts. If Christians' minds are unclear on this point, it will be difficult for them to understand and respond to the presence of Christ in their worship services.

The mysterious Spirit of the Old Testament
The Old Testament refers to the Holy Spirit as *ruach* in Hebrew and *pneuma* in the Greek Septuagint. These words have been interpreted variously as wind, breath, spirit, and Spirit.[5] *Ruach* is used for the spirit in man and in various places refers to the life of man (his emotions, volitional ability, and intelligence), but it primarily "insists that this powerful, mysterious Spirit belongs to God, and to God alone. It is essentially the personal God, Yahweh, in action," according to Michael Green.[6]

George Ladd agrees: "the *ruach Yahweh* in the Old Testament is not a separate, distinct entity; it is God's power—the personal activity in God's will achieving a moral and religious object."[7] Succinctly stated, "The Spirit is no other than God himself" (Küng).[8]

This book will not investigate all the Old Testament contains about the Spirit,[9] but this quote from Hans Küng summarizes:

Perceptible and yet not perceptible, invisible and yet powerful, real like the energy-charged air, the wind, the storm, as important for life as the air we breathe: this is how people in ancient times frequently imagined the "Spirit" and God's invisible working. According to the beginning of the creation account, "spirit" . . . is the "roaring," the "tempest" of God over the waters. "Spirit" as understood in the Bible means—as opposed to "flesh," to create, perishable reality—the force or power proceeding from God: that invisible force of God and power of God that is effective, creatively or destructively, for life or judgment, in creation and history, in Israel and later in the Church.[10]

Sometimes the Old Testament pictures the Spirit of God as a "violent, invading force"[11] that withers grass and topples cedars (Isa. 40:7). The Spirit gave unusual prophetic manifestations and visions as He forcefully moved upon His people. After moving so fitfully and unpredictably, the Spirit would someday rest upon a Messiah who would be a servant and a king for His people, according to the prophets. That Messiah would be (in some mysterious way) the channel whereby the Spirit would come to rest upon all God's people.[12]

Jesus bearer of the Spirit

Salvation history holds only a handful of pivotal events. Jesus' receipt of the Holy Spirit in the Jordan is one of them.[13] A unique moment in history, it began the endtime, the messianic age, the New Covenant. Jesus, upon whom the Spirit rests, now appears among men as the promised Messiah. He brings the benefits of that Spirit to all responsive people.

Just as rain ends drought and refreshes the earth, Jesus' ministry broke a long, divinely imposed silence. Matthew describes the anointed Jesus as a rising sun that dispels darkness and brings hope to all people (Matt. 4:15,16 to fulfill Isa. 9:1 and probably Mal. 4:2). Mark describes Jesus—with the Spirit still upon Him—coming into Galilee proclaiming the Good News of God to a people who had forgotten what good news was (Mark 1:14, 15). Luke records the dramatic moment when Jesus declares the fulfillment of Isa. 61:1 to His hometown folks at Nazareth:

> The Spirit of the LORD is upon Me, Because He anointed Me to preach the Gospel to the poor. He has sent Me to proclaim release to the captives, And recovery of sight to the blind, To set free those who are downtrodden, To proclaim the favorable year of the LORD (Luke 4:18, 19).

He came as the Spirit-endowed Messiah, but Jesus also came as the Suffering Servant of the Lord to fulfill the four "Servant Songs" of Isa. 42:1-4; 49:1-6; 50:4-9; 52:13-53:12.[14] In this capacity, He would have God's Spirit "upon Him" (Isa. 42:1; fulfilled in Matt. 12:18-21). Thus, the dual roles of Messiah and Suffering Servant blended in Jesus, "the unique Man of the Spirit."[15]

The Paraclete

John's gospel records five references to the Holy Spirit as the *paraclete* (14:15-18; 14:25-27; 15:26-27; 16:7,13-15). The Greek word *parakletos* is peculiar to the Johannine writings, and the essential meaning is vigorously debated. No single word provides an adequate rendering. The King James Version gives the popular translation of comforter, with origins in Wycliffe's fourteenth century English translation. The word came from the Latin *confortare* and meant to make strong or to fortify.[16] Supporter or helper perhaps best translate the meaning, although advocate provides the basic concept and sustaining religious idea.[17] Jesus deliberately waited until His "farewell discourse" to introduce this special term that would illustrate the oneness, as well as the distinction between the Spirit and Himself.

Various Translations: Comforter (KJV, LB, M), Helper (NAS, TEV, NKJV), Counselor (RSV, NIV), Advocate (NEB, JB), someone to stand by you (PHILLIPS).

The followers of Jesus have two Paraclete-Helpers, the Holy Spirit being the second. Generally, Jesus is not thought of as a helper; but in actual fact, He was (see 1 John 2:1, where Jesus is called a Paraclete in the forensic sense). He came as a tangible expression of God's concern for people. John's elaborate opening statement in the first epistle, verses 1-3, indicates a relational experience with Jesus that clearly establishes Jesus as a Helper who was heard, seen, handled, and fellowshipped. The disciples saw Jesus hungry, wet, tired, triumphant, lonely, prayerful, and compassionate. Yet He always was present to help those who believed in Him.

The Gospels show how Jesus physically led His people as a Paraclete. He taught, guided, helped, and presided over His disciples. By the end of His earthly ministry, the disciples had grown accustomed to the Teacher-Leader-Helper. Imagine their wonder when He announced one day:

> If you love Me, you will keep My commandments. And I will ask the Father, and He will give you *another* Helper, that He may be with you forever; that is the Spirit of truth, whom the world cannot receive, because it does not behold Him or know Him, but you know Him because He abides with you, and will be in you. I will not leave you as orphans; I will come to you (John 14:15-18, emphasis added).

Later, in the same message, He brings an even more amazing thought:

> But I tell you the truth, it is to your advantage that I go away; for if I do not go away, the Helper shall not come to you; but if I go, I will send Him to you (John 16:7).

When Jesus said that He would send another Helper, He meant He already had functioned with His disciples as a Paraclete. The Spirit being sent would simply assume Jesus' responsibilities and continue His ministry with the disciples.[18] However, the new Paraclete would not be with them as He had been in Jesus, but He actually would be *in* each individual disciple.

It was necessary for Jesus to leave them physically so that He might return in the person of the Holy Spirit to indwell each of them separately. When Jesus said "I will come to you" (14:18), He meant that He would come in the person of the Holy Spirit. That is why 1 John 3:24 states: "We know by this that He abides in us, by the Spirit which He has given us." Catherine Marshall makes this helpful comment:

> We wonder how anything could be more wonderful than the physical presence of our Lord .... And here we have His solemn word in His Last Supper talk with His apostles that there is something better—His presence in the form of the Holy Spirit.[19]

Two pages later she suggests a beautiful prayer that matches her thoughts:

I also begin to see, Lord, that since the Helper is really Your presence in another form, what You were telling Your apostles—and me—is that You Yourself will be in me.

The Spirit as Jesus

To be recognizable, the diffused, universal Spirit of God became clearly focused and sharply localized in Jesus. Jesus gave definition and delineation to the Spirit. In a sense, the Spirit was clothed with Jesus. The Spirit was so marked by and identified with the character of Jesus that He can be called "the Spirit of Jesus" (Acts 16:7).

The Spirit descended on Jesus and remained on Him (John 1:32). This event publicly announced the anointing of Jesus with the Holy Spirit. It also introduced Jesus' association with the Spirit that would continue throughout His earthly ministry and reach highest fulfillment in His heavenly exaltation. When he departed, Jesus left His personality with the disciples in the form of the New Paraclete.[20] The Spirit that represents Jesus will "remain bound to the person and character of Jesus."[21] The believer who has the Spirit has the presence of Jesus.

This concept is developed in John's gospel. The tandem relationship is too noticeable to ignore. "In many ways the Paraclete is to Jesus as Jesus is to the Father."[22] Here is a summary of the parallels:

Similarity	Jesus	Spirit
Came into the world	16:28; 18:37	16:8
Came forth from the Father	16:27-28; 17:8	15:26
Given & sent by Father	3:16	14:16, 26
Taught the disciples	6:59; 7:14, 28; 8:20	14:26; 16:13
Unrecognized by the world	16:3	14:17
Sent as a representative	3:17; 5:43	14:26
Remained with & guided	17:12	14:16-18
The Truth	14:6	14:17; 15:26; 16:13
Unpretentious	8:28; 12:28; 17:4	16:14
Bore witness to another	8:14	15:26, 27

The Acts of the Apostles opens with two verses that confirm the Holy Spirit continues the earthly ministry of Jesus.

The first account I composed, Theophilus, about all that Jesus *began* to do and teach, until the day when he was taken up, after He had by the Holy Spirit given orders to the apostles whom He had chosen (Acts 1:1-2, emphasis added).

While on earth, Jesus initiated a ministry which He planned to continue through the Holy Spirit in the church. F. Dale Brunner comments:

Luke wishes here in an impressive introductory manner to connect the work of Jesus with the ministry of the Spirit. What Jesus did or continues to do was and is "through the Holy Spirit." Luke does not wish for the Holy Spirit, who is to play such an important role in Acts to be separated from the work of Jesus Christ as though the Holy Spirit could be understood to have a separate, independent, or even analogous work of his own. Luke's first sentence makes clear an intention of his entire book: the Spirit is not to be dissociated from Jesus. The Spirit IS Jesus at work in continuation of his ministry.[23]

In the Gospels Jesus *physically* leads His people, and the Spirit is in Jesus. In the Acts and the Epistles Jesus *spiritually* leads His people, but by that time Jesus is in the Spirit! In this sense, Jesus and the Holy Spirit are equivalent. Christ became a "life-giving spirit" through the resurrection (1 Cor. 15:45), and He has continued to lead His people in the person of the Holy Spirit. Hans Küng capsulizes this thought: "The Spirit is . . . the earthly presence of the glorified Lord."[24] Paul Hoon says: "The Spirit is conceived as the power or presence of the ascended Jesus energizing His body, the church."[25]

The New Testament writers consider the Spirit of God and the Spirit of Jesus the same functionally. For instance, "the Holy Spirit . . . the Spirit of Jesus" (Acts 16:6, 7), "the Spirit . . . the Spirit of God . . . the Spirit of Christ" (Rom. 8:9), "God sent forth the spirit of His Son" (Gal. 4:6), and the unusual "Now the Lord is the Spirit: and where the Spirit of the Lord is, there is liberty. But we all . . . are being transformed into the same image from glory to glory, just as from the Lord, the Spirit" (2 Cor. 3:17, 18). Two references in 1 Peter can be added: "the Spirit of Christ within them" (1:11), and "put to death in the flesh, but made alive in the Spirit" (3:18).

Functionally, "Jesus equals Spirit" in the church, but "the Spirit is not Jesus; the Spirit is another Paraclete. If John reflected upon it he would probably say that Christ was present in the Spirit."[26] This could easily cause confusion! Is the Holy Spirit really a distinct person, merely a replacement for Jesus, a mode of Christ's continuing presence, or what?[27]

Words get frustrating at this point because people do not have the mental capacity to breathe the rarefied air surrounding this summit of New Testament Trinitarian Theology. This touches the mystery of God (1 Tim. 3:16). It would be best simply to accept the Paraclete as the presence of Jesus while Jesus is physically absent. Yes, He is a person, but also, somehow, He is the personal, spiritual presence of the Father and Son. That is where the mystery lies.[28]

The breath of Jesus

Jesus undoubtedly realized the mental consternation and theological wrangling that would follow His teaching on the Paraclete.[29] To ease the confusion among His disciples, Jesus performed a dramatic act to illustrate all He had taught. He breathed on them and told them to receive the Holy Spirit. None of the disciples would forget that incident.

Jesus therefore said to them again, "Peace be with you; as the Father has sent Me, I also send you." And when He had said this, He breathed on them, and said to them, "Receive the Holy Spirit. If you forgive the sins of any, their sins have been forgiven them; if you retain the sins of any, they have been retained (John 20:21-23).

Jesus signified that His life and breath were synonymous with the Holy Spirit that they would receive in Acts, chapter 2. Ray Anderson describes the John 20 scene:

> Having touched his body and having seen his familiar features with their own eyes, they now feel his breath on them, and thus are led to experience the Holy Spirit as an intimate and familiar presence rather than as a strange and unknown power. The Holy Spirit would come charged with the familiarity of his own bodily breath and bearing to them the presence of his own person.[30]

We do not encounter God separately from the Lord Jesus or the Holy Spirit. The Holy Spirit mediates actions of the one God to His people, individually and collectively.

> Through Him we both have our access in one Spirit to the Father (Eph. 2:18).

> The grace of the Lord Jesus Christ and the love of God and the fellowship of the Holy Spirit be with you all (2 Cor. 13:14).

Jesus and the Spirit share such harmony and spiritual unity that they function as one. Christ is the ascended Lord and head of the church, yet in the Spirit He is present among men!

Christ here and now

Karl Barth titled one of his books: *God Here and Now*.[31] In the translator's introduction, Paul M. Van Buren explains Barth's meaning by dynamically enlarging the title: "*God Here and Now* really *God* and really *here and now*." Barth said in his book "that faith knows nothing about God in general, but only about the God who has made Himself 'here and now' in Jesus of Nazareth."

I take Barth's thesis a step further. Yes, God was in Christ, and He was Here. However, now Christ has gone, sending the Paraclete as His replacement. Evangelical believers may confess that God is now here in the sense that Jesus was manifested among mankind. But—and this is a critical point for our worship services—we may also say in full confidence that Christ is *here now* in the person of the Holy Spirit.

The Spirit-filled church declares in the midst of worship: *Christ, here and now! REALLY Christ, and REALLY here and now!*

John had a vision of the spiritual presence of Christ. He saw the church as a seven-branched candelabra with Christ standing in the midst of it. The seven burning lamps represented "the seven spirits of God" (or, the fullness of the Holy Spirit; "seven-fold Spirit," AMP). The basis for the entire unfolding of John's Revelation was that Jesus and His Spirit are in the church, and they act as one (Rev. 1:12-20; 4:5).

A man who did not believe in the existence of God had written above his bed, "God is nowhere." But his granddaughter was just learning to read, and words of more than one syllable were beyond her. In her own way she spelled out what her grandfather had written, and for her it read "God is now here."

Worship services take on new life for people who believe Jesus is present and active among them in the person of the Holy Spirit. How else can the following verse be fulfilled? "For where two or three have gathered together in My name, there I am in their midst" (Matt. 18:20).

The only true worshiper leads us

The Bible says Jesus leads the worship of God. He "once and for all" offered the ultimate sacrifice to God, worship so perfect that it stands as the eternal standard of excellence (Heb. 5:9; 7:27, 28; 9:12, 26, 28; 10:10, 12). His leadership and participation makes believers' worship truly authentic. Worship actually has little benefit apart from Jesus. The epistle to the Hebrews, which teaches much on worship, gives exciting insight to Jesus' role as mediator. Jesus is the "one true worshiper" and as such becomes "the leader of our worship" (*leitourgos*, Heb. 8:2).[32]

The Lamb in the midst of God's throne room in Revelation, chapter 5, is both the perfect worship sacrifice as well as the perfect worship leader for all creation. Standing alive with the marks of crucifixion upon Him, Jesus offers to the Father, through the Holy Spirit, his own adoration and devotion and the grateful praise of all the redeemed. He opened a door to God that forever antiquated the priestly, Levitical system.

Heaven's worship focuses upon the Lamb, Jesus, who perfects it and offers it to the Father. The church's approach should reflect this heavenly principle that allows believers to offer worship in Spirit and Truth.

> Through Him then, let us continually offer up a sacrifice of praise to God, that is, the fruit of lips that give thanks to His name (Heb. 13:15).

The Lamb worships not only in heaven. Jesus sings God's praise in church gatherings here on earth. He sings in and through the saints by His Holy Spirit. The Paraclete draws the highest expressions of adoration and praise from worshipers' hearts. Then He offers the spiritual sacrifice to God who accepts it because it has been blended with the worship and sacrifice of the only true worshiper, the Lord Jesus Christ.

> I (Jesus) will proclaim Thy name to My brethren, In the midst of the congregation I (Jesus) will sing Thy praise (Heb. 2:12).

HALLELUJAH, What a thought! JESUS SINGS THROUGH THE CHURCH BY THE SPIRIT.

Reflections

This simple belief that He was still living and present with them was one of the supremely creative factors in the growth and worship of the Church.

—*Alexander B. Macdonald*[33]

For the Spirit of Jesus to be in the church was simply for Jesus himself to be there in a way as real as his physical presence among his disciples.

—*George T. Montague*[34]

The Spirit does not come to us as "naked" Spirit, to be clothed with our own subjective human feelings and possibilities. Rather, the Spirit comes to us "clothed" with the subjective feelings, experiences and possibilities of Jesus Christ himself.

—*Ray S. Anderson*[35]

With the outpouring of the Holy Spirit on the Day of Pentecost Jesus appeared—although He remained physically invisible—to His followers and entered into them as Pneuma.

—*Peter Brunner*[36]

31

The Sacraments

Do this to remember me.
—1 Corinthians 11:24 LB

A favorite sermon illustration of the late Peter Marshall was "the King is in the audience."[1] In dramatic fashion he would describe a scene typical of the London theater. He portrayed the audience filing in engaged in cheerful conversation, the orchestra tuning their instruments, the stagehands preparing the ropes, cables, and lights, and the actors finishing last-minute makeup and preparation. Finally, warning lights blink. The overture begins.

Suddenly the orchestra stops! After a moment of deathly silence, the strains of the National Anthem powerfully fill the theater. Excitement fills the backstage as the stage manager and director excitedly urge everyone, "Give it all you've got tonight. Play as you've never played before!"

Building to the climax, Peter asks, "Why? Why this commotion? Because the King is in the audience!"

Jesus Christ, a living reality

In every church service, the greatest concern must be for the presence of Jesus Christ our King. Ideal New Testament worship allows people who believe doctrinally in Jesus' presence to realize it experientially in the church service. Without Jesus' presence, the service would be only a theatrical performance. His electrifying presence makes the service a living encounter with the risen Jesus. Like theater-goers and actors in Marshall's illustration, every Christian must be acutely aware that the purpose for gathering to worship in a group is suddenly enhanced by the presence of the King. What a dramatic thought.

Gathered in a church building, people realize, "The King is actually here—walking these aisles, sitting beside me! He loves me! He is concerned about my feelings and needs at this very moment! The presence of God and Christ in the person of the Holy Spirit is here now. Really and truly God is here—NOW!"

The whole objective of a church service is for individual worshipers and the collective church body to encounter God. Robert Simpson, in his famous lectures, strongly concurs:

> But let us hold high with insistence, that the central thing in worship is the Presence of God, that a worshiping congregation comes to church to give to God and to get from God, that the ruling thought in every worshiper's mind as he enters a church should be that of coming to meet with God, and the one question that should be in his mind as he leaves what we call the place of worship, should be, "Have I or have I not met God?"[2]

But how, when, and why does the presence of God come? Is it even right to expect some type of encounter with God that is meaningful? These questions have settled particularly on the *sacramental* means or forms by which Christ's presence is known in the church.

The following is not an extended investigation of the sacraments. I offer a few key thoughts and suggestions on how the working of the Holy Spirit and the use of Davidic worship forms can increase people's awareness of the divine presence. But first, consider some fundamentals.

Basic questions about the sacraments

What Is A Sacrament? Christian sacraments are symbolic demonstrations performed in a worship service, which were commanded or recognized by Jesus "as means of initiating and nurturing persons as Christians."[3] These visible activities are meant to intensify Christ's spiritual relationship with the church as well as with individual Christians. "They are the outward and visible signs of the blessings of the Gospel that are given by God's grace and received by faith."[4]

Augustine, the fifth-century bishop of Hippo in North Africa, defined a sacrament as a visible work or an outward, visible sign of an inward and spiritual grace. Augustine, quoted by Calvin, calls a sacrament "the Word made visible."[5]

The Meaning of the Term. The word *sacrament* comes from the Greek word *mysterion* (Eph. 5:32) which was translated by Jerome into the Latin word *sacramentum.* The word referred to things set apart as sacred (spiritual mysteries) and to an oath of obedience taken by Roman soldiers.

The term came "to designate any sign which possessed a hidden meaning . . . . It became increasingly evident that the religious significance of the term was too free and broad for careful biblical precision, although the word itself is not used in the Bible."[6] Various rites and ceremonies, such as the sign of the cross, anointing with oil, preaching, confirmation, prayer, aid to the sick, etc., were all termed sacraments. The efforts of church theologians to standardize the meaning of the term brought "neither agreement on the essence nor on the number of the sacraments."[7]

What Are The Two Main Parts of a Sacrament? A sacrament has two parts: (1) the outward visible sign, act, or ceremony that should be carefully observed in the way it is taught in the Scriptures, and (2) the inward, spiritual work of the Holy Spirit that imparts life and change.[8]

What Are the Components in Every Sacrament? Every sacrament has four important components as follows:

1) the ministry of the church that performs the action,[9]
2) the scriptural words of the institution,[10]
3) the material elements used to establish the sign,[11] and
4) the physical action required.

What is the Value of a Sacrament? Throughout the Old Testament, the people of God followed ceremonies in worship (see Leviticus and Psalms). Their hearts grasped religious truths as they shared spiritual experiences through prescribed rites, visible symbols, and physical actions. New Testament sacraments share similarities but are more than religious ceremonies. They are instruments the Holy Spirit uses to make Christ real in the church.[12]

How Many Sacraments are There? Most Protestant churches teach two: water baptism and Communion.[13] The Methodist church "recognizes two sacraments: baptism is the initiation sacrament; Holy Communion is the nurturing sacrament."[14] The Roman Catholic church has traditionally held to five additional sacraments: Penance, Confirmation, Consecration, Marriage, and Extreme Unction. However, since Vatican II, The Anointing of the Sick has been added as a sacrament. Some Protestant churches also include Anointing with Oil, Foot Washing, and Dedication of Children.[15] The safest rule distinguishes sacraments as actions instituted by the Lord Jesus Christ. To each of them is attached the promise of His grace and presence.[16]

Water baptism and Communion are almost universally accepted as authentic because of their clear teaching in the New Testament. An interesting footnote in *The Celebration of the Gospel* by the three Methodist authors:

> Though the Methodist Church recognizes only two SACRAMENTS, it may be said that the ordinances of confirmation, ordination, marriage, and burial are taken with that devout seriousness that causes them to be sacramental in tone and effect.[17]

Jesus is the primary sacrament

Sacramental actions of the church are based on Jesus as the prototype. The revelation of Jesus Christ—His life, death, and resurrection—is the one event, or the one sacrament, in which God revealed Himself in the form of a creature to mankind.[18] The true mystery of God resides in the ministry of Jesus Christ.

The word sacrament refers to spiritual mysteries. The primary mystery in Christianity is how Christ manifests His presence in the church. Revealing God's presence, Jesus performed the original sacrament by walking among men almost two thousand years ago. Today, a liturgical vehicle is used to reveal—through the Holy Spirit—a special manifestation of Jesus to believers assembled for worship. Christ lived a liturgical life in the sense that His adoration of God was so genuine that He demonstrated the supreme worship of God the Father. Catholic scholar E. Schillebeeck, provides insights in his *Christ the Sacrament of the Encounter with God*; for instance:

> Because this divine power to save appears to us in visible form, the saving activity of Jesus is SACRAMENTAL . . . a bestowal of salvation in historical visibility . . . .
> The man Jesus, as the personal visible realization of the divine grace of redemption, is THE sacrament, the primordial sacrament, because this man, the son of God himself, is

intended by the Father to be in his humanity the only way to the actuality of redemption.[19]

The life Jesus lived among men was a tangible, visible demonstration of the salvation God has freely bestowed on us. Water baptism and Communion preserve the opening and closing events of His earthly ministry: His baptism in Jordan and the happenings of Passion Week. All other worship components and activities find their place and significance in relationship to these two great pillars of truth.

By the Holy Spirit, believers are baptized with Christ in His baptism and participate with Him in His death, burial, and resurrection through the Eucharist. In His prayers we pray, in His worship we worship, and in His service we serve. The sacraments make visible today what was visible in Christ.[20] Now, by the Spirit, the life of the church becomes sacramental in the sense that the presence of Christ shows through the church, just as the life of the Father showed through the Son.

Re-presenting Christ

Sacraments and related ceremonies join Christians with the salvation events of history. They encourage believers to remember or memorialize Christ, and they re-present the reality of the life of Christ (1 Cor. 11:24; Matt. 18:20; John 14:21, 23.[21] They also allow the Spirit of Christ to act in and through them to fulfill God's desire for worship in Spirit and Truth (John 4:23).

While Christ re-presents Himself spiritually in baptism and Communion,[22] today's worshipers also must recapture the awareness of Christ's presence in other spiritual activities mentioned in the New Testament.

Early Christians enjoyed more frequent, diverse manifestations of Christ in their worship services than most churches do today. If believers allowed the Spirit more opportunity to work, they might see more of the Spirit's activities!

Robert N. Schaper comments:

> The real presence of Jesus is a doctrine that has perhaps suffered because it has been too narrowly rather than broadly defined. Christ is truly present in Word and sacrament. He is present in the continued expression of his servants in worship. It is we who are sadly absent in our blindness and unbelief.[23]

Baptism and Communion stand by themselves and must retain their basic format. All branches of the Christian church recognize the importance of water baptism in bringing new believers into the body of Christ.[24] Similarly, the Eucharist, or Lord's Supper, keeps the church mindful of Christ's supreme sacrifice and worship.[25]

Christ's presence must not be restricted to these two sacraments. Since the word *sacrament* is not in the Bible, Christians do not need to doggedly use this term and, through its use, relegate other biblical activities to less significant positions.

John wrote his Gospel possibly as a reaction to the human tendency to over-institutionalize and suffocate the Spirit's working.[26] In his final years, he saw a growing tendency in the church to limit Jesus' presence exclusively to the sacraments and to find solace in these sacred acts as believers waited for His delayed second coming.[27]

The Sacraments

Although time passes, the church does not drift farther away from the Christ of the Gospels. It is unnecessary to over-emphasize the sacraments, rites, or offices to compensate for His physical absence. Jesus is present in the person of the Holy Spirit in the church of every generation, every culture, and every place. What we should seek is the vivifying presence of the Holy Spirit in both sacraments and other Scriptural channels. James D.G. Dunn captures this thought masterfully:

> Each generation is as close to Jesus as the last—and the first—because the Paraclete is the immediate link between Jesus and his disciples in every generation. That is to say, the link and continuity is provided not by sacraments or offices or human figures, but by the Spirit.
>
> The vitality of Christian experience does not cease because the historical Jesus has faded into the past and the coming of Jesus has faded into the future; it retains its vitality because the Spirit is at work here and now as the other Paraclete.[28]

If Christ is indeed *the* sacrament of God, and He is being re-presented through the church by the Holy Spirit, perhaps we should consider the church herself as a sacrament. David Watson suggests:

> It seems that part of the trouble is that we have regarded the sacraments as institutions OF the church and WITHIN the church; and it may well be that some of this tension would be resolved if, with the Eastern Orthodox church, we saw the church in itself as the sacrament of Christ's presence and action in the world.[29]

Consider the fascinating possibilities of Christ being re-presented in, to, and through the church by:
* Anointing the sick with oil for divine healing (Mark 6:13; James 5:14, 15).
* Lifting our hands in prayer for blessing (1 Tim. 2:8).
* Singing psalms, hymns, and spiritual songs to glorify God (Eph. 5:19; Col. 3:16; Heb. 2:12).
* Praying audibly together for God's help (Acts 4:24; 12:5)
* Allowing spiritual gifts to manifest the revelation, power, and utterance of Jesus Christ (1 Cor. 12).
* Praising God as a New Testament sacrifice (Heb. 13:15; Ps. 22:3).
* Using the Davidic forms of worship to glorify God (Rom 15:9-11; Phil. 3:3; 1 Pet. 2:9).
* Acknowledging apostolic government as it develops (Eph. 4:11, 12).

Protestants discuss the preaching of the Word of God as a possible sacrament.[30] Should Christians approach the preaching and teaching of the Bible with the same prayerful expectation that they do Communion? I have found it helpful to preface a sermon with a strong prayer to invoke God's blessing and to ask God to manifest His presence—inherent in the Word—in the hearts of people. Preaching the Word is momentous, and we do respect the theory but struggle in practice. "We would like to feel," Robert Schaper honestly confesses, "that the preaching is verbal sacrament, mediating a present Christ, but we are not sure."[31]

Anamnesis: A new significance

In today's church, Christians speak of "remembering what Christ did for us." Jesus and Paul said to partake of Communion in "remembrance" of Him (Luke 22:19; 1 Cor. 11:25, 26).[32] The word *anamnesis*, translated as "remembering," has new significance in biblical theology. As Christians observe Communion, they remember the historical event of Christ's passion but also sense the event as if it is presently happening.

The Lord's Supper is similar to the Jewish Passover. The Passover celebration gave Israel a routinely scheduled time to remember the great redemptive act that God performed for Israel (Exodus, chapter 12). Every Israelite, regardless of when and where he lived, was to receive—by faith—deliverance from Egypt as if he were one of the original generation of freed slaves. Early Christians celebrated the Eucharist not only to remember the historical event of Christ's passion, but also to experience immediate fellowship with their risen Lord! The events of the Lord's life, death, and resurrection were experienced through the living presence of the Spirit of Jesus. Throughout the age, Christians receive Communion to participate in Christ's experience with Him!

Most people struggle with the effort to "remember" a Christ they have never seen, one that has been represented in numerous ways by various painters. As a boy growing up in a military family, I attended Protestant communion services in chapels on bases where my father was stationed. I struggled to visualize or "remember" Christ. My mind would flash back and forth between a suffering Victim on a cross and a solemn Jesus at a supper table surrounded by twelve men with strange expressions on their faces. Sometimes I envisioned Jesus praying in the Garden of Gethsemane with a beam of light shining on Him. I welcomed the variation.

The apostle Paul recognized the futility and danger of using mental recall or viewing things from a natural viewpoint: He wrote, "Even though we once regarded Christ from a human point of view, we regard Him thus no longer" (2 Cor. 5:16 RSV). The Holy Spirit has to help believers see the significance and reality in anamnesis. Bible truths are not "words taught by human wisdom, but in those taught by the Spirit, combining spiritual thoughts with spiritual words" (1 Cor. 2:13). Michael Green explains, "it takes God to reveal God. And Paul claims that God has done so through the Spirit interpreting spiritual truths to men who possess the Spirit."[33]

The need for dependence on the Spirit motivated John to write his Gospel. In the sixth chapter, John points to Jesus' own spiritual emphasis of the Eucharistic concept of body and blood. When crowds turned away from Jesus after hearing His offensive invitation to eat His flesh and drink His blood (6:53, 54), Jesus further mystified them by asking how they could eat His body if He were to ascend up? In other words, if it seemed impossible with Him standing there, how much more impossible would it be after He is taken away? Jesus answered his own question by saying, "It is the Spirit who gives life" (6:63). By the Spirit, Jesus' followers would be able to ingest His life.

My point is that we cannot "remember" Christ in Communion merely by thinking about those events, as sacred a they may be. We must have the Holy Spirit working in us to properly experience Communion.

The abiding presence
Striking displays of divine activity characterized the early church. The manifestations were considered to have supernatural origin and, therefore, to attest to the presence of Christ among His people. Prophecy was treated as if it actually was Christ speaking among people. Miraculous signs were recognized as the continuing personal concern Christ shows for mankind. Revelations that came in visions to worshiping saints were received as revelations of Jesus in the midst of His church. Early Christians believed in the very real presence of Jesus at all times.

I am with you always, even to the end of the age (Matt. 28:20).

For where two or three have gathered together in My name, there I am in their midst (Matt. 18:20).

And the disciples were continually filled with joy and with the Holy Spirit (Acts 13:52).

Communion was not the only revelation of the risen Christ to the church. The Lord's Supper, structured as it was, could more easily be retained and maintained in congregational life than the spontaneous manifestations of His presence, which would be affected by lack of prayer and dedication. However, the evidence of the supernatural also could diminish in sacramental activities by increased concern and fussiness over predetermined prayers and formal activities. It is easy for a structured form to substitute for a life-flow that originates with the Spirit of God.

Of all the various activities of worship, the sacrament of His body and blood retains the best dynamic, reciprocal motion in the minds of most Christians. God does something, and people do something. The simple, dramatic act of the church eating and drinking together "in remembrance" of Him, has perpetuated a wonderful truth that could have been easily lost.

It is unfortunate when the genuine awareness of His presence yields to a casual recall of an historical event. Religious forms alone cannot communicate or perpetuate spiritual experience. The ritual is not meant to replace the reality.

Jesus Christ is Lord, and He is in the midst of His church! As believers sing, praise, pray, preach, and fellowship, He constantly abides, faithfully concerned about their welfare.

And I turned to see the voice that was speaking with me. And having turned I saw seven golden lampstands; and in the middle of the lampstands one like a son of man (Rev. 1:12, 13).

For both He who sanctifies and those who are sanctified are all from one Father; for which reason He is not ashamed to call them brethren, saying, "I WILL PROCLAIM THY NAME TO MY BRETHREN, IN THE MIDST OF THE CONGREGATION I WILL SING THY PRAISE" (Heb. 2:11, 12).

271

Let us maintain our awareness of His presence in the two great sacraments of baptism and Eucharist, but let us also allow His presence to infuse meaning into every biblical activity carried on in the church. We have been given broad freedom for spiritual expression. Let us encourage a flower garden of sacramental diversity to spring up, making church life to be sacrament in itself.

Reflections

At least for St. Paul the Lord's Supper was no mere recalling of a memory from the past, nor only a looking forward to the future, but a potent means of present contact with the risen Lord.
—*C.F.D. Moule*[34]

To recall, in Biblical thought, means to transport an action which is buried in the past in such a way that its original potency and vitality are not lost, but are carried over into the present. 'In remembrance of me', then, is no bare historical reflection upon the Cross, but a recalling of the crucified and living Christ in such a way that He is personally present in all the fullness and reality of His saving power, and is appropriated by the believer's faith.
—*Ralph P. Martin*[35]

This ANAMNESIS or memorial . . . is something quite different from a mere exercise of memory. It is a restoration of the past so that it becomes present . . . . In the world of Biblical culture "to remember" is to make present and operative . . . . Past and present are merged . . . . the present becomes possible.
—*J.J. von Allmen*[36]

The very word implies that the mind turns back to the past action—Christ's world-redeeming work—to bring it down to the present moment and into the midst of the celebrating community . . . . through the memorial, which is more than mere subjective recalling. Thus . . . the emphasis is on the object . . . more than on the Church's commemorative act.
—*Josef A. Jungmann*[37]

The force of the phrase is . . . not 'with a view to preserving my memory' or even 'celebrating my memory' but 'with a view to recalling me' . . . . It recalled Christ so vividly . . . that He was felt to be actually present.
—*Charles A.A. Scott*[38]

Celebration links us to the past and the future in a rich continuity of life. In its . . . historical sense, [it] is the symbolic reenactment of a meaningful event, a reconstruction of certain essential symbols which stand for an event of extraordinary meaning . . . . [It] points to a reality which extends a past event into the living present . . . . reaffirms values that are meant to endure . . . .
—*Dwight H. Small*[39]

Take account of the clear understanding then general in a largely Greek-speaking church of . . . ANAMNESIS as meaning a "re-calling" or "re-presenting" of that thing in such a way that it is not so much regarded as being "absent", as itself PRESENTLY OPERATIVE by its effects.
—*Dom Gregory Dix*[40]

273

32

The Local Church
as a House of Prayer

*If my people, which are called by my name, shall humble themselves, and pray, and
seek my face, and turn from their wicked ways; then will I hear from heaven, and will
forgive their sin, and will heal their land. Now mine eyes shall be open, and mine ears
attend unto the prayer that is made in this place.*
—2 Chronicles 7:14,15 KJV

Prayer and worship have much in common. Strictly speaking, prayer is talking to
God. Worship is expressing love and adoration to God. However, people with a life of
prayer know that it, especially long periods of it, involves thanksgiving and praise as
well as petition. The word *worship* can be viewed as a generic term covering all
activities of prayer, praise, thanksgiving and worship.[1] Prayer and worship are so
intertwined that it is impossible and unnecessary to separate them. A person or
congregation that lives a life of prayer finds a direct relationship between prayer and
the glorious manifestations of the Spirit that occur when their church worships
together.

Dick Eastman devoted an entire section of his well-known book *School of Prayer*
to "The Prayer Warrior's Praise-Life" because praise is so vital to prayer.[2] E.M.
Bounds, a famous authority on prayer from Civil War days, clearly associates prayer
and worship:

> Praise is so distinctly and definitely wedded to prayer, so inseparably joined, that they
> cannot be divorced.[3]

It is possible for a person to function in elementary forms of prayer without
being much of a worshiper; nevertheless, the person who has become an in-depth
worshiper will be strong in prayer. A deepening prayer life predictably produces
an enhanced worship experience.

Prayer and the house of God

Jesus' most definitive description of the local church was quoted from Isaiah
56:7: "My house shall be called a house of prayer" (Matt. 21:13; Mark 11:17; Luke
19:46). The place where God's people gather could be described as home to a variety
of activities, such as preaching, education, music, evangelism, etc. These things are all

275

very important, but the aspect Jesus focused on and considered most important was prayer.

Charlie Shedd commented, "It might be argued whether this was Jesus' most specific expression of his desire for his church." Then he hastens to add, "But serious students of the Word will hold it for prime consideration."[4] E.M. Bounds, in his typically direct fashion, says that Jesus in this statement, "makes prayer preeminent, that which stands out above all else in the house of God."[5]

Jesus used the expression "a house of prayer" to emphasize the necessity of congregating people for prayer. Individual prayer is important, but in both Old and New Testaments the gathering of people at scheduled times and specific places for collective, congregational prayer is too significant to be overlooked. The sacred pursuit of prayer and worship with a church family makes a person's religious heritage rich.

People in the local church find occasions to gather together in "the house of God."[6] While the church is not a place or a building, people inherently want to set apart a place for worship and prayer that is free from unhallowed and secular uses. Without unnecessary distractions, it becomes a sacred place where God meets with His children. Significantly, when heathen people from any of the cultures around the world are converted to Christ, they immediately desire to gather in a house of worship with other believers.[7]

King David understood this human tendency—this innate desire to gather with others unto God. Naturally, he wanted to build a great temple. It was to be a place "for the name of the Lord" (in the sense of being a memorial), and it was to be a place for people to gather to seek the Lord. David prepared to build the magnificent structure, but his son, Solomon, actually carried out the plan. The parallel accounts in 1 Kings, chapter 8, and 2 Chronicles, chapters 6 and 7, confirm that Solomon's temple was indeed a house of prayer above everything else.

When both Isaiah and Jesus used the expression "house of prayer," they referred back to the original intent for the building as stated in Kings and Chronicles. At the temple's dedication, Solomon prayed with extraordinary spiritual insight and revealed what the heart and mind of God wanted His house to be. Standing on a small bronze platform about five feet high, he called the people to prayer. Then, dropping to his knees before all the people and lifting his hands to heaven, the humbled king prayed one of the great prayers of the Bible. His prayer designated the temple as a focal point for prayer in Israel. Eight times he urged God to hear His people when they "pray and make supplication before Thee in this house."[8] His climactic words were:

> Now, O my God, I pray Thee, let Thine eyes be open, and Thine ears attentive to the prayer offered in this place (2 Chron. 6:40).

God quickly responded to Solomon's prayer, and gave His famous answer in 2 Chron. 7:12-22. Every great prayer movement uses verse 14 as a key text, and Christians around the world recite and claim it. Verse 15 proves God's concern for His house of prayer:

If my people, which are called by my name, shall humble themselves, and pray, and seek my face, and turn from their wicked ways; then will I hear from heaven, and will forgive their sin, and will heal their land. Now mine eyes shall be open, and mine ears attend unto the prayer that is made in this place (KJV).

For all nations

With prophetic insight, Isaiah enlarged the Davidic concept of "a house of prayer" to become "a house of prayer *for all the peoples.*" Of the three synoptic Gospel writers, only Mark records Jesus' use of this last phrase of Isaiah's quotation:

> And He began to teach and say to them, "Is it not written, 'MY HOUSE SHALL BE CALLED A HOUSE OF PRAYER *FOR ALL THE NATIONS*'? But you have made it a robbers' den" (Mark 11:17, emphasis added).

Jesus knew that the privilege of prayer was extended to all nations, and Mark, writing to a Gentile audience, carefully included the whole quotation of Jesus in his record. The basic meaning of this expanded version is: "God's house of prayer is for all people." Barnes says the Isaiah passage has two basic ideas: "first, that the temple should be regarded as a house of prayer; and, second, that privileges of that house should be extended to all people."[9]

In Jesus' day, the great Temple of Herod made token provision for heathen converts and worshipers. The Court of the Gentiles provided sanctuary for devout pagans, but those who came were restricted to that area. It is so ironic that such a beautiful, provisional concept could be so abused. This special area became desecrated by commercial activities initiated and maintained by the temple authorities. Under the guise of supplying sanctified, sacrificial animals and appropriate, blessed money for worshipers, the priests and their associates committed graft, extortion, and desecration of the house of prayer. In the very area where sincere seekers of other nations were confined, the house of God was made into a marketplace of merchandise, a bazaar of bargains, and an emporium of evil. Swete says:

> Who could pray in a place which was at once a cattle-market and an exchange, where the lowing of oxen mingled with the clinking of silver and the chaffering and haggling of the dealers and those who came to purchase?[10]

Small wonder that Jesus manifested such wrath and indignation at the desecration of His Father's house—the place of prayer had become a den of scheming robbers.

In 70 A.D., Herod's temple, with its mixture of evil and blessing, was destroyed by the Roman army. Fortunately, the church understood how the original concept would be transferred from a temple of dead stones to Christ's church of living believers. The church—composed of Christians from all nations—is now the "temple of God" (1 Cor. 3:16); we are the "household of God" (1 Tim. 3:15). Heb. 3:6 says: "but Christ was faithful as a Son over His house whose house we are." The church has become the house of prayer for all nations—whether we pray individually in our prayer closets or collectively in buildings—and so we fulfill Malachi 1:11:

"For from the rising of the sun, even to its setting, My name will be great among the nations, and in every place incense is going to be offered to My name, and a grain offering that is pure; for my name will be great among the nations," says the LORD of hosts (Mal. 1:11).

The church as a prayer closet

What Jesus said about prayer in the Sermon on the Mount has become His most famous teaching on the subject. Jesus pointed to differences between a hypocrite praying on the street corner and a sincere believer praying secretly and alone. Without considering other Scriptures on prayer, it would be easy to assume that authentic prayer occurs only in private and in a prayer closet.

> And when thou prayest, thou shalt not be as the hypocrites are: for they love to pray standing in the synagogues and in the corners of the streets, that they may have glory of men. Verily I say unto you, they have their reward. But thou, when thou prayest, enter into thy closet, and when thou hast shut thy door, pray to thy Father which is in secret and thy Father which seeth in secret shall reward thee openly (Matt. 6:5-6 KJV).

The term *closet* conveys a strange, negative connotation to some readers. As a child, I envisioned our small, family broom closet as the focus of Jesus' words. Actually the Greek word *tameion* is translated variously as: "your room" (RSV, TEV, NIV), "your inner room" (NAS), "your own room" (PHILLIPS, BECK), "your private room" (JB), "room by yourself" (NEB), and "your most private place" (W). The Living Bible gives the basic meaning: go away by yourself, all alone.

Jesus did not routinely pray in broom closets, but He did regularly practice private, uninterrupted communion with His heavenly Father in out-of-the-way places. For instance, He used a secluded wilderness area (Luke 5:16), a remote mountain top (Luke 6:12), and an unoccupied garden (Luke 22:41). Such places may seem uninviting—even frightening—to commune with the Almighty, but it was where the Son of Man learned the ways and thoughts of God. Jesus' teaching was born from real-life situations, in which He found for Himself the deep pleasure and inspiration in private, devotional times. This truth about closet praying may have occurred to Jesus while reflecting on Isaiah 26:20, a portion of which He quoted in the text above. It says, "Come my people, enter into your rooms, and close your doors behind you."

God is everywhere, yet Jesus promised that the Father will particularly meet individual believers "there in the secret place" (NEB). He takes an interest in any prayer that is offered without attracting attention. Our heavenly Father is concerned about what is secretly and privately important to you! The Phillips translation says it succinctly: "Your Father who sees all private things . . . ." Our invisible Friend from heaven who has unlimited power and resources desires to meet with us individually and regularly in a private, secluded place where He can personally hear, evaluate and give help to bring your secret desires to pass.[11]

These thoughts on personal prayer need not conflict with the concept of congregational prayer. Instead, they help illustrate that the prayer closet is for individual prayer, and the house of God is a sanctified place for united prayer. In fact, the local church building can be considered a closet of prayer. There are times when

Christians, especially city dwellers, find it difficult to have secluded prayer, so the use of a church building for both private and corporate prayer becomes a necessity. Thus, the church building is a closet for the body of Christ. It is a sanctuary in the best sense of the word.

The building may also be used for preaching, evangelism, dramatic productions, and film showings to reach non-Christians, but its primary function is to be a meeting place for prayer and worship. Outreach programs for unbelievers are important, but prayer and worship is essential for those who already believe.

Many think of church gatherings as programs designed to appeal to sinners. The thought has staggering implications. It leads to watered-down sermons and worship services. In contrast, the needs of the saints will be met only when they gather for spiritual edification.

The local church building should be a hub of activity for Christians. This sanctified place invites church people to travel from all directions for united prayer to God. The gathering of Christians for collective prayer is a closet experience in the sense that people come out of various environments to seek the living God. In the devoted atmosphere of the Christian community and secluded from the secular city, they face few distractions and interruptions. Although other believers may pray nearby—even audibly—each Christian finds the setting conducive to prayer. In fact, the spiritual power that attends praying people enhances and empowers personal prayer.

The morning I wrote these words I attended early morning prayer meeting at the church building. Traveling 2.8 miles by car, and arriving at 5:55 a.m., I found people already present for prayer. As I entered the sanctuary, I asked the woman coming in at the same moment how long it took her to come. She said, "Twenty minutes, but I don't mind." She felt it was worth the trip.

Fifty people prayed for an hour with a leader pacing us through the main points of the Lord's prayer. During that hour people sat, knelt, stood, and even walked as they prayed. Some prayed silently and some audibly. Although I pray alone at home, I find a group prayer service fulfilling. Praying with the rest of the body of Christ, I join the church in a collective closet experience.

Spurgeon's prayer meeting

One of the most successful pastors of all times was Charles Haddon Spurgeon (1834-1892). At the age of twenty-two, he was the most popular preacher in his day. By the age of twenty-seven he had built a church in London seating 6,000 people to accommodate the crowds that flocked to hear him preach. For more than thirty years he pastored the same church, which came to be known as the largest church in the world. His published sermons fill sixty-three volumes.

Spurgeon believed deeply in the value of prayer. He made his Metropolitan Tabernacle a true house of Prayer. Listen to this account of his world-famous Monday night prayer meeting by Justin D. Fulton:

His Prayer Meeting

No sooner did I enter than his eye caught mine, and I was invited to the platform, and was permitted to enjoy the greatest privilege of my life, and trace to its source the marvelous power of the man. The prayer meeting was a colossal fact. It surpassed anything I ever saw before. Its size was surprising. Without anything of an extraordinary nature, the ground floor was full at the opening. And still they came, until the first gallery was full, and the crowd began to darken the second gallery. Then the meeting began promptly on time. The singing was not extra. No instrument. A good leader, and all sang old tunes in an old-fashioned way. Nothing yet to explain the marvelous crowd. The Scripture was read, and the comment on it was good, but nothing surprising. The secret was not in the reading of the Scripture. The prayers were in no way extraordinary. On the platform sat the father, mother, wife, and brother of the great preacher. Deacon Olney read the requests for prayer, and told us all something about the extent of the work in London, and throughout the world, and then he prayed; the meeting was still dead. Then Spurgeon arose and talked, and said: 'I want to introduce to you the noblest and best of living men, my honoured father.' Up arose the honoured man, but nothing came of it. Then came Deacon Olney and said to the pastor, 'You had better take the meeting.' I looked at his face and I think I will remember how it looked in heaven. The red lines ran up and down his cheeks. He was in silent prayer. Whether he said anything preceding his prayer, I do not remember, but if he did, it was only to get ready for the prayer. Then in a humble manner he said, 'Let us all go to the throne of grace,' No British regiment ever followed Havelock into a terrific charge with more determination, or with a greater sense of the crisis to be met, than did that praying host on that occasion. In a moment the enemy of souls was charged.[12]

Congregational prayer times

Local church people should gather periodically for prayer in their church buildings or meeting places. Whether in a home or cathedral, the church is to be a house of prayer. The New Testament teaches and illustrates congregational prayer.

> Again I say to you, that if two of you agree on earth about anything that they may ask, it shall be done for them by My Father who is in heaven. For where two or three have gathered together in My name, there I am in their midst (Matt. 18:19, 20).

Others sometimes attended Jesus' devotional prayer times. For instance, Luke 11:1 reads: "And it came about that *while He was praying in a certain place,* after He had finished, one of His disciples said to Him . . . ." Jesus' most awesome time of personal prayer, in the Garden of Gethsemane, was attended by several disciples. At least they heard some of His words and recorded them in Mark 14:32-42. Luke 9:18 says, "While He was praying alone, the disciples were with Him." Ten verses later, the Scripture says, "He took Peter and John and James, and went up into a mountain to pray" (Luke 9:28).

Acts 1:14 records the first prayer meeting of the church. Prayer lasted for several days, and at one point 120 people were present. Herbert Lockyer makes the point, "Historically, the church of Jesus Christ was born in a prayer meeting," and then he adds with feeling, "and her life can only be maintained in the same atmosphere."[13]

Prevailing prayer in the Upper Room precipitated the mighty outpouring of the Holy Spirit on the day of Pentecost. The Modern Language Bible states it like this:

> All these engaged constantly and with one mind in prayer, together with the women and Mary the mother of Jesus, and with His brothers.

Prayer became one of the important activities of the Christians. Apparently they prayed together frequently.

> And they were continually devoting themselves to the apostles' teaching and to fellowship, to the breaking of bread and to prayer (Acts 2:42).[14]

After being ridiculed and castigated by the Jewish council, Peter and John returned to the church and held a glorious prayer meeting:

> And when they heard this, they lifted their voices to God with one accord . . . . And when they had prayed, the place where they had gathered together was shaken, and they were all filled with the Holy Spirit, and began to speak the word of God with boldness (Acts 4:24, 31).

Leaders of the early church were not content with a few mighty prayer meetings. They prayed together frequently. Their watch-cry was: "We will devote ourselves to prayer and the ministry of the word" (Acts 6:4).

The early church did not have church buildings but they met wherever and whenever they could. When Peter was thrown into prison, Acts 12:5 says, "but prayer for him was being made fervently by the church to God." This intense prayer time took place in the home of Mark's mother. After Peter had been miraculously delivered, the Bible says, "He came to the house of Mary . . . where many were gathered together and were praying" (v. 12).

Other illustrations of collective prayer include the gathering of the church at Antioch (Acts 13:2, 3), the times of prayer preceding ordination in the churches (Acts 14:23), the place of prayer that birthed the church at Philippi (Acts 16:13, 16), Paul's prayer with the elders of Ephesus (Acts 20:36), and the prayer meeting with men, women, and children on the seashore (Acts 21:5).

Early morning prayer around the world

An amazing and encouraging sign of church renewal in this day is the emphasis on prayer. There have always been books on prayer and prayer seminars, but there now seem to be genuine efforts to reinstitute the praying characteristic of the New Testament church. Christians around the world rise every day to early morning prayer.[15] As the earth turns and the sun rises, people in every time zone wake up to pray. If enough people throughout the world in the various hemispheres participate, God hears literally unceasing prayer "from the rising of the sun, even to its setting" (Mal. 1:11). Then prayer encircles the earth![16]

Perhaps the greatest praying churches today are in Korea. Prayer is practiced, not just discussed. Well-known church growth expert C. Peter Wagner recently commented:

> I think my deepest impression of Korea was the extraordinary pervasive sense of prayer I found in all the churches. Every church has a dawn prayer meeting at 4:30 or 5:00 a.m. every single day. It is so important that the senior pastor of most multiple-staff churches visits or leads that meeting every morning. When I asked why, several said simply, "That's where the power comes from," Most churches have an all-night prayer meeting on Friday nights that the pastor often attends.[17]

One of the most famous churches in the world is also the largest, the Full Gospel Central Church of Seoul led by Pastor Paul Y. Cho. It has more than 700,000 members and sponsors a mountain retreat dedicated to fasting and prayer that defies description. Thousands gather daily for fasting and prayer and receive miraculous answers to their prayers. All the evangelical churches believe in morning prayer, and some have similar mountain prayer retreats. Many Americans have been forced by the success of Korean church growth to reexamine Scriptures such as:

> My voice shalt thou hear in the morning, O Lord; in the morning will I direct my prayer unto thee, and will look up (Ps. 5:3).[18]

Pastor Alec Rowlands, of the First Assembly of God in Cedar Rapids, also testifies to the amazing results of regularly scheduled congregational prayer. He says that seventy-five percent of the people in his church who have become committed to a ministry of prayer became involved in corporate prayer when the church took a visible stand on it. He said, "I believe the congregation must have a visible, tangible expression for their commitment—that is, regularly scheduled prayer meetings."[19]

Church renewal depends on a foundation of prayer, and the vitality and fruitfulness of Christian worship directly reflects the church's state of prayer. The sobering fact is that ministers in America spend an average of one hour per week in prayer. "It is quite natural and inevitable," wrote Dean Inge, " that if we spend sixteen hours daily of our waking life in thinking about the affairs of the world, and five minutes in thinking about God . . . this world will seem 200 times more real to us than God."[20]

Spiritual leaders will produce praying, worshiping churches if their own lives, ministries, and messages are shaped by staying in vital union with God, by praying in the Holy Spirit, by abiding in the vine (Eph. 6:18; Jude 20; John 15:5). Pastor Cho says it plainly:

> As a pastor, I have learned from the beginning of my ministry that the only way to cause my members to want to pray is to pray myself. If I did not have a life of prayer, I would not have a praying church, and I certainly would not be in the midst of revival. Christ's disciples were only ready to be taught how to pray after they had expressed the desire to learn because of His example.[21]

Prepare for worship with pre-service prayer

Conducting a church prayer meeting before the start of every worship service can revolutionize corporate worship services. We use it, and wherever I have seen this procedure followed in a local church, it produces positive results. It is often called pre-service prayer or preparatory prayer.

Corporate prayer prepares people for dynamic, spiritual worship. Consider what might happen if people could be trained to come early to the church building, before the service is scheduled to begin, and gather in some designated area for serious, concentrated, united prayer. Families would arrive early at the church property and fill the prayer room to seek the Lord. A church that develops a large prayer group (i.e., a high percent of the number attending services) will powerfully and easily move into the charismatic realm.

A house of prayer should accommodate prayer. It should schedule prayer, designate a place to pray, and appoint people to be in charge of prayer. A large carpeted room with seats arranged in rows provides comfort as well as privacy from the eyes of church visitors.

People should be encouraged to pray fervently. If they wish to change prayer posture, encourage them to do so; their attention to prayer should not be hindered by tiredness. The prayer time (specify at least thirty minutes) can be structured or unstructured, but the objective must be to bring the people into an experience of faith and confidence in their God. Faith, in turn, lifts the worship service into a dynamic dimension of grace.

> And without faith it is impossible to please Him for he who comes to God must believe that He is, and that He is a rewarder of those who seek Him (Heb. 11:6).

In our own local church we use pre-service prayer to:
* acknowledge that God is the church's only source.
* invite His presence.
* invoke His blessing.
* humble our souls.
* exercise faith for a great service.
* prepare to receive God's living Word.
* praise and thank Him for His goodness.
* pray for specific requests.

Pre-service prayer generates an excitement and expectancy that carries right over into the scheduled worship celebration. R.S. Simpson fervently comments:

> Still, I am persuaded that if prayer, corporate prayer, is to attain unto the fullness of its fruit and have lasting reality in the public worship of God, we must hold today that prayer does something—does something almost objectively; that personal prayer does it; that corporate prayer does it; and that through the prayers of the church there is given to God material, as it were, which He uses for the working out of the ends of His kingdom.[22]

Effort is required to build a consistently large, enthusiastic attendance at pre-service and early morning prayer, but the results are remarkable. The pastor, by his announcements and attendance, must show it holds major significance for him. Also, if elders, deacons, and teachers actively join in, the example will stimulate church-wide, voluntary cooperation.

Benefits of pre-service prayer
Benefits of scheduled pre-service prayer include:
1. People are in the church building when it is time to start the service, and they are eager to enter into dynamic worship.
2. Prayer constantly reminds church people of their dependence on God, and it provides them with a time and place for prayer if they want and need it.
3. God is presented with petitions which He will honor, thereby building the church's confidence in a miracle-working God as prayers are answered and testimonies are given.
4. Children and youth see by the examples of their parents and leaders that a church needs congregational prayer to fulfill its calling.
5. Prayer is like "seeding the heavenly clouds," which in turn pour out copiously the blessings of the Spirit during the worship service.
6. Fervent corporate prayer stimulates personal prayer lives and vitalizes the people's praise and worship.
7. Everyone is made to realize that prayer and worship go hand-in-hand.

A leading proponent of pre-service prayer was the late Pastor Reg Layzell, who influenced many churches to begin it. He made this classic statement:

> The pastor must recognize the greatest thing that could happen to his church is a strong united praying people. He must set the example by leading in such a prayer life so that the people see that he does it and is with them. The pastor needs to recognize that the anointed prayer time of the church is the powerhouse of the church. Persistent effort must be made to have every member of the congregation participate. Prayer life has to be deliberately cultivated. Generally speaking, prayer is a sacrifice and requires personal discipline. To have a large number of the congregation participating in the prayer time is difficult and requires a persistent example on the part of the pastor and all the ministry. It is the most important meeting of the congregation.[23]

Praying people will be worshipers
Nothing will enhance the worship services of a church and create an appreciation of God's majesty like active prayer by the church body. An ongoing prayer program allows a continuous release of joyous, spontaneous, spiritual worship in people. Judson Cornwall confirms the relationship between prayer and worship:

> Worship begins in prayer, and it must flow Godward through the prayer channel. Where there is no prayer, there will be no worship! Because this is true, prayerlessness is the greatest enemy to worship in the churches of America.[24]

The majesty of God that seems so distant to the average person, suddenly becomes wonderfully accessible through humble prayer. When people realize their carnal poverty and weakness, they are moved to pray. In prayer they meet the God they worship, and He transforms them—lifting them up into heavenly realms by His blessed Holy Spirit. Bob Sorge stated:

> If we invest ourselves diligently in prayer for the worship service, we will be amazed at our level of concern for and participation in the service. If we spend quality time praying for the service, we will be eager to see a return on that investment and will be ready to become involved to help make it a glorious session.[25]

The "bottom line" of worship—the foundation for it all—is a humble, broken spirit that manifests itself in sincere prayer, seeking God's blessing. This prostration of soul and body before God does not degrade people. It provides the necessary vehicle for lifting up the person into communion with his or her loving-yet-majestic heavenly Father. Strength and vitality come from brokenness and prepare the soul to adore God in triumphant celebration!

The search for reality in worship begins humbly on the knees. It should not seem strange. A praying church will reel in the majesty of their God. They will be a worshiping people.

Reflections

The prayer meeting ought to be the most important meeting in the church. It is the most important meeting if it is rightly conducted. Of course the church prayer meeting in many churches is more a matter of form than a center of power. The thing to do in such a case is not to give up the prayer meeting, but to make it what it ought to be.

—*R.A. Torrey*[26]

Any church calling itself the house of God, and failing to magnify prayer; which does not put prayer in the forefront of its activities; which does not teach the great lesson of prayer, should change its teaching to conform to the Divine pattern or change the name of its building to something other than a house of prayer.

—*E.M. Bounds*[27]

The prayer-meeting is a meeting for prayer. That is so obvious a statement as to appear unnecessary . . . . there is nothing the Church needs more at the present hour than to understand what a real prayer meeting is.

—*G. Campbell Morgan*[28]

Satan does not care how many people read about prayer if only he can keep them from praying. When a church is truly convinced that "prayer is where the action is" that church will so construct its corporate activities that the prayer program will have the highest priority . . . . Unless a church is satisfied to merely operate an ecclesiastical treadmill, prayer will become her main occupation.

—*Paul E. Billheimer*[29]

All who are familiar with Mr. Spurgeon's writings, know that he regarded the prayer-meeting as the thermometer of the church; and, judging by the test, the spiritual temperature of the large community under his charge stood very high . . . . the world-wide testimony was that the meeting was altogether unique . . . . He often said that it was not surprising if churches did not prosper, when they regarded the prayer-meeting as of so little value that one evening in the week was made to suffice for a feeble combination of service and prayer-meeting . . . .

From the introduction to Charles H. Spurgeon's Autobiography

Prayer is the act by which the community of faith surrenders itself, puts aside all other concerns, and comes before God Himself.

—*Charles Colson*[30]

33

Gathering the Called-Out Ones

Let us not give up the habit of meeting together,
as some are doing.
—Hebrews 10:25 TEV

Christians gathered to worship have an effect more grand than the sum of their individual experiences. An exciting, synergistic power goes to work in the assembly. Alone, each believer has a quality and quantity of personal experience with God; however, God delights as believers come together in unity in a cooperative action of worship.[1]

Use of the term body in New Testament writings to describe Christ's church continues to remind Christians that they flow and function best when they are part of the metabolism of a local church. Robert Rayburn said, "The unattached Christian is an impossibility."[2] God intended for dedicated Christians to gather frequently with each other.[3] By concentrating in combined, unified worship, believers produce the best example of how a whole can be greater than the sum of its parts. Scattered Christians become the gathered church. Raymond Abba suggests:

> Christian worship is the corporate approach to God of the people of God. It is a family activity.[4]

God's grace or presence comes in two manners: personal and corporate. God's bestowal of corporate grace can be experienced only in the assembled church. Matt. 18:19 states the principle. A person may assume his Christianity is a personal matter and stay home—perhaps even watch religious TV—instead of gather with the saints. He misses the advantages of corporate grace and forfeits divine blessings intended for him.

The gathering of Christians in a congregation to worship the true and living God releases spiritual vitality. Together, believers experience spiritual rejuvenation not possible through private, individual devotions. Each believer should have a scheduled place for private prayer where personal nurture occurs (Matt. 6:6), but he also should meet with fellow believers at a specific location for the even more grand experience of

287

congregational nurture and worship. Certain major issues will respond only to corporate prayer (Acts 4:24-31; 12:12; Matt. 18:19).[5] Believers need their own personal prayer closets as well as a corporate prayer closet.

Truths of the Bible can be understood by personal study, but special understanding comes in the context of the assembled church. When Paul described the activities of a worship gathering, he constantly emphasized edification (1 Cor. 14:3, 4, 5, 12, 17, 26). As the Word of God is preached and taught in the local assembly, a special spiritual strengthening takes place. This strengthening comes only in the assembled company of the saints!

The assembled congregation

Although a place is necessary for worship, that location is merely a meeting place for the church. It is NOT the church. When the word *church* is used in the Bible, it refers to Christians who assemble together for corporate worship and NOT to church buildings which they use.[6] Walter Oetting cleverly illustrates this point:

> If you had asked, "Where is the church?" in any important city of the ancient world where Christianity had penetrated in the first century, you would have been directed to a group of worshiping people gathered in a house. There was no special building or other tangible wealth with which to associate "church," only people![7]

The Greek word *ekklesia,* translated church signifies that believers are a chosen, called-out group (*ek* = out of; *klesis* = a calling).[8] However, the meaning is as much "assembled together" as it is "called out." The term in non-biblical Greek referred to the recognized citizen body of a town assembled for political purposes, and in the Greek Old Testament it translates the Hebrew word *qahal* which referred to the assembled people of God.

Both Jesus and Paul apply *ekklesia* to the universal and local expressions of the body of Christ. C.K. Barrett suggests, "the word means not simply the people of God, but the people of God assembled."[9] Watchman Nee, in his characteristic clarity, simply states: "*Ecclesia* means 'the called-out ones assembled.' Today God has not only called out a people but He also wants them to assemble together."[10]

During times of church renewal, it is not uncommon for zealous people to challenge institutionalized structure, governmental oversight, or worship form. This mentality springs from dissatisfaction—or disenchantment— with the established church. It causes some to swing away from what they see as the problem and to create a fanatical freedom that is as detrimental as frozen formality. They may even question the validity of gathering for a worship service.

During the 1960s, young Jesus people were accepting Christ and having their own "hang-loose" type of gatherings. To some of them a structured service—even a church building—was anathema.[11] Some felt that if God wanted to gather people together, His Holy Spirit would move upon them and draw them. Naturally, this approach did not produce lasting fruit.

The churches of Bible days did meet regularly with scheduled programs as their situations allowed and at designated places where the specific objective was congregational worship. Some of those places were houses, caves, etc.

For where two or three are gathered together in my name, there am I in the midst of them (Matt. 18:20 KJV).

And they continued steadfastly in the apostles' doctrine and fellowship, in the breaking of bread and in prayers (Acts 2:42 KJV).

So for a whole year Barnabas and Saul met with the church and taught great numbers of people (Acts 11:26 NIV).

ALSO: Acts 14:27; 15:6, 22, 30; 20:7, 8.

So, my dear brothers, what conclusion is to be drawn? At all your meetings, let everyone be ready with a psalm or a sermon or a revelation, or ready to use his gift of tongues or to give an interpretation; but it must always be for the common good (1 Cor. 14:26 JB).

ALSO: 1 Cor. 5:4; 14:23, 28, 34; 1 Tim. 3:15; James 2:2.

Does the Bible furnish a form?

Did the early church have a set form or structure for their worship services? Did their liturgy have a defined shape? When they gathered together did they expect to follow a certain format?

First, the worship references in the New Testament do not give a clear focus on the actual mechanics. They merely excite our imaginations and whet our appetites.[12] 1 Corinthians, chapters 12-14, portray a thought-provoking and awe-inspiring charismatic format. Unfortunately, these same chapters have been fogged by Christians' unbelief and inexperience.

Second, a public assembly of people cannot be conducted without a form or structure for the meeting. Every church has some type of form or order, and this is commonly known as liturgy or ritual. Even churches that insist they have no liturgy follow some form or order. Robert Rayburn comments:

> The fact that Christians worship in groups makes certain demands upon them. A group is more than a crowd of individuals. In a true church gathered for worship there is a unity of the believers with a self-consciousness of its own. Corporate or group action always requires a certain form. An individual who worships alone may act in his own way, but when an aggregate of individuals comes to be what is called a congregation or community of believers they must have form and order in their worship.[13]

Lutheran scholar Peter Brunner, in his classic book, *Worship in the Name of Jesus*, devotes one third of his text to "The Form of Worship."[14]

> So long as we sojourn in this body, our worship bears the features of our earthly, physical existence and thus has a physical form. The importance of this form is seen

especially when we are assembled with others. This necessarily involves and stipulates order and form.[15]

Nearly forty years ago, the monumental *The Shape of the Liturgy* by Dom Gregory Dix was first published. This piece of massive scholarship traces the development of the Eucharist or breaking of bread, which he perceives to be the heart and core of the Christian worship. His general definition of liturgy follows:

"Liturgy" is the name given ever since the days of the apostles (Acts 13:2) to the act of taking part in the solemn corporate worship of God by the "priestly" society (1 Pet. 2:5) of Christians, who are "the Body of Christ, the church" (Eph. 1:22,23). "The Liturgy" is the term which covers generally all that worship which is officially organized by the church, and which is open to and offered by, or in the name of, all who are members of the church.[16]

Author's recommendations on form

I am not persuaded that a church needs to renounce its entire religious tradition to have a present-day moving of the Spirit. Radical changes need not be made just to be contemporary, but churches should rediscover the originality and spontaneity that characterized the early church. A wooden liturgy imparts no life to people. To bring back the sincerity, freshness, variety, and ardor of the early church's worship, church leaders must honestly face the dangers inherent in ecstatic worship yet never waver in confidence in the Spirit's leading.

Most churches have easily retained certain basic concepts of worship such as communion (Eucharist), water baptism, hymn singing, forms of prayer and preaching. These ingredients of the worship service have assumed various shapes in different churches, but generally the liturgic expression has tended to become so standardized and institutionalized that there is no "sense of the unexpected" or excitement of the unpredictable."[17]

Therefore, I propose following three radical but reasonable imperatives to revive and renew worship in today's church:

1. *Be willing to be flexible and expandable.* The New Testament mentions nineteen ingredients that were part of the worship experience. Today's church can enjoy all of them. It can overcome the scourge of monotonous drudgery in every Sunday service. Everything needs to be scrutinized, including the printed bulletin, with its strict regimentation, and the right-to-the-minute closure of the service (the "racing the clock" mentality). Every activity should be evaluated in the light of whether or not it produces vibrant Christians.

2. *Be open to the pneumatic flow.* "The flow of the church service," says Jack Hayford, "is a significant factor in determining the release of a congregation's life and the individual's ministry."[18] He adds that the order—the sequence, design and direction—of the meeting will bring either fruitfulness or frustration. Order should not be set in cement, but it should be the means God can use to meet with and move among His people as He so desires.

The active presence of the Holy Spirit makes the difference. A person "going to church" must meet God. He should not walk away with just a blind, unfeeling, take-it-by-faith experience. Believers gathering for worship must expect God to be present in a distinct and profound way! They also should expect to hear a divine directive, a Word from God that is actually "what the Spirit is saying to the Church."

This requires leadership and people who are filled with the Holy Spirit. It also requires prayer and waiting on God for direction. It requires being willing to allow the Holy Spirit to move in directions that sometimes are unanticipated. For example, during one of our worship services, I felt strongly impressed by the Lord to minister prophetically to a young couple seated halfway back in the sanctuary. Momentarily, I interrupted the hymn singing and asked the couple to come forward. I knew a little about their marital friction, but in that moment I felt that God would bring healing. Taking their hands in mine I ministered a prophetic prayer and release. Then I prayed for her chronic, migraine headaches to cease. The people stood with me and lifted their hands with joyful thanksgiving. The couple returned to their seats, and the woman later testified that she had not had that type of headache reoccur.

The pneumatic flow of the Holy Spirit understands the present needs of people in attendance. In a moment, the Spirit can accomplish more than we can with hours of counseling. Here is my plea: Let the Holy Spirit be welcome and made comfortable in our worship services. Let us flow with Him.

3. *Be comfortable with Psalmic worship forms.* Davidic worship forms are important adjuncts to traditional sacraments in releasing the transcendent presence of God among the people. If they are allowed and encouraged during the church service under proper pastoral guidance, a renewed excitement and interest will be generated in the people, particularly among the young people and serious Christians.

Such worship is a catalyst to initiate an actual spiritual encounter with Christ in the prophetic realm. The key to God's presence is not in a meticulous rendition of an ancient liturgy. The key is in the attitude of the assembled church. What are the people thinking? What are they expecting? God will indeed move through an ancient form or sacrament, or through a freshly inspired ode or spiritual song, but these things are merely vehicles for the Spirit's flow. We must not become too dogmatic about the form and the basis for the form in our liturgical expression to God. There is actually a great freedom of choice that is given to us in our expression. A spontaneous yet controlled form of worship helps people in a biblical way to open up their hearts and emotions to the living God.

David discovered that God wanted all of him in His worship. He responded, and the result is the book of Psalms. For years people have been reading the Psalms in church services. Now, leaders may simply invite people to do what they have been reading. This great heritage of the church needs to be taken out of mere responsive readings and made into living liturgy. Davidic styles of worship are for all peoples of every generation. Let us not only read the Psalms but also *do* them!

Peter Brunner makes a point that should be given serious consideration:

> The peculiar problem in the formation of worship service is posed by the wide area that remains between the two boundary lines of the *absolutely forbidden* and the *absolutely commanded* (emphasis added).

Brunner states that the church age lies between the time of the highly regulated Old Testament worship and the future worship of the New Jerusalem which has not yet appeared. New Testament believers are being led by the Holy Spirit to experience the worship of heaven without comprehending its guidelines. He continues:

> The formation of worship in that wide space between the absolutely forbidden and the absolutely commanded remains a matter of the believer's liberty . . . . If the church lives in the Word and in the Spirit, it will not be without guidance, without directives in the formation of that free space.[19]

One of the grand ways to use this liberty of expression in the free space afforded to us by the openness of the New Testament is to use Psalmic worship forms that have historical precedent throughout the Bible.

Ingredients of New Testament worship

The New Testament gatherings had both form and freedom. In 1 Corinthians, chapter 11, Paul repeated how Jesus conducted the Last Supper. He also stressed the need for a functional decorum that is not offensive and allows for courteous participation by all (1 Cor. 14:26, 33, 40).

The New Testament gives no fixed liturgy,[20] however, it does mention an interesting collection of elements or components which were part of the early church's services.[21] These ingredients were combined in various ways for different types of meetings. They formed the skeletal structure of worship services, which were ordered by the pastoral oversight of local eldership and embellished by the charismatic spontaneity of the Holy Spirit. They allowed liberty for varied expression but were dedicated to basic content for the mutual encouragement of the Christian community.

They give the impression that New Testament worship was void of any routineness, regularity, or sameness that could destroy the freshness necessary for authentic worship. Meaningful worship was maintained. The following list tells what they did but not *how* they did it:

Reading of Scripture. The scriptural content of the recorded sermons indicates a great use of Scripture (Acts, chapters 3, 7, and 11). The Bereans examined the Scriptures daily (Acts 17:11), the disciples continued in the Apostles' teaching (Acts 2:42), and the Word of God spread abroad (Acts 13:49). Paul expected his writings to be read in the churches (Col. 4:16; 1 Thess. 5:27; 2 Thess. 3:14). This is particularly necessary when people do not have their own Bibles.

Singing and worship. The joyful spirituality of early Christians was expressed in both spontaneous and routine song, praise, and giving thanks (Eph. 5:19; Col. 3:16; 1 Cor. 14:15, 26; Heb. 13:15). See chapter 16.

Peaceful greetings. Both Paul and Peter mention the great warmth of fellowship that was evidenced in the greeting of fellow Christians (Rom. 16:16; 1 Cor. 16:20; 2 Cor. 13:12; 1 Thess. 5:26; 1 Pet. 5:14). Everyone must feel welcome and needed whether it is by hugging, hand shaking, or kissing (depending on cultural limitations). Because Peter seems to connect the kiss with the peace of God, some feel that the kiss was a high point of early Christian worship.[22]

Lifting of hands in prayer. 1 Tim. 2:8. See chapter 19.

The people's 'Amen.' When what is said or done in a service is endorsed by a hearty "Amen!" a positive climate of faith is created. Amen means "let it be so" and voices approval in a striking way (1 Cor. 14:16). The Amen not only indicates the close of a prayer, but it also can effectively demonstrate congregational unity in response to a prayer.[23]

Giving of offerings. Giving tangible tokens always has been a part of religious worship. Christian giving should be "spontaneous, personal, individual, voluntary, and from a willing heart" (1 Cor. 16:1, 2; 2 Corinthians, chapters 8 and 9; Rom. 15:26; 1 Tim. 6:18).[24] In some cultures people give bananas, in others chickens. Most Americans give money. Giving should be done with enthusiasm and dignity. People may bring their offerings and march past ushers who hold receptacles. This method adds vitality to the service. At other times, offering bags may be passed. If not ostentatious, sacrificial giving pumps new life into any church's worship.[25]

Prayers. New Testament Christians were people of prayer (Acts 2:42, 46, 47; 3:1, 2; 4:24-31; 1 Tim. 2:1). They prayed for each other and they banded together to tackle impossible problems through prayer. Thoughts on prayer fill Paul's writings (Eph. 1:16; Col 1:9). Use every innovative approach to develop more effective prayer, including the Psalmic form of kneeling. See chapter 32.

Preaching and teaching. See Acts 8:4, 12; 15:35; 20:7-11. Teachers and teaching are mentioned numerous times (Acts 15:35; Rom. 12:7, 8; 1 Cor. 12:28; Eph. 4:11).

Prophecy. A person's initiation into the early church involved the experience of the Holy Spirit and prophetic activity.[26] The new convert found that this wonderful consciousness of the Spirit brought him into direct contact with God. He also discovered that the people to whom he was joined were prophetic people in the sense that they all experienced the same Spirit of Jesus. Their gatherings for worship gave the church members purpose and direction in living.

The unusual frequency of prophecy in its various forms throughout 1 Corinthians, chapters 11-14, indicates how important this manifestation was in the church worship services. Prophecy was given in the worship setting. David Aune says:

> On the basis of the evidence in 1 Cor. 12-14 it appears that prophets, or those who prophesied, were active only within the framework of Christian worship. Further, it appears that prophets were particularly active during particular segments of the service.[27]

Perhaps the most thoroughly prophetic book in the New Testament is Revelation. Significantly, John's prophetic experiences occur in the congregational worship setting of heaven itself. The enthusiastic, extravagant, praise and worship of heaven was the ideal setting for the grandest display of prophetic activity ever recorded. Heaven's expression is so reminiscent of Davidic enthusiasm in the Psalms that it is hard to conceive of the New Testament churches being content with just formal, structured worship. Revelation and 1 Corinthians, chapter 14, indicate that the Psalmic forms of expressive, audible worship set the best atmosphere for the manifestation of Jesus and His Spirit.

Spiritual gifts. Many books on spiritual gifts have flooded the market in recent years, but few mention how these gifts would function in the context of the church worship service. The nine "manifestations" of the Spirit mentioned in 1 Corinthians, chapter 12, seem to be those gifts best suited for the congregational meeting.

Laying on of hands. This was a broad ordinance (sacrament?) that included praying for the sick, ordination to ministry, prayer to receive the Holy Spirit, encouragement to people, blessing children and spiritual impartation (Heb. 6:2; Acts 6:6; 13:3; 8:17; 9:17; 19:6; 1 Tim. 4:14; 2 Tim. 1:6).

Anointing the sick with oil. One reference indicates that the disciples of Jesus anointed the sick with oil during Jesus' earthly ministry (Mark 6:13). This apparently became a standard procedure because James tells the sick to call for the elders to anoint with oil (James 5:14).

The breaking of bread. See Acts 2:42; Jude 12; 2 Pet. 2:13; 1 Cor. 11.

The Lord's Supper. See 1 Cor. 10:21; 11:20. See chapter 31.

Water baptism. See Acts 2:41; 8:36; 16:29-34. Also discussed in chapter 31.

Contributions by individuals. Eager Christians can be directed and controlled.[28] It need not be the terrible risk that some would suggest. The key verse here is 1 Cor. 14:26: "When you assemble, each one has a psalm, has a teaching, has a revelation, has a tongue, has an interpretation." Although the Corinthian services experienced some abuses, this cooperative participation was a brilliant principle. In our church, we place a microphone in the front for the spiritual contributions that people in the congregation wish to make. Without this provision we would have missed beautiful, spiritual odes, challenging prophecies, stirring exhortations, ringing testimonies, wise direction, and a host of other enrichments.

Confession of faith. To hear the church affirm her faith through the great creeds is a grand thing. Many great hymns allow these statements to be sung. I have found it helpful to have people audibly repeat phrases or portions I use in messages. To have people stand—even in the middle of a sermon—and repeat three times in ever louder tones: *Jesus is Lord!* can be exhilarating. To have one section of the congregation make a statement followed by another section's "Amen!" is another way of actually confessing our faith in the worship setting (1 Tim. 6:12; 2 Cor. 9:13).

Musical instruments. Instruments are used throughout the Old Testament, and they are used in the book of Revelation (Rev. 5:8; 14:2; 15:2). Why should there be a gap in their use—especially in our day when musical expression has become such a glorious, sophisticated art? See chapter 20.

The benediction. Closing remarks in the epistles indicate what probably was a church service tradition. It seems that a benediction would have been a natural way to close the services (Rom. 16:25-27; 1 Cor. 16:23, 24; 2 Cor. 13:14; Gal 6:18; Eph. 6:23, 24; 1 Thess. 5:28; Jude 24, 25).

Summary of New Testament charismatic worship

The people of a local church set aside a time of celebration to collectively express their love and devotion to God and to one another and, at the same time, to allow God to express His loving grace to them.[29] People hungry to meet with God come together to worship. Eagle-winged saints gather in Christ's presence in a local church. Such a meeting is not for people who "play church" but for the people in a given area who are the church!

Leaders structure the service time and the format at such a festival. They carefully consider their own approach, the building environment, and the movement and control of people so that:

There can be praise and worship which allows the people to be enthusiastic, sincere, and reverent in an emotional release as they adore and proclaim God. The atmosphere should be conducive to Psalmic worship forms. The people need a frame of mind open to the inspiration of the Holy Spirit, and the leadership must desire to flow with God and the people in pneumatic dialogue. The goal should be a charismatic worship celebration which proclaims joyfully the Lordship of Jesus in that particular church.

There can be ways of releasing the maximum power of the Holy Spirit through a maximum number of participating members. Flexible methods will allow the different kinds of gifts, ministries, and operations of the Spirit to take place, be properly evaluated, and publicly acknowledged for the edification of the church and any interested non-members.

There can be biblical instruction and preaching which will give substance, verification, and application to the Gospel as well as to the Spirit's activities. Pastoral leadership must interpret the Bible and what God is presently saying to His people at home and abroad. When people understand and appropriate the Bible, it guides their morality and spirituality. God's will, the Gospel of Christ, becomes known through the exposition of the Bible.

There can be opportunity for people to pray personally, for each other, encouraging one another. The local church needs more than teaching about prayer. It needs to provide example and exhortation for the people to pray collectively as well as individually. People who desire salvation, healing, Holy Spirit baptism, etc., should have opportunity for counseling and prayer by trained workers.

The people's tithes and offerings can be received in the spirit of faith and dignity which proclaims God as the source of all blessing. People want to be happy, responsive, and filled with faith to do the impossible. The challenge of missionary giving, building expansion, helping the needy, etc., are made possible in an atmosphere of worshiping Christians.

The Sacraments can be performed in such a way that the presence of Christ is manifest. Rather than being performed as isolated forms, the Communion, water baptism, preaching, anointing with oil, and confirmation can be integrated as part of the total manifestation of Christ in the midst of His church.[30] Every aspect of worship by the assembled company should be in and through the perfect worship and sacrifice of Christ—not just in the mechanical operation of a traditional Eucharist but in the Spirit of the living, worshiping Christ Himself!

There can be the public reading of the Bible. Because of the variety of translations, leaders need to be flexible and use modern techniques to obtain a unified, verbal statement of Scriptural truth. Use every legitimate expression to make the story known. Song, music, interpretive dance, drama, and the employment of modern multimedia tools should not be neglected for this TV generation.

Implementing Psalmic worship in the local church

If the Spirit of God is moving and the groundwork of Bible teaching has been laid, a congregation will gradually grow into a comfortable, expressive relationship with the nine Psalmic worship modes. It is not reasonable to ask uninformed and uninspired people to participate immediately in worship forms that are meaningless to them. Many people will respond immediately and enjoy Psalmic worship immensely. Others will need teaching and will carefully watch what is being modeled for them and how sincere other worshipers are. In any church, if people enjoy meaningful worship, they will participate for an hour. If they do not enjoy it, two minutes can be too long.

A leader who attempts to lead people into more spiritually demanding forms of worship, probably will need to draw most of his personal satisfaction from private devotions. As he sustains himself personally, he can patiently begin to teach what he wants to produce. He should teach it until the people demand that the church do it. Even then, enter gradually, and allow the whole congregation to begin participating. As people's hearts find spiritual fulfillment, they automatically will do what had seemed impossible previously.

Small congregations must be particularly careful about introducing extreme modes of worship, especially if many of the people are visitors or non-Christians. In a large church, visitors can hide more easily in the congregation and be less self-conscious of their lack of participation.

By praying and being prepared, and enthusiastic, the responsible people of the church insure that their services are meaningful and done in Spirit and truth. They can create an atmosphere conducive to worship. Present God in a way that makes people want to worship Him.

If every service is electric with excitement and enthusiasm, even the unbeliever will be swept up in the tide of spiritual worship. Sinners have walked down the aisles of our church to accept Christ as people fervently praise God, standing with uplifted hands. I am excited about the Lord and rejoice to see worshipers loving Him, because He loves them in return. I know Psalmic worship thrills the heart of God. A healthy, praying, evangelistic church can have great worship services. Yours can be one of them!

Reflections

What I wish to suggest is this, that it is for the most part through the public worship for the Christian church that the sense of God is kept alive in the community, and further, that it is by our regular habit of taking part in church worship that most of us seriously practice the Presence of God.

—*Robert S. Simpson*[31]

Surely there is in the NT nothing which prescribes or suggests the use of fixed forms, but neither is there anything which forbids or discourages such use. The rule of the Holy Spirit seems to be, "love God, and then worship according to your heart's desire." In such worship there is perfect freedom.

—*Andrew Blackwood*[32]

The tendency to standardize a specific type of worship . . . is alien to the Bible . . . . There is in the NT a greater variety of forms and expressions of worship than in the majority of divided churches and traditions today.

—*Paul W. Hoon*[33]

Believers are to gather to provide a time and place for the living Lord to manifest His glory . . . . We present ourselves in worship purposing to provide a place for God to make an entrance among us, to shape us, to work among and through us.

—*Jack Hayford*[34]

There is something added to the individual as he worships, not by himself, but in fellowship with others. Modern psychology is quite clear about that, and that is an argument for the corporate worship of God, as contrasted with the worship of the individual. As I have said before, there will always be natures that prefer to worship alone, and due allowance must be made for such. At the same time it must be asserted that, even on scientific principles, men and women who withdrew from the corporate worship of God in religion are missing much, because they are not joining in the group of Christian people for common worship.

—*Robert S. Simpson*[35]

A form should never be allowed to shackle or cage the spirits of the worshipers. Used rightly, it can channel what might otherwise be emotional foundering into a life-giving movement toward God. As form in music makes melody possible, so form in worship can free the worshiping spirit for the highest of all human expressions: the act of worship.

—*Clarice Bowman*[36]

Notes

Chapter 1

1. Leon Joseph Cardinal Suenens. *A New Pentecost*. (NY: The Seabury Press, 1974): 90.
2. Illion T. Jones. *A Historical Approach to Evangelical Worship*. (Nashville: Abingdon Press, 1954): 85.
3. Ernest F. Scott. *The Nature of the Early Church*. (New York: Charles Scribner's Sons, 1941): 95.
4. J. Winston Pearce. *Come, Let us Worship*. (Nashville: Broadman Press, 1965): 19.

Chapter 2

1. Walter M. Abbott, Gen. Ed. *The Documents of Vatican II*. (New York: Guild Press, 1966): 179.
2. J.J. von Allmen. *Worship: Its Theology and Practice*. (New York: Oxford University Press, 1965): 55.
3. Marianne H. Micks. *The Future Present*. (New York: The Seabury Press, 1970): X.
4. Paul W. Hoon. *The Integrity of Worship*. (Nashville: Abingdon Press, 1971): 36.
5. The complete story is given by: David J. DuPlessis, *The Spirit Bade Me Go*. (Published by the author): 17-18.
6. Raymond Abba properly reminds us: "Worship therefore which is truly prompted by the Spirit will be subject to a theological constraint; it will be restricted as well as evoked by the Christian revelation." *Principles of Christian Worship*. (London: Oxford University Press, 1957): 8.
7. Clark Pinnock. "Opening the Church to the Charismatic Dimensions," *Christianity Today*. (12 June 1981): 16.
8. Paul Hoon makes a statement along these lines that deserves our serious consideration: "The contrast between the God presented to us in much theological writing and the God we know in the actual experience of worship is often bewildering if not shattering. It seems not to be understood that God *becomes real as an object of truthful knowledge only insofar as he is an object of devotion at the same time*, and that a God *who can be worshipped* is as necessary to any adequate theology as *a believable God* is necessary to authentic worship." (italics mine): 89.

299

9. R. Laird Harris, Gleason L. Archer, Jr., Bruce K. Waltke, eds. *Theological Wordbook of the Old Testament*. (Chicago: Moody Press, 1980): I: 836.

10. It is a matter of personal interpretation as to whether the Greek word *pneuma* is to be translated Spirit with a capital S.

11. Oscar Cullmann. *Early Christian Worship*. (London: SCM Press Ltd, 1953): 32-33.

12. Michael Green. *I Believe in the Holy Spirit*. (Grand Rapids: Eerdmans, 1980, first printed 1975): 210.

13. Although I have never heard this hymn, the words were so striking that I thought it good to include them here. Taken from a hymnal given to me while visiting the well-known Martyrs' Memorial Free Presbyterian Church, Belfast, Ireland.

14. Joseph C. Aldrich. *Life-Style Evangelism*. (Portland: Multnomah Press, 1981): 120.

15. Taken from the Foreword of a delightful book by Ronald Barclay Allen and Gordon Lamar Barror: *Worship—Rediscovering the Missing Jewel*. (Portland: Multnomah Press, 1982): 10.

16. Andrew W. Blackwood. *The Fine Art of Public Worship*. (New York: Abingdon, 1939): Foreword.

17. Marilee Zdenek and Marge Champion. *Catch the New Wind*. (Waco, Texas: Word Books, 1972): 147.

18. Robert Webber. *Signs of Wonder*. (Nashville: Star Song Publishing Group, 1992): 17.

Chapter 3

1. Robert G. Rayburn. *O Come, Let Us Worship*. (Grand Rapids: Baker Book House, 1980): 14.

2. My wife and I visited Jacob's well in 1987, and the experience was one of the highlights of our Israel tour. The well which was once on ground level and in the open air, is at present twenty feet below the level of the ground. A small chapel covers the well itself, and is the showpiece for the small buildings, garden, and uncompleted church of the Greek-Orthodox Monastery that surrounds it. Entering through a small wooden door, we proceeded down stone steps. The well itself is a rock-faced shaft 105 feet deep that remains unchanged by the centuries. About three feet above the floor level a rectangular stone caps the well, with a hole about two feet wide in the center of the stone. A windlass lowered a bucket, by which water was drawn up, and we drank the cool, perfectly clean water. An interesting pamphlet on the well and Samaria is sold in that area: *Jacob's Well* by Emmanuel Dehan (Tel-Aviv, Israel: Published by author, 1977).

3. These additional references clearly associate "the gift of God" with the Holy Spirit: Ac 2:38; 8:20; 10:45; 11:17; Heb 6:4.

4. John's Gospel mentions water in several significant passages: 3:5; 4:10-15; 7:38; 19:34. C.K. Barrett comments: "The 'water' is preeminently the Holy Spirit, which alone gives life (cf. 6:63). It proceeds from the side of the crucified Jesus; it is the agent of the generation of Christians; and it forms the fountain of life which forever springs within Christians, maintaining their divine life." *The Gospel of St. John*. (London: S.P.C.K., 1967): 195.

5. James M. Freeman. *Manner and Customs of the Bible*. (Plainfield, New Jersey: Logos, International, reprinted 1972): 425.

6. Paul Yonggi Cho. *The Fourth Dimension*. (Plainfield, New Jersey: Logos, International, 1979): 152-153.

7. Robert E. Webber in his excellent book, *Worship Old and New*. (Grand Rapids: Zondervan Publishing House, 1982): 151, makes these appropriate remarks: "It is a fundamental axiom of Christianity that worship can be conducted at any place . . . . Throughout the history of the Christian Church, believers have worshiped everywhere—in the fields, in the catacombs, by the river, in homes, in prison, on ships, and on planes. Yet, it has been normal for Christians to have a

Notes

place of worship . . . the church has long acknowledged that what we do in worship ought to be expressed in the use we make of worship space."

8. Jesus used this unusual teaching tool of the "coming-yet-present" in regard to: (1) the resurrection, John 5:25, (2) the scattering of the disciples because of persecution, John 167:32, and (3) the present-yet-future appearance of the Kingdom of God, as Luke 11:20, etc. One of the best explanations of this concept as it applies to the Kingdom would be found in *The Presence of the Future*, by leading theologian George Eldon Ladd (Grand Rapids: Eerdmans, 1974).

9. "According to Carl Schneider the Greek word *stenazeim* or *anastenazein*, which means 'sighing,' 'groaning,' was a technical term in the Hellenistic world of that day for prayer that did not involve the mind, but was called forth by the Spirit. According to Mark 7:34 and 8:12 Jesus prayed in this way." Arnold Bittlinger. *Gifts and Graces*. (Grand Rapids: Eerdmans, English Trans., 1967): 49.

10. Raymond E. Brown. *The Gospel According to John, I-XII*. (Garden City, New York: Doubleday and Co., 1966): 49.

11. George Eldon Ladd. *A Theology of the New Testament*. (Grand Rapids: William B. Eerdmans Publishing Co., 1974): 292.

12. Rayburn: 105-111.

13. James D.G. Dunn. *Jesus and the Spirit*. (Philadelphia: The Westminster Pres, 1975): 353-354.

14. Joachim Jeremias. *The Parables of Jesus*. (New York: Charles Scribner's Sons, 1963): 191.

15. Ralph P. Martin. *Worship In the Early Church*. (Grand Rapids: Wm. B. Eerdmans, 1974): 35.

16. Dunn: 26. One of the most enlightening commentaries on *Abba* that I have read is found on pp. 21-20. His evaluation of Jeremias' painstaking research lends appropriate balance to that well-known work.

17. The following references show Jesus' use of "Father." It seems apparent, as Dunn points out (p 365), that the Aramaic *Abba* underlies the Greek *Pater* (simply "Father" in the English Versions). Mark 11:25f/Matt. 6:14f.; Matt. 5:48/Luke 6:36; Matt. 6:9/Luke 11:2; Matt. 6:32/Luke 12:30; Matt. 7:11/Luke 11:13; Matt. 23:9.

18. C.F.D. Moule. *Worship in the New Testament*. (London: Lutterworth Press, 1962): 76.

19. Zane Clark Hodges. *The Hungry Inherit*, rev. ed. (Portland: Multnomah Press, 1982): 33.

20. William Temple. *Reading in St. John's Gospel*. (London: MacMillan, 1955): 64.

21. Bob Sorge. *Exploring Worship*. (New Wilmington, PA: Son-Rise Publications, 1987): 77.

22. Brown: 180.

23. Graham Kendrick. *Learning to Worship as a Way of Life*. (Minneapolis: Bethany House Publishers, 1984): 91.

Chapter 4

1. As Luis Bush says, "We must do all in our power to show Muslims that the highest prophet described in the Koran is not Mohammed, but Jesus Christ. And that He is not only the greatest prophet, but the Son of God Himself who died and resurrected in order that millions of Muslims may be saved." *The 10/40 Window*. (Colorado Springs: AD 2000 & Beyond Movement): 3.

2. Kalafi Moala. "The World of Islam," one of many fine articles in the best informational fact book on missions I have ever seen. *Target Earth*, Frank Kaleb Jansen, Gen. Ed. (Pasadena: Global Mapping International, 1989): 128.

3. Figures from Bush: 3.

4. All around the earth remarkable breakthroughs in reaching every people group with the gospel have occurred. For an exciting glimpse into what God is doing, read *Catch the Vision 2000* by Bill and Amy Stearns (Minneapolis: Bethany House Publishers, 1991).

5. C.K. Barrett. *The Gospel of St. John.* (London: S.P.C.K., 1967): 198.
6. Charles Colson. *The Body.* (Dallas: Word Publishing, 1992): 158.
7. George Barna. *What Americans Believe: An Annual Survey of Values and Religious Views in the United States.* (Ventura, California: Regal, 1991).
8. Lawrence O. Richards. *Creative Bible Teaching.* (Chicago: Moody Press, 1970): 56
9. Paul W. Hoon. *The Integrity of Worship.* (Nashville: Abingdon Press, 1971): 114-115.
10. Geoffrey Wainwright says that "this verse from Ephesians expresses exactly a classic pattern in the history of Christian worship." *Doxology.* (NY: Oxford University Press, 1980): 91.
11. © 1975, Maranatha Music.
12. Raymond E. Brown. *The Anchor Bible, The Gospel According to John, I-XII.* (Garden City, NY: Doubleday and Co., 1966): 180.
    In agreement with this approach would be H. Schonweiss and C. Brown who feel this interpretation would "fit better the train of thought." C. Brown, ed., *The New International Dictionary of New Testament Theology.* (Grand Rapids: Zondervan Publishing House, 1979): 2:875.
13. James D. G. Dunn, for instance, says: " 'In truth' most probably refers again to the definitive revelation of God in Jesus as testified to in the original kerygmas. In short, true worship for John is worship in terms of Jesus—inspired by the Spirit of Jesus and according to the truth revealed in Jesus." *Jesus and the Spirit.* (Philadelphia: The Westminster Press, 1975): 354.
14. Barrett: 199.
15. George Eldon Ladd. *A Theology of the New Testament.* (Grand Rapids: Eerdmans, 1974): 292.
16. Wainwright: 89.
17. Ray S. Anderson, ed. *Theological Foundations for Ministry.* (Grand Rapids: Eerdmans, 1979): 380, quoting from *Theology in Reconstruction.* (Grand Rapids: Eerdmans, 1966).
18. Malcom Hunter. "Tracking the Gospel Among the Nomadic Pastoralists." Jansen. p. 130.
19. George T. Montague. *The Holy Spirit: Growth of a Biblical Tradition.* (NY: Paulist Press, 1976): 346, 347.
20. Raymond Abba. *Principles of Christian Worship.* (London: Oxford University Press, 1957): 9.
21. Bob Sorge. *Exploring Worship: A Practical Guide to Praise and Worship.* (New Wilmington, PA: Son-Rise Publications, 1987): 80.
22. Calvin H. Chambers. *In Spirit and in Truth.* (Ardmore, PA: Dorrance and Co., 1980): 22.
23. Judson Cornwall. *Let Us Worship.* (North Plainfield, NJ: Bridge Publishing, 1983): 97.
24. Graham Kendrick. *Learning to Worship as a Way of Life.* (Minneapolis: Bethany House Publishers, 1984): 96.

Chapter 5

1. Ferdinand Hahn's blunt appraisal is: "1 Corinthians 14 is the only text in the New Testament that takes a position with respect to Christian worship." *Worship in the Early Church.* (Philadelphia: Fortress Press, 1973): 68.
2. I must agree with Illion T. Jones when he says that it is "an oversimplification of the problem of New Testament worship to state that the Christian church took over bodily the form and order of worship to which they were accustomed in the synagogue . . . what they did with these same elements made the difference--and it was a tremendous difference between the old worship and the new." *A Historical Approach to Evangelical Worship* (Nashville: Abingdon Press, 1954): 69.
    The more traditional and formal evaluation of synagogue-church relationship would be found in: C.W. Dugmore. *The Influence of the Synagogue Upon the Divine Office.* (Westminster: The

Notes

Faith Press, 1964); W.O.E. Oesterley. *The Jewish Background of the Christian Liturgy*. (Gloucester: Peter Smith, 1965).
3. Alexander B. Macdonald. *Christian Worship in the Primitive Church*. (Edinburgh: T&T Clark, 1934): 2.
4. James F. White. *New Forms of Worship*. (Nashville: Abingdon, 1971): 31-32.
5. Howard Hendricks in an interview, "Discussing First Things First," *Leadership* (Summer 1980): 108.
6. Robert E. Webber. *Worship Old and New*. (Grand Rapids: Zondervan, 1982): 20.
7. Robert G. Rayburn. *O Come, Let Us Worship*. (Grand Rapids: Baker Book House, 1980): 11.
8. Paul Waitman Hoon. *The Integrity of Worship*. (Nashville, New York: Abingdon Press, 1971): 30.
9. Andrew W. Blackwood. *The Fine Art of Public Worship*. (New York: Abingdon Press, 1939): 17.
10. Donald Gee. *A New Discovery*. (Springfield: Gospel Publishing House, 1932): 23.
11. Robert S. Simpson. *Ideas in Corporate Worship*. (Edinburgh: T&T Clark, 1927): 23.
12. Paul E. Billheimer. *Destined for the Throne*. (Ft. Washington, Pennsylvania: Christian Literature Crusade, 1975): 118.
13. D. Gerhard Delling. *Worship in the New Testament*. (London: Darton, Longman and Todd, 1962): 10.
14. Nelson: 136.
15. Donald P. Hustad. *Jubilate!* (Carol Stream, Illinois: Hope Publishing Company, 1981): XII.
16. Robert E. Webber. *Common Roots*. (Grand Rapids: Zondervan, 1978): 103.
17. Calvin H. Chambers. *In Spirit and in Truth*. (Ardmore, PA: Dorrance & Co., 1980): x.

Chapter 6
1. Paul Waitman Hoon. *The Integrity of Worship*. (Nashville/NY: Abingdon Press, 1971): 88.
2. The book, *Knowing God*, by I.J. Packer (Downers Grove, Illinois: Inter Varsity Press, 1973), is a sample of positive discussion about God.
3. One of the most clearly articulated statements on this subject would be that by Robert H. Schuller. *Self Esteem, the New Reformation*. (Waco: Word Books, 1982).
4. J. Winston Pearce. *Come Let Us Worship*. (Nashville: Broadman Press, 1965): 52.
5. Ray C. Stedman. *Body Life*. (Glendale: Regal Books, 1972).
6. Robert G. Rayburn gives a good explanation and application in his Chapter 2, "Corporate Worship in the Old Testament." *O Come, Let us Worship*. (Grand Rapids: Baker, 1980).
7. James D.G. Dunn. *Jesus and the Spirit*. (Philadelphia: The Westminster Press, 1975): 13.
8. Robert E. Webber comments in *Worship Old and New*: "A major problem for pastors and congregations is finding adequate sources of information for worship renewal. Gimmicks and so-called innovative approaches to worship become threadbare all too quickly. So where should they turn? My argument is that the most powerful sources of worship renewal are found first in the Scripture and second in the history of the church," pp. 13,14.
9. Two books might be suggested for the average reader. Both have quotations concerning worship by the Church fathers grouped in certain sections. Henry Bettenson, ed., *Documents of the Christian Church*. (Oxford University Press, 1963); and Everett Ferguson. *Early Christians Speak*. (Austin: Sweet Publishing Co., 1971).
10. Evelyn Underhill. *Worship*. (Harper & Bros., 1937): 89.
11. See for instance, "The Fastest-growing American Denomination," *Christianity Today*. (7 Jan 1983): 28, 30-31.
12. G.C. Berkouwer. *The Person of Christ*. (Grand Rapids: Wm. B. Eerdmans, 1954): 59.

13. Leonard Ravenhill. *Why Revival Tarries*. (Minneapolis: Bethany Fellowship, 1959): 59.
14. C. Ellis Nelson. *Where Faith Begins*. (Atlanta: John Knox Press, 1971): 174.
15. Berkouwer: 55.
16. Quote by Arthur Wallis, *In the Day of Thy Power*. (Ft. Washington, PA: Christian Literature Crusade, 1956): 94.
17. Evelyn Underhill. *Worship*. (Harper & Bros, 1937):14.
18. Ernest F. Scott. *The Nature of the Early Church*. (New York: Charles Scribner & Son, 1941): 87.
19. Judson Cornwall. "Worship," *New Wine*. (November 1976): 8.
20. Leslie Earnshaw. *Worship for the Seventies*. (Nutfield, Surrey: Denholm House Press, 1973): 42.
21. Nelson: 154.
22. Webber: 13.
23. Underhill: 299.
24. Charles Kraft. "Fear of Change is Like Acting on a Shaky Stage," *Worship Leader*. (October/November 1992): 9.

Chapter 7

1. Robert E. Webber. *Worship Old and New*. (Grand Rapids: Zondervan Publishing House, 1982): 14,15.
2. Although doctrines of secondary nature may be tolerated, it goes without saying that we must not compromise the primary doctrines of historic Christianity (such as the deity of Christ, the efficacy of Christ's atonement, the virgin birth, the literal resurrection of Christ, etc.).
3. R.V.G. Tasker. *The Gospel According to St. Matthew, The Tyndale N.T. Commentaries*. (Grand Rapids: Wm. B. Eerdmans Publishing Co., 1961): 140.
4. David Hill. *The Gospel of Matthew, New Century Bible*. (Greenwood, SC: The Altic Press, 1972): 240.
5. T.W. Manson. *The Sayings of Jesus*. (Grand Rapids: William B. Eerdmans Publishing Co., 1957): 178.
6. It seems overly simplistic to see here the conversion of a literal scribe to the teaching of Jesus, since the record does not indicate that any of the apostles or early leaders were scribes. Tasker points out that such an interpretation "would make the saying somewhat irrelevant to the context" (p. 140). It is the function, not the office, that Jesus stresses.
7. Manson: 198.
8. Hill: 240.
9. James D.G. Dunn. *Jesus and the Spirit*. (Philadelphia: The Westminster Press, 1975): 40.
10. Manson: 254, 255.
11. William Rennie Caird. *On Worship in Spirit and in Truth*. (London: Thomas Bosworth, 198 High Holborn, 1877): IV.
12. As Evelyn Underhill has so correctly stated: "It is only too easy for the best and most significant cults to lose spiritual content when it is not a vehicle for the worship of spiritual men." *Worship*. (New York: Harper and Row, 1957): 77.
13. Alexander B. Bruce. *The Training of the Twelve*. (Grand Rapids: Kregel Publications, 1971, reproduced from the Fourth Edition, 1894 by A.C. Armstrong and Son): 77.
14. Dunn: 349.
15. Clyde Reid and Jerry Kerns. *Let It Happen*. (New York: Harper & Row, 1973): 40.
16. Illion T. Jones. *A Historical Approach to Evangelical Worship*. (Nashville: Abingdon Press, 1954): 289.

Notes

17. David Watson. *I Believe in the Church*. (Grand Rapids: Eerdmans, 1978): 73,74.
18. Dunn: 360.
19. Snyder: 15, 16.
20. Leslie Earnshaw. *Worship for the Seventies*. (Nutfield, Surrey: Denholm House Press, 1973): 42.
21. Robert G. Rayburn. *O Come, Let Us Worship*. (Grand Rapids: Baker, 1980): 143.
22. Charles Kraft. "Worship: tradition or just follow the leader?" *Worship Leader*. (February/March, 1992): 7.
23. Ronald A. Knox. *Enthusiasm*. (Westminster, Maryland: 1983, ©1950): 1.

Chapter 8
1. David Randolph. *God's Party*. (Nashville: Abingdon, 1975): 13.
2. A more complete analysis of societal and church change would include the excellent insights of: Francis A. Schaeffer. *The Church at the End of the 20th Century*. (Downers Grove, Illinois: Inter Varsity Press, 1970): chapter 6; Howard A. Snyder. *The Problem of Wine Skins*. (Downers Grove: Inter-Varsity Press, 1975): chapter 2; Gene A. Getz. *Sharpening the Focus of the Church*. (Chicago: Moody Press, 1974): chapter 19; Randolph: 31-37; Robert E. Webber. *Common Roots*. (Grand Rapids: Zondervan Publishing House: 1978): chapters 5 & 6.
3. Walter M. Abbot, gen. ed. *The Documents of Vatican II*. (New York: Guild Press, 1966).
4. *What is the Liturgical Renewal?* (Washington, D.C.: The Liturgical Conference, 1964): 3.
5. An interesting biography of Pope John XXIII by Lawrence Elliott is *I Will Be Called John*. (New York: Reader's Digest Press, E.P. Dutton & Co., 1973). The chapter on "Open Windows" reflects his brave action.
6. See the astounding statistics presented by David B. Barrett. "Annual Statistical Table on Global Mission: 1993," *International Bulletin of Missionary Research*. (January 1993): 23. There is, of course, an overlap with the figures presented for the various Christian bodies.
7. An estimate of 100 million Pentecostals and Charismatics was given in David B. Barrett's massive *World Christian Encyclopedia*. (NY: Oxford University Press, 1982) and presented in *Time* Magazine for May 3, 1982 (p. 67).

   Those figures by Barrett were significantly increased, however, and the startling announcement was made by Barrett in July 1987 in a press release at the North American Congress on the Holy Spirit and World Evangelization at New Orleans that there now existed a grand total of 277 million Christians in the world counted as part of the renewal. They are, he said, in 90% of the nations of the world and are growing at an astounding rate. *AD 2000 Together*, Vol 1 Number 7 (Fall 1987): 2.

   In 1987 Catholic theologian Kilian McDonnell edited a fascinating three-volume series which "draws together 104 documents on the charismatic renewal, resulting in an almost exhaustive assemblage of such documents." These documents were initially published by the historic churches and classical Pentecostal denominations between 1960 and 1980, and they show remarkable insight as well as illustrate the far-reaching impact of the Holy Spirit's Charismatic emphasis throughout all the churches during those twenty years. Worship, naturally, is a topic frequently mentioned. *Presence, Power, Praise*. (Collegeville, Minnesota: The Liturgical Press, 1988): I, II & III.
8. Chart taken from *AD 2000 Together*, 2 Number 1 (Jan-Feb 1988): 14, with the later figures and projections drawn in.
9. Stephen B. Clark. *Building Christian Communities*. (Notre Dame, Indiana: Ave Maria Press, 1972): 158, 159.
10. Lyle E. Schaller, ed. *Creative Leadership Series*, "Church Growth Strategies That Work." (Nashville: Abingdon, 1980): 7.

11. Donald A. McGavran. *Understanding Church Growth*. (Grand Rapids: Eerdmans, 1970).
12. One of the best books on the subject would be by a Southern Baptist, Charles L. Chaney. *Church Planting at the End of the Twentieth Century*. (Wheaton: Tyndale House Publishers, 1982). His emphasis on reaching ethnic groups in a meaningful way has significance for contemporary church worship.
13. Schaller: 107,108.
14. Webber: 77.
15. *Charisma* (August 1985).
16. "The Church in the '80s: A Survey of Opinion" from the Office of the Provost, Fuller Theological Seminary. This preliminary survey was later published in better form for Fuller's *Theology, News & Notes* (June 1979), but unfortunately the above information was deleted.
17. Henry E. Horn. *Worship In Crisis*. (Philadelphia: Fortress Press, 1972): 3.
18. Clyde Reid and Jerry Kerns. *Let It Happen*. (New York: Harper and Row, 1973): 8.
19. Synan: 138.
20. Myron Widmer. "Adventist Worship—Celebration-Style," *Adventist Review*. (November 1, 1990): 12.
21. Robert E. Webber. "9 Proposals for Worship Renewal," *Theology, News and Notes*. (March 1991): 23.
22. J. David Newman. " 'Celebration' is a Naughty Word," *Ministry*. (December 1990): 26.
23. Deanna Davis. "Raised Hands, Raised Eyebrows—Adventists learn to Celebrate," *Theology, News and Notes*. (March 1991): 20.

Chapter 9

1. Keith Miller. *The Taste of New Wine*. (Waco: Word Books, 1965): 106.
2. Leslie Earnshaw. *Worship for the Seventies*. (Nutfield, Surrey: Denholm House Press, 1973): 24.
3. Anne Ortlund. *Up With Worship*. (Glendale: Regal Books, 1975): 100.
4. David R. Mains. *Full Circle*. (Waco: Word Publishers, 1971): 52.
5. Ralph Martin. *Worship in the Early Church*. (Grand Rapids: Eerdmans, 1974): 10.
6. D.C. Benson. *Electric Liturgy*. (Richmond: John Knox Press, 1972): 7.
7. James F. White. *Introduction to Christian Worship*. (Nashville: Abingdon, 1980): 22.
8. Two different happenings involving different women is credible and acceptable; as in *A Harmony of the Gospels* by Robert L. Thomas and Stanley N. Gundry (San Francisco: Harper and Row, 1987): Sections 77 and 186.
    Also, see the quite complete discussion given by Raymond E. Brown in *The Anchor Bible, The Gospel According To John (i-vii)*. (Garden City: Doubleday, 1966): 447-454.
9. For a more comprehensive study, consult the eight pages devoted to the study of this word by: Gerhard Kittel and Gerhard Friedrich, eds. *Theological Dictionary of the New Testament*. (Grand Rapids: Wm. B. Eerdmans Publishing Co., 1968): VI, 758-766. Also, three pages in: Colin Brown, ed. *The New International Dictionary of New Testament Theology*. (Grand Rapids: Zondervan Publishing House, 1979): 2, 875-876.
10. W.E. Vine. *An Expository Dictionary of New Testament Words*. (Westwood, New Jersey: Fleming H. Revell Co., 1940): IV, 235.
11. Colin Brown: 875, 876.
12. Martin: 11.
13. A.S. Herbert. *Worship in Ancient Israel*. (London: Lutterworth Press, 1959): 47.

14. I agree with C.F.D. Moule that "These words are used of obeisance before men as well as before God. But they come to denote more generally, 'worship', as in John 4:20-23 . . . . " *Worship in the NT*. (London: Lutterworth Press, 1961): 79, 80.

    The Context in both testaments indicate that in most cases the words apply to the worship of the true God or of false gods. See Kittel: 761.

15. Frank S. Mead, ed. and comp. *The Encyclopedia of Religious Quotations*. (Old Tappan, New Jersey: Fleming H. Revell Co., MCMLXV): 480.

16. One will not find proskynesis in the average dictionary, although Kittel's *Dictionary* uses this noun form of proskyneo twenty-four times in the nine pages of text as though it were an English word (see note #9).

    Some additional gleanings from D. Gerhard Delling are helpful: ". . . the renunciation of the claim to one's own dignity is expressed . . . a sign of respect . . . . It is quite clear that by proskynesis that act of submission and unconditional acknowledgment is meant . . . proskunesis proper involves the deep bowing of the facing of the kneeler . . . for more than the matter of external form is involved. It would mean that the inner attitude . . . was therein made figuratively visible." *Worship in the New Testament*. (London: Darton, Longman and Todd, 1962): 105,106,108.

17. Peter Brunner comments: "The Bible knows of no 'mute adoration.' Word and gesture belong together." *Worship in the Name of Jesus*. (St. Louis: Concordia Publishing House, 1968): 212.

18. "Ultimately, only one thing is needful in the sense that without it worship cannot be worship: the posture of adoration before the Lord." Paul W. Hoon. *The Integrity of Worship*. (New York: Abingdon, 1971): 24.

19. Watchman Nee. *Worshipping the Ways of God*. (Published by The Stream, P.O. Box 20755, Los Angeles, CA 90006, USA): 1.

20. "When in New Testament reports kneeling and proskunesis are mentioned together, the action is portrayed in its different phases; first one falls on one's knees, then bows the face downwards; Rev. 4:10, 19:10, 22:8; Matt. 2:11, 4:9, 18:26; Acts 10:25." Delling: 10 (footnote).

21. Colin Brown. *The New International Dictionary of New Testament Theology*. (Grand Rapids: Zondervan Publishing House, 1979): 2, 877.

22. Thomas Kimber. *The Worship of God*. (New York: David S. Taber & Co., 1890): 24.

23. Evelyn Underhill. *Worship*. (New York: Harper & Row, 1957): 9.

24. Willard L. Speery. *Reality in Worship*. (New York: The MacMillan Co., 1925): 164.

25. Edward K. Ziegler. *Book of Worship for Village Churches*. (New York: Agricultural Missions Foundation, Inc., 1939): 19.

26. Ronald Allen and David Borror. *Worship—Rediscovering the Missing Jewel*. (Portland: Multnomah, 1982): 18.

27. Bob Sorge. *Exploring Worship*.(New Wilmington, PA: Son-Rise Pub., 1987): 83-84.

28. H. Greeven. "*Proskyneo* [to bow down, worship]," from the abridged one volume edition of Kittel's *Theological Dictionary of the New Testament*. (Grand Rapids: Eerdmans, 1985): 949, done by Geoffrey W. Bromiley.

Chapter 10

1. In a recent book, *The Worship of God* (Grand Rapids: Eerdmans, 1982), Ralph P. Martin addresses the problem of the "meager" results of the so-called "renewal of worship" during the past two or three decades. One element that he feels has worked against a recovery of vital worship in our day is "secularization." The picture of a God "out there" or "up there" is one that has lost credibility. "The

secular world view refuses to accept the dichotomy of 'secular' over against 'sacred'" (p. 3). This is a challenge that the church must squarely face, for the "holiness of God" is at the heart of the Christian idea of worship (p. 18).

2. Contrast between majestic God and poverty-stricken man is graphically presented in Ezekiel's repeated use of two terms. *Today's English Version (Good News Bible)* gives a striking translation. The first words spoken by God to Ezekiel were: "Mortal man, stand up, I want to talk to you" (Ezek. 2:1). Rising from his prostrated position on the ground, the prophet hears his commission from "the Sovereign lord" (v. 4). Then, with monotonous consistency, the TEV continues to use these terms that so clearly establish God's majesty ("the Sovereign LORD") and man's poverty ("mortal man").

3. Delivered at the Canadian World MAP Family Camp at Penticton, BC, August 1984.

4. An outline presented by Bruce Leafblad at a Fuller Seminary lecture in 1979.

5. Hebrews 7:27, 9:12,28, 10:10; Romans 6:10; 1 Peter 3:18; John 10:17.

6. ©1981 Rocksmith Music, c/o Trust Music Management, 6225 Sunset Blvd., Hollywood, CA 90028. For a most interesting account of how this wonderful song was born and for a fascinating book on worship, see *Worship His Majesty* by Jack W. Hayford. (Waco, Texas: Word Books, 1987).

7. Paul David Y. Cho. *Key to Revival.* (Waco: Word Books, 1984):20,30.

8. Henry Sloane Coffin. *The Public Worship of God.* (Philadelphia: The Westminster Press, 1946): 17.

9. Robert E. Webber. *Worship Is A Verb.* (Waco: Word, 1985): 111.

10. Ralph P. Martin. *The Worship of God.* (Grand Rapids: Eerdmans, 1982): 173.

11. C.F.D. Moule. *The Holy Spirit.* (Grand Rapids: Eerdmans, 1978): 13.

12. As quoted in "How's your 'Oh!' Factor?" *Closer Walk* 3, Number 12. (. ember 1990): Last page.

13. Charles Colson. *The Body.* (Dallas: Word Pub., 1992): 382.

Chapter 11

1. Paul W. Hoon. *The Integrity of Worship.* (Nashville: Abingdon Press, 1971): 31.

2. David Watson comments: "Evangelical or social activities can never be a substitute for this worship. If we neglect our foremost calling, we become spiritually arid in ourselves. We have nothing of lasting value to offer the world, and we dishonor God." *I Believe in the Church.* (Grand Rapids: Wm. B. Eerdmans, 1978): 179.

3. Clarice Bowman. *Restoring Worship.* (Nashville: Abingdon Cokesbury Press, 1951): 48.

4. "We need to be caught up in the wonder of the person of Jesus Christ of Nazareth, to know Him intimately and deeply: then we will find that our ministry Godward will urge us manward with a new freshness and power, and then we will not only talk of God's power but will also see it demonstrated." Roxanne Brant. *Ministering to the Lord.* (Florida: Roxanne Brant Crusades, 1973): 7.

5. Thomas Kimber. *The Worship of God.* (New York: David S. Tabor & Co., 56 LaFayette Place, 1890): 24.

6. C.F.D. Moule. *Worship in the New Testament.* (London: Lutterworth Press, 1961): 80.

7. William Nicholls. *Jacob's Ladder.* (Richmond: John Knox Press, 1958): 15.

8. Everett F. Harrison. "Romans" *The Expositor's Bible Commentary.* Frank E. Gaebelein, gen. ed. (Grand Rapids: Zondervan, 1976): 10: 128.

9. Robert N. Schaper adds: "A distinction worth noting is that in the Greek version of the Old Testament, *latreia* is used to translate the service of the cult, the worship of the people, but

Notes

leitourgia is used for the work of the priests. In the New Testament that distinction is not maintained. In fact, the service of God, though cultic at times, is ultimately the entire life of the worshiping Christian." *In His Presence*. (NY: Thomas Nelson Pub, 1984): 49.
10. John Reumann, ed., Ferdinand Hahn. *The Worship of the Early Church*. (Philadelphia: Fortress Press: 1973): Introduction: xvi.
11. Ibid: xvii.
12. Peter Brunner. *Worship in the Name of Jesus*. (St. Louis: Concordia, 1968): Titles of chapters 7 and 8.
13. Millar Burrows. *An Outline of Biblical Theology*. (Philadelphia: The Westminster Press, 1946): 262.
14. John Ruskin: ". . . any place where God lets down the ladder. And how are you to know where that will be? Or how are you to determine where it may be, but by being ready for it always?" Quoted in: *The Torah: A Modern Commentary*. W. Gunther Plaut, ed. (NY: Union of American Hebrew Congregations, 1981): 197).
15. Nicholls: 31.
16. Wendell Willis. *Worship*. (Austin, Texas: Sweet Publishing Co., 1973): 5.
17. Judson Cornwall. "Worship," *New Wine*. (November 1976): 7.
18. A.W. Tozer. *Born After Midnight*. (Harrisburg, Penn.: Christian Publications, Inc., 1959): 126.
19. Ernest F. Scott. *Nature of the Early Church*. (New York: Charles Scribner's Sons, 1941): 70.
20. G. Campbell Morgan. *God's Last Word to Man: Studies in Hebrews*. (Grand Rapids: Baker, Reprinted 1974): 98.
21. E. Leroy Lawson. *The New Testament Church Then and Now*. (Cincinnati: Standard Publishing, 1981): 71.

Chapter 12
1. Massey H. Shepherd. *The Paschal Liturgy and the Apocalypse*. (Richmond: John Knox Press, 1960): 97.
2. Paul W. Hoon. *The Integrity of Worship*. (Nashville: Abingdon, 1971): 132.
3. I like Barry Liesch's discussion of how Revelation gives us a model of worship. He says that "Revelation worship is the culminating model of worship." *People in the Presence of God*. (Grand Rapids: Zondervan, 1988): 233.

Conformation is also given by Evelyn Underhill, *Worship*. (New York: Harper and Row, 1957): 91-93.

An interesting premise that the Paschal Liturgy of the Church is seen in the basic structure of Revelation is given by Massey H. Shepherd, Part Two. (See footnote 1 above.)

Note D. Gerhard Delling's approach in showing how the creatures of primitive worship are reproduced in the book of Revelation in *Worship in the New Testament*. (London: Darton, Longman and Todd, 1962): 64.

Two recent books, beautifully done in an inspirational manner: Robert E. Coleman. *Songs of Heaven*. (Old Tappan, New Jersey: Fleming H. Revell Company, 1980). Anne Murchison. *Praise and Worship In Earth As It Is In Heaven*. (Waco, Texas: Word Books, 1981).
4. Timothy Ware. *The Orthodox Church*. (Baltimore, Maryland: Penguin Books, 1963): 269, 270, 277, 278.
5. Ibid.
6. Ibid.
7. Robert S. Simpson. *Ideas in Corporate Worship*. (Edinburgh: T. and Clark, 1927): 108.

8. Seeley D. Kinne. *The Prophetic State*. (Published by the author, 1922): 76.
9. As an example, the author was pleased to hear noted theologian Ralph P. Martin at Fuller Theological Seminary confirm this concept in a Doctor of Ministry class on the theology of worship.
10. A.W. Tozer. *Worship: The Missing Jewel of the Evangelical Church*. (Harrisburg, PA: Christian Publications, Inc., 1961).
11. Marianne H. Micks. *The Joy of Worship*. (Philadelphia: The Westminster Press, 1982): 43.
12. Robert E. Webber. "Church Buildings: Shapes of Worship," *Christianity Today*. (7 August 1981): 18.
13. Alexander B. Macdonald. *Christian Worship in the Primitive Church*. (Edinburgh: T.&T. Clark 38, George Street, 1934): 38.
14. C.F.D. Moule. *Worship in the New Testament*. (Richmond: John Knox Press, 1967): 39.
15. Henry H. Halley. *Halley's Bible Handbook*. (Grand Rapids: Zondervan, 1965, 24th ed.): 655.

Chapter 13

1. Robert Webber of Wheaton says: "The central act of Christian worship in the history of the church has always been the communion." *Common Roots*. (Grand Rapids: Zondervan, 1978): 86.
   The Communion or Mass in and of itself, however, has not successfully maintained (in the average church goer's mind) the spiritual quality present in the worship and people of Bible days. There is a missing dimension in many churches that allows the Sacrament to become merely an acknowledgment of a worthy historical event. In later chapters we will investigate the "when" and "how" of Jesus' presence in the church, and suggest proper balancing of Communion with other worship events.
2. "*We know that in heaven we shall do nothing other than ceaselessly repeat Amen and Alleluia, with insatiable satisfaction,*" St. Augustine. Sermon 362,29, P.L. 39 1632ff.
3. Martin Luther provided an interesting discussion on this passage. *Works of Martin Luther*. (Philadelphia: Muhlenburg, 1931): 5:23-24.
4. Basilea Schlink. *Patmos: When the Heavens Opened*. (Carol Stream, Illinois: Creation House, 1976): 7, 8.
5. John Bunyan. *The Pilgrim's Progress*. (Philadelphia: Universal Book and Bible House, no date [originally published in 1678]): 168.
6. Paul E. Billheimer. *Destined for the Throne*. (Ft. Washington, Pennsylvania: Christian Literature Crusade, 1975): 116.
7. Ralph P. Martin. *Worship in the Early Church*. (Grand Rapids: Eerdmans, 1974): 45.
8. Charles R. Erdman. *The Revelation of John*. (Philadelphia: The Westminster Press, 1936): 13,14.
9. Anne Ortlund. *Up with Worship*. (Glendale: Regal Books, 1975): 64.
10. Schlink: 20.
11. Bob Sorge. *Exploring Worship*. (New Wilmington, PA: Son-Rise Pub., 1987): 76.

Chapter 14

1. Later in life, David was the prolific inventor of musical instruments (1 Chron. 23:5; 2 Chron. 7:6).
2. Charles Haddon Spurgeon. *The Treasury of David*. (Byron Center, MI: Associated Publishers and Authors, a 1970 reprint): II: 22.
3. For a more complete discussion of the joyful worship found in the Tabernacle of David, see the following two works: Kevin J. Conner. *The Tabernacle of David*. (Portland, Oregon: Bible Temple

Notes

Publishing, 1976); Graham Truscott. *The Power of His Presence*. (Burbank, CA: World MAP Press, originally published 1969).

4. This was a potentially dangerous move. Fortunately, David's popularity increased. Jacob M. Myers in the *Anchor Bible* Commentary on 1 Chronicles (Garden City, NY: Doubleday and Company, 1965): 122, gives this interesting observation: "In Chronicles David virtually displaces Moses. The name of Moses occurs only 31 times in Chronicles, Ezra, Nehemiah, whereas that of David occurs there more than 250 times. While statistics cannot be regarded as proof, they do indicate certain trends that cannot be ignored . . . . There was surely some reason for this emphasis. For the Chronicler, the temple and its services were central, and for this David was the key person since, in the Chronicler's theory, he was responsible for the whole of temple worship. He connected Moses with the tabernacle, which was only of antiquarian interest, because the temple had inherited its tradition."

5. C.F. Keil and F. Delitzsch. *Commentary on the Old Testament*. (Grand Rapids: Eerdmans, reprinted 1978): II: 327.

6. *Matthew Henry's Commentary on the Whole Bible*. (reprinted by Fleming H. Revell): II: 476.

7. H.L. Ellison, F. Davidson, ed. *The New Bible Commentary - I and II Chronicles*. (Grand Rapids: Eerdmans, 1953): 348.

8. Keil: 326.

9. David James Randolph. *God's Party*. (Nashville: Abingdon, 1975): 53.

10. James I. Packer. "Knowing Notions or Knowing God?" (An Interview), *Pastoral Renewal*. (6 March 1982, Number 9): 67.

11. C.S. Lewis. *Reflections on the Psalms*. (New York: Harcourt, Brace and World, Inc. 1958): 45.

12. Marilee Zdenek and Marge Champion. *Catch the New Wind*. (Waco: Word Books, 1972: 47.

13. Clyde Reid and Jerry Kerns. *Let It Happen*. (New York: Harper and Row, 1973): 80.

14. C.F.D. Moule. *Worship in the New Testament*. (London: Lutterworth Press, 1961): 12.

15. Peter E. Gillquist. *The Physical Side of Being Spiritual*. (Grand Rapids: Zondervan, 1979): 15, 16.

Chapter 15

1. C.F. Keil and F. Delitzsch. *Commentary on the Old Testament*. (Grand Rapids: Eerdmans, reprinted 1978): III, 325.

2. Keil and Delitzsch: 325.

3. Jack Hayford. *The Church on the Way*. (Lincoln, VA: Chosen Books, 1982): 81.

4. Frances Metcalfe. *Living the Life of Praise*. (Idyllwild, CA: The Golden Candlestick): 17.

5. Raymond Abba. *Principles of Christian Worship*. (London: Oxford University Press, 1957): 5.

6. Douglas Horton. *The Meaning of Worship*. (NY: Harper and Brothers, 1959): 16.

7. Evelyn Underhill. *Worship*. (NY: Harper and Brothers, 1937): 339.

8. Underhill: 170.

9. Underhill: 177.

10. Andrew W. Blackwood. *The Fine Art of Public Worship*. (NY: Abingdon Press, 1939): 14.

11. H. Grady Davis. *Why We Worship*. (Philadelphia: Fortress Press, 1961): 14.

12. Davis: 37.

13. Henry Sloane Coffin. *The Public Worship of God*. (Philadelphia: The Westminster Press, 1946): 19.

14. J. Winston Pearce. *Come, Let Us Worship*. (Nashville: The Broadman Press, 1965): 65.

15. Edward K. Ziegler. *Book of Worship for Village Churches*. (NY: Agricultural Missions Foundation, Inc., 1939): 28.

16. David K. Blomgren. *The Song of the Lord*. (Portland, Oregon: Bible Temple Publishing, 1978): 13.
17. Paul E. Billheimer. *Destined for the Throne*. (Ft. Washington, PA: Christian Literature Crusade, 1975): 120.
18. Billheimer: 121.
19. C.S. Lewis. *Reflections on the Psalms*. (New York: Harcourt, Brace & World, 1958): 93.
20. Graham Truscott. *The Power of His Presence*. (Burbank, Calif: World MAP Press, 1969 copyright): 260.
21. Ralph Mahoney. "True Spiritual Worship: Key to a Dynamic Spiritual Life," *World MAP Digest*. (July/August, 1981): 21.
22. David R. Mains. *Full Circle*. (Waco: Word Publisher, 1971): 53.

Chapter 16

1. The other references would be: 18:6; 28:2; 28:6; 40:1; 55:17; 64:1; 66:19; 77:1; 86:6; 102:5; 116:1; 119:149; 130:2; 141:1.
2. Consider the following Psalms: 109, 119, 139, 141, 143.
3. Judson Cornwall. *Elements of Worship*. (South Plainfield, NJ: Bridge Publishing, 1985): 146.
4. Ralph P. Martin. *Worship in the Early Church*. (Grand Rapids: Eerdmans, 1976 ed.): 69.
5. Gordon D. Fee. *The First Epistle to the Corinthians, The New International Commentary on the New Testament*. (Grand Rapids: Eerdmans, 1987): 672.
6. James D.G. Dunn. *Jesus and the Spirit*. (Philadelphia: Westminster, 1975): 292.
7. See the comments by Ronald Allen and Gordon Borror. *Worship: Rediscovering the Missing Jewel*. (Portland: Multnomah Press, 1982): 112ff.
8. Robert G. Rayburn. *O Come, Let Us Worship*. (Grand Rapids: Baker, 1980): 150.
9. For more discussion on this see G.C. Berkouwer. *The Person of Christ*. (Grand Rapids: Eerdmans, 1954): Chapter 3, "Ecumenical Decisions."
10. G.Campbell Morgan. *The Practice of Prayer*. (Grand Rapids: Baker Book House, 1971 reprint): 66.
11. Andrew Murray. *The Prayer Life*. (Grand Rapids: Zondervan, 1988 ed.): 33.
12. Morgan points out that this prayer follows the pattern of the "index prayers" which the Jewish rabbis taught the people. These prayers were actually brief sentences, each of which suggested a subject of prayer. Each petition was recited in sequence as the person endeavored to fulfill the intent by prayerfully thinking and elaborating on each subject: 66.
13. Charles H. Spurgeon. *The Treasury of David*.(Byron Center, MI: Associated Publishers and Authors, a 1970 reprint): III: 182.
14. A.S. Herbert. *Worship in Ancient Israel*. (London: Lutterworth Pres, 1959): 28.
15. Terry Law. *The Power of Praise and Worship*. (Tulsa: Victory House, 1985): 146.
16. Rayburn: 150f.
17. A.W. Tozer (ed., Gerald B. Smith). *Whatever Happened to Worship?* (Camp Hill, Penn.: Christian Publications, 1985): 15.

Chapter 17

1. David J. Beattie. *The Romance of Sacred Song*. (London/Edinburgh: Marshall, Morgan & Scott, Ltd., 1931 4th ed.): 21.
2. See F.F. Bruce's interesting comments on the Psalms and OT theology in *New Testament Development of Old Testament Themes*. (Grand Rapids: Eerdmans, 968 copyright, The Paternoster Press): 17f.

Notes

3. Newton Marshall Hall and Irving Francis Wood, eds. *The Book of Life.* (Chicago: John Rudin & Co., 1951, 19th printing): 227.
4. Ian R.K. Paisley. *Psalms, Paraphrases, and Hymns.* (Belfast, Ireland: The Puritan printing Co., 1973): Foreword.
5. Verse 4 of "Joyful, Joyful, We Adore Thee," by Henry Van Dyke, Arr. from Ludwig van Beethoven.
6. Psalms 7:17; 9:2; 9:11; 13:6; 18:49; 21:13; 27:6; 30:4; 30:12; 33:2; 47:6,7; 51:14; 57:7, 9; 59:16, 17; 61:8; 66:2; 66:4; 67:4; 68:4, 32; 71:22, 23; 75:9; 81:1; 89:1; 92:1; 95:1; 96:1; 96:2; 98:1, 4, 5; 101:1, 2; 104:33; 105:2; 108:1, 3; 126:2; 135:3; 138:1; 144:9; 146:2; 147:1, 7; 149:1, 3, 5.
7. Taken from *Dynamic Preaching* (Feb, 1990): V, 2, 21.
8. Taken from *Eternity Magazine* (July, 1975).
9. From an article in *Christianity Today:* "Returned POW: How We Overcame." (July 20, 1973): 18. Taken from *In the Presence of Mine Enemies* by Howard and Phyllis Rutledge with Mel and Lyls White (Fleming H. Revell Co., 1973).
10. Tom Fettke, sen. ed., Charles R. Swindoll. *The Hymnal for Worship and Celebration.* (Waco: Word, 1986): Foreword.
11. As stated by Lowell P. Beveridge, "Church Music: Pop or Pro?", *Christianity Today.* (March 14, 1969): 7: "Throughout the history of the church, advocates of congregational singing have maintained that wholehearted participation in song based upon the words is one of the foundations of liturgical worship, and there is a long tradition of protest against the tendency to obscure this principle, whether through inertia and neglect or by deliberate interference."
12. Fred Bock, gen. ed. *Hymns for the Family of God.* (Nashville: Paragon Associates, 1976): Preface.
13. Wayne Lukens. *Eternity Magazine* (March 1977): 24.
14. *The Mennonite Hymnal.* (Scottsdale, PA: Herald Press, 1969): Preface.
15. Donald P. Hustad, ed. *Hymns for the Living Church.* (Carol Stream: Hope Publishing Co., 1974): 2.
16. For example, these three: David K. Blomgren. *The Song of the Lord.* (Portland: Bible Temple Publishing, 1974). 47 pages, all very good; Kevin J. Conner. *The Tabernacle of David.* (Portland: Bible Temple Publishing, 1976): chapter 18; Donald P Hustad. *Jubilate!* (Carol Stream: Hope Publishing Co., 1981): chapters VII and VIII.
17. Ralph P. Martin. *New Testament Foundations: A Guide for Christian Students.* (Grand Rapids: Eerdmans, 1975): I, 257.
18. Gerhard Kittel and Gerhard Friedrich, eds., G. Gerhard Delling. "Humnos," *Theological Dictionary of the New Testament.* (Grand Rapids: Eerdmans, 1972): VIII, 500.
19. Ronald Allen and Gordon Borror. *Worship: Rediscovering the Missing Jewel.* (Portland: Multnomah, 1982): 159.
20. Jack Hayford. *Worship His Majesty.* (Waco: Word Books, 1987):146.
21. Robert Rayburn. *O, Come Let Us Worship.* (Grand Rapids: Baker, 1980): 95.
22. Hustad: 89. He refers to Wellesz, "Early Christian Music," *The New Oxford History of Music*, Vol. 2: 2
23. Curtis Vaughan. "Colossians," *The Expositors Bible Commentary.* (Grand Rapids: Zondervan, 1978): 216.
24. Peter T. O'Brien. "Colossians," *Word Biblical Commentary.* (Waco: Word, 1982): 44, 208.
25. Blomgren: 5.
26. Ibid.
27. Hustad: 89.
28. Luke 20:42, 24:44; Acts 1:20, 13:33 (cp. v. 35); 1 Cor. 14:26; Eph. 5:19; Col. 3:16.

29. Eph. 5:19; Rom. 15:9; 1 Cor. 14:15; James 5:13.
30. Blomgren: 33.
31. Hayford: 149.
32. The Greek word *humnos* basically means a religious song and appears only in Eph. 5:19 and Col. 3:16. See note #37 below for a comment on hymns in the Greek text of the New Testament.
33. This is one of Hustad's translations (p. 90). Note that to the Greeks, any words that were sung would be considered an "ode."
34. This spiritual activity is developed more fully in chapters 30, 31, and 33.
35. "Sacred Songs" is used by both the Living Bible and The Bible in Today's English Version, but I would prefer the translation "spiritual songs" as in the New International Version, New English Bible, New King James Version, Revised Standard Version, Phillips Translation and the familiar Authorized King James Version.
36. Hayford: 150.
37. For lack of space, I have not discussed the possibility of hymns or hymn forms in the New Testament Greek text. These so-called *Christ-hymns* embedded within the New Testament material, have provoked much scholarly debate. Some examples would be: Phil. 2:6-11; Col. 1:15-20; John 1:1-16; Heb. 1:3; 1 Tim. 3:16; Rev. 4:8. It would seem that if these passages are, in fact, hymns of that day it would strengthen our thesis that the early church used Psalmic worship. For further information, consult these two references: 1) James D.G. Dunn. *Unity and Diversity in the New Testament.* (Philadelphia: Trinity Press International, 1990, 2nd ed.): 132-141. And this book that I heard Bernard Ramm call "the best book on the subject," 2) J.T. Sanders. *The New Testament Christological Hymns.* (Cambridge University Press, 1971).
38. Dick Eastman. *The Hour that Changes the World.* (Grand Rapids: Baker, 1978): 111.
39. Ralph Carmichael, pres. *The New Church Hymnal.* (Lexicon Music, Inc., 1976): Introduction.
40. Charles H. Spurgeon. *The Treasury of David.* (Byron Center, MI: Associated Publishers and Authors, a 1970 reprint): IV: 27.
41. John Wesley. *The Works of John Wesley.* (Grand Rapids: Baker Book House, a 1978 reprint of the 1872 edition): 346.
42. James L. Beall. *The Ministry of Worship and Praise.* (Detroit: Bethesda Missionary Temple): 12.

Chapter 18

1. As stated by Lutherans. See for instance Peter Brunner. *Worship in the Name of Jesus.* (St. Louis, Missouri: Concordia, 1968): 208-210.
2. As stated by Robert G. Rayburn. *O Come, Let Us Worship.* (Grand Rapids: Baker Books House, 1980): 150.
3. Quoted from Robert E. Coleman, *Songs of Heaven.* (Old Tappan, New Jersey: Fleming H. Revell Co., 1980): 112.
4. C.F. Keil and F. Delitzsch. *Biblical Commentary on the Old Testament.* (Grand Rapids: Eerdmans, 5th printing, 1978): 1 - The Pentateuch, 184.
5. Judson Cornwall. *Let Us Praise.* (Plainfield, New Jersey: Logos International, 1973): 34.
6. C. Peter Wagner. *Spiritual Power and Church Growth.* (Lake Mary, Florida: Creation Hose, 1986): 103.
7. Brunner: 208-209.
8. A.S. Herbert. *Worship in Ancient Israel.* (London: Lutterworth Press, 1959): 11.
9. John W. Peterson and Norman Johnson, compilers and ed. *Praise! Our Songs and Hymns.* (Grand Rapids: Zondervan, 1982): Foreword.

Notes

10. Marilee Zdenek and Marge Champion. *Catch the New Wind.* (Waco: Word Books, 1972): 36.
11. Charles H. Spurgeon. *The Treasury of David.* (Byron Center, MI: Associated Publishers and Authors, a 1970 reprint): I: 94.
12. A.W. Tozer (ed., Gerald B. Smith). *Whatever Happened to Worship?* (Camp Hill, Penn.: Christian Publications, 1985): 14.
13. LaMarr Boschman. "With a Loud Voice," *The Trumpet.* (Spring 1987): 1.
14. Graham Truscott. *The Power of His Presence.* (Burbank: World MAP, 1972): 244.

Chapter 19
1. Walter Lowrie. *Art in the Early Church.* (NY: Harper Torchbooks, Harper and Row, 1947): 22.
2. Lowrie: 21.
3. Theodor Filthaut. *Learning to Worship.* (Westminster, Maryland: The Newman Press, Translation Copyright 1965 by Burns and Dates Ltd.): 138,139.
4. Lowrie: 46.
5. Ralph F. Wilson comments in "Lifting Hands," *Paraclete.* (Winter, 1986): 4-8. "It is strange to find no references to lay people lifting hands in prayer in Rabbinic writings. Jewish writers explain the cessation of this prayer form in the synagogue as a reaction against the prevalence of the custom among Christians." Based on: Abraham E. Millgram. *Jewish Worship.* (Philadelphia: Jewish Publication Society of America, 1971): 356-357; and Avrohom Chaim Fuer. *Tehillim: A New Translation with a Commentary Anthologized from Talmudic, Midrashic and Rabbinic Sources.* (Brooklyn: Mesorah Publications, Ltd. 1977-80, 5 vols.): 4:1094.
6. Peter E. Gillquist. *The Physical Side of Being Spiritual.* (Grand Rapids: Zondervan, 1979): 119.
7. Ralph E. Wilson says (p. 5), "The lifting of the hands so characterizes prayer in the Bible that it becomes a metonymy, a symbol for supplication without the need to identify it as prayer. For example, Jeremiah urges, 'Lift your hands to him for the lives of your children . . .' (Lam. 2:19; Ps. 44:20; and perhaps Lam. 1:17). To lift the hand to God means invoking His help."
8. Charles Spurgeon. *The Treasury of David.* (Byron Center, MI: Associated Publishers and Authors, a 1970 reprint): II: 23.
9. J.J. von Allmen. *Worship: Its Theology and Practice.* (NY: Oxford University Press, 1965): 95.
10. Exodus 7:19; 8:5-6, 16-17; 10:12, 13, 21, 22; 14:16, 21, 26, 27; 15:12.
11. W. Gunther Plaut, ed. *The Torah: A Modern Commentary.* (NY: Union of American Hebrew Congregations, 1981): 505.
12. *Keil-Delitzsch Commentary.* (Grand Rapids: Eerdmans, 1978): I, 82.
13. November 1983 conference at Church on the Way, Van Nuys, California.
14. Filthaut: 139.
15. Cp. Numbers 6:22-27. The last glimpse the early church had of Jesus was as He was blessing them with upraised hands (Luke 21:50, 51). Raising the hands is easily identified with the laying on of hands. For instance, the transference of sins to a sacrifice (Lev. 1:4; 16:21-22), or the bestowing of authority, consecration, or special gifts through ordination (Num. 27:18-23; Deut. 34:9; 1 Tim. 4:14). Jesus blessed children and healed the sick with his hands, and the early church conveyed the Holy Spirit by laying on hands (Acts 8:17-18; 19:6). Thus, the idea of transference is easily applied to "blessing" God.
16. 2 Sam. 22:50; 1 Chron. 16:4, 7, 8, 34, 35, 41; 23:30; 25:3; 29:13; 2 Chron. 5:13; 31:2; Ezra 3:11; Neh. 12:24; Ps. 6:5; 18:49; 30:4, 12; 35:18; 75:1; 79:13; 92:1; 97:12; 105:1; 106:1, 47; 107:1; 118:1, 29; 119:62; 122:4; 136:1 , 2, 3, 26; 140:13.
17. Some of the references: Psalm 42:4; 50:23; 56:12; 69:30, 31; 95:2; 100:4.

315

18. Allen and Borror: 124.
19. *Concerning Prayer:* XIV, as quoted by Hennie Stader. "Lifting Up of Hands," *Paraclete* (Winter 1986): XX: 9.
20. James Lee Beall. *The Armory Church Bulletin.* (Detroit: Bethesda Missionary Temple, May 1972).
21. E.M. Bounds. *The Weapon of Prayer.* (Grand Rapids: Baker, reprinted, 1975): 52.
22. Billheimer: 128.
23. Barry Liesch. *People in the Presence of God: Models and Directions for Worship.* (Grand Rapids: Zondervan, 1988): 175.

Chapter 20

1. A.L. and Joyce Gill. *Praise and Worship Study Guide.* (Fawnskin, CA: Powerhouse Publishing, 1989): 37.
2. Psalm 21:13; 27:6; 30;4, 12; 33:2; 47:6, 7; 57:7, 9; 59:17; 61:8; 66:2, 4; 68:4, 32; 71:22, 23; 92:1; 98:4, 5; 101:1; 104:33; 105:2; 108:1, 3; 135:3; 138:1; 144:9; 146:2; 147:1,7; 149:3.
3. A translation published in *Christianity Today* magazine many years ago which I filed, but failed to note the date or the author.
4. As mentioned in the margin of the NAS.
5. See: Kevin Conner. *The Tabernacle of David.* (Portland: Bible Temple Publishing, 1976): 149-165.
6. See the information given in chapter 15.
7. Psalm 33:2, 3; 43:4; 57:8; 68:25; 71:22; 81:2, 3; 87:7; 92:3; 98:5, 6; 108:2; 137:2; 144:9; 147:7; 149:3; 150:3-5.
8. Note 1 Chron. 6:31; 13:8; 15:16, 19, 24, 28; 16:5, 6, 42; 23:5; 25:1-8; 2 Chron. 5:12-14; 7:6; 8:14; 15:14; 20:28; 23:13; 26:15; 29:25-27; 30:21; 34:12; Ezra 3:10; Neh. 12:36.
9. Markus Barth. *The Anchor Bible, Ephesians 4-6.* (Garden City, NY: Doubleday & Co., Inc., 1974): 584.
10. See article by Darryl Miller, "The Organ: 'King of the Instruments.'" *Worship Leader Magazine.* June/July 1993: 26ff.
11. C. Peter Wagner. *Look Out! The Pentecostals Are Coming.* (Carol Stream: Creation House, 1973): 115f.
12. Conner: 165.
13. Gill: 7.
14. Frank Longino. *The Orchestra in Worship.* (Mobile, AL: Selah Music Ministries, 1987): 22.
15. Bob Sorge. *Exploring Worship.* (New Wilmington, PA: Son-Rise Publications, 1987): 18.
16. Millar Burrows. *An Outline of Biblical Theology.* (Philadelphia: The Westminster Press, 1946): 268.

Chapter 21

1. R. Laird Harris, ed. *Theological Wordbook of the Old Testament,* Vol 2. (Chicago: Moody Press, 1980): 979.
2. Bob Sorge. *Exploring Worship.* (New Wilmington, PA: Son-Rise Publications, 1987): 17,18.
3. As reported by Ken Walker. "Correction for Charismatics," *Charisma & Christian Life.* (May 1989): 40; quoting from Kenneth E. Hagin. *Plans, Purposes & Pursuits.* (Faith Library Publications).
4. ©1972 by Lexicon Music, Inc./ ASCAP.
5. ©1986 by Sharon L. Dermer.

Notes

6. Matthew Henry. *Matthew Henry's Commentary on the Whole Bible.* (reprinted by Fleming H. Revell Co.): III:413.
7. Charles H. Spurgeon. *The Treasury of David.* (Byron Center, MI: Associated Publishers and Authors, a 1970 reprint): III: 135.
8. Barry Liesch. *People in the Presence of God.* (Grand Rapids: Zondervan, 1988): 169f.

Chapter 22

1. See C.H. Spurgeon's interesting comments on Psalm 134. *The Treasury of David.*(Byron Center, MI: Associated Publishers and Authors, a 1970 reprint). Also, W. Graham Scroggie. *The Psalms.* (Old Tappan: Fleming H. Revell, 1972): 297-302; and Bernard C. Mischke. *Meditations on the Psalms.* (New York: Sheed and Ward, 1963): 265-266.
2. Phillip Schaff. *History of the Christian Church.* (Grand Rapids: Eerdmans, 1950): I, 460.
3. Helene Lubienska de Lenval. *The Whole Man At Worship.* (New York: Desclee Co., 1961): 18.
4. Theodor Filthaut. *Learning How to Worship.* (Westminister, Maryland: The Newman Press, Translation copyright 1965 by Burns and Dates Ltd.): 134.
5. Mildred Sendrey and Alfred Norton. *David's Harp.* (New York: The New American Library of World Literature, 1964): 222, 223.
6. de Lenval: 18.
7. G. Duffield and G.J. Webb. *"Stand Up For Jesus."*
8. Filthaut:134
9. Ibid.
10. Quoted from Cureton's *Ancient Syria Documents.* Page 27, by William D. Maxwell. *A History of Christian Worship.* (Grand Rapids: Baker Book House, 1982 paperback reissue of 1936 publication): 16 (footnote).
11. Marianne H. Micks. *The Joy of Worship.* (Philadelphia: Westminster, 1983): 53.
12. Paul Waitman Hoon. *The Integrity of Worship.* (Nashville/NY: Abingdon Press, 1971): 321.
13. C. Peter Wagner. *Look Out! The Pentecostals Are Coming.* (Carol Stream, Illinois: Creation House, 1973): 111.

Chapter 23

1. Opening story taken from Dean Merrill's article, "Whatever Happened to Kneeling?" *Christianity Today* (February 10, 1992): 24.
2. Clyde Reid and Jerry Kerns. *Let It Happen.* (NY: Harper and Row, 1973): 17.
3. Quoted by Paul Waitman Hoon. *The Integrity of Worship.* (Nashville/NY: Abingdon Press, 1971): 321.
4. Hoon: 129.
5. G.W. Bromiley, "Worship," Merrill C. Tenney, Gen. Ed.. *The Zondervan Pictorial Encyclopedia of the Bible.* (Grand Rapids: Zondervan, 1975): 5, 970.
6. John Wesley. *The Works of John Wesley.* (Grand Rapids: Baker Book House, reprinted 1978): VIII, 317.
7. As quoted by Jean-Jacques von Allmen. *Worship: Its Theology and Practice.* (NY: Oxford University Press, 1965): 94.
8. C. Peter Wagner. *Look Out! The Pentecostals Are Coming.* (Carol Stream, Illinois: Creation House, 1973): 111.
9. As quoted by Merrill: 25.

10. Theodor Filthaut. *Learning How to Worship*. (Westminister, Maryland: The Newman Press, translation copyright 1965 by Burns and Dates Ltd.): 136f.
11. As quoted by Edward K. Ziegler. *Book of Worship for Village Churches*. (NY: Agricultural Missions Foundation, Inc., 1939): 28.
12. Helene Lubienska de Lenval. *The Whole Man at Worship*. (NY: Desclee Co., 1961): 18.
13. Quoted by Peter Brunner. *Worship in the Name of Jesus*. (St. Louis: Concordia, 1968): 333.
14. Margaret Fisk Taylor. *A Time to Dance*. (Philadelphia/Boston: United Church Press, 1967): 22.
15. H.H. Rowley. *Worship in Ancient Israel*. (Philadelphia: Fortress Press, 1967): 257.
16. Merrill: 24.
17. Brunner: 212.
18. E.M. Bounds. *Prayer and Praying Men*. (Chicago: Moody Press ed., 1980): 126.

Chapter 24

1. "Dancing before the Lord," *Presbyterian Life* (April 1972): 34.
2. For further study, see the selected bibliography of over sixty titles provided by Margaret Fisk Taylor, *A Time to Dance* (Philadelphia/Boston: United Church Press, 1967): 177-180. Also, an additional bibliography of over sixty titles: Doug Adams, Diane Apostolos-Cappadona, eds., *Dance as Religious Studies*. (NY: Crossroad, 1990): 218-221.
3. Jess Stein, ed. in chief. *The Random House Dictionary of English Language*. (NY: Random House, 1967): 366.
4. Adams, *Dance*. Margaret Taylor, "A History of Symbolic Movement in Worship": 15.
5. Debbie Roberts. *Rejoice: A Biblical Study of the Dance*. (Little Rock, Arkansas: Revival Press, 1982): 1.
6. James Orr, gen. ed. *The International Standard Bible Encyclopedia*. (Grand Rapids: Eerdmans, 1960): I, 1169.
7. Richard Wurmbrand. *In God's Underground*. (Glendale: Diane Books Pub. Co., 1960): 75.
8. Helene Lubienska de Lenval. *The Whole Man at Worship*. (NY: Desclee Co., 1960): 75.
9. Evelyn Underhill. *Worship*. (Harper and Brothers, 1937): 23.
10. Dennis C. Benson. *Electric Liturgy*. (Richmond: John Knox Press, 1972): 39.
11. Peter E. Gillquist. *The Physical Side of Being Spiritual*. (Grand Rapids: Zondervan, 1979): 126.
12. For a better, more detailed discussion see Adams, *Dance*. Mayer I. Gruber, "Ten Dance-Derived Expressions in the Hebrew Bible": 48-66.
13. John H. Eaton, "Dancing in the Old Testament," *The Expository Times* (February 1975): 136.
14. Mildred Sendrey and Alfred Norton. *David's Harp*. (NY: The New American Library of World Literature, 1964): 207.
15. By permission. David Fischer. *The Restoration of the Worship of the Psalms in the Twentieth Century Church*. (Pasadena: Living Word Bible College, 1985): 17.
16. Adams, *Dance*. Hal Taussig, "Dancing the Scriptures": 67, 68.
17. As done by Marilyn Daniels. *The Dance in Christianity*. (NY/Ramsey: Paulist Press, 1981): 9. For an analysis of ancient Hebrew dance, the classic and most quoted text remains: W.O.E. Oesterley. *The Sacred Dance*. (NY: Macmillan, 1923).
18. Roberts: 89ff.
19. David Fischer (see endnote 15), whom I asked to review this chapter, expressed his opinion on this point: "Didn't the cultural experience become what it was because of the Spirit-experience that produced it? . . . in other words, Jewish culture **became what it was** (utilizing dance) because of

Notes

the God-breathed word that introduced these worship forms into the culture. Thus, I see them as normative for all cultures and ages."

20. Daniels: 13.
21. David Watson. *I Believe in the Church*. (Grand Rapids: Eerdmans, 1978): 195. Also see Sam L. Sasser. *The Dance: To Be or Not To Be*. (Melbourne, Florida: Zionsong Publications, 1984).
22. As told by Robert E. Webber. *Worship is a Verb*. (Waco: Word, 1985): 189.
23. James Lee Beall. "Is Congregational Dancing a Part of New Testament Worship," an article in *Voice of the Armory* (their Sunday bulletin) (Detroit: Bethesda Missionary Temple, Sept. 16, 1973): 4.
24. See for instance, Adams, *Dance*. Margaret Taylor, "A History of Symbolic Movement in Worship," Chapter 2.
25. For some simple suggestions see Margaret Palmer Fisk. *The Art of the Rhythmic Choir*. (NY: Harper and Brothers, 1950).
26. Watson: 195.
27. C. Peter Wagner. *Look Out! The Pentecostals Are Coming*. (Carol Stream, Illinois: Creation House, 1973): 112.
28. Smith Wigglesworth. *Ever Increasing Faith*. (Springfield, Missouri: Gospel Pub. House, 1971).
29. F.W. Bourne. *Billy Bray the King's Son*. (London: Lutterworth Press, 1959): 47.
30. Taylor: 10.
31. Daniels: 12.
32. A.S. Herbert. *Worship in Ancient Israel*. (London: Lutterworth Press, 1959): 47.
33. Lucien Deiss and Gloria Weyman. *Dance for the Lord*. (Schiller Park: World Library Publications, 1975): 3.

Chapter 25
1. Leslie S. M'Caw. "The Psalms," *The New Bible Commentary*. (Grand Rapids: Eerdmans, 1953): 412.
2. Samuel Terrien. *The Psalms and Their Meaning Today*. (NY: Bobbs-Merrill Co., Inc., 1951): VII (Preface).
3. Elmer A. Leslie. *The Psalms*. (Nashville/NY: Abingdon Press, 1949): 17.
4. Andrew W. Blackwood. *The Fine Art of Public Worship*. (NY: Abingdon Press, 1938): 36.
5. Leslie: 18.
6. Robert G. Rayburn. *O Come, Let Us Worship*. (Grand Rapids: Baker Book House, 1980): 94.
7. Larry Lea. *Mending Broken Nets & Broken Fishermen*. (Rockwall, Texas: Church on the Rock, 1985): 81.
8. Anne Murchison. *Praise and Worship in Earth as It Is In Heaven*. (Waco: Word Books, 1981): 55.
9. John Wimber. *Worship Seminar*. By the author, circa 1985: 4.
10. G.W. Anderson. "Israel's Creed: Sung not Signed," his inaugural lecture for installation in the presidential chair of the (British) Society for Old Testament Study, January, 1963. Quoted by F.F. Bruce. *NT Development of OT Themes*. (Grand Rapids: Eerdmans, 1969): 18.
11. Claus Westermann. *The Living Psalms*. (Grand Rapids: Eerdmans, 1989, reprint): 1.

Chapter 26
1. R.C. Sproul. *Knowing Scripture*. (Downers Grove, Ill: InterVarsity Press, 1977): 48. Leland Ryken. *How to Read the Bible as Literature . . . and Get More Out of It*. (Grand Rapids: Zondervan, 1984): 11.

2. Bernard Ramm. *Protestant Biblical Interpretation*. (Grand Rapids: Baker, 1970, Third Revised Edition): 123.
3. J. Robertson McQuilkin. *Understanding and Applying the Bible*. (Chicago: Moody Press. 1973): 63.
4. David L. Cooper. *Messiah: His Glorious Appearance Imminent*. (Los Angeles: Biblical Research Society, 1961): 52.
5. Ryken: 102.
6. McQuilkin: 123.
7. Ramm: 138.
8. Ramm: 191.
9. J. Edwin Hartill. *Principles of Biblical Hermeneutics*. (Grand Rapids: Zondervan, 1947): 76.
10. Milton S. Terry. *Biblical Hermeneutics*. (Grand Rapids: Zondervan, 1974): 186.
11. Hartill: 89.
12. Sproul: 66. The initial formulation of this principle is credited to Kierkegaard. See Ramm's discussion of this: 75-77.
13. McQuilkin: 239, 245.
14. McQuilkin: 242.
15. An exciting book that develops the importance and centrality of praise is *The Hallelujah Factor* by Jack R. Taylor (Nashville: Broadman Press, 1983).
16. Ramm: 101-104.
17. Kevin J. Conner and Ken Malmin. *Interpreting the Scriptures*. (Portland: Bible Temple Publishing, 1976): 153-166.
18. Hartill: 13-29.
19. Ramm: 2
20. McQuilkin: 254.
21. F.F. Bruce. *NT Development of OT Themes*. (Grand Rapids: Eerdmans, 1969 [American ed.]): 18.
22. David J. Randolph. *God's Party*. (Nashville: Abingdon, 1975): 49, 50.

Chapter 27

1. The eleven Psalms, commonly known as the Messianic Psalms, would have been of particular interest because of His concern to fulfill all things. Those Psalms are: 2, 8, 16, 22, 45, 69, 72, 89, 110, 118, and 132.
2. See Matthew 26:38.
3. Charles H. Spurgeon. *The Treasury of David*. (Byron Center, Mich.: Associated Publishers and Authors, a 1970 reprint): I: 365.
4. Stanley A. Ellisen. *Knowing God*. (Nashville/Camden/NY: Thomas Nelson Publishers, 1984): 144. Note: no one figure seems agreeable to all.
5. One of the best studies is written by Gleason L. Archer and G.C. Chirichigno. *Old Testament Quotations in the New Testament: A Complete Survey*. (Chicago: Moody Press, 1983). In four parallel columns they present the Masoretic Hebrew, Septuagint, Greek NT texts pertinent for each quotation, and a critical commentary. Sections 132-198 lists the Psalms quoted.
6. F.F. Bruce. *New Testament Development of Old Testament Themes*. (Grand Rapids: Wm. B. Eerdmans, original copyright 1968): 68.
7. For a fuller discussion see: Kevin Conner and Ken Malmin. *The Covenants*. (Portland: Bible Temple Publications, 1983): Chapter 8, "The Davidic Covenant."
8. Luke 1:32; Acts 2:30; 2 Tim. 2:8; Heb. 1:8; Rev. 3:7.

Notes

9. Kevin Conner. *The Tabernacle of David*. (Portland: Bible Temple Publishing, 1976): 34.
10. Matthew 1:1-17 (generally considered Christ's descent through Joseph), and Luke 3:23-38 (His descent through Mary).
11. George Eldon Ladd. *A Theology of the New Testament*. (Grand Rapids: Eerdmans, 1974): 335f.
12. Bruce: 69, says "The 'holy and sure blessings of David' are the steadfast, reliable covenant-mercies which Yahweh confirmed to David and his house."
13. Note the fascinating way in which Bill and Amy Stearns weave many of the Hebrew scriptures about God's desire for all peoples into their challenging missionary book, *Catch the Vision 2000*. (Minneapolis: Bethany House Publishers, 1991).
14. E.W. Hengstenberg. *Christology of the Old Testament*. (A reprint of the 1854 translation: Mac Donald Publishing Co., P.O. Box 6006, Mac Dill AFB, Florida 33608): 1: 284.
15. E.B. Pusey. "Zechariah," *Barnes' Notes*. (Grand Rapids: Baker Book House, reprinted from the 1885 edition): 2: 373.
16. C.F. Keil and F. Delitzsch. "Minor Prophets," *Commentary on the Old Testament*. (Grand Rapids: William B. Eerdmans, reprinted 1980): 10, Second Part: 298.
17. Keil and Delitzsch: 10, Second Part: 298.
18. We have no actual proof that the crown was made or hung in the temple, but there is a talmudic notice in Middoth iii about where the crown was hung.
19. Bruce: 79.
20. Hebrews 5:6, 10; 6:20; 7:1, 10, 11, 15; 7:17, 21.
21. Hebrews 9:12, 26, 28; 10:10.
22. Bruce: 81, 82.
23. Spurgeon: V: 185.
24. G. Campbell Morgan. *God's Last Word to Man*. (Grand Rapids: Baker, 1974, reprint): 85.
25. Kenneth S. Wuest. *Wuest's Word Studies (Hebrews)*. (Grand Rapids: Eerdmans, 1947): 239.

Chapter 28

1. Two of the best books that address this subject in both a scholarly yet relatable way would be: Jack R. Taylor. *The Hallelujah Factor*. (Nashville: Broadman Press, 1983); and Ronald Barclay Allen. *Praise! A Matter of Life and Breath*. (Nashville: Thomas Nelson Publishers, 1980).
2. Paul E. Billheimer. *Destined for the Throne*. (Ft. Washington, PA: Christian Literature Crusade, 1975): 116.
3. As, (1) *Psalmist* Magazine, Kent Henry, ed. , 9820 Watson Road, St. Louis, MO 63126. (2) *Worship Leader*, write CCM Publications, 1913 21st Ave S., Nashville, TN 37212.
4. See the following three books: 1) Graham Kendrick. *Learning to Worship as a Way of Life*. (Minneapolis: Bethany House, 1985); 2) John MacArthur, Jr. *The Ultimate Priority*. (Chicago: Moody, 1983); and 3) Warren W. Wiersbe. *Real Worship*. (NY: Thomas Nelson, 1986).
5. Jim Hayford, Sr. *Contending for the Authentic*. (Santa Barbara, CA: Servant Ministries, 1992): 67.
6. In the early years of the Greek language, the Greek verb *dokeo* produced the Greek noun *doxa* (meaning "glory"). The verb originally meant "to appear" or "to seem," consequently the derived noun meant "an opinion," which is the way something appears or seems to the observer. In time, *dokeo* was used only for having a good opinion about some person; thus, to glorify came to mean giving the "praise" or "honor" due to one of whom the good opinion was held. This concept was easily applied to God. I appreciate the simple but adequate explanation given by James Montgomery Boice, *Foundations of the Christian Faith* (Downers Grove: InterVarsity, 1986, revised ed.): 589f.

7. John R.W. Stott. *Christ the Controversialist: A Study in Some Essentials of Evangelical Religion.* (London: Tyndale Press, 1970): 160.
8. Barry Liesch. *People in the Presence of God.* (Grand Rapids: Zondervan, 1988): 40.
9. Bob Sorge. *Exploring Worship.* (New Wilmington, PA: Son-Rise Publications, 1987): 65.
10. Quoted by Kent R. Wilson, "Monday Morning Worship," *Discipleship Journal* (Issue Seventy, July/August 1991, Vol 12, Number 4): 26. Incidentally, this issue is devoted to the theme of worship and has some very good information.
11. *Worship Leader* (Vol 2, No. 2): 26.
12. Hayford: 70.
13. David Watson. *I Believe in the Church.* (Grand Rapids: Eerdmans, 1978): 198.
14. For the most thoroughly readable discussion, see Taylor, Chapter 10, "Praise: A Word Study in Hebrew," prepared with the help of linguist Robert D. Beren. A table listing forty-five of the lesser-known Hebrew words for praise is included.
15. Robert Young. *Young's Analytical Concordance*: 766,767.
16. Admittedly, *Young's* does not give us the complete meanings for these seven words, so other sources will be consulted to fill out the definitions, but the format serves my purpose.
17. James Strong. *The Exhaustive Concordance of the Bible.* (Copyright by author, 1890).
18. The summaries given for each word are based on the information available in the standard lexicons and are generally used by the various authors. If, however, it seems to me that some source gives a unique insight, I will use and footnote it.
19. Jay Green, ed. *The New Englishman's Hebrew and Chaldee Concordance.* (Wilmington, DE: Assoc. Publishers, 1975). This is a reprint of *The Englishman's Hebrew and Chaldee Concordance of the Old Testament*, first published in 1843, with Strong's number system added.
20. Ronald B. Allen. "When the Psalmists Say, 'Praise the Lord!'" *Worship Leader*, October/November 1992: 8.
21. In its various forms. William Wilson. *Wilson's Old Testament Word Studies.* (McLean, VA 22102: Mac Donald Publishing Co., reprinted), "Praise," p. 322. *The New Englishman's Concordance* lists some 154 occurrences of the word with its various translations.
22. William Gesenius. *Gesenius' Hebrew and Chaldee Lexicon to the Old Testament Scripture.* Trans. Samuel P. Tregelles (Grand Rapids: Eerdmans, 1976 12th printing): 226.
23. Wilson's: 322.
24. From Gesenius: 226 — "In the sacred writers, the more any one boasts, the more he is regarded as being foolish; just as, on the other hand a modest person is looked upon as wise and pious.
25. Allen: 114.
26. R. Laird Harris, ed. *Theological Wordbook of the Old Testament.* (Chicago: Moody Press, 1980): 1, 217.
27. Harris: 218.
28. Terry Law. *The Power of Praise.* (Tulsa: Victory House Publishers 1985): 130.
29. As, Taylor: 83.
30. Endnote 16 in that Section lists the references.
31. *Young's*: 766.
32. See Allen's discussion: 65.
33. Harris: 1: 364.
34. *Wilson's*: 322.
35. Harris: 1: 132.
36. *Gesinius*:142.

Notes

37. *Young's*: 766.
38. Some Old Testament references that use *bârak* as praise to God: Gen. 9:26; 14:20; 24:27; Exod. 18:10; 1 Sam. 25:32,39; 2 Sam. 18:28; 1 Kings 1:48, 5:7, 8:15,56, 10:9; 1 Chron. 16:36; 2 Chron. 2:12, 6:4, 9:8; Ezek. 7:27; Job 1:21; Ps. 16:7, 18:46, 26:12, 28:6, 31:21, 34:1, 66:8,26, 68:26,32,35; 72:18-19; 96:2; 100:4b; 103:1,2,20,21,22; 104:1,35; 106:48; 115:18; 119:12; 124:6; 134:1,2; 135:19,20,21; 144:1; 145:1,2,10,21.
39. *Gesinius*: 766.
40. Anne Murchison. *Praise and Worship in Earth as It Is in Heaven*. (Waco: Word, 1981): 81.
41. Taylor: 88.
42. A.H. Leitch, "Praise," Merrill C. Tenney, gen. Ed., *The Zondervan Pictorial Encyclopedia of the Bible*. (Grand Rapids: Zondervan, 1975): Four, 834.
43. *Young's*: 766, lists the following OT references where *tehillâh* appears: Exod. 15:11; Deut. 10:21; 26:19; 1 Chron. 16:35; 2 Chron. 20:22; Neh. 9:5; 12:46; Ps. 9:14; 22:3,25; 33:1; 34:1; 35:28; 40:3; 48:10; 51:15; 65:1; 66:2,8; 71:6,8,14; 78:4; 79:13; 100:4; 102:21; 106:2,12,47; 109:1; 111:10; 119:171; 145 title; 15:21; 147:1; 148:14; 149:1; Isaiah 42:8,10,12; 43:21; 48:9; 60:6,18; 61:3,11; 62:7; 63:7; Jer. 13:11; 17:14; 33:9; 49:25; 51:41; Hab. 3:3; Zeph. 3:19,20.
44. OT references for *zâmar*: Judges 5:3; 2 Sam. 22:50; Ps. 7:17; 9:1,11; 18:49; 21:13; 27:6; 30:4,12; 33:2; 47:6,7; 57:7,9; 61:8; 66:2,4; 68:4,32; 71:22,23; 75:9; 92:1; 98:4,5; 101:1; 104:33; 105:2; 108:1,3; 138:1; 144:9; 146:2; 147:1,7; 149:3; Isa. 12:5.
45. Law: 133.
46. Thought from the notes at a LaMarr Boschman worship seminar, "Praise versus Worship: What is the Difference?" (PO Box 130, Bedford, TX; published by author): 6.
47. Allen: 66.
48. *Strong's*, Hebrew Dictionary entry #2167.
49. *Wilson's*: 322.
50. Harris: 1: 365. See End Note 17 in Chapter 17, Section I, for listing of references.
51. *Gesenius*: 801.
52. J. Winston Pearce. *Come, Let Us Worship*. (Nashville: Broadman Press, 1965): 55f.
53. Billheimer: 116.
54. Walter Brueggmann. *Israel's Praise: Doxology against Idolatry and Idealogy*. (Philadelphia: Fortress Press, 1988): 1.
55. Delling: 65.
56. Charles H. Spurgeon. *The Treasury of David*. (Byron Center, MI: Associated Publishers and Authors, a 1970 reprint): IV: 110.

Chapter 29

1. W. White, Jr., provides an interesting 14-page discussion in "Synagogue," *The Zondervan Pictorial Encyclopedia of the Bible*, Merrill C. Tenney, Gen. ed. (Grand Rapids: Zondervan, 1975): 5: 554.
    Also see Robert N. Schaper's discussion: *In His Presence*. (NY: Thomas Nelson, 1984): chapter 3, "Worship in the Synagogue," p. 38ff.
2. C.W. Dugmore. *The Influence of the Synagogue Upon the Divine Office*. (Westminster: The Faith Press LTD, 1964): 1-2.
3. Dugmore: 5. Also cf. *The Jewish Background of the Christian Liturgy*, by W.O.E. Oesterley (Oxford Press, 1925).
4. William D. Maxwell. *A History of Christian Worship*. (Grand Rapids: Baker Book House, 1936): 1-5.

5. Illion T. Jones. *A Historical Approach to Evangelical Worship*. (Nashville, Tennessee: Abingdon Press, 1954): 84. His excellent insights confirm our thesis.
6. Ernest F. Scott. *The Nature of the Early Church*. (NY: Charles Scribner's Sons, 1941): Chapter IV.
7. Jones: 83.
8. Alexander B. Macdonald. *Christian Worship in the Primitive Church*. (Edinburgh: T.&T. Clark, 1934): 2.
9. Dugmore: 2.
10. Scott: 77.
11. Dietrich Ritschl. *A Theology of Proclamation*. (Richmond: John Knox Press, 1963): 90f.

Chapter 30

1. About fifty years ago, Alexander B. Macdonald wrote *Christian Worship in the Primitive Church*. (Edinburgh: T.& T. Clark, 1934). Although done in a scholarly fashion, the book captures in a unique way the Spiritual quality of the early church experience. Chapter V, "The Worship as Spirit-Controlled" is very thought-provoking.
2. Illion Jones. *A Historical Approach to Evangelical Worship*. (Nashville: Abingdon Press, 1954): 68.
3. B.H. Streeter. *The Primitive Church*. (New York: The Macmillan Co., 1929): 73.
4. Ernest F. Scott. *The Spirit in the NT*. (New York: George H. Doran Co., 1923): 246.
5. Strangely, the term *Holy* Spirit appears only three times in the OT: Psalm 51:11; Isaiah 63:10,11.
6. Michael Green. *I Believe in the Holy Spirit*. (Grand Rapids: Eerdmans, 1975): 19.
7. George Eldon Ladd. *A Theology of the New Testament*. (Grand Rapids: Eerdmans, 1974): 287.
8. Hans Küng. *Does God Exist? An Answer for Today*. (Garden City, New York: Doubleday, 1980): 697.
9. An informative (somewhat liberal) book by a Roman Catholic scholar who covers all the major biblical texts dealing with the Spirit is: George T. Montague. *The Holy Spirit: Growth of a Biblical Tradition*. (New York: Paulist Press, 1976). I feel that Michael Green's study (Note 6 above) is an excellent study help.
10. Küng: 696,697.
11. Green: 19.
12. Green: 23-28.
13. An interesting discussion on this theme by James D.G. Dunn, *Baptism in the Holy Spirit* (Philadelphia: The Westminster Press, 1970): 23-26. His hypothesis is that the baptism of the Holy Spirit is a conversion-initiation event experienced by all believers. For a scholarly response to that work by a Pentecostal theologian see *Conversion-Initiation and the Baptism in the Holy Spirit* by Howard M. Ervin (Peabody, Mass.: Hendrickson Publishers, 1984).
14. For a brief, exciting review: F.F. Bruce. *New Testament Development of Old Testament Themes*. (Grand Rapids: Eerdmans, 1968): 83-99.
15. I like Green's description: 32.
16. Ladd: 293.
17. Gerhard Kittel and Gerhard Friedrich, eds. *Theological Dictionary of the NT*. (Grand Rapids: Eerdmans, 1977): V: 814.
18. Dunn: 175. "The dominant theme is the continuity between the ministries of Jesus and the Paraclete. The Spirit takes over as the *allos parakletos* (other Paraclete) where the first Paraclete leaves off. Indeed we might say that Jesus continues to be present with and in his disciples through

Notes

the Paraclete. In other words, a purely spiritual relationship is to supersede what was also a physical one (14:18-23)."
19. Catherine Marshall. *The Helper*. (Waco: Word Books, 1979): 33.
20. James D.G.Dunn. *Jesus and the Spirit*. (Philadelphia: The Westminster Press, 1975): 351.
21. Green: 45.
22. Raymond E. Brown. "The Paraclete in the Fourth Gospel," *New Testament Studies* 13, 1966-67: 126. Brown's insights are very enlightening.
23. Frederick Dale Brunner. *A Theology of the Holy Spirit*. (Grand Rapids: Eerdmans, 1970): 156.
24. Hans Küng. *The Church*. (Garden City, New York: Image Books, 1976): 221.
25. Paul Waitman Hoon. *The Integrity of Worship*. (Nashville/New York: Abingdon, 1971): 118.
26. Ladd: 294, 295.
27. For a brief, but adequate explanation of the formulation of the Christian church's understanding of the Holy Spirit, which took shape in the two centuries following the NT period, see C.F.D. Moule. *The Holy Spirit*. (Grand Rapids: Eerdmans, 1978): IV, "Subsequent Doctrinal Developments."
28. I am grateful here for the insights of Montague: 354.
29. See Dunn, *Baptism*: XIV, "The Johannine Pentecost?"
30. Ray S. Anderson *On Being Human: Essays in Theological Anthropology*. (Grand Rapids: Eerdmans, 1982): 182.
31. Karl Barth. *God Here and Now*. (New York: Harper & Row, 1964).
32. For a more complete discussion, see: James B. Torrance. *Church Service Society Annual*, No. 40, May 1970: 41-62; as used in: James B. Torrance. "The Place of Jesus Christ in Worship": 348-362, Chapter 12, Ray S. Anderson, ed., *Theological Foundations for Ministry*. (Grand Rapids: Eerdmans, 1979).
33. Macdonald: 30.
34. Montague: 296.
35. Anderson: 200.
36. Peter Brunner. *Worship in the Name of Jesus*. (St. Louis, Missouri: Concordia Publishing, 1968): 77.

Chapter 31
1. Peter Marshall. *John Doe, Disciple*. (New York: McGraw-Hill Book Co., 1963): 71,72.
2. Robert Stephenson Simpson. *Ideas in Corporate Worship*. (Edinburgh: T.&T. Clark, 1927): 91.
3. H. Grady Hardin, Joseph D. Quillian, and James F. White. *The Celebration of the Gospel*. (Nashville: Abingdon, 1964): 110.
4. David Watson. *I Believe in the Church*. (Grand Rapids: Eerdmans, 1978): 225.
5. *Verbum visible*, Augustine in *Johan. Ev. Tract.* lxxx:3; Calvin, *Institutes*, 1536, cap. iv.
6. C.M. Horne. "Sacraments", *The Zondervan Pictorial Encyclopedia of the Bible*. Merrill C. Tenney, gen. ed. (Grand Rapids: Zondervan, 1975): Vol 5, 192.
7. Horne: 192.
8. Patricia Beall Gruits. *Understanding God*. (Whitaker Books, 1972): 351.
   Also, compare G.C. Berkouwer, "The Sacraments as Signs and Seals," *The Sacraments*. (Grand Rapids: Eerdmans, 1969): 134ff. He pursues the difficult explanation of the sign (the external) and the seal (the internal) being inseparable.
9. I feel that the person doing the baptizing must represent in some meaningful way the Church of Jesus Christ. This attitude is based on meeting self-baptized hippies that see no necessity of being rooted in the local church.

On this point see, "Encounter," *Theological Foundations for Ministry*, by Ray S. Anderson, ed. (Grand Rapids: Eerdmans, 1979): 433.

Also, Watson's comments, p. 277: ". . . no man baptised himself . . . ."

Also, Hans Küng, *The Church*. (Garden City, NY: Image Books, 1976): 273.

10. The Bible actually does not say that any words must be said, so various statements have come into use. The use of clear biblical words does enhance the action and follow the scriptural precedent of invoking the name of the Lord upon people (as, Num. 6:27). If God and His name are one in essence, the use of God's name becomes a powerful vehicle for communicating God to the person.

11. H.S. Coffin: "In the Sacraments there are physical symbols—water and bread and wine. These elements are essential factors in the Sacraments, as words are in a sentence; but it is the whole sentence which effectually conveys meaning, and it is the Gospel portrayed in sacramental actions in their entirety through which God in Christ conveys himself to us." *The Pubic Worship of God*. (Philadelphia: The Westminster Press, 1946): 136,137.

12. Note particularly Michael Green's, "The Spirit enlivens the Sacraments", *I Believe in the Holy Spirit*. (Grand Rapids: Eerdmans, 1975): 111ff.

13. See Berkouwer's discussion on chapter 2, "The number of the Sacraments:" 27ff.

14. Hardin: 110,111.

15. For instance, Gruits: chapters 54-61.

16. Rayburn: 243.

17. Hardin: 110.

18. cf. Karl Bath. *Church Dogmatics*, IV/4: 108-109.

19. E. Schillebeeckx. *Christ the Sacrament of the Encounter with God*. (NY: Sheed and Ward, 1963): 19.

20. Schillebeeckx: 19,45.

21. Berkouwer discusses Kuyper's ideas on the special grace of the sacrament. I like the thought: "If this working from heaven does not accompany the administration of the sacrament on earth, the sacrament is not present; there is then nothing left but an appearance" (P. 83).

22. James B. Torrance. "The Place of Jesus Christ in Worship," included by Anderson; note particularly page 363.

23. Robert N. Schaper. "Worship and the Presence of Christ," *Theology, News and Notes* (October 1977): 26.

24. "Membership in the Christian community is brought to a sacramental focus in Christian baptism," says C.F. D. Moule. *The Holy Spirit*. (Grand Rapids: Eerdmans, 1978): 33.

25. "The central act of Christian worship in the history of the church," says Robert E. Webber, "has always been the Communion." *Common Roots*. (Grand Rapids: Zondervan, 1978): 86.

26. cf. Ralph P. Martin's discussion, *The Worship of God*. (Grand Rapids: Eerdmans, 1982): 205,206.

27. James D.G. Dunn. *Baptism in the Holy Spirit*. (Philadelphia: The Westminster Press, 1970): 194.

28. James D.G. Dunn. *Jesus and the Spirit*. (Philadelphia: The Westminster Press, 1975): 351.

29. Watson: 225.

30. Berkouwer: Chapter 3, "Word and Sacrament."

31. Schaper: 26.

32. Although some scholars argue that the Lukan account is not authentic, the term itself stands irreproachable.

33. Green: 14.

34. C.F.D. Moule. *Worship in the NT*. (London: Lutterworth Press, 1961): 36.

35. Ralph P. Martin. *Worship in the Early Church*. (Grand Rapids: Eerdmans, 1974): 126.

Notes

36. Jean-Jacques von Allmen. Worship: *Its Theology and Practice*. (NY: Oxford University Press, 1965): 34.
37. Joseph Jungmann. *The Mass*. (Collegeville: The Liturgical Press, 1976): 116.
38. Charles A.A. Scott. *Christianity According to St. Paul*. (Cambridge: The University Press, 1961): 191.
39. Dwight H. Small. *Christian: Celebrate Your Sexuality*. (Old Tappan, New Jersey: Revell, 1974): 203.
40. Dom Gregory Dix. *The Shape of the Liturgy*. (London: Dacre Press, Adam & Charles Black, 1945): 245.

Chapter 32

1. See the very practical explanation given by Bob Sorge in *Exploring Worship*. (New Wilmington, PA: Son-Rise Publication, 1987): Chapter 4, "What Is Worship?" He diagrams his explanation with four overlapping circles which represent praise, prayer, worship, and thanksgiving.
2. Dick Eastman. *Change the World! School of Prayer*. (Studio City, Calif.: World Literature Crusade, 1976): Section VI.
3. E.M. Bounds, Compiled by Leonard Ravenhill. *A Treasury of Prayer*. (Minneapolis: Bethany House, 1981): 151.
4. Taken from an excellent little book: *How to Develop a Praying Church* by Charlie W. Shedd (NY/Nashville: Abingdon Press, 1964): 10.
5. Edward M. Bounds. *The Necessity of Prayer*. (Grand Rapids: Baker Book House, 1976 edition): 137.
6. The Greek word for church, *ekklesia*, denoted an assembly or congregation of free citizens summoned or "called out" by a herald for public affairs. The term is increasingly perceived to mean as well, however, "called together." The church of an area is the Christian community called out of a secular community who periodically gather together for spiritual affairs.
7. This thought reminds me of Isaiah 2:3: "Come, let us go up to the mountain of the Lord, to the house of the God of Jacob."
8. 2 Chron. 6:21, 23, 25, 27, 30, 33, 35, 39.
9. Albert Barnes. *Barnes' Notes on the Old Testament*. (Grand Rapids: Baker Book House, 1950): Isaiah, Vol 2: 309.
10. Quoted by K.S. Wuest. *Wuest's Word Studies from the Greek New Testament*. (Grand Rapids: Eerdmans, 1950): 1: 221.
11. Some examples of secret praying are: Moses (Deut. 9:25), Samuel (1 Sam. 15:11), Elijah (1 Kings 17:19), Daniel (Dan. 6:10), Peter (Acts 10:9), Cornelius (Acts 10:30), and Jesus Himself (Mark 1:35; 6:46, 47; Luke 5:15, 16; 6:12; 9:18; 22:41, 42.)
12. This account was taken from an out-of-date publication personally sent to me by Eric W. Hayden, considered the leading expert on Spurgeonic materials.
13. Herbert Lockyer. *All the Prayers of the Bible*. (Grand Rapids: Zondervan, 1959): 229.
14. Note that the mark of a true widow is continuance in supplications and prayers (1 Tim. 5:5).
15. See *Awaken the Dawn!* by Ernest B. Gentile (Portland: Bible Temple Publishing, 1990), a book that details the blessings, joy and power of early morning prayer.
16. This idea was advocated at the Lausanne II Conference in Manila, July 1989. For a free copy of the *Global Prayer Strategy Manual* write: Senior Associate for Prayer LCWE, P.O. Box 888-850, Atlanta, Georgia 30356, USA.
17. C. Peter Wagner. "The Korean Experience," *World Evangelization Bulletin* No. 24. (September 1981): 6.

18. Note also: Psalm 57:8; 59:16; 88:13; 90:14; 92:2; 108:2; 119:147; 143:8; Isa. 50:4; Mark 1:35; Luke 5:16; 6:12.
19. Alec E. Rowlands. "How Prayer Transformed Our Church," *Ministries: The Magazine for Christian Leaders:* Vol 3, Number 3 (Summer 1985): 41.
20. Quoted by Dick Eastman: E-2.
21. Paul Y. Cho. *Prayer: Key to Revival.* (Waco: Word Books, 1984): 62. Also note the ringing challenge of E.M. Bounds in his chapter 6, "Prayer, the Great Essential" in *Power through Prayer.* (Grand Rapids: Baker, 1976): 32ff.
22. Robert S. Simpson. *Ideas in Corporate Worship.* (Edinburgh: T.&T. Clark, 1927): 126.
23. Reg Layzell. *Prayer.* (Published by the author, 1981): 8, 9.
24. Judson Cornwall. *Elements of Worship.* (South Plainfield, NJ: Bridge Publishing, 1985): 80.
25. Bob Sorge. *Exploring Worship.* (New Wilmington, PA: Son-Rise Pub., 1987): 36.
26. R.A. Torrey. *How to work for Christ.* (Westwood, New Jersey: Fleming H. Revell Co. [no date]): 205.
27. Bounds,*The Necessity of Prayer*: 140, 141.
28. G. Campbell Morgan. *The Practice of Prayer.* (Grand Rapids: Baker Book House, reprinted 1971 from 1960 Revell ed.): 114.
29. Paul E. Billheimer. *Destined for the Throne.* (Ft. Washington, Penn.: Christian Literature Crusade,1975): 131.
30. Charles Colson. *The Body.* (Dallas: Word, 1992): 142.

Chapter 33

1. Ferdinand Hahn makes this comment about the avoidance of cultic terminology in the NT: "The only term that occurs with a certain regularity is *synerchestai* ('come together') or *synagesthai* ('be gathered together'). The 'coming together' of the faithful is the significant feature of Christian worship." *The Worship of the Early Church.* (Philadelphia: Fortress Press, 1973): 36.
2. Robert G. Rayburn. *O Come, Let Us Worship.* (Grand Rapids: Baker, 1980): 91.
3. In his Chapter 7 on "Principles of New Testament Edification," Gene A. Getz makes a strong point that a local church is a body of believers that *meets regularly. Sharpening the Focus of the Church.* (Chicago: Moody, 1974): 76.
4. Raymond Abba. *Principles of Christian Worship.* (London: Oxford University Press, 1957): 10.
5. I am grateful for Watchman Nee's thoughts along this line in, *Assembling Together.* (New York: Christian Fellowship Publishers, 1973): 33ff.
6. David Watson, in *I Believe in the Church*, has made a fine presentation of the basic meaning, also amplifying the meaning to include "called out," "called for," "called together," and "called to". (Grand Rapids: Eerdmans, 1978): Chapter Five.
7. Walter Oetting. *The Church of the Catacombs.* (St. Louis: Concordia, 1964): 25.
8. W.E. Vine. *An Expository Dictionary of NT Words.* (Westwood, NJ: Fleming H. Revell Co., 1940): 83f.
9. C.K. Barrett. *A Commentary on the First Epistle to the Corinthians.* (New York/Evanston: Harper & Row, 1968): 261.
   Also, note Peter Brunner's statement: ". . . 'assembly' is surely the most important meaning of *ekklesia." Worship in the Name of Jesus.* (St. Louis: Concordia, 1968): 315.
10. Nee: 36.
11. This question of the necessity of church buildings has always been a challenge. Howard A. Snyder asks the question in his chapter 5: "Are Church Buildings Superfluous?" *The Problem of Wineskins.*

Notes

(Downers Grove: InterVarsity Press, 1975). He correctly concludes that any church building must be functional—means, not an end.

12. Hahn: "It is a well-known fact that the earliest evidences from which we can derive a complete picture of the structure and sequence of Christian worship date from the middle of the second century" (page 1).
13. Rayburn: 116.
14. Brunner: 215ff.
15. Brunner: 215, 217.
16. Dom Gregory Dix. *The Shape of the Liturgy*. (London: Dacre Press, Adam & Charles Black, 1945): 1.
17. Snyder 97.
18. Jack Hayford. *The Church on the Way*. (Lincoln, Virginia: Chosen Books, 1982): 94.
19. Brunner: 225.
20. ". . . there is, of course, no place in the New Testament which clearly states that the church had any set order of service, and very little information is supplied to us about the outward forms which were in use." Ralph P. Martin. *Worship in the Early Church*. (Grand Rapids: Eerdmans, 1964): 134.
21. Reference should be made to Illion Jones' presentation of thirteen elements in the New Testament worship, to which these notes were much indebted. *A Historical Approach to Evangelical Worship*. (Nashville: Abingdon, 1954): 69-82.

    See also, Barry Liesch. *People in the Presence of God*. (Grand Rapids: Zondervan, 1988): Chapter Five.

    Also, see Rayburn's thoughts, page 86ff. Ralph P. Martin gives a most helpful discussion of the contents throughout his book, *Worship in the Early Church*.
22. Robert E. Webber. *Worship Is A Verb*. (Waco: Word, 1985): 54,55.
23. This suggestion by Rayburn (page 148ff.) is one way to encourage participation in a church that is not so accustomed to vocal participation. See Chapter 16.
24. Jones: 72.
25. Teaching such as that by Pat Robertson will do much to stimulate a responsiveness in people. *The Secret Kingdom*. (Nashville: Nelson, 1982): Chapter Seven, "The Law of Reciprocity."
26. James D.G. Dunn clearly establishes the importance of prophecy among the spiritual gifts when he says: "In all the various lists and discussion of charismata in Paul's letters the only constant member is 'prophecy' or 'prophet' (Rom. 12:608; 1 Cor. 12:8-10, 28ff; 14:1-5, 6ff; Eph. 4:11; 1 Thess. 5:19-22)." *Jesus and the Spirit*. (Philadelphia: The Westminster Press, 1975): 227,228.
27. David E. Aune. *Prophecy in Early Christianity and the Ancient Mediterranean World*. (Grand Rapids: Eerdmans, 1983): 196.
28. See for instance, the interesting suggestions scattered by Bruce Yocum throughout his book, *Prophecy* (Ann Arbor: Servant Books, 1976).
29. I am in accord with Peter Wagner's famous formula C+C+C = C (Celebration + Congregation + Cell = Church). He is saying that the Church body will have healthy, vital growth if every member can participate in a great celebration, worship service with all the other Christians, and if that same member can also be an active part of a smaller congregational group within the large church body, and last of all if that person can meet regularly with a small cell of believers from the church body. I am here dealing with the larger celebration meeting, realizing that some of the ingredients mentioned in my chapter will find application in smaller meetings. See Wagner's, *Your Church Can Grow*. (Glendale: Regal Books, 1976): Chapter 7.

30. Alexander B. Macdonald: "For there can be little question that they thought of their meeting, with all its varied procedure, as a compact unity, because controlled from beginning to end by the Spirit of God" : 17. *Christian Worship in the Primitive Church.* (Edinburgh: T.&T. Clark, 1934).

31. Robert S. Simpson. *Ideas in Corporate Worship.* (Edinburgh: T.&T. Clark, 1927): 116.

32. Andrew W. Blackwood. *The Fine Art of Public Worship.* (New York: Abingdon Press, 1939): 46.

33. Paul Waitman Hoon. *The Integrity of Worship.* (Nashville: Abingdon Press, 1971): 47.

34. Hayford: 80.

35. Simpson: 48.

36. Clarice Bowman. *Restoring Worship.* (Nashville, Tenn.: Abingdon-Cokesbury Press, 1951): 114.

A Selected Bibliography

Here are sixty-five significant worship books that impressed the author. They are representative choices, arranged in five arbitrary categories, and they do not, of course, represent the same viewpoints. Additional bibliographic information can be found under each book's listing in the regular bibliography.

Worship in the New Testament Church

Cullman, Oscar. *Early Church Worship.*
Delling, D. Gerhart. *Worship in the New Testament.*
Dunn, James D.G. *Unity and Diversity in the New Testament* (Chapters VII-IX).
Hahn, Ferdinand. *The Worship of the Early Church.*
Jones, Illion. *A Historical Approach to Evangelical Worship* (Chapters 3 & 4).
Macdonald, Alexander. *Christian Worship in the Primitive Church.*
Martin, Ralph. *Worship in the Early Church.*
Moule, D.F.D. *Worship in the New Testament.*
Scott, Ernest. *The Nature of the Early Church* (Chapter IV).
Streeter, Burnett. *The Primitive Church.*

The Theology of Worship

Abba, Raymond. *Principles of Christian Worship.*
Allmen, J.J. von. *Worship: Its Theology and Practice.*
Brunner, Peter. *Worship in the Name of Jesus.*
Dix, Dom Gregory. *The Shape of the Liturgy.*
Hayford, Jack. *Worship His Majesty.*
Hoon, Paul. *The Integrity of Worship.*

331

Jungmann, Josef. *Public Worship.*
Martin, Ralph. *The Worship of God.*
Nee, Watchman. *Worshipping the Ways of God.*
Nicholls, William. *Jacob's Ladder.*
Simpson, Robert. *Ideas in Corporate Worship.*
Underhill, Evelyn. *Worship.*
Wainwright, Geoffrey. *Doxology.*
Webber, Robert. *Worship Old and New.*

General Information

Adams, Doug, ed. *Dance as Religious Studies.*
Allen, Ronald, and Gordon Borror. *Worship: Rediscovering the Missing Jewel.*
Blackwood, Andrew. *The Find Art of Public Worship.*
Davies, J.G. *The New Westminster Dictionary of Liturgy and Worship.*
Hustad, Donald. *Jubilate!*
Lenval, H. Lubienska de. *The Whole Man at Worship.*
McDonnell, Killian, ed. *Presence, Power, Praise* (3 Vols).
Rayburn, Robert. *O Come, Let Us Worship.*
Shaper, Robert. *In His Presence.*
Spurgeon, Charles. *The Treasury of David.*
Webber, Robert, ed. *The Topical and Illustrated Encyclopedia of Christian Worship* (7 Vols. when completed).
White, James. *Introduction to Christian Worship.*
_____. *New Forms of Worship.*

Inspirational/Innovative/Contemporary

Allen, Ronald. *Praise! A Matter of Life and Breath.*
Coleman, Robert. *Songs of Heaven.*
Cornwall, Judson. *Elements of Worship.*
Gillquist, Peter. *The Physical Side of Being Spiritual.*
Hayford, Jack, John Kittinger, and Howard Stevenson. *Mastering Worship.*
Taylor, Jack. *The Hallelujah Factor.*
Liesch, Barry. *People in the Presence of God.*
Ortlund, Anne. *Up with Worship.*
Tozer, A.W. *Worship: The Missing Jewel of the Evangelical Church.*
_____. *Whatever Happened to Worship?*
Webber, Robert. *Worship Is a Verb.*
_____. *Signs of Wonder.*

A Selected Bibliography

Charismatic/Restoration

Beall, James. *The Ministry of Worship and Praise.*
Blomgren, David. *Song of the Lord.*
_____, ed. *Restoring Praise and Worship to the Church*
Chambers, Calvin. *In Spirit and in Truth.*
Conner, Kevin.*The Tabernacle of David.*
Cornwall, Judson. *Let us Worship.*
_____. *Let Us Praise.*
Gill, A.L. and Joyce. *Praise and Worship Study Guide.*
Griffing, Barry, David Fischer, Larry Dempsey, and Steve Griffing. *The Restoration of the Worship of the Psalms in the Twentieth Century Church.*
Hayford, Jack. *The Church on the Way.*
Law, Terry. *The Power of Praise and Worship.*
Murchison, Anne. *Praise and Worship in Earth as it is in Heaven.*
Nee, Watchman. *Assembling Together.*
Sassor, Sam. *The Dance: To Be or Not to Be.*
Sorge, Bob. *Exploring Worship.*
Truscott, Graham. *The Power of His Presence.*

Bibliography

Abba, Raymond. *Principles of Christian Worship*. London: Oxford University Press, 1957.

Abbott, Walter M., gen. ed. *The Documents of Vatican II*. New York: Guild Press, 1966.

Adams, Doug, and Diane Apostolos-Cappadona, eds. *Dance as Religious Studies*. New York: Crossroad, 1990.

Allen, Ronald B., and Gordon L. Borror. *Worship: Rediscovering the Missing Jewel*. Portland, Oregon: Multnomah Press, 1982.

Allmen, Jean-Jacques von. *Worship: Its Theology and Practice*. New York: Oxford University Press, 1965.

Anderson, Ray S., ed. *Theological Foundations for Ministry*. Grand Rapids: Eerdmans, 1966.

_____. *On Being Human*. Grand Rapids: Eerdmans, 1982.

Barrett, C.K. *The Gospel of St. John*. London, S.P.C.K., 1967.

Barth, Marcus. *Ephesians 4-6, The Anchor Bible Series*. Garden City, NY: Doubleday & Co., Inc., 1974, Vol. 34A.

Beattie, David J. *The Romance of Sacred Song*. London/Edinburgh: Marshall, Morgan & Scott, 1960.

Beall, James Lee. *The Ministry of Worship and Praise*. Detroit: Bethesda Missionary Temple.

_____. "Is Congregational Dancing a Part of New Testament Worship?" *Voice of the Armory Bulletin*. Detroit: Bethesda Missionary Temple, Sept. 16, 1973.

Benson, Dennis C. *Electric Liturgy*. Richmond, Va.: John Knox Press, 1972.

Berkouwer, G.C. *The Person of Christ*. Grand Rapids: Eerdmans, 1954.

Billheimer, Paul E. *Destined for the Throne*. Ft. Washington, Pa.: Christian Literature Crusade, 1975.

Bittlinger, Arnold. *Gifts and Graces*. Grand Rapids: Eerdmans, Eng. Tr., 1967.

Blackwood, Andrew W. *The Fine Art of Public Worship*. New York: Abingdon Press, 1939.

Blomgren, David K. *The Song of the Lord*. Portland, Or.: Bible Temple Publications, 1978.

_____, ed. *Restoring Praise and Worship to the Church*, Shippensburg, PA: Revival Press, 1989.

Bounds, E.M. *The Weapon of Prayer*. Grand Rapids: Baker Book Edition, 1975.

_____. *The Necessity of Prayer*. Grand Rapids: Baker Book Edition, 1976.

_____. *Prayer and Praying Men*. Chicago: Moody Press Edition, 1980.

_____. *A Treasury of Prayer*. Minneapolis: Bethany House, 1981.

Bowman, Clarice. *Restoring Worship*. Nashville: Abingdon-Cokesbury Press, 1951.

Brant, Roxanne. *Ministering to the Lord*. Florida: Roxanne Brant Crusades, 1973.

Brown, Colin, ed. *The New International Dictionary of New Testament Theology*. Grand Rapids: Zondervan, 1979. Vol. 2: 875-876.

Brown, Raymond E. *The Gospel According to John, I-XIII, The Anchor Bible*, Vol 29. Garden City, NY: Doubleday & Co., 1966.

Bruce, Alexander B. *The Training of the Twelve*. Grand Rapids: Kregel Publications, 1971, reproduced from 4th Ed., 1894 by A.C. Armstrong and Son.

Bruce, F.F. *The New Testament Development of Old Testament Themes*. Grand Rapids: Eerdmans, reprinted 1982.

Brunner, Peter. *Worship in the Name of Jesus*. St. Louis: Concordia, 1968.

Brueggemann, Walter. *Israel's Praise: Doxology against Idolatry and Idealogy*. Philadelphia: Fortress Press, 1988.

Burrows, Millar. *An Outline of Biblical Theology*. Philadelphia: The Westminster Press, 1946.

Caird, William Rennie. *On Worship in Spirit and in Truth*. London: Thomas Bosworth, 198 High Holborn, 1977.

Chambers, Calvin H. *In Spirit and in Truth*. Ardmore, PA: Dorrance and Company, 1980.

Cho, Paul Yonggi. *The Fourth Dimension*. Plainfield, NJ: Logos International, 1979.

_____. *Prayer: Key to Revival*. Waco: Word Books, 1984.

Clark, Stephen B. *Building Christian Communities*. Notre Dame: Ave Maria Press, 1972.

Coffin, Henry Sloane. *The Public Worship of God*. Philadelphia: The Westminster Press, 1946.

Coleman, Robert E. *Songs of Heaven*. Old Tappan, NJ: Fleming H. Revell Co., 1980.

Colson, Charles. *The Body*. Dallas: Word, 1992.

Conner, Kevin J. *The Tabernacle of David*. Portland, OR: Bible Temple Publishing, 1976.

_____, and Ken Malmin. *Interpreting the Scriptures*. Portland, OR: Bible Temple Publications, 1976.

Cooper, David L. *Messiah: His Glorious Appearance Imminent*. Los Angeles: Biblical Research Society, 1961.

Cornwall, Judson. "Worship," *New Wine*, November 1976.

_____. *Let Us Praise*. Plainfield, NJ: Logos International, 1973.

_____. *Let Us Worship*. South Plainfield, NJ: Bridge Publ., 1983.

_____. *Elements of Worship*. South Plainfield, NJ: Bridge Publ., 1985.

Daniels, Marilyn. *The Dance in Christianity*. NY/Ramsey: Paulist Press, 1981.

Davis, H. Grady. *Why We Worship*. Philadelphia: Fortress Press, 1961.

Deiss, Lucien, and Gloria G. Weyman. *Dancing for God*. Cincinnati: World Library Publ., 1969.

Delling, D. Gerhart. *Worship in the New Testament*. London: Darton, Longman and Todd, 1962.

Dix, Dom Gregory. *The Shape of the Liturgy*. London: Dacre Press, Adam and Charles Black, 1945.

Dugmore, C.W. *The Influence of the Synagogue upon the Divine Office*. London: Faith Press LTD, reprinted 1964.

Dunn, James D.G. *Baptism in the Holy Spirit*. Philadelphia: The Westminster Press, 1970.

_____. *Jesus and the Spirit*. Philadelphia: The Westminster Press, 1975.

_____. *Unity and Diversity in the New Testament*. Philadelphia: Trinity Press International, 1990 (2nd ed.).

DuPlessis, David J. *The Spirit Bade Me Go*. Published by author.

Earnshaw, Leslie. *Worship for the Seventies*. Nutfield, Surrey: Danholm House Press, 1973.

Eastman, Dick. *Change the World! School of Prayer*. Studio City, CA: World Literature Crusade, 1976.

Eaton, John H. "Dancing in the Old Testament," *The Expository Times*, February 1975.

Edwards, Jonathan. *Eternity*. July 1975.

Erdman, Charles R. *The Revelation of John*. Philadelphia: The Westminster Press, 1936.

Ervin, Howard M. *Conversion-Initiation and the Baptism in the Holy Spirit*. Peabody, MA: Hendrickson Publishers, 1984.

Fee, Gordon D. *The First Epistle to the Corinthians, The New International Commentary on the New Testament*. Grand Rapids: Eerdmans, 1987.

Filthaut, Theodor. *Learning to Worship*. Westminster, MD: The Newman Press, Tran. copyright 1965 by Burns and Dates Ltd.

Freeman, James M. *Manners and Customs of the Bible*. Plainfield, NJ: Logos International, reprinted 1972.

Gesenius, William. *Gesenius' Hebrew and Chaldee Lexicon to the Old Testament Scriptures*, trans. by Samuel P. Tregelles. Grand Rapids: Eerdmans, 1976 (12th printing).

Getz, Gene A. *Sharpening the Focus of the Church*. Chicago: Moody Press, 1974.

Gill, A.L. and Joyce. *Praise and Worship Study Guide*. Fawnskin, CA: Powerhouse Publishing, 1989.

Gillquist, Peter E. *The Physical Side of Being Spiritual*. Grand Rapids: Zondervan, 1979.

Green, Jay, ed. *The New Englishman's Hebrew and Chaldee Concordance*. Wilmington, DE: Assoc. Publishers, 1975. A reprint of *The Englishman's Hebrew and Chaldee Concordance of the Old Testament*, first published in 1843.

Green, Michael. *I Believe in the Holy Spirit*. Grand Rapids: Eerdmans, 1980.

Griffing, Barry, David Fischer, Larry Dempsey, and Steve Griffing. *The Restoration of the*

Worship of the Psalms in the Twentieth Century Church. Pasadena: Living Word Bible College, 1985.

Gruits, Patricia Beall. *Understanding God.* Whitaker Books, 1972.

Hahn, Ferdinand. *The Worship of the Early Church.* Philadelphia: Fortress Press, 1973.

Harris, R. Laird, ed. *Theological Wordbook of the Old Testament.* Chicago: Moody Press, 1980.

Hayford, Jack W. *The Church on the Way.* Lincoln, VA: Chosen Books, 1982.

_____. *Worship His Majesty.* Waco: Word Books, 1987.

Hayford, Jim. *Contending for the Authentic.* Santa Barbara: Servant Ministries, 1992.

Hedley, George. *Christian Worship.* New York: The MacMillan Co., 1953.

Hendricks, Howard. "Discussing First Things First," *Leadership,* Summer 1980.

Hengstenberg, E.W. *Christology of the Old Testament.* (A reprint of the 1854 translation: MacDonald Publishing Co., P.O. Box 6006, MacDill AFB, Florida 33608), Vol 1: 284.

Herbert, A.S. *Worship in Ancient Israel.* London: Lutterworth Press, 1959.

Hill, David. *The Gospel of Matthew, New Century Bible.* Greenwood, SC: The Attic Press, 1972.

Hoon, Paul Waitman. *The Integrity of Worship.* Nashville: Abingdon Press, 1971.

Horton, A.S. *The Meaning of Worship.* New York: Harper & Brothers, 1959.

Hustad, Donald P. *Jubilate!* Carol Stream, IL: Hope Publishing co., 1981.

Jones, Illion T. *A Historical Approach to Evangelical Worship.* Nashville: Abingdon Press, 1954.

Jungmann, Josef A. *The Mass.* Collegeville, MN: The Liturgical Press, 1976.

Kantzer, Kenneth S. "The Charismatics Among Us," *Christianity Today,* February 22, 1980.

Kendrick, Graham. *Learning to Worship as a Way of Life.* Minneapolis: Bethany House Publ., 1984.

Kimber, Thomas. *The Worship of God.* New York: David S. Tabor & Co., 56 LaFayette Place, 1890.

Kinne, Seeley D. *The Prophetic State.* By the author, 1922.

Kittel, Gerhard, and Gerhard Friedrich, eds. *Theological Dictionary of the New Testament.* Grand Rapids: Eerdmans, 1968.

Kittler, Glenn D. *The Wings of Eagles.* Garden City, NY: Doubleday, 1966.

Ladd, George Eldon. *A Theology of the New Testament.* Grand Rapids: Eerdmans, 1974.

_____. *The Presence of the Future.* Grand Rapids: Eerdmans, 1974.

Law, Terry. *The Power of Praise and Worship.* Tulsa: Victory House Publishers, 1985.

Lawson, E. Leroy. *The New Testament Church Then and Now.* Cincinnati: Standard Publishing, 1981.

Layzell, Reg. *Prayer.* By the author, 1981.

Lea, Larry. *Mending Broken Nets and Broken Fishermen.* Rockwall,TX: Church on the Rock, 1985.

Leitch, A.H. "Praise." Tenney, Merrill C., gen. ed. *The Zondervan Pictorial Encyclopedia of the Bible.* Grand Rapids: Zondervan, 1975. Vol 4: 834.

Lenski, R.C.H. *The Interpretation of St. John's Gospel.* Columbus, OH: Lutheran Book Concern, 1942.

Bibliography

Lenval, Helene Lubienska de. *The Whole Man at Worship*. New York: Desclee Co., 1961.

Leslie, Elmer A. *The Psalms*. Nashville/New York: Abingdon Press, 1949.

Liesch, Barry. *People in the Presence of God*. Grand Rapids: Zondervan, 1988.

Lockyer, Herbert. *All the Prayers of the Bible*. Grand Rapids: Zondervan, 1959.

Longino, Frank. *The Orchestra in Worship*. Mobile, AL: Selah Music Ministries, 1987.

Lowrie, Walter. *Art in the Early Church*. New York: Harper Torchbooks, Harper and Row, 1947.

Luther, Martin. *Works of Martin Luther*. Philadelphia: Muhlenberg Press, Volume 5.

MacArthur, John Jr. *The Ultimate Priority*. Chicago: Moody Press, 1993.

Macdonald, Alexander B. *Christian Worship in the Primitive Church*. Edinburgh: T.&T. Clark, 1934.

Mains, David R. *Full Circle*. Waco: Word Publishers, 1971.

Manson, T.M. *The Sayings of Jesus*. Grand Rapids: Eerdmans, 1957.

Martin, Ralph P. *Worship in the Early Church*. Grand Rapids: Eerdmans, 1974.

_____. *New Testament Foundations: A Guide for Christian Students*, Vol 2. Grand Rapids: Eerdmans, 1978.

_____. *The Worship of God*. Grand Rapids: Eerdmans, 1982.

Maxwell, William D. *A History of Christian Worship*. Grand Rapids: Baker Book House, 1982 reprint.

McDonnell, Kilian, ed. *Presence, Power, Praise*. Collegeville, MN: The Liturgical Press, 1980. Vols 1, 2, & 3.

McGavran, Donald. *Understanding Church Growth*. Grand Rapids: Eerdmans, 1970.

McQuilkin, J. Robertson. *Understanding and Applying the Bible*. Chicago: Moody Press, 1973.

Merrill, Dean. "Whatever Happened to Kneeling?" *Christianity Today*, February 10, 1992.

Metcalfe, Frances. *Living the Life of Praise*. Box 458, Idyllwild, CA, 92349: The Golden Candlestick, 1952.

Micks, Marianne H. *The Future Present*. New York: The Seabury Press, 1970.

_____. *The Joy of Worship*. Philadelphia: The Westminster Press, 1982.

Miller, Keith. *The Taste of New Wine*. Waco: Word Books, 1965.

Montague, George T. *The Holy Spirit: Growth of a Biblical Tradition*. New York: Paulist Press, 1976.

Morgan, G. Campbell. *The Practice of Prayer*. Grand Rapids: Baker Book House, reprinted 1971 from 1960 Revell ed.

_____. *God's Last Word to Man: Studies in Hebrews*. Grand Rapids: Baker, reprinted 1974.

Moule, C.F.D. *Worship in the New Testament*. London: Lutterworth Press, 1961.

Murchison, Anne. *Praise and Worship in Earth as It Is in Heaven*. Waco: Word Books, 1981.

Nee, Watchman. *Worshipping the Ways of God*. Los Angeles: The Stream.

_____. *Twelve Baskets Full*. The World Outreach, 1966.

_____. *Assembling Together*. New York: Christian Fellowship Publ., 1973.

Nelson, C. Ellis. *Where Faith Begins*. Atlanta: John Knox Press, 1971.

Nicholls, William. *Jacob's Ladder: The Meaning of Worship*. Richmond: John Knox Press, 1958.

O'Brien, Peter L. *Word Biblical Commentary*, Vol. 44. Waco: Word Books, 1982.
Osterley, W.O.E. *The Jewish Background of the Christian Liturgy*. Gloucester: Peter Smith, 1965.
_____. *The Sacred Dance*. New York: Macmillan, 1923.
Ortlund, Anne. *Up with Worship*. Glendale: Regal Books, 1975.
Packer, J.I. *Knowing God*. Downers Grove, IL: Inter-Varsity Press, 1973.
Pearce, J. Winston. *Come, Let Us Worship*. Nashville: Broadman Press, 1965.
Pinnock, Clark. "Opening the Church to the Charismatic Dimension," *Christianity Today*, 12 June 1981.
Plaut, W. Gunther, ed. *The Torah: A Modern Commentary*. New York: Union of American Hebrew Congregations, 1981.
Randolph, David James. *God's Party*. Nashville: Abingdon, 1975.
Ravenhill, Leonard. *Why Revival Tarries*. Minneapolis: Bethany Fellowship, 1959.
Rayburn, Robert G. *O Come, Let Us Worship*. Grand Rapids: Baker, 1980.
Reader's Digest Editors. *Family Word Finder*. Pleasantville, NY: The Reader's Digest Association, 1975.
Reid, Clyde, and Jerry Kerns. *Let It Happen*. New York: Harper and Row, 1973.
Ritschl, Dietrich. *A Theology of Proclamation*. Richmond: John Knox Press, 1963.
Roberts, Alexander, and James Donaldson, ed. *The Ante-Nicene Fathers*. Grand Rapids: Eerdmans, 1970. Vol. VII.
Roberts, Debbie. *Rejoice: A Biblical Study of the Dance*. Little Rock, AR: Crossroad, 1990.
Rowlands, Alec E. "How Prayer Transformed Our Church," *Ministries*, Vol 3, Number 3, Summer 1985.
Rowley, H.H. *Worship in Ancient Israel*. Philadelphia: Fortress Press, 1967.
Rutledge, Howard. "Returned POW: How We Overcame," *Christianity Today*, July 10, 1973.
Sassor, Sam L. *The Dance: To Be or Not To Be*. Melbourne, FL: Zionsong Publications, 1984.
Schaefer, Francis A. *The Church at the End of the 20th Century*. Downers Grove: Inter-Varsity, 1970.
Schaller, Lyle E., ed. *Creative Leadership Series, Church Growth Strategies that Work*. Nashville: Abingdon, 1980.
Schaper, Robert N. "Worship and the Presence of Christ," *Theology, News and Notes*, October 1977.
_____. *In His Presence*. New York: Nelson, 1984.
Schillebeeckx, E. *Christ the Sacrament of the Encounter with God*. New York: Sheed and Ward, 1963.
Schlink, Basilea. *Patmos: When the Heavens Opened*. Carol Stream, IL: Creation House, 1976.
Schuller, Robert H. *Self Esteem, the New Reformation*. Waco: Word Books, 1982.
Scott, Charles A. Anderson. *Christianity According to St. Paul*. Cambridge: The University Press, 1961.
Scott, Ernest F. *The Spirit in the New Testament*. New York: George H. Doran, 1923.

Bibliography

_____. *The Nature of the Early Church*. New York: Charles Scribner's Sons, 1941.

Sendrey, Mildred, and Alfred Norton. *David's Harp*. New York: The New American Library of World Literature, 1964.

Shedd, Charlie W. *How to Develop a Praying Church*. New York/Nashville: Abingdon Press, 1964.

Shepherd, Massey H. *The Paschal Liturgy and the Apocalypse*. Richmond: John Knox Press, 1960.

Simpson, Robert Stevenson. *Ideas in Corporate Worship*. Edinburgh: T.& T. Clark, 1927.

Snyder, Howard A. *The Problem of Wine Skins*. Downers Grove: Inter-Varsity Press, 1975.

Sola, Carla de. *Learning Through Dance*. New York: Paulist Press, 1974.

Sorge, Bob. *Exploring Worship: A Practical Guide to Praise and Worship*. New Wilmington, PA: Son-Rise Publications, 1987.

Speery, Willard L. *Reality in Worship*. New York: The MacMillan Co., 1925.

Spurgeon, Charles H. *The Treasury of David*. Byron Center, MI: Associated Publishers and Authors, Inc., reprinted 1970. Vols. 1 and 2, containing all the original volumes.

Stander, Hennie. "Lifting Up of Hands," *Paraclete*, Winter 1986.

Stedman, Ray C. *Body Life*. Glendale: Regal Books, 1972.

Stott, John R. W. *Christ the Controversialist: A Study in Some Essentials of Evangelical Religion*. London: Tyndale Press, 1970.

Streeter, Burnett Hillman. *The Primitive Church*. New York: The Macmillan Co., 1929.

Strong, James. *The Exhaustive Concordance of the Bible*. Copyright by author, 1890.

Suenens, Leon Joseph Cardinal. *A New Pentecost*. New York: The Seabury Press, 1974.

Sunday Mercury News, 11 December 1977.

Swindoll, Charles R. Foreword: *The Hymnal for Worship and Celebration*. Waco: Word, 1986.

Synan, Vinson. *In the Latter Days: The Outpouring of the Holy Spirit in the 20th Century*. Ann Arbor, MI: Servant Publications, 1984.

Tasker, R.V.G. *The Gospel According to St. Matthew*, The Tyndale N.T. Commentaries. Grand Rapids: Wm. B. Eerdmans Publishing Co., 1961.

Taylor, Margaret Fisk. *A Time to Dance*. Philadelphia/Boston: United Church Press, 1967.

_____(as Margaret Palmer Fisk). *The Art of the Rhythmic Choir*. New York: Harper and Brothers, 1950.

Taylor, W. "Twelve Favourite Hymns," quoted in *The Expositor's Dictionary of Texts*. Grand Rapids: Baker Book House, reprinted 1978.

Temple, William. *Readings in St. John's Gospel*. London: MacMillan and Co. Ltd., 1955.

Tozer, A.W. *Born After Midnight*. Harrisburg, PA: Christian Publications, Inc., 1955.

_____. *The Root of the Righteous*. Harrisburg: Christian Publications, 1955.

_____. *Worship: The Missing Jewel of the Evangelical Church*. Harrisburg: Christian Publications, 1961.

_____. Gerald B. Smith, ed. *Whatever Happened to Worship?* Camp Hill, PA: Christian Publications, 1985.

Truscott, Graham. *The Power of His Presence*. Burbank: World MAP, 1972.
Underhill, Evelyn. *Worship*. Harper and Brothers, 1937.
Vine, W.E. *An Expository Dictionary of New Testament Words*. Westwood, NJ: Fleming H. Revell Co., 1940.
Wagner, C. Peter. *Look Out! The Pentecostals Are Coming*. Carol Stream, IL: Creation House, 1973.
_____. "The Korean Experience," *World Evangelization Bulletin* No. 24, September 1981.
Wainwright, Geoffrey. *Doxology*. New York: Oxford University Press, 1980.
Wallis, Arthur. *In the Day of Thy Power*. Ft. Washington, PA: Christian Literature Crusade, 1956.
Ware, Timothy. *The Orthodox Church*. Baltimore: Penguin Books, 1963.
Watson, David. *I Believe in the Church*. Grand Rapids: Eerdmans, 1978.
Webber, Robert E. *Common Roots*. Grand Rapids: Zondervan, 1978.
_____. "Church Buildings: Shapes of Worship," *Christianity Today*, August 7, 1981.
_____. *Worship Old and New*. Grand Rapids: Zondervan, 1982.
_____. *Worship Is a Verb*. Waco: Word Books, 1985.
_____. *Signs of Wonder*. Nashville: Star Song Publishing Group, 1992.
_____, ed. *The Topical and Illustrated Encyclopedia of Christian Worship*. Nashville: Abbott Martyn Press, 1992.
Wesley, John. *The Works of John Wesley*, 3rd ed. Grand Rapids: Baker Book House, reprinted 1978. Volumes VIII and XIV.
Westermann, Claus. *The Living Psalms*. Grand Rapids: Eerdmans, 1989 (reprint).
What Is the Liturgical Renewal? Washington, D.C.: The Liturgical Conference, 1964.
White, James F. *New Forms of Worship*. Nashville: Abingdon, 1971.
_____. *Introduction to Christian Worship*. Nashville: Abingdon, 1980.
Wiersbe, Warren W. *Real Worship*. New York: Thomas Nelson, 1986.
Wigglesworth, Smith. *Ever Increasing Faith*. Springfield, MO: Gospel Publishing House, 1971.
Willis, Wendell. *Worship*. Austin, TX: Sweet Publishing Co., 1973.
Wilson, Ralph F. "Lifting Hands in Worship," *Paraclete*, Winter 1986.
Wilson, William. *Wilson's Old Testament Word Studies*. McLean, VA: MacDonald Publ. Co., reprinted.
Wuest, Kenneth S. *Wuest's Word Studies* (Hebrews). Grand Rapids: Eerdmans, 1947.
Wurmbrand, Richard. *In God's Underground*. Glendale: Diane Books, 1968.
Young, Robert. *Young's Analytical Concordance*.
Zdenek, Marilee, and Marge Champion. *Catch the New Wind*. Waco: Word Books, 1972.
Ziegler, Edward K. *Book of Worship for Village Churches*. New York: Agricultural Missions Foundation, Inc., 1939.

Index

Authors whose books or articles appear in the Bibliography have their names appear here in regular type.

343

Index

More books by Ernest Gentile
www.ernestgentile.com

The Major & Minor Prophets $15

The book is about the history of Israel and their God, as chronicled through the Holy Scriptures. Throughout the Old Testament, the Lord raised up prophets to speak to the nation of Israel, and communicate the heart of God. The Spirit of Prophecy moved on holy men and women of God at key moments in Israel's history to affect change, direction, repentance, warning, encouragement and much more, including some prophecies that foretold events that would end up having their fulfillment centuries later with stunning detail and accurac

Why Apostles Now $15

As the apostolic movement develops, the literature continues to increase both in quantity and quality. I am delighted that Ernest Gentile has stepped up to the plate, and, drawing on his well-honed research skills, has given us a superb textbook on apostolic ministry. An outstanding feature of Why Apostles Now? is the presentation of the different views of those who have addressed each of the major issues along with a fair analysis of the strengths and weaknesses of each. I strongly recommend this book.

C. PETER WAGNER
Vice President and Apostolic Ambassador, Global Spheres, Inc.

More books by Ernest Gentile
www.ernestgentile.com

Your Son's and Daughters Shall Prophesy $22

Today there is a great concern about the prophetic and its checks and balances, as well as the prophet's ministry. Though there are a number of books on the subject, this book is one of the most balanced and proven that I have read

DICK IVERSON

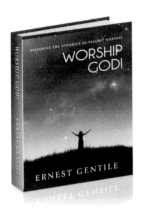

Worship God $17

"This book is also available in Spanish (Adora a Dios), and can be ordered from this website."

Ernest Gentile may have just written this century's [1994] most important book on biblical worship! His research will satisfy the scholar, his study will meet the exegete's expectations, and best of all his practical points for application will gratify pastors and worship leaders. I believe sensitive shepherds who yearn for help in directing their flock into spiritually vital worship will rejoice as I have in discovering Worship God!

JACK HAYFORD

More books by Ernest Gentile
www.ernestgentile.com

Awaken The Dawn $10

Discover from the author how you too can walk the road of prayer and develop an intimate, personal relationship with God through exciting experience in the realm of prayer. The fresh insights in this book, particularly those surveying the prayer ministry of Jesus, will arouse a new anticipation of meeting God in the morning.

The Glorious Disturbance $15

The Glorious Disturbance refers to the outpouring of the Holy Spirit on the Day of Pentecost when the church was launched. It is called the baptism with the Holy Spirit-and it is still available today. Ernest Gentile helps Christians of all backgrounds understand Holy Spirit baptism more clearly. Is it real? Is it necessary? And what about speaking in tongues? Gentile answers these questions and many more. He shows how important Spirit baptism was in the life of Jesus and in the early church. And he demonstrates scripturally that the empowerment of the Spirit isn't just for biblical times or certain groups of Christians; it's for every one of us.

More books by Ernest Gentile
www.ernestgentile.com

The Final Triumph $15

In this book Ernest is able to take a fresh look at this subject while showing appropriate respect for traditional views. He is passionate without being polemic in his approach. I believe this book to be an important contribution because Ernest brings to this subject a unique combination of scholarly integrity, pastoral concern and prophetic passion.

KEN MALMIN
Dean of Portland Bible College and textbook author